CORPORATE INCOME TAXES UNDER PRESSURE

Why Reform Is Needed and How It Could Be Designed

EDITORS

RUUD DE MOOIJ
ALEXANDER KLEMM
VICTORIA PERRY

Cataloging-in-Publication Data
IMF Library

Names: Mooij, Ruud A. de. | Klemm, Alexander. | Perry, Victoria J. | International
Monetary Fund, publisher.
Title: Corporate income taxes under pressure : why reform is needed and how it
could be designed / Editors: Ruud de Mooij, Alexander Klemm, Victoria
Perry.
Description: Washington, DC : International Monetary Fund, 2021. | Includes
bibliographical references.
Identifiers: ISBN 9781513511771 (paper)
Subjects: LCSH: Corporations—Taxation. | International business
enterprises—Taxation.
Classification: LCC HD2753.M66 2021

Recommended citation: De Mooij, Ruud, Alexander Klemm, and Victoria Perry,
eds. 2021. *Corporate Income Taxes under Pressure : Why Reform Is Needed and How
It Could Be Designed*. Washington, DC: International Monetary Fund.

ISBN: 978-1-51351-177-1 (paper)
978-1-51356-399-2 (ePub)
978-1-51356-397-8 (PDF)

Please send orders to:

International Monetary Fund, Publication Services
P.O. Box 92780, Washington, D.C. 20090, U.S.A.
Tel.: (202) 623–7430 Fax: (202) 623–7201
E-mail: publications@imf.org
Internet: www.elibrary.imf.org
www.bookstore.imf.org

Table of Contents

Foreword

International corporate taxation has been a core element of the IMF's tax work for decades.

In the IMF's capacity development work, the tax treatment of multinational corporations has been a recurring theme covering wide-ranging topics, including advice on tax incentives intended to attract foreign direct investment, the tax treatment of companies in extractive industries, and the safeguarding of revenue against profit shifting. This work, especially in developing countries, has significantly intensified. International tax issues are also being analyzed more deeply as part of the IMF's regular macroeconomic surveillance of members. Over the last few years, a diverse range of countries has undergone in-depth assessment of their international corporate taxation, prepared by or with Fiscal Affairs Department staff and published with the standard annual surveillance (Article IV) reports.

On the analytical front, international tax issues came into increased prominence after the global financial crisis of 2009, and IMF staff have contributed to the global tax discussions. The IMF published two policy papers in 2014 and 2019 that directly addressed issues in the international tax debates—based upon several underlying research papers. In 2015 a book about international tax issues in extractive industries was published, and in 2017 another on the implications of digitalization for the public finances.

While much work was embodied in the 2019 IMF Policy Paper "Corporate Taxation in the Global Economy," space constraints did not allow for a deep explanation of core concepts and issues, nor to completely exhibit the underlying research and analysis. This volume therefore complements the 2019 IMF Policy Paper, providing additional background and detailed research. Of course, it does not mark the end of the IMF's work in this area. On the contrary, we expect the field to be very busy for many years to come. For example, we expect and hope that 2021 will be the year of deepening of international cooperation. International taxation is crucial for this agenda.

Vitor Gaspar
Director, Fiscal Affairs Department
International Monetary Fund

Preface

This book complements the 2019 IMF Policy Paper "Corporate Taxation in the Global Economy," providing additional background and detailed research. It is organized so as to guide readers in a structural manner through the issues in international taxation. Apart from readers who go through the entire book, however, each of the chapter is self-contained to facilitate reading of selected chapters. While the book was mostly prepared prior to the COVID-19 crisis, the topics covered are likely only to have increased in importance. Notably, the need for globally coordinated efforts to further reduce profit shifting and tax competition is likely to be greater in a world in which many countries will want to raise revenues to cover the cost of the crisis in a progressive manner. And the desire of many countries to shift the long-standing allocation of the international tax base has likewise intensified.

We are grateful to the many contributing authors of this book for sharing their deep knowledge of the issues and their enthusiasm and efforts to put in significant work during a time of already heavy work pressures. Many other IMF staff members have contributed to its completion by reviewing and commenting on chapters, sharing ideas in brainstorming meetings, and formatting tables and figures, among many other tasks. While they are too many to name, we are indebted to them.

We would like to thank the management of the Fiscal Affairs Department, notably Vitor Gaspar and Michael Keen, for their support of this book. It has also benefited greatly from the expertise and advice of colleagues in the Communications Department, including our primary counterparts Joe Procopio and Gemma Diaz.

Contributors

EDITORS

Ruud de Mooij is an Advisor in the IMF's Fiscal Affairs Department. Before that, he was Division Chief of the IMF's Tax Policy Division. He has published extensively on tax issues in leading academic journals, including in the *American Economic Review* and the *Journal of Public Economics*.

Alexander Klemm is Deputy Division Chief of the IMF's Tax Policy Division, leading capacity development and research on tax policy. He holds a PhD from University College London and has work experience at the Institute for Fiscal Studies and the European Central Bank. He has published on tax policy and other public finance issues, investment, and the balance of payments.

Victoria Perry is Deputy Director of the Fiscal Affairs Department of the IMF, where she previously headed the Revenue Administration and Tax Policy Divisions. She was formerly President of the National Tax Association and the American Tax Policy Institute, was past Chair of the VAT Committee of the American Bar Association Section of Taxation, and currently serves on the Board of the International Institute of Public Finance. She received her JD from Harvard Law School.

AUTHORS

Aqib Aslam is Deputy Division Chief of the Regional Studies Division in the African Department of the IMF. Prior to joining the IMF, he studied for a PhD at the University of Cambridge and worked at Goldman Sachs International, the Bank of England, and the UK Government Economic Service.

Irving Aw was Counsel (Tax Law) of the IMF's Financial and Fiscal Law Unit, Legal Department, and currently works as a tax law expert with the IMF. He holds a JD from Columbia Law School and an LLB (Hons.) from the London School of Economics and Political Science. His publications include books and articles on tax laws, commercial transactions, and investment funds.

Thomas Baunsgaard is a Deputy Division Chief in the IMF's Tax Policy Division, leading capacity development and analytical work on natural resource taxation. He previously served as IMF Resident Representative to Tanzania and Malawi, and prior to joining the IMF worked in Papua New Guinea and the West Bank and Gaza.

Sebastian Beer is an Economist in the IMF's Tax Policy Division. He conducts research on a broad range of tax-related issues and provides technical assistance to member countries. Before joining the IMF, Sebastian worked at the Austrian central bank and at the Vienna University of Economics and Business.

Maria Coelho is an Economist in the IMF's Tax Policy Division. She holds a PhD in Economics from UC Berkeley, and her research focuses primarily on optimal tax design and the impact of fiscal policy on financial markets and macroeconomic activity.

Dan Devlin is part of the IMF's Tax Policy Division, specializing in providing support to developing countries on extractive industries, fiscal modeling, and international profit shifting. Previously, Dan worked in tax and public policy at the OECD, Australian Treasury, and the United Nations. He has an MA in Economic Policy from the Australian National University.

Shafik Hebous is a Senior Economist in the IMF's Tax Policy Division. Shafik has provided tax policy advice in countries in Asia, Africa, and Europe. His research covers various fiscal issues and has been published in academic peer-reviewed journals. Shafik was Adjunct Professor at Oslo Fiscal Studies at the University of Oslo and Assistant Professor at the Economics Department at the Goethe University Frankfurt, where he obtained his PhD in Economics.

Cory Hillier is a Tax Lawyer and Senior Counsel in the IMF's Legal Department. He provides legal advice on, and drafts legal instruments in, all major areas of tax law, including domestic direct and indirect taxes, tax administration and procedures, and international taxation. He is also extensively involved in the IMF's legal and international tax policy work.

Sébastien Leduc is an Economist in the IMF's Tax Policy Division, which he joined in 2016 after serving as Senior International Tax Policy Economist in the Department of Finance Canada. He leads multiple technical assistance activities, undertakes analytical work, and contributes to the various outputs from the Platform of Collaboration on Tax.

Li Liu is a Senior Economist in the IMF's Tax Policy Division. Previously, she was Senior Research Fellow at Oxford University Centre for Business Taxation. Her research focuses on public economics and development economics. Li is also a Research Fellow at the University of Oxford and the Leibniz Centre for European Economic Research (ZEW) in Mannheim, and an Associate Editor of *International Tax and Public Finance.*

Oana Luca is an Economist in the IMF's European Department and has extensive experience in capacity development, policy advice, and macroeconomic surveillance in over 20 member countries. She is a graduate of the Johns Hopkins University's School of Advanced International Studies, and her publications cover the taxation of extractive industries, financial sector debt bias, and capital flows to developing countries.

Thornton Matheson is a Senior Fellow at the Urban-Brookings Tax Policy Center, where she specializes in business and environmental taxation. She holds a PhD from the University of Maryland, College Park, and has published on international corporate taxation, financial transaction taxes, and natural resource taxation.

Geerten Michielse is a Senior Economist in the Tax Policy Division at the IMF and formerly a university Professor of international tax law. He has published extensively on corporate and international tax issues.

Kiyoshi Nakayama is an Advisor in the Fiscal Affairs Department of the IMF. He has led many technical assistance missions on tax policy and tax administration to Asian and African countries. Before joining the IMF, he was Professor of Tax Law at the Graduate School of Business Science, University of Tsukuba, Tokyo. He also worked for the National Tax Agency and the Ministry of Finance in Japan.

Narine Nersesyan is a Senior Economist at the Tax Policy Division of the IMF, with over 20 years of experience in tax policy capacity development and applied economic analysis. Previously, she served as a Senior Economist at the OECD and as a Senior Manager at Deloitte Consulting/US.

Roberto Schatan is a Senior Economist in the IMF's Tax Policy Division. He holds a PhD from the National University of Mexico and worked for many years at the Ministry of Finance and the Tax Administration Service in Mexico. He was a delegate to the OECD's working party on the taxation of multinational enterprises and later joined the OECD as a Senior Advisor.

Alpa Shah is an Economist in the IMF's Tax Policy Division. Her work encompasses a range of technical assistance, research, and analysis on income, consumption, and natural resource tax policy issues. She holds an MA in Economics from the University of Cambridge and an MSc from the School of Oriental and African Studies, University of London.

Christophe Waerzeggers is a Senior Counsel in the Financial and Fiscal Law Unit of the IMF's Legal Department. Previously he was a Lecturer in tax and comparative tax law at Utrecht University. He started his career as a tax lawyer in Brussels consecutively with the Belgian firms de Bandt, van Hecke & Lagae (Linklaters in Belgium), and the US firm Hogan & Hartson. He holds LLMs in law and tax law from the Katholieke Universiteit Leuven.

PART I

Introduction and Background

CHAPTER 1

Introduction

Ruud de Mooij, Alexander Klemm, and Victoria Perry

In recent years, newspaper headlines have featured terms such as "digital service taxes," "paradise papers," and "tax wars," all referring to various issues in international taxation. These and related topics have long been discussed among tax experts from academia, businesses and policy circles. Recently, increased strains on government budgets after the global financial crisis and information that journalists have revealed about the very low global taxation of some large and profitable multinational corporations have triggered political and popular upheaval going far beyond the small group of tax insiders.

The COVID-19 crisis has only amplified the importance of the international tax debate. While several multinational businesses—and many domestically oriented ones in all countries—are hard hit and fighting for survival, others are thriving and report record-high stock-market values and profits—most notably companies that are highly digitalized and those operating in the pharmaceutical sector. At the same time, the necessary and life-saving government interventions during the pandemic have increased public debt ratios to record levels, raising concerns about how to recover from this through future tax collections. This reinforces the need to fix what is sometimes called "a broken international tax system," the revenue-raising ability of which has been under severe stress as a result of tax competition, issues in allocation of the tax base, and aggressive tax planning techniques.

The debate has led to several global, regional and national initiatives to address the most pressing problems in the century-old international tax architecture—which dates back to the League of Nations in the 1920s. Most notably, the G20/OECD project on base erosion and profit shifting that concluded in 2015 is a landmark in the history of international tax coordination in its effort to resolve some of the most urgent issues of perceived tax avoidance ("loopholes")—even though it left the main building blocks of the framework itself untouched. It induced many countries to implement changes in domestic laws to mitigate the most egregious forms of tax avoidance by multinational enterprises. More recently, discussions in the OECD's Inclusive Framework have focused on more fundamental changes in the international tax architecture itself, with the aim to resolve the key weaknesses that form the root cause of the problems.

Understanding the economic aspects of international tax rules is complex since many current design features are not based on clear economic principles, but rather determined by a pragmatic compromise between countries. Still, for policy makers it is critical to understand the scale and scope of the current problems as well as the economic implications of reforms in the overall framework. This book aims to contribute to such better understanding by providing a thorough but comprehensible analysis of key issues in international tax design and reform.

The IMF has long played an active role in research and advice on international tax issues. In its work with developing country members, it has been advising governments for decades on the design and implementation of effective tax laws, including on fiscal regimes for extractive industries, (model) tax treaties, anti-avoidance measures and other policies to safeguard revenue while maintaining an attractive investment climate. On the analytical side, IMF staff has played an active role in identifying problems and providing solutions. A study was released in 2014 about the character, scope and scale of international tax spillovers from corporate taxes and how these could be addressed (IMF 2014)—with multiple research papers underlying that analysis. Together with partner organizations of the Platform for Collaboration on Tax, the Fund developed a toolkit in 2015 on the effective and efficient use of tax incentives for investment in low-income countries (IMF, OECD, WB, and UN 2015), building on a wealth of earlier research by IMF staff. In a series of papers, IMF research also dealt specifically with the inherent distortion of corporate income tax systems toward debt finance by corporations, an issue that is particularly relevant for financial stability (IMF 2009; 2016). More recently, the IMF published a comprehensive policy paper on options for reform of the international tax framework, entitled "Corporate Taxation in the Global Economy" (IMF 2019). That study documents the unprecedented stress on the current international corporate tax system and the need for fundamental redesign. It explores alternative directions for progress, quantifying their impact where that is possible to inform the ongoing policy debate. IMF staff also participated in a book project of Oxford University, which deepens the analysis of alternative systems of international taxation (Devereux and others 2021).

The present volume elaborates further on the series of studies conducted by IMF staff on international tax issues, releasing extensive background research that underlay the 2019 study and building further on it. Where appropriate it has a special focus on developing countries. The aim of this book is to provide a complete and self-contained assessment of the current international tax framework and possible alternative architectures, grouped in a logical manner and accessible to a relatively broad audience. We hope that this will offer useful analytical background to support the global debate on this important and topical matter.

OVERVIEW

The book is divided into three parts. Part I sets the scene by providing a basic introduction of the international aspects of the corporate income tax. For instance, it discusses why the corporate income tax exists in the first place, how it works when companies operate internationally, and how recent economic developments have changed the corporate—and therefore the tax—landscape. Part II then discusses the challenges that the current international tax framework is facing, in part as a result of these economic developments. Part III analyzes potential solutions to these problems, including both incremental and more fundamental reforms.

Part I: Fundamentals of International Corporate Taxation

Before getting into the issues of international taxation, the first question that must be answered is why countries have a corporate income tax and how it should be designed (Chapter 2, De Mooij and Klemm). Understanding the *why* is essential for everything that follows, as all difficulties would be moot if there were no clear rationale to have a corporate income tax. In that case, one could simply use other taxes that are more efficient and/or simpler to administer and enforce. As there does appear to be a strong rationale for a corporate income tax from a domestic perspective, the next question is *how* to design a good corporate income tax. Here, the chapter discusses both the standard corporate income tax and more innovative designs such as rent taxes.

One of the key issues of international taxation is that multiple jurisdictions can impose a tax claim on the income earned by a multinational corporation. The interaction of domestic laws, multilateral guidance, international norms, and bilateral treaties have led to a highly complex international tax architecture (Chapter 3, Nersesyan). It is marked by the need to distinguish among source, residence, and destination countries. The chapter explains these concepts, as well as systems of territorial and worldwide taxation that aim to implement these principles. These concepts play a key role throughout the rest of the book.

Current problems in the international tax framework were not foreseen at their inception. A century ago, most firms were domestic, and capital was tied to a location and mostly tangible in nature. The rise of multinational corporations (Chapter 4, Hebous) and the growing importance of intangible assets have changed the corporate landscape drastically. This raises significant challenges for the current system, which would not have materialized if businesses were still mostly operating in one country and international transactions were limited to exports and imports between unrelated parties.

Part II: Problems of the Current International Tax Architecture

A major issue in designing the international tax system is how to attribute taxable profits of multinational enterprises to different jurisdictions. One key characteristic of the current framework is that the accounts of the multinational are separated between jurisdictions, that is, in each country where the multinational operates, its accounts terminate at the border. Determining the profits in each jurisdiction is then achieved by using transfer prices for internal transactions. Here, the international convention is to use the arm's-length principle, which prescribes that prices between related parties should be used as if they were transactions between unrelated parties operating in the market. Determining these transfer prices, however, can be practically challenging, especially when there are no obvious comparable transactions among unrelated parties. Determining arm's-length prices can also be conceptually difficult, as explained using the example of allocating risk and debt of a multinational across its subsidiaries (Chapter 5, Schatan). Especially developing countries may suffer from these difficulties by seeing their tax base eroded.

Under current international tax rules, primary taxing rights are allocated to source countries, that is, where the productive activities take place. Multinationals might choose the location of these activities and associated profits based on the tax burden imposed by different jurisdictions. This creates incentives for jurisdictions to engage in tax competition, that is, to use their tax system strategically to attract reported profits and real activities (Chapter 6, Hebous). Such tax competition can be harmful for global welfare, although there is no consensus on how harmful it is or what form is particularly harmful.

While source-based taxation is associated with profit shifting and tax competition, one alternative is to tax multinational profits on a residence basis. Enforcing residence-based taxes, however, encounters its own difficulties, such as avoidance through deferral, manipulation of the place of residence, and the need for complicated anti-avoidance rules (Chapter 7, Nakayama and Perry). And even a pure residence-based system would face major challenges. Further, from the point of view of lower income developing countries, which are nearly always primarily "source" countries, allocating the entire tax base to the residence of multinational enterprises would be disadvantageous. In practice, interactions between source and residence-based taxation further complicate matters.

A key principle of the international tax framework is to avoid double taxation, by which is meant more than one claim by different jurisdictions on the profit earned by a multinational company. The allocation of taxing rights between source and residence countries and the attribution of profits is traditionally agreed in detailed double-taxation treaties (Chapter 8, Leduc and Michielse). Treaties often assign more taxing rights over passive income to residence countries, for example, by setting maximum withholding tax rates on cross border bilateral payments of interest, dividends, and royalties from income earned in source countries. Treaties can raise challenges, however. Multinational companies can use complex treaty networks to reroute transactions through the most beneficial treaty jurisdictions (treaty shopping). Developing countries are often particularly vulnerable to loss of tax bases through this channel.

The impact of taxes can sometimes be counterintuitive, and this is critical for understanding the impact of policies. For instance, corporate income taxes are known to affect both the location of reported profits of multinationals and the location of their real capital. These channels may interact in various ways (Chapter 9, Klemm and Liu). For example, a high corporate tax rate may not discourage real investment in a country if it is possible for the multinational to shift profits out of that country at low cost. Somewhat surprisingly, it appears that profit shifting may even increase real investment in both low and high-tax jurisdictions. Such effects imply that measures to curb profit shifting can have ambiguous effects on tax revenues, investment and welfare.

The rapid digitalization of the economy reinforces the tax challenges for the international tax framework identified in other chapters, but also raises new issues (Chapter 10, Aslam and Shah). For instance, digital companies can be active in markets and earn profits there, without being physically present—and physical presence is the long-standing basis for claiming taxing rights over corporate income, in treaties and also in most domestic tax laws. Moreover, by using data generated from users or consumers, the destination of digital services also becomes partly the source of its profits. This raises new issues and creates debate as to whether taxing rights should be exercised by countries where users and consumers reside, that is, destination countries and not (only) by the country in which the multinational company "resides," or "is physically present."

Part III: Reform options

One way to address the problems associated with profit shifting is through efforts that strengthen source-based taxation (Chapter 11, Beer and Michielse). For instance, changes in the definition of a permanent establishment (which determines the right for a jurisdiction to tax) and adaptations in profit attribution rules (such as transfer pricing rules) can reduce opportunities for profit shifting. They should be combined with improved international cooperation and transparency. Tax competition is harder to address and minimize under source-based taxation and might even intensify if source-based elements are strengthened. However, tax competition can be reduced by the application of minimum taxes on the returns to inbound foreign direct investment.

A different option would be rather to strengthen residence taxation. Recent attempts and proposals to reduce the opportunities for tax minimization by means of manipulation of residence focus on specific rules for controlled foreign corporations, anti-inversion rules and exit taxes, and anti-avoidance rules related to hybrid entities. Yet, more radical possibilities could more strongly strengthen the reach of residence-based taxation, including minimum taxes on outbound investment, or an outright shift toward worldwide taxation—in contrast to the recent trend to eliminate worldwide taxation in favor of taxation of business profits only where they are deemed to be generated ("territorial taxation") (Chapter 12, Nakayama, Perry, and Klemm). Even more radical and forward looking would be to impose all taxes on business profits on a look through basis, that is, on the ultimate (human) owners of the capital in their places of residence.

A third option for reform discussed in the book would entail a much more fundamental change, by moving toward a destination-based international tax system (Chapter 13, Hebous and Klemm). This would be the most effective way to eliminate profit shifting and tax competition. There is an important dilemma, however: it needs to be adopted in a coordinated fashion around the world, which will be difficult to achieve due to varying interests. Indeed, the direct revenue consequences, at least in the short run, are potentially very large for individual countries, both positive and negative. Favorable dynamic effects might, however, relax these implications in the medium term.

Profit shifting can also be effectively addressed by replacing separate accounting with transfer pricing by unitary taxation with formula apportionment (Chapter 14, Matheson, Beer, Coelho, Liu, and Luca). The formula may contain production factors, such as assets and employment to sustain elements of source taxation. It can also be based on sales factors, consistent with destination-based taxation. Instead of formula apportionment for the entire profit of a multinational company, also a hybrid system of residual profit allocation is considered, whereby routine profits are allocated to countries of production and formulary methods are used for the allocation of residual profits, that is, those exceeding a normal rate of return.

Specific international tax challenges arise in the natural resource sector (Chapter 15, Baunsgaard and Devlin). Given the large profits generated by this sector, special regimes are usually in place to ensure that a fair share of these location-specific rents are captured by the state where the resources are located. These regimes are especially important for developing economies where extractive industries can be responsible for a major share of all revenue. These special regimes, however, create their own challenges regarding international taxation, discussed in the chapter.

Reforms in the international tax system can have important legal implications (Chapter 16, Waerzeggers, Hillier, and Aw). The current system is grounded in a complex network of domestic law, bilateral tax treaties and multilateral agreements, such as tax directives in the European Union. The complexity as well as tax uncertainty of these legal provisions provide an additional argument for change—most importantly for developing countries for whom administrative capacity is generally a major obstacle for enforcement of these laws. The legal aspects of fundamental reform options, however, might generate their own obstacles with respect to adoption and implementation—especially in light of existing double tax treaties. Irrespective of the chosen path, international cooperation will likely be needed.

CONCLUSION

The chapters in this book yield a variety of insights and policy conclusions. Some that are worth noting include:

- It becomes very clear that the current international tax architecture is no longer fit for purpose. The past century has seen dramatic changes in technologies, a surge of globalization and major changes in how businesses are organized and operate. The international tax framework has not kept pace with these developments. Issues of profit shifting are increasingly challenging, tax competition continues, major concerns arise for developing countries and digitalization requires new ways to design the framework.

- Partial solutions can help resolve some issues but run the risk of magnifying other problems—with unknown implications for welfare. Tackling the most common forms of profit shifting, for example, can intensify tax competition for real investment.

- While fundamental reforms often have the appeal of offering powerful solutions to the existing problems, they might create new ones that are yet unforeseen and untested. Moreover, they can have major distributional implications—and thus international agreement on these reforms will be very difficult to achieve.

- Economic forces will likely induce a continuing tendency toward to the adoption of destination-based elements in the taxation of multinationals. Fundamental proposals, such as the destination-based cash-flow tax or formulary apportionment with a sales factor, are likely a step too far at this point, although a partial step in this direction is currently being discussed and could pave the way for future reforms. At the same time, trends toward a greater use of consumption taxes at the expense of corporate and labor taxes achieve much the same effect and are pervasive.

- International cooperation is essential to make progress. Unilateral reforms will run the risk of large spillovers to other economies. Even incremental reforms of the current system require strong cooperation to ensure consistency.

REFERENCES

Devereux, Michael P., Alan J. Auerbach, Michael Keen, Paul Oosterhuis, Wolfgang Schön, and John Vella. 2021. "Taxing Profit in a Global Economy", Oxford University Press.

International Monetary Fund (IMF). 2009. "Debt Bias and Other Distortions: Crisis-Related Issues in Tax Policy." IMF Policy Paper, Washington, DC.

International Monetary Fund (IMF). 2014. "Spillovers in International Corporate Taxation," IMF Policy Paper, Washington, DC.

International Monetary Fund (IMF). 2016. "Tax Policy, Leverage, and Macroeconomic Stability." IMF Policy Paper, Washington, DC.

International Monetary Fund (IMF). 2019. "Corporate Taxation in the Global Economy." IMF Policy Paper, Washington, DC.

International Monetary Fund (IMF), Organisation for Economic Co-operation and Development (OECD), World Bank (WB), and United Nations (UN). 2015. "Options for Low Income Countries' Effective and Efficient Use of Tax Incentives for Investment." Report to the G-20 Development Working Group, Washington, DC.

CHAPTER 2

Why and How to Tax Corporate Income

Ruud de Mooij and Alexander Klemm

INTRODUCTION

The question whether countries should tax corporations on their income is an old one, yet it has never been more topical than it is today. Tax competition is driving down corporate tax rates in a race to the bottom, and 12 countries today levy no corporate income tax at all. The pressure from tax competition and the major complications that arise in administering and enforcing current corporate income tax systems are so vast that one may wonder whether it is worth dealing with them or whether it would not be much easier simply to give up on taxing corporate income, replacing lost revenues with other taxes.

This chapter starts by discussing why it is worthwhile for countries to maintain a corporate income tax, even if possibly in a reformed manner. It starts, in the first section, by discussing the role of the corporate income tax as part of the broader income tax system. Corporate income is a subset of capital income, and so the first question to answer is whether capital income should be taxed or not ("Why Tax Capital Income?"). If that is answered in the affirmative, the next question is whether there is a role for the corporate income tax in the enforcement of capital income taxation ("Why Tax Corporate Income?"). If one accepts that, the subsequent issue that arises is how corporate income should be taxed and how such a tax should be implemented. While details of corporate income tax systems around the world differ, there are some common principles underlying them—including with respect to the taxation of international business income ("The Standard Corporate Income Tax"). Yet there are alternative systems that are based on different principles and that might avoid some of the distortions and complexities of the current corporate income tax. The chapter discusses in particular the comprehensive business income tax, which broadens the base of the corporate income tax by disallowing deductions for interest expenses ("Comprehensive Business Income Tax"). Finally, the chapter discusses various implementations of rent taxes, which exempt the normal return on capital at the corporate level.

WHY TAX CAPITAL INCOME?

Income generally arises from labor effort, be it wages or entrepreneurial activity, and capital returns in the form of interest, dividends, or capital gains. The distinction between labor and capital income is not always easy to make. For instance, self-employed entrepreneurs do not distinguish between payment for the labor effort they put into their own company and their capital investment. The entrepreneurial income they earn is simply the sum of both. Attempts to distinguish labor and capital income for tax purposes then become arbitrary and prone to avoidance: entrepreneurs can easily present income as either labor or capital income, depending on which is being taxed least.

This arbitrage between capital and labor income is at the heart of discussions on the design of the income tax system. For some, the theoretical ideal is to tax the sum of labor and capital income at a progressive rate structure, consistent with the ability-to-pay principle. This "global income tax" prevents arbitrage between labor and capital that could otherwise arise for the taxation of self-employed entrepreneurs.

Others have argued, however, that only labor income should be taxed, while capital income should be exempt. Their argument goes as follows: a tax on (the normal return to) saving increases the relative price of future consumption relative to present consumption. Chamley (1986) and Judd (1985) show that, in an infinite horizon model, this is inefficient and violates horizontal equity principles: it is always better to tax only labor income and avoid the intertemporal distortion to savings. The optimal tax on the normal return is therefore zero (see also Atkinson and Stiglitz 1976). This result has led economists to argue for an exemption of the normal return (see, for example, Mirrlees and others 2011). However, the income tax literature has also criticized the Chamley–Judd outcome for relying on too-specific assumptions, such as optimization over an infinite horizon. Models that relax the assumptions arrive at different conclusions and offer several rationales for a positive capital income tax rate, both for efficiency reasons and to address equity concerns (see, for example, Banks and Diamond 2010). Recent contributions further suggest that the classical Chamley-Judd results are misinterpreted, providing further theoretical ground for the taxation of capital income (Straub and Werning 2020). Overall, the theoretical consensus has been shifting away from the question whether capital income should or should not be taxed towards the question to what extent it ought to be taxed.

Yet others favor an intermediate position between comprehensive taxation of income and zero taxation of capital income. They support separate taxation of labor and capital income under a "dual income tax," with a progressive rate scheme applying to labor income, and with a flat rate applying to capital, usually at a relatively low rate. The motivation for this is twofold: first, the lower tax on capital mitigates distortions in saving and investment, which tend to be relatively severe; second, flat capital income taxes do not need to be personalized, which eases enforcement by using withholding schemes.

When discussing the taxation of capital income, it is useful to distinguish between the normal return on capital and economic rents. The normal return on capital is generally defined as the minimum return required to make investors equally well off (with an adjustment for risk) compared to some benchmark investment, such as a government bond. The remaining profit, over and above the normal return, is called "rents." While the normal return can be called capital income, rents might in fact be subject to bargaining between workers and capital owners—and thus can be reflected either as capital income or as labor income (in the form of higher wages).

Public finance literature is unanimous in advocating taxes on rents as they are in principle nondistortionary. A classic result from theory is therefore that they should in fact be taxed at 100 percent. Practical considerations lead to lower tax burdens, however, because rents are also often "quasi rents," arising from specific investments with a fixed cost. Rent taxes are also deemed equitable since assets are typically owned by the well-off. The more controversial debate outlined earlier in this section on whether capital income should be taxed thus refers to the normal return, not to economic rents.

Another important dimension of capital income taxes arises in open economies, as the supplier of the capital might be based in a different country from where capital is demanded and used. Here, there are two principles of taxation: source or residence. "Source" refers to the country where the capital is installed and where it yields its return. "Residence" is the country where the owner of the capital resides (see Chapters 3 and 4). Residence-based capital income taxes are consistent with taxation based on the ability to pay of domestic residents, as they are taxed on their worldwide capital income—irrespective of where the source of that return is. This generally applies to the personal income tax. Source-based taxes impose tax on investment returns irrespective of their residence. This generally applies to the corporate income tax, which thus imposes tax on the return earned by foreign investors. Again, the distinction between normal returns and economic rents is important. For instance, if after-tax normal returns on investment are fixed on world capital markets, any source-based tax on the normal return will lead to adjustment in the amount of capital such that the before-tax return rises enough to restore equilibrium. Less capital means lower wages, and so the incidence of a source-based tax on the normal return will fall on workers. This, however, will not apply to location-specific rents: to the extent that a source-based tax reduces this rent, the foreign owner will not be able to escape the tax and will bear its full incidence.

WHY TAX CORPORATE INCOME?

There are different types of systems to tax capital income (detailed in the following paragraphs). The so-called classical corporate income tax considers corporations as separate entities from their ultimate owners. As wages and interest are generally deductible, the corporate income tax effectively becomes a withholding tax on equity returns at the company level. Corporate income tax is thus levied separately, besides the personal income tax on equity returns (in the form of dividends and capital gains). Hence, the classical corporate income tax system implies double taxation. If the combined burden of corporate income tax and personal income tax is higher for corporate businesses than for sole proprietorships, it could induce entrepreneurs to run their businesses in the latter legal form so as to avoid paying the double tax. To mitigate such distortions from the double-tax burden on equity returns, classical systems often apply relatively low flat personal income tax rates on equity income.

In contrast to the classical corporate income tax system, the so-called integration system looks through the corporation and acknowledges that, ultimately, legal entities are owned by people. As only people can ultimately bear the true incidence of taxes, this clearly makes more economic sense. The corporate income tax then operates as a withholding mechanism for the full income tax, and imputation credits are provided for individuals when calculating their personal income tax liability. The difficulty with integration systems, however, arises from international transactions: imputation credits are generally not provided for foreign corporate income tax paid. This can lead to distortions in international capital markets. In the European Union, imputation systems have therefore been abolished, as they are an infringement to the freedom of establishment.

As the integration system illustrates, governments do not necessarily have to tax capital income through corporations. Indeed, the alternative would be to tax capital income solely and directly on the income that people receive, that is, through personal income tax, without any withholding of tax at the corporate level. So why is there a corporate income tax? There are two main reasons—none of which is of a fundamental nature; they rather provide a pragmatic case for its existence.[1]

The first reason is based on the relative ease of administration and particularly the withholding role of the corporate income tax. Corporations are convenient collection agents for governments. For instance, besides corporate income tax, value-added tax (VAT) and personal income tax (through pay-as-you-earn schemes) are also often withheld by corporations, as they hold proper books and records and can efficiently be monitored by tax inspectors. Relying on individuals or consumers to pay their tax, based on filed tax returns, would be considerably costlier to enforce. The withholding role is especially important for profits that are retained in the company, as distributed profits can also be taxed through a withholding tax on dividends. Retained profits, however, simply lead to higher value of the firm and, therefore, to capital gains for the owners. For practical reasons, capital gains at the personal level are seldom taxed on an accrual basis but rather upon realization. Capital owners can then postpone their tax payment by not realizing these gains. Moreover, capital gains in small nontraded companies are especially hard to value and might escape taxation altogether. The attraction of the corporate income tax is that it withholds tax on all profits as they arise, thus eliminating the difficulty in taxing capital gains and the distortions it would induce.

---

[1] Other reasons that are often mentioned are less convincing. These include (1) the benefit principle, that is, the idea that corporates should pay something for the use of public goods, and (2) the value of limited liability. The weakness of these arguments is that the amount of tax paid has little relationship to these benefits.

The second reason for taxing corporations relates to taxing the rents earned by international businesses. Under the current international tax convention, source countries have the primary taxing right to tax multinational income. To the extent that this reflects a normal return, it might be shifted onto employees—as was noted before. But to the extent that it reflects economic rent, it would fall on foreign capital owners. For an individual country, taxing foreign capital owners on their rents has significant appeal and provides a major attraction to the corporate income tax. The taxation of rents that accrue to foreigners is particularly important if rents arise from natural resources. Numerous developing countries have abundant resources that are extracted by multinational companies that have their residence elsewhere. Fiscal regimes are generally in place to ensure that a significant portion of these natural resource rents accrues to the local governments.

THE STANDARD CORPORATE INCOME TAX

The most common corporate income tax system applies tax on corporate profits, defined along similar principles as accounting profits but with some adjustments. The tax definition may, for example, be more prescriptive to reduce the amount of judgment in calculating tax bases[2] and to simplify compliance and enforcement. Deviations could also occur for policy reasons, as governments can encourage or discourage certain behaviors by changing their tax implications.

Using a definition of profits as the tax base has the implication that, as in accounting, investment is not a deductible expense. As the company merely changes one type of asset (cash) for another (capital), such a transaction is not a cost. The cost to the company is, instead, the loss of value of the capital due to obsolescence or wear and tear, and this depreciation is deductible. The permissible deduction for depreciation is in many countries specified by law, for example as an annual percentage of the acquisition cost ("straight line") or the written-down value ("declining balance"). Such rules are meant to prevent abuse and to reduce compliance and administrative costs, but they can also be used to purposefully encourage investment. Hence, the exact depreciation allowance for tax purposes is likely to differ from true economic depreciation, that is, the exact loss in value of the asset, and it may also differ from accounting depreciation, although in some countries both are aligned.

Also, following the accounting logic, issuing or repaying debt is treated as a change in the asset composition with no impact on profit, while interest is treated as a deductible expense. Profits are taxed, irrespective of whether they are retained in the company or distributed as dividends. The result is a difference in treatment in interest and dividends, only the former of which is deductible. This generally implies

---

[2] Judgment is often allowed in accounting, and, combined with explanatory notes, can improve the quality of information. It would not be good to allow firms judgment in determining their tax base; moreover, there is a strong benefit to the quality of accounting if judgmental decisions can be made without impact on taxation.

a debt bias in corporate income tax systems, although this also depends on the integration with personal-level income taxes: if personal income tax on interest is higher than on dividends, this may offset the discriminatory effect associated with the corporate income tax. It is unlikely to completely undo it, though, because there are typically some taxpayers (for example, pension funds, foreign investors) who benefit from a tax exemption or rate reduction on both interest and dividends.

Debt bias is not only a distortion that exists in theory but has been shown to be of significant importance empirically. A meta-analysis by Feld, Heckemeyer, and Overesch (2013) finds that the debt ratio of nonfinancial firms increases on average by 0.27 percentage point for each percentage point increase in the corporate income tax rate. Another metastudy by De Mooij (2011) finds that these responses are increasing over time, suggesting that distortions relating to debt bias have become more important. De Mooij and Keen (2016) and Luca and Tieman (2016) analyze debt bias among, respectively, banks and nonbank financial firms. Both find significant and sizable effects on leverage ratios, which is particularly worrisome in light of the implications high debt can have on financial stability. The IMF (2009; 2016) argues that such biases are hard to justify, and alternative systems have been proposed by economists that address this bias.

Standard corporate income tax systems not only distort the financial structure of corporations, but also the level of investment. By allowing a deduction for both depreciation and interest, marginal investments that just break even and that are financed by equity are discouraged by taxation as taxes increase the cost of capital.

COMPREHENSIVE BUSINESS INCOME TAX

If interest deductibility creates debt bias, the obvious solution is not to allow it. A US Treasury report (Department of the Treasury 1992) works out a concrete proposal for how such a system would work, including its international implications. Clearly, to prevent double taxation, such a proposal also means that interest receipts of corporations are untaxed. This would also apply to banks and other financial intermediaries, which would no longer be taxed on profit associated with the interest margin between lending and borrowing. Moreover, the personal income tax on interest might be abolished or reduced to bring it in line with dividends and capital gains. The main impact of a comprehensive business income tax is hence to move the point of ultimate taxation from the lender to the borrower. So instead of collecting corporate income tax from financial intermediaries and personal income tax on interest from any savers providing funds, the comprehensive business income tax would collect the tax in one step from the borrower.[3] This would thus mirror the treatment of dividends, which are equally

---

[3] The specific comprehensive business income tax proposal by the US Treasury argues for exempting interest and dividend income throughout, but, in principle, additional personal-level taxation could be maintained, as long as treatment on interest and dividend is the same. Such treatment would be required if progressive taxation of comprehensive income is desired. A governmental commission in Sweden proposed the introduction of a comprehensive business income tax in 2014.

nondeductible, and—at least under certain circumstances—typically nontaxable when received by corporations.

A comprehensive business income tax would effectively mean that the normal return on capital, irrespective of whether financed by debt or equity, is taxed in the source country and at the level of the firm. This would raise taxes and redistribute revenues across countries. The increase in taxation would be the result of current tax structures, under which some interest recipients are exempt from tax or are tax favored. Pension funds, for example, are often tax exempt, implying that their interest income is not taxable. A shift to a comprehensive business income tax would change this, as the pension funds' interest income would be taxed at the corporate level of the firms in which they invest. International redistribution would occur because foreign debtors are currently only subject to a possible withholding tax on interest in the country where they invest. These tax rates are typically lower than full corporate income tax or personal income tax rates and may even be zero in some cases (notably if the investor is a sovereign wealth fund). The country where the investor is located may, in turn, collect taxes, typically crediting the withholding tax. A move to a comprehensive business income tax would mean higher revenues for the source country, and either lower revenues in the residence country (if the system is adapted there too) or higher total taxation of interest (assuming no credit is given for corporate income tax).

A comprehensive business income tax effectively taxes the return on debt at the level of the corporation, instead of at the level of the owner of the capital. If this is to be integrated with the personal income tax, it serves as a withholding tax for the personal income tax. Yet a comprehensive business income tax can also serve as a final withholding tax on all capital returns if the personal income tax on interest, dividends, and capital gains is abolished. By taxing the normal return, a comprehensive business income tax would discourage investment. The incidence of the comprehensive business income tax might thus to a significant extent be shifted onto workers in the form of lower wages.

RENT TAXES

Instead of taxing the full normal return to capital at the corporate level, as under a comprehensive business income tax, another class of corporate tax systems exempts the normal return entirely at the corporate level. These can be labeled "rent taxes." There are different ways to implement rent taxes, as this section will discuss. Note that normal returns can still be taxed at the personal level. The systems discussed here refer only to the taxation of capital returns at the corporate level.

Cash-Flow Taxes

One class of rent taxes is known as cash-flow taxes, first systematically classified in Meade (1978). The simplest form is the real ("R")-base cash-flow tax, first described by Brown (1948). As suggested by its name, it is defined as the net sum of all real—meaning nonfinancial—flows. On the incoming side, this is simply a company's sales, including of capital goods. On the outgoing side, this includes all costs, such as labor and purchases of intermediate and capital goods. Financial flows, such as interest payments, net debt issuance, and net dividends, are excluded from the tax base.

Compared to the standard corporate income tax, there are two key differences: First, disregarding financial flows means that interest is nondeductible. This aspect of the cash-flow tax is similar to a comprehensive business income tax, and it means that there is no debt bias in the system, as dividends also remain nondeductible. Second, investment can be immediately expensed. This deduction of the cost of capital goods is significantly more generous than the depreciation allowances under the standard corporate income tax system: while such allowances also permit deduction of the full cost over the lifetime of a capital good, the amount is worth less in net present value terms (and if, as is typically the case, there is no adjustment for inflation, there is a real erosion of the cumulative value of deductions). This more generous treatment of investment implies an exemption of the normal return on assets from tax, restricting the tax base to economic rent (see Box 2.1). As a result, the cash-flow tax is neutral with respect to investment: any investment that is worthwhile in the absence of taxation remains profitable under such tax, because the investors are not taxed on their required rate of return.

Various tax reform proposals incorporating R-base cash-flow taxes have been made. For example, the Hall and Rabushka (2007) flat tax is essentially an R-base cash-flow tax combined with a flat-rate tax on wages. Bradford's (2004) X tax is equally an R-base cash-flow tax, but in this case combined with a graduated tax on wages. Moreover, Bradford discusses a destination-based version of this tax, a topic that is covered in Chapter 13.

A second type of cash-flow tax is levied on real and financial ("R+F") cash-flows. The inclusion of financial flows means that interest deductibility is back, but changes in net debt are also included. Specifically, any inflows from issuing loans are taxed, while outflows, such as repayments, are deductible. This ensures the neutrality of the tax: if interest deductibility were simply combined with expensing of investment, the result would be subsidized investment, as the expensing alone already achieves neutrality. By taxing the debt issuance, this effect is undone.

The R and R+F cash-flow taxes thus both tax economic rents. The difference is mostly in implementation and in where tax is collected, but there is one exception. Suppose the financial sector earns economic rents in its lending activity. Under an R+F base, such rents are always taxed. Under an R-base tax, the taxation of rents depends on the type of borrower. If the borrower is a taxable business, then rents are taxed because interest is not deductible. If the borrower is, however, an individual not covered by the cash-flow tax, then rents would go untaxed, unless another mechanism to recover tax on them is introduced (for example, if interest is not deductible for individuals, it is covered by the personal income tax).

A third type of cash-flow tax discussed by Meade (1978) is the share transactions ("S")-base cash-flow tax. This simply taxes the net distributions of companies; that is, dividends and share buybacks are taxable, while capital increases are deductible. In net present value terms, this tax can be shown to be identical to an R+F-base tax. It is therefore also neutral. To see this intuitively, note that capital raised is deductible, which results in the same effect as the deduction of investment in Box 2.1.

Box 2.1. Why Does Expensing Capital Imply Rent Taxes?

The R-base cash-flow tax, which allows expensing of investment but no deduction for interest, is an example of a tax on economic rents. As it may not be intuitive why expensing implies rent taxation, the following provides an illustration.

Suppose a firm plans an investment I held for one year, yielding a rate of return p, and facing a cost of capital r. In the absence of taxes, the economic rent of such an investment would be:

$$R = -I + \frac{I(1+p)}{1+r} = I\frac{p-r}{1+r}. \tag{1}$$

A cash-flow tax imposed at rate t would then raise the following present value tax payment T:

$$T = -tI + \frac{tI(1+p)}{1+r} = tI\frac{p-r}{1+r}. \tag{2}$$

This equation shows that no tax is payable in present value terms whenever the rate of return equals the cost of capital at which the firm discounts future flows. If the government's discount rate is lower, the present value of tax revenue would still be positive.

Rent-earning investments would be taxed, but tax would never turn a profitable investment into a loss-making one. The cash-flow tax is therefore a neutral tax. This can also be seen by deducting tax (equation (2)) from pretax rents (equation (1)), which yields $R(1-t)$.[4] Another interpretation is that the government turns into a silent partner of the investment, cushioning the firm's losses in case of a bad outcome and receiving a share of the upside. To achieve neutrality in practice, tax authorities need to refund (or carry forward with interest) negative tax liabilities when investment is undertaken (left part of equation (2)).

In a traditional tax system, investment is not deductible, so the tax payment would be:

$$T = \frac{tIp}{1+r}. \tag{3}$$

The rent net of tax would then be:

$$R = I\frac{p(1-t)-r}{1+r}. \tag{4}$$

Hence, a project that just breaks even before tax ($p = r$) turns unprofitable. To be undertaken, an investment needs to yield a higher return, specifically, the cost of capital is increased from r to $r/(1-t)$.

---

[4] These results continue to hold if the asset is held forever or is subject to depreciation d. In that case, the pretax rent would be $R = -I + \sum_{i=1}^{\infty} \frac{p(1-d)I}{(1+r)^i} = I\frac{p-d-r}{r+d}$. The cash-flow tax allows deduction of investment. Depreciation is not deductible, so that the posttax rent is still $R(1-t)$. With or without tax, the investment is worthwhile if the real return ($p - d$) exceeds the cost of capital r.

Allowances for Corporate Equity or Capital

A different class of rent taxes achieves the exemption of the normal rate of return by offering directly an allowance for it (see Boadway and Bruce 1984). One way to implement this in a way that is relatively close to the current system is the allowance for corporate equity. This maintains deductibility of interest on debt and complements it with a deduction for notional interest on equity, where the notional interest rate is fixed administratively. This method achieves approximate rent taxation, and works better the more closely the prescribed notional interest rate matches the normal rate of return. It also reduces the debt bias but may not fully eliminate it if the interest rate on debt exceeds the notional interest rate on equity.

A related further step is the allowance for corporate capital, which is similar to an allowance for corporate equity, but replaces the deductibility of actual interest on debt with the same notional interest rate as applied on equity. This always achieves a full abolition of debt bias at the corporate level, and achieves rent taxation, whenever the notional rate is set at the level of the normal rate of return.

The allowance for corporate equity and the allowance for corporate capital are consistent with rent taxation (assuming an appropriate notional rate is chosen) without a need for expensing. Hence, the current depreciation system can be kept in place. Interestingly, one of the features of these taxes is that the depreciation rate becomes irrelevant for tax purposes. A higher depreciation rate provides a greater initial deduction but also reduces a firm's equity and hence the amount on which the notional interest is applicable. It therefore even allows expensing, in which case investment does not add to equity at all, and the allowance for corporate equity or allowance for corporate capital mirrors a cash-flow tax.

Practical Experiences with Rent Taxes

In practice, only the allowance for corporate equity has been implemented, sometimes only for a few years, in a number of countries (for example, Belgium, Croatia, Cyprus, Italy, Latvia, Liechtenstein, Malta, Turkey). Other countries moved partially toward an allowance for corporate equity by allowing a reduced tax rate on the notional return (Austria), by offering it to small firms (Portugal), or by restricting it to dividends paid out (Brazil).[5]

Pure cash-flow taxes are rare, but there are many examples of countries implementing some of their features. Many countries, for example, have temporarily allowed expensing of investment, but without restricting interest deductibility. This leads to subsidization of marginal investments rather than neutrality. Some countries use cash-flow tax features on surtaxes, for example in the natural resource sector, to capture resource rents. Mexico had a tax that came close to an R-base cash-flow tax,[6] but it served as a minimum rather than final corporate tax. A few countries have taxes that are charged only on distributions, thus resembling S-base cash-flow taxes (for example, Estonia), but they do not offer a deduction for capital increases.

Finally, the VAT also allows expensing of investment and denies interest deductibility. It thus resembles an R-base cash-flow tax, with the major difference

---

[5] For details of the years these taxes were applicable, as well as their main features, see Table 2 in Hebous and Klemm (2020).

[6] Impuesto Empresarial a Tasa Única (IETU, "Flat Rate Business Tax"), applicable from 2008 to 2013.

being the nondeductibility of labor costs. Value added is the sum of profits and wages, but the VAT is actually a tax only on rents and wages, leaving normal profits untaxed.

CONCLUSION

While taxing corporate income is common around the world, the case for doing so is certainly not undisputed. First, the role of the corporate income tax as a withholding mechanism at the source of profits has come under intense pressure due to profit shifting, distortionary effects on (international) investment and corporate finance decisions, and ongoing tax competition. Second, economists have raised serious doubts as to the fundamental question of whether the normal return to capital income should be taxed at all, in light of the distortionary effects these taxes have on saving and investment. This latter view is disputed among economists, however, especially in recent contributions that question the validity of the classical zero-tax results. One option to tax the normal return might be a comprehensive business income tax, which taxes interest at the corporate level. This would eliminate the inherent bias toward debt finance in current corporate income tax systems, and it could eliminate the need to have complicated schemes for taxing the normal return at the personal level. Given that such a system would increase the tax base, it could come along with a lower tax rate to yield the same corporate tax revenue.

Consensus does exist on the taxation of economic rents, which provides a strong rationale for some type of corporate income tax. Moreover, there is generally broad support for the withholding function of the corporate income tax for enforcing the income tax, most notably for developing countries where administrative capacity is limited. These motivations do not, however, unequivocally support a corporate tax system as countries currently have it. More efficient design would point, for instance, to some kind of rent tax—with the possibility to tax the normal return at the personal level. A corporate rent tax can be based on a simple cash-flow tax system. Alternatively, it can be implemented by allowing a deduction for the normal return on equity. To the extent that rent taxes at the source are subject to spillovers, for example from profit shifting or tax competition, they can also be based on a destination basis, which is generally more robust to spillovers. These aspects are discussed in more detail in subsequent chapters.

REFERENCES

Atkinson, Anthony B., and Joseph E. Stiglitz. 1976. "The Design of Tax Structure: Direct versus Indirect Taxation." *Journal of Public Economics* 6(1–2): 55–75.

Banks, James, and Peter Diamond. 2010. "The Base for Direct Taxation." In *Dimensions of Tax Design,* edited by Stuart Adam, Tim Besley, Richard Blundell, Stephen Bond, Robert Chote, Malcolm Gammie, Paul Johnson, Gareth Myles, and James Poterba, 548–674. Oxford, UK: Oxford University Press.

Boadway, Robin, and Neil Bruce. 1984. "A General Proposition on the Design of a Neutral Business Tax." *Journal of Public Economics* 24: 231–39.

Bradford, David F. 2004. "The X Tax in the World Economy." NBER Working Paper 10676, National Bureau of Economic Research, Cambridge, MA.

Brown, E. Cary. 1948. "Business Income Taxation and Investment Incentives." In *Income, Employment and Public Policy*, edited by Lloyd A. Metzler and others, 300–16. New York: Norton.

Chamley, Christophe. 1986. Optimal Taxation of Capital Income in General Equilibrium with Infinite Lives. *Econometrica* 54(3): 607–22.

De Mooij, Ruud. 2011. "The Tax Elasticity of Corporate Debt: A Synthesis of Size and Variations." IMF Working Paper 11/95, International Monetary Fund, Washington, DC.

De Mooij, Ruud, and Michael Keen. 2016. "Debt, Taxes, and Banks." *Journal of Money, Credit, and Banking* 48(1): 5–33.

Department of the Treasury. 1992. *Integration of the Individual and Corporate Tax Systems: Taxing Business Income Once*. Washington, DC: Government Printing Office.

Feld, Lars P., Jost H. Heckemeyer, and Michael Overesch. 2013. "Capital Structure Choice and Company Taxation: A Meta-Study." *Journal of Banking and Finance* 37(8): 2850–66.

Hall, Robert E., and Alvin Rabushka. 2007. *The Flat Tax*. Stanford, CA: Hoover Institution Press.

Hebous, Shafik and Alexander Klemm. 2020. "A Destination-Based Allowance for Corporate Equity." *International Tax and Public Finance* 27: 753–77.

International Monetary Fund (IMF). 2009. "Debt Bias and Other Distortions: Crisis-Related Issues in Tax Policy." IMF Policy Paper, Washington, DC.

International Monetary Fund (IMF). 2016. "Tax Policy, Leverage and Macroeconomic Stability." IMF Policy Paper, Washington, DC.

Judd, Kenneth L. 1985. "Redistributive Taxation in a Simple Perfect Foresight Model." *Journal of Public Economics* 28(1): 59–83.

Luca, Oana, and Alexander Tieman. 2016. "Financial Sector Debt Bias." IMF Working Paper 13/217, International Monetary Fund, Washington, DC.

Meade, James. 1978. *The Structure and Reform of Direct Taxation*. London: George Allen and Unwin.

Mirrlees, James, Stuart Adam, Tim Besley, Richard Blundell, Stephen Bond, Robert Chote, Malcolm Gammie, Paul Johnson, Gareth Myles, and Jim M. Poterba. 2011. *Tax by Design*. Oxford, UK: Oxford University Press.

Straub, Ludwig and Ivan Werning. 2020. "Positive Long-Run Capital Taxation: Chamley-Judd Revisited." *American Economic Review* 110(1): 86–119.

CHAPTER 3

The Current International Tax Architecture: A Short Primer

Narine Nersesyan

INTRODUCTION

When a business activity crosses national borders, the question arises as to where the profits resulting from that activity should be taxed. In principle, there are at least three possibilities for assigning a taxing right:

- *Source:* the countries where production takes place
- *Residence:* the countries where a company is deemed to reside
- *Destination:* the countries where sales take place

The generally applied tax architecture for determining where profits are taxed is now nearly 100 years old—designed for a world in which most trade was in physical goods, trade made a less significant contribution to world GDP, and global value chains were not particularly complex. This chapter describes briefly that traditional architecture and sets the stage for following chapters that provide more detailed explanations and set out various possible approaches to developing a framework better suited to modern economic circumstances—one which could potentially be perceived as fairer among countries that now play different roles in global value chains.

The current international tax framework is based on the so-called "1920's compromise" (Graetz 2001, p. 262).[1] In very basic outline, under the "compromise" the primary right to tax active business income is assigned where the activity takes place—in the "source" country—while the right to tax passive income, such as dividends, royalties and interest, is given up to the "residence" country—where the entity or person that receives and ultimately owns the profit resides. The system has, however, evolved in ways that considerably deviate from this historic "compromise," and international tax arrangements currently rest on a fragile and contentious balance of taxing rights between residence and source countries (IMF, 2014).

---

[1] The *Report on Double Taxation*, submitted to the Financial Committee of the League of Nations in 1923 (League of Nations 1923), defines not only the fundamental structure of the current international tax system but also its key concepts.

The determination of where income is to be taxed when activities cross borders therefore requires the following: determining the nature of the income (active versus passive); where the source of the income is; where the residences of the parties involved are; and, importantly, whether the activity has sufficient linkages to the source country ("nexus") to be deemed allocable there.[2] In the current architecture, assuming that the income in question is "active" *and* that there is sufficient nexus with the source country, the net profit is allocated by the parties by means of the "arm's length principle"—pricing all individual transactions between related entities as if they were taking place between unrelated entities in a competitive market—and thus determining the profits deemed to arise in each country involved in the chain of business transactions.

While domestic laws of each individual country set out the rules generally described in the preceding paragraph, the international taxation system is—very importantly—overlain with a network of more than 3,000 bilateral double-taxation treaties. These typically add (among other functions) a layer of definitions and income allocation rules that try to bring into alignment, and therefore can alter, the rules imposed by the individual signatories. Most of these treaties follow fairly closely one of two models— the OECD or the UN. Most significantly, tax treaties (1) define the necessary nexus for a source country to impose tax on active business income, and (2) give up (some or all) taxing rights in regard to "passive" income payments from within the source country to the "residence" country of the recipient. The key role of the international tax architecture is to govern the allocation of taxing rights between the potential tax-claiming jurisdictions to avoid both excessive taxation of a single activity and a nontaxation of a business activity.

In the course of a century-long evolution, the current international tax framework has turned into a hybrid construct, defined by a complex web of interactions between domestic laws and tax treaty obligations. The rules for assigning income to a particular geographical area reflect political, legal, economic, historic, and administrative realities. The resulting fairness—or unfairness—of the balance of taxing rights between jurisdictions with legitimate taxation claims is an increasing concern for the international tax community.

CORPORATE RESIDENCE

A corporation is a set of complex legal relationships; shoehorning it into the concept of "resident"—a word that would normally apply with respect to natural persons—presents definitional challenges (Couzin 2002). A corporation does not live and does not have a home. It can have a "residence," therefore, only if the law assigns it one (McIntyre 2003). Since there is no "real" home for a corporation, various residence criteria have developed over time, leading to significant divergences, overlap, and coverage gaps across countries.

---

[2] For a more detailed explanation of these issues, see, inter alia, Richard Vann (1998).

Defining the residence of a modern corporation is becoming increasingly difficult. In the early 20th century, when the concept of corporate residence was established as one of the international tax doctrines, the exercise appeared more straightforward. Considering any of the possibilities—jurisdiction of incorporation, the place of management and control, the country where most of the assets and jobs were located, or the country in which the company's main shareholders resided—would tend to point in the same direction with reasonable consistency (Graetz 2016). But such a classic multinational corporation, with an exact national identity and a fixed headquarters, is largely extinct. The manipulability of corporate residence allows multinationals to "mutate with remarkable ease" (Desai 2009, p. 1). The indicators that could establish a nexus with one particular state—where the company "was incorporated, where it was listed, the nationality of its investor base, the location of its headquarters functions"—now point in different directions, making it difficult to credibly assign where "home" lies (Desai 2009, p. 1).

A modern multinational corporation may have very good non-tax-related reasons to have more than one residence. In a context of a highly integrated global corporate operation, a multinational that aims at business optimization, value creation, and improved competitiveness in many cases will distribute its corporate and business functions among members of the corporate group that are primarily located in different places. As Michael Graetz notes: "It is no accident that we call corporations doing business around the world 'multinationals'" (2001, p. 320). These issues are further discussed in Chapter 7.

Residence criteria for corporations largely use two approaches in establishing a corporate residence.[3] One approach tests for a formal legal connection to the jurisdiction, such as place of incorporation or registration in the commercial register—a historical fact that cannot be changed, at least easily. The other establishes an economic or commercial connection of a business with the taxing jurisdiction, such as place of effective management, place of substantial ownership and control, or place where the board of directors meets (Ault and Arnold 2010). A combination of these two approaches is also used. Table 3.1 provides by way of example an overview of approaches used by several OECD countries in establishing corporate residence.

---

[3] Predictably, the discrepancies in corporate residence rules have become a fertile ground for tax avoidance and minimization schemes. An example was the "double Irish sandwich." Prior to 2015 companies were only deemed to be Irish tax resident if their place of effective management was in Ireland. A member of a "US multinational" could therefore be legally incorporated in Ireland but be a nonresident there for tax purposes if it was managed and controlled outside of Ireland. Since it was not incorporated in the United States, it would also not be legally resident in the United States. In 2015 Ireland changed the definition of tax residence to include not only entities that are effectively managed in Ireland but also those incorporated there (IMF 2018).

TABLE 3.1.

Tests to Establish Corporate Residence in Select OECD Countries		
	Formal Legal Test	**Economic or Commercial Connection**
United States	Yes, a corporation is resident if organized under the law of the United States	No
Japan	Yes, a corporation is resident if its headquarters or principal office is organized in Japan	No
Sweden	Yes, a corporation is resident if registered under Swedish corporate law	No
United Kingdom	Yes, place of incorporation under UK law	Yes, place of central management and control, considered the place where the board of directors meets
Canada	Yes, place of incorporation under Canadian law	Yes, place of meetings of the board of directors
Australia	Yes, place of incorporation under Australian law	Yes, place of central management and control; additionally, the residence of shareholders, if a majority of voting power is held by shareholders
Germany	Yes, a corporation is resident if its statutory seat is in Germany	Yes, place of management, with focus on day-to-day management

Source: Ault and Arnold (2010).

DEFINING "SOURCE" OF INCOME

The principle of taxing net profit based at its source requires a method for dividing and allocating income and deductions to geographic locations. To do that, the current international tax system relies on the arm's length principle that requires that transfer prices—the prices charged in transactions of one party "related" to another—generally defined by reference to overlapping ownership—are the same as if the parties were not affiliated.

The application of the arm's length principle, in turn, assumes that the tax system is based on so-called separate accounting, where each part of an integrated multinational business is treated as a separate entity and is taxed on income determined from its separate accounts. Determining the source of income for related parties through implementation of the arm's length principle involves significant practical difficulties. Indeed, observing a fair arm's length price for related-party dealings, establishing a third-party transaction that is *comparable* to an intragroup operation of a multinational, is far from easy.[4] The system

---

[4] Moreover, under certain conditions the arm's length price might not exist, especially in a context of highly integrated global corporate operations. For example, suppose that two laboratories each invented and patented a single element of a highly valuable technological breakthrough. Viewed separately, at the arm's length, each patent would be priced at close to zero; the patents are valuable only when priced together. Here, the arm's length pricing of a single patent is pointless (Auerbach,

facilitates profit shifting through transfer price manipulation between related entities to minimize their global income tax liability by allocating income to jurisdictions in which income will be lightly taxed, if at all. This, in turn, leads to aggressive competition between governments to attract the mobile "shiftable" taxable income (Green 1993).

Pinpointing a jurisdiction where income is sourced has become increasingly difficult with globalization of cross-border production chains. Services could be considered sourced either where the service is performed, where the provider resides, or where the provider mastered the skills that allowed for the provision of the service. A royalty income could be sourced in the jurisdiction where the license of a patent is funded, where the patent is developed, or where it is registered.

Moreover, recent years have witnessed a technological revolution and expansion of digital products that have put further strain on the source-of-income concept (see Chapter 10).

Some question the normative foundations of source-based taxation, arguing that the source of income is not a sound economic concept. Income does not have a source; physical location is not a property that can be attributed to income (Ault and Bradford 1990). Income is a number, calculated by adding and subtracting other numbers; it cannot be interpreted as having a spatial property according to this view. Assigning geographical location to income is described as a "category mistake" by Mitchell Kane,[5] who notes that "the factual determination of income being located in a given jurisdiction . . . is conceptually incoherent" (2015, p. 328). Nonetheless, certainly an assertion by sovereign states of their right to tax activities within their jurisdictions is viewed by many as fair.

Pragmatic and administrative considerations gave rise to source-based taxation and may still be the most valid rationale. The country of source is in the best position to impose income tax (Graetz 2001). The jurisdiction that is best positioned to monitor an income-generating transaction should have the primary taxing rights over that item of income (Cui 2017). Indeed, the country of source is normally in a position to enforce a tax on cross-border income, as it can require both the reporting by local enterprises of the income and withholding taxes on payments thereof (Green 1993).

SO WHERE DOES THE TAX BASE FINALLY LIE?

In practice, essentially every country taxes active business income deemed sourced within it—provided that the activity giving rise to the income is sufficiently closely linked to the country under the standards of the current international

---

Devereux, and Simpson 2010). Equally meaningless would be an attempt to apply the arm's length principle as a pricing solution for transactions that create value from synergies, which a group of companies, if acting independently, could not create (Devereux and Vella 2014).

[5] Mitchell Kane, in turn, borrows the term from Gilbert Ryle (1949 [2002], pp. 8–12).

architecture. This typically requires a degree of physical presence (reflecting its origins in a world of commodities and physical goods, in a predigital age). This is the so-called permanent establishment or nexus concept. Legal incorporation in the country normally would constitute this, as would physical business locations in the country, and certain activities meeting minimum time or degree of activities such as construction work.

And source countries may also retain the right to tax profits remitted abroad in the form of passive income payments made by local corporations—to foreign lenders, owners, holders of intellectual property used by the company (in the form of royalties), or even payments to related providers of certain services—normally through withholding a certain percentage of such payments. Adjusting those withholding amounts downward from the level provided in domestic law—sometimes to zero, ceding the entire tax base of such payments to the receiving country—is one primary function of tax treaties.

Countries may, in addition to taxing passive income payments received by their corporate residents from foreign sources, assert taxing rights over active business income of their corporate residents where such income is sourced outside the country (earned abroad). This is referred to as a "worldwide tax system." Obviously, this approach would give rise to taxing that foreign-earned income twice—once in the source country, and again in the residence country. This is typically mitigated by a provision in domestic law granting a tax credit for the tax paid to the source country (a "foreign tax credit"). And tax treaties normally, too, impose the requirement to grant such credits.

The other approach for residence countries is to give up worldwide taxation—at least in regard to active income sourced abroad—and adopt a so-called territorial system, in which foreign-sourced active income of corporate residents is not taxed, through exclusion from the tax base. This approach, once uncommon, has now been adopted by essentially all advanced economies—most recently by the United States in its 2017 tax reform.

In practice, though, no country implements a pure territorial or worldwide model; there is a broad spectrum of variations between these extremes. Notably, for example, territorial systems may contain anti-avoidance mechanisms to prevent profits being shifted artificially abroad (for example, controlled foreign company rules) or may grant exemption only to selected countries through tax treaties. Box 3.1 explores the issue further and shows the evolution of taxation systems in the OECD over the last century.

TAXING CORPORATE INCOME BASED ON DESTINATION?

An alternative to assigning taxing rights based on source or residence is taxation at the destination. While this is not part of the current architecture for corporate income taxes, the destination-based principle has been long been accepted for VAT.

Chapter 13 explores the pros and cons of such destination-based allocation of taxing rights. Such an approach, while far removed from current norms, would be

Box 3.1. Territorial or Worldwide?

If the territorial and worldwide taxation systems are visualized as two opposite sides of a spectrum, the overwhelming majority of countries will fall somewhere in between. Nevertheless, for classification purposes, the countries with predominately territorial taxation elements—for example, some type of foreign dividend exemption system—are categorized as territorial, and countries with significant worldwide taxation elements are classified as having a worldwide tax system. With that in mind, as of June 2019, 31 out of 36 OECD member states have territorial tax systems (Figure 3.1.1). Interestingly, the pace of the shift from a worldwide to a territorial taxation model has been significantly accelerating over the last 30 years.

To the extent the foreign tax rate equals or exceeds the domestic tax rate, the foreign tax credit granted under the worldwide system for taxes paid abroad minimizes or eliminates the differences between a worldwide and a territorial system. Further, a system of deferrals—the postponement of current taxation on the net income or gain economically accrued by a taxpayer—such as existed in the United States before the introduction of the Tax Cuts and Jobs Act in 2017, can further blur the distinctions between worldwide and territorial systems.

Figure 3.1.1. Evolution of Taxation Model in OECD Countries: Shifting from Worldwide to Territorial System

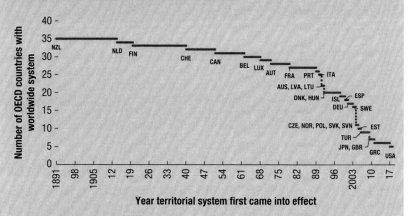

Sources: PWC (2013) and the author.
Note: New Zealand and Finland effectively repealed (in 1988 and 1990, respectively) and reinstated (in 2009 and 2005 respectively) territorial systems. The year when the territorial system *first went into effect* is shown. Data labels use International Organization for Standardization (ISO) country codes.

more robust to profit shifting and tax competition. To apportion profit between jurisdictions, there would be "no need for massive economic studies that try to "estimate" arm's length prices in the absence of meaningful benchmarks" (Avi-Yonah, Clausing, and Durst 2009, p. 511). Further, the need for the whole host of anti-avoidance rules—including exit taxes, controlled foreign company rules, and anti-inversion rules—is also eliminated (Auerbach and others 2017). Thus, such a system is considerably more practical and robust from a tax administration point of view. On the other hand, the transition to such an approach would entail a massive reallocation of the tax base across countries, and in its pure form is not under serious consideration now. Nonetheless, destination-based elements are now being introduced in the current international discussions of overhauling the architecture.

CONCLUSION

The existing international tax framework is complicated, reflecting the diverging interests of the jurisdictions that designed it, as well as historical developments. There is a broad agreement on the framework of the system, but there are also plenty of exceptions, inconsistencies, loopholes, and ad hoc solutions. The compliance and administrative costs are enormous, and some definitions are not even conceptually clear—and are becoming harder to enforce and understand as the economy becomes less and less geographically attached. Changing the system to address specific difficulties occurs continuously. Introducing fundamental reform to shift to a coherent principles-based alternative is much harder and will entail intense political compromises.

REFERENCES

Auerbach, Alan J., Michael P. Devereux, Michael Keen, and John Vella. 2017. "Destination-Based Cash Flow Taxation." Oxford University Centre for Business Taxation Working Paper 17/01, Oxford University Centre for Business Taxation, Oxford, UK.

Auerbach, Alan, J., Michael P. Devereux, and Helen Simpson. 2010. "Taxing Corporate Income." In *Dimensions of Tax Design*, edited by Stuart Adam, Timothy Besley, Richard Blundell, Stephen Bond, Robert Chote, Malcolm Gammie, Paul Johnson, Gareth Myles, and James Poterba, 837–93. Vol. 1 of *The Mirrlees Review*. Oxford: Oxford University Press.

Ault, Hugh J., and Brian J. Arnold. 2010. *Corporate Income Taxation: A Structural Analysis.* 3rd ed. Alphen, Netherlands: Wolters Kluwer.

Ault, Hugh J., and David F. Bradford. 1990. "Taxing International Income: An Analysis of the U.S. System and Its Economic Premises." In *Taxation in the Global Economy,* edited by Assaf Razin and Joel Slemrod, 11–52. Chicago: University of Chicago Press.

Avi-Yonah, Reuven S., Kimberly Clausing, and Michael C. Durst. 2009. "Allocating Business Profits for Tax Purposes: A Proposal to Adopt a Formulary Profit Split." *Florida Tax Review* 9(5): 497–553.

Couzin, Robert. 2002. *Corporate Residence and International Taxation.* Amsterdam: International Bureau of Fiscal Documentation.

Cui, Wei. 2017. "Minimalism about Residence and Source." *Michigan Journal of International Law* 38(2): 245–269.

Desai, Mihir A. 2009. "The Decentering of the Global Firm" *World Economy* 32(9): 1271–90.

Devereux, Michael, and John Vella. 2014. "Are We Heading towards a Corporate Tax System Fit for the 21st Century?" *Fiscal Studies* 35(4): 449–75.

Graetz, Michael J. 2001. "Taxing International Income: Inadequate Principles, Outdated Concepts, and Unsatisfactory Policies." *Tax Law Review* 54: 261–336.

Graetz, Michael J. 2016. Remarks at Corporate Tax for the 21st Century conference, Tax Policy Center, Washington, DC, July 14.

Green, Robert. 1993. "The Future of Source-Based Taxation of the Income of Multinational Enterprises." *Cornell Law Faculty Publications.* Paper 952.

International Monetary Fund (IMF). 2014. "Spillovers in International Corporate Taxation." IMF Policy Paper, Washington, DC.

International Monetary Fund (IMF). 2018. "Ireland: Selected Issues." IMF Country Report 18/195, Washington, DC.

Kane, Mitchell A. 2015. "A Defense of Source Rules in International Taxation." *Yale Journal on Regulation* 32(2): 311–361.

League of Nations. 1923. *Report on Double Taxation.* Document E.F.S.73 F.19. Geneva, Switzerland: League of Nations.

McIntyre, Michael J. 2003. "The Use of Combined Reporting by Nation States." Tax Notes International (35): 917–48.

PricewaterhouseCoopers LLP (PWC). 2013. Evolution of Territorial Tax Systems in the OECD. Prepared for The Technology CEO Council. April 2.

Ryle, Gilbert. (1949) 2002. *The Concept of Mind.* Chicago: University of Chicago Press.

Vann, Richard. 1998. "International Aspects of Income Tax." In *Tax Law Design and Drafting,* edited by Victor Thuronyi, 2:718–810. Washington, DC: International Monetary Fund.

CHAPTER 4

Global Firms, National Corporate Taxes: An Evolution of Incompatibility

Shafik Hebous

How did the rise of multinational enterprises put pressure on the prevailing international corporate tax framework? Multinational enterprises, and firms with market power, are not new phenomena, nor is the corporate income tax, which dates to the early 20th century. This prompts the question, what is distinctly new (about multinational enterprises)—if anything—that has triggered unprecedented recent concerns about vulnerabilities in international tax arrangements and the taxation of multinational enterprises? This chapter presents a set of empirical observations and a synthesis of strands of the literature to answer this question. A key message is that multinational enterprises of the 21st century operate differently from prior periods and have evolved to become global firms—with important tax ramifications. The fragility of international tax arrangements was present at the outset of designing international tax rules, but the challenges have drastically intensified with the global integration of business, the increased international trade in hard-to-price services and intangibles, and the rapid growth of the digital economy.

INTRODUCTION

In December 1600, long before the Industrial Revolution (1760–1820) or the first long-distance telephone call (by Alexander Graham Bell in 1876), the East India Company was established with a royal charter awarding the company a monopoly on English trade in the Indies. It is one of the first multinational enterprises. Historical records suggest that the company accounted for half of world trade in the 18th century (Farrington 2002). As of today, a significant number of key multinational enterprises are not young. For example, in 2018 only about 26 companies in the Fortune 500 were established after 2000—about half of the rest are older than 100 years.[1] However, multinational enterprises today, as

---

[1] Compiled by the author based on *Fortune 500*, http://fortune.com/fortune500/.

this chapter will argue, are different in important respects—with important tax implications—from those of previous centuries.

Thinking of international trade—whether the crawling caravans on the Silk Road or the giant vessels of the 21st century—we tend to picture goods and containers or merchants seeking to exploit comparative advantages, regional differences in endowments, economies of scale, and benefits from agglomeration and specialization. While these economic fundamentals still largely explain current observed patterns of international trade, a distinctive recent feature—which emerged at the end of the 2nd millennium—is the rise of international trade in services and intangible assets. With a mere mouse click, a company can import or export management services, sell patents and other hard-to-price know-how assets to its own affiliated companies abroad, engage in operational leasing services with other group members, purchase an insurance contract from an offshore company— just to name a few examples. Beyond benefits of specialization, as this chapter will argue, taxes play an important role in explaining observed patterns of international trade in services.

The corporate income tax, in its current form (that is, the notion that corporations are taxpayers regardless of their owners), is slightly more than 100 years old. For example, in 1909 the federal corporate income tax in the United States was introduced.[2] The rate reached 52.8 percent in 1968 to finance the Vietnam War, comparable with other corporate income tax rates in Europe at the time. Currently, statutory corporate income tax rates in advanced and developing countries are 22.3 and 24 percent on average, respectively, but significant differences across countries remain (not only regarding corporate income tax rates but also more generally concerning tax systems), enabling multinational enterprises to minimize taxes and shift income to low-tax jurisdictions using various schemes. One popular tax-minimizing practice is to violate or misuse the arm's length principle—the notion that intragroup prices should be valued at the prices charged to unrelated parties—for example, by overpricing imports from affiliated companies in low-tax jurisdiction (that is, inflating costs in high-tax countries) or underpricing exports to these affiliates (that is, understating incomes in high-tax countries).[3]

Since multinational enterprises and international trade were existent at the inception of the corporate income tax and its international arrangements, the question arises, what new developments, if any, have created vulnerabilities and increased concerns about the prevailing international tax framework and tax avoidance by multinational enterprises? In other words, what is it that makes the 2000s different from, say, the 1920s or 1960s? In fact, concerns about international tax planning and tax competition, in particular, took off in 1998 when the

---

[2] For detail, see Kornhauser (1990). It was enacted in 1894 but eventually implemented in 1909.

[3] Other strategies include the use of intragroup borrowing to benefit from interest deductions in high-tax countries. For an overview of tax avoidance practices, see, for example, Chapter 6 (this volume); Beer, De Mooij, and Liu (2020); Dharmapala (2014); Hebous and Weichenrieder (2014); and IMF (2014).

OECD launched a report on "harmful tax practices" (OECD 1998), and reached the top of the international policy agenda with the 2015 G20/OECD Base Erosion and Profit Shifting (BEPS) initiative, which lays out a set of "minimum standards" and common approaches for the corporate income tax to address profit-shifting practices. The salience of the issue in the public eye reached an unparalleled level with leaked records such as Lux Leaks and other major news headlines (see, for example, Bergin 2012). During the COVID-19 pandemic, some countries (including Belgium, Denmark, France, and Poland) denied, or invoked the possibility of denying, tax reliefs for companies registered (or doing businesses) in what they refer to as "tax havens." This gesture reflects an attempt to respond to the general public dissatisfaction with the taxation of multinationals.[4]

This chapter summarizes a set of empirical observations and insights from three strands of the literature (international trade, public finance, and recent studies on firm market power) to shed light on the interlinkages between the current international tax framework and the evolution of multinational enterprises. The theme that emerges is that the fundamental challenges facing the corporate income tax framework at present are not distinctively new. However, the new "global" enterprise (as opposed to the term "multinational enterprises") exacerbates existing weaknesses, thereby exposing major flaws of the fundamental concepts of current arrangements.

The major challenges that grow as a result of global firms difficulties in (1) applying the arm's length principle, (2) identifying the location of "value creation"—which is a conceptual issue, and (3) identifying source and residence countries (economically speaking)—key concepts for the current international tax system, whereby broadly a source country refers to where production takes place and the resident country is the primary location of the company (where it is "effectively managed" or incorporated).[5] As a result of these challenges, profit shifting has become a serious concern and the debate about the allocation of taxing rights across countries has intensified.

Key reasons behind these difficulties arise from the following facts: (1) the typical global firm of today produces in and for the *global* market, which vitiates the notion that production and business can be easily separated by national boundaries; (2) increasing importance of intragroup trade particularly in hard-to-price services and intangibles; and (3) increased digitalization of the economy, which—beyond enabling doing business with little (or even without a) physical presence in a country (significantly weakening the existing concept of source country)—prompts serious rethinking about the value created by consumers or users.

This chapter is structured as follows: The second section provides a summary of the evolution of multinational enterprises. The third section presents a set of

---

[4] Also, the pandemic has sparked off considerable debate about taxing "excess profits" of companies that benefited from the pandemic.

[5] See also Chapter 3, Chapter 9, and Chapter 12.

empirical observations about international trade and digital trade. The fourth section briefly discusses firm market power and the tax implications thereof, and the fifth illustrates the difficulties in taxing the global firms based on the arrangements of today. The chapter ends with concluding remarks.

MULTINATIONAL ENTERPRISES TODAY ARE BETTER TERMED "GLOBAL FIRMS"

Observations about Multinational Enterprises

Observation 1: Multinational enterprises today are different from multinational enterprises in the last century or earlier periods and should be called global firms.

The evolution of multinational enterprises can be thought of in terms of three phases:

Phase I (trading company): Early multinational enterprises, up to the middle of the 19th century, were mostly established by states to perform specific functions. For example, early chartered companies essentially focused on trade in cotton, silk, tea, spices, and other raw material.[6] In the mid and late 19th century, with the spread of the limited liability concept, the business model of multinational enterprises evolved to become international distribution of home-manufactured products, but those multinational enterprises remained important importers of raw material.

Phase II (international company): In the early 20th century, during World War I and the interwar period, the spread of trade protectionism led companies to establish local plants to serve national markets and escape trade barriers (what we may call "international companies"). This meant that the prime purpose of the foreign presence of multinational enterprises was tariff jumping and serving local markets. These companies produced close to where they sold.

Phase III (global firm): Starting from the late 20th century (early 1970s) the liberalization of international trade and investment, coupled with improved information technology and decreasing transportation costs, created a new era for multinational enterprises and transformed them to what we may call "global firms" (see Palmisano 2006). Two defining features of this era have been particularly salient since the late 1990s and early 21st century: (1) the integration of production and (2) outsourcing functions. The latter, to the extent outsourcing is to unrelated parties (that is, the function is being undertaken by a nonrelated company as opposed to within the multinational group), has no direct

---

[6] Examples include the East India Company (an English company that was established in 1600 as a trading company in the Indian Ocean region), the Dutch East India Company (an amalgamation of various Dutch companies that traded in the Indian Ocean region), and the Emden Company (a Royal Prussian Asiatic Company that traded with China).

consequences on corporate tax avoidance,[7] but tax competition between countries remains relevant, among other factors. The global integration of production (a global supply chain) means that the multinational enterprise has become a globally integrated enterprise that supplies to *the global market* as opposed to fragmented markets defined within national boundaries.[8]

The falling costs of information technology have facilitated the coordination of a global complex production process entailing multiple locations. This constitutes a shift from foreign investment that is entirely driven by the host market (that is, producing goods and services close to where they are supposed to be sold) to an integrated production model shaped by the question of how to supply globally, that is, a worldwide value delivery. A product might be designed in a country where there is little or no demand for it, and thus the question becomes, what is the exact location that creates the value of this design? Examples of global supply activities are abundant, including marketing strategies for the brand, research and development activities, legal services, human resource services, and other services for the entire worldwide group. As Palmisano (2006), p. 129, states, "[N]ew perceptions of the permissible and the possible have deepened the process of corporate globalization by shifting its focus from products to production." This is a key change in the multinational enterprise business model, with significant implications on taxation, as we will argue in the fifth section, "Multinational Enterprises and Taxation."

Observation 2: Multinational enterprises are important employers and value-added generators in the economy.

In 2018 the world's 500 largest companies (Fortune Global 500) employed 67.7 million people worldwide, generated $30 trillion in revenues (that is, a multiple of 1.5 of US GDP) and $1.9 trillion in profits, and are headquartered by 33 countries.[9]

The share of value added by multinational enterprises in total value added is significant, reaching more than 50 percent in some advanced countries (Figure 4.1). While typically the number of multinational enterprises constitute a low share in the total number of enterprises in a country (not exceeding 5 percent in most economies), their share of total employment is close to or above 20 percent in many economies (Figure 4.1). In the United States, in 2016, the value-added generated by majority-owned US affiliates of foreign multinational enterprises reached $910.6 billion, accounting for 6.4 percent of total US business-sector GDP and

---

[7] However, somewhat distinctly but relatedly, as jobs are increasingly transformed into tasks done by outside contractors (for example, freelancers and the gig economy), there will be important implications for personal income taxes resulting, for instance, from a vanishing tax-withholding function of firms, increasing mobility of labor, and existing different tax treatments of employees (wage earners) and the self-employed.

[8] It remains to be seen how the COVID-19 pandemic and recent international trade tensions affect the supply chains of the global firm.

[9] See *Fortune 500*, http://fortune.com/fortune500/2018.

Figure 4.1. Value-Added and Employment of Multinational Enterprises
(% of Total)

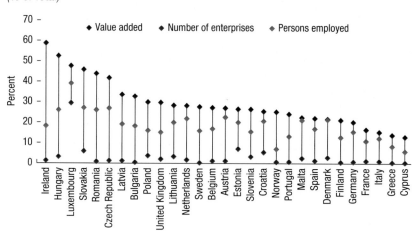

Source: Data are from the Eurostat. Numbers are for nonfinancial foreign-controlled enterprises, 2015.

5.6 percent of total private-industry employment (ignoring US-owned multinational enterprises).[10]

Multinational Enterprises and Taxation

In a way, the evolution of multinational enterprises through the above mentioned phases (under Observation 1) is similar to that of the theory of international trade and foreign direct investment that progressed from initially modeling a single-plant production firm with all activities in a single location to "horizontal" firms—which produce the same goods in several countries—and "vertical" firms—which split stages of production by location (see Markusen 2004). This literature, however, focuses on explaining bilateral foreign direct investment by variables such as relative endowment differences across countries (differences in production costs), market access costs (trade costs and investment costs), and market size (for example, Carr and others 2001; Markusen and Maskus 2001; Egger and Köthenbürger 2018).

The question of how international tax differences affect foreign direct investment decisions has been almost exclusively addressed in a separate strand of (mostly empirical) literature, which generally finds the following:

- High taxes reduce foreign direct investment flows—that is, the intensive margin of foreign direct investment (De Mooij and Ederveen 2008; Feld and Heckemeyer 2011).

---

[10] US Bureau of Economic Analysis: https://apps.bea.gov/scb/2018/12-december/1218-affiliates.htm

- High taxes reduce the propensity to host a new foreign direct investment— that is, the extensive margin of foreign direct investment (see, for example, Devereux and Griffith 1998).

- Greenfield investments are more responsive to taxes than mergers and acquisitions, because in the latter case the tax effect is partially capitalized in the acquisition price (Hebous, Ruf, and Weichenrieder 2011).

- Vertical foreign direct investment appears to be more sensitive to taxation than horizontal foreign direct investment (Overesch and Wamser 2009).

While the above studies look at *real* responses to taxes, another strand of the literature, discussed under the following observation, looks at the effects of taxation on the location of profits.

Observation 3: Multinational enterprises face lower effective taxation than domestic firms but tend to be important contributors to total corporate income tax revenues in many countries.

Multinational subsidiaries, especially in relatively high-tax countries, tend to report lower profits than comparable domestic companies (as found in, for example, Bilicka 2019, for UK firms; and Egger, Eggert, and Winner 2010, for a panel of European firms). However, at the consolidated group level, multinational enterprises tend to be highly profitable companies—some reach after-tax profits of multibillions of US dollars. For instance, profits of Apple reached $45.7 billion in 2016. Profits of SAP, a German-based software company, reached about $4 billion in 2016. To put it differently, the five-year (2012–2017) cumulative return on $100 invested in Netflix stock yielded $1,400 (that is, a return of 1,400 percent). A similar investment in Alphabet (parent company of Google) would have yielded $300 (that is, 300 percent return).[11] Anecdotal evidence suggests that the effective tax rate of some giant multinational enterprises hardly reaches 1 percent or is even close to zero in some locations.[12]

Strategies of international tax planning to lower effective taxation in higher-tax jurisdictions include, beyond the violation of the arm's length principle, locating asset sales in low-tax jurisdictions to avoid capital gains taxes, arranging business operations in high-tax jurisdictions on a contractual basis ("risk transfer"), and exploiting mismatches in the legal characterization of financial instruments or transactions between countries (generating tax arbitrage, for example, in the form of double deductions), to name a few.[13] Surveying the literature on profit shifting is beyond the scope of this chapter, but Table 4.1 summarizes recent evidence on transfer mispricing. Overall,

---

[11] See Annual Reports published on U.S. Securities and Exchange Commission: https://www.sec.gov.

[12] See, for example, NY Times: https://www.nytimes.com/2019/04/29/us/politics/democrats-taxes-2020.html.

[13] Beer, De Mooij, and Liu (2020) and IMF (2014) provide an overview. Macro-based estimates generally find larger magnitudes of profit shifting, in part because estimates include total profit shifting--not only focusing on one strategy such as transfer mispricing (see, for example, Tørsløv, Wier, and Zucman 2018).

TABLE 4.1.

Recent Evidence on Transfer Mispricing		
Study	Country	Revenue Foregone (% of Corporate Income Tax Revenue)
Cristea and Nguyen (2016)	Denmark	3.2
Davies and others (2018)	France	1
Flaaen (2018)	USA	0.73
Hebous and Johannessen (2019)	Germany	2
Liu, Schmidt-Eisenlohr, and Guo (forthcoming)	UK	0.37
Wier (2018)	South Africa	0.5

Source: Author.
Note: The above studies look at mispricing of goods, except for Hebous and Johannessen (2019), which studies mispricing of services.

available results, which are largely based on examining trade in goods (not services, except for Hebous and Johannessen 2019), suggest that failing to adhere to the arm's length principle has had a negative impact on corporate income tax revenues in several countries. Unfortunately, country-specific evidence for developing countries is rather scarce. Further, several studies find evidence for profit shifting though intragroup lending—also in developing countries (see, for example, Feld, Heckemeyer, and Overesch 2013; and Fuest, Hebous, and Riedel 2011).

However, multinational enterprises contribute a large share of corporate income tax revenues in some countries. UNCTAD (2015) estimates that multinational enterprises, on average, contribute about 23 percent of total corporate income tax revenues in developing countries. Bilicka (2017) shows that 55 percent of corporate income tax revenue in the United Kingdom is paid by multinational enterprises. In many countries, the distribution of corporate income tax payments is highly skewed toward a relatively small number of large taxpayers that pay a large fraction of the aggregate revenue.

EMPIRICAL OBSERVATIONS ABOUT INTERNATIONAL TRADE AND DIGITALIZATION

International Trade and Activities of Multinational Enterprises

Observation 4: A small fraction of firms engage in international trade, and an even smaller fraction of firms engage in related-party trade.

Bernard and others (2018) document that only a small share of firms in the United States export (and import), not exceeding 35 percent. Moreover, remarkably, only 8.5 percent of all firms are responsible for about 85 percent of the total value of US exports (approximately 2,000 firms). Similar patterns are found in other countries (Freund and Pierola, forthcoming).

Furthermore, only the very largest firms tend to engage in related-party trade, accounting for a disproportionately large share of aggregate value of international trade (Bernard and others, 2009; 2018). According to the WTO (2018), about

80 percent of global trade is within multinational enterprises. This high concentration of international trade and substantial overlap between traders and multinational enterprises imply that taxation and transfer pricing issues are particularly relevant for a minority of "superstar" firms (considering the universe of all firms).

The degree of intrafirm trade varies across products and partner countries. For instance, as documented in Bernard and others (2010), more than 70 percent of US imports of autos, medical equipment, and instruments involve intrafirm trade, but in the case of rubber it is only 2 percent.

Observation 5: International trade in services has rapidly risen, reaching more than 6 percent of world GDP, and a significant share of international trade in services is related-party trade in hard-to-price business services.

Figure 4.2 shows that world imports of services have been upward trending since the 1980s. According to WTO statistics, international trade in services accounted for more than 22.7 percent of world trade in 2017. This development reflects changes in technology (demand for services as inputs) and growing demand by final consumers. Figure 4.3 shows, however, that business services, together with financial, telecommunication, computer, and information services, account for more than 55 percent of commercial services (the rest is mainly transport and travel).

The WTO (2018) states that developing economies accounted for 30.6 percent of world commercial services exports and 38.1 percent of imports. Furthermore, there are key regional players. For example, Singapore is a leading

Figure 4.2. World Imports of Services
(Ratio to world GDP)

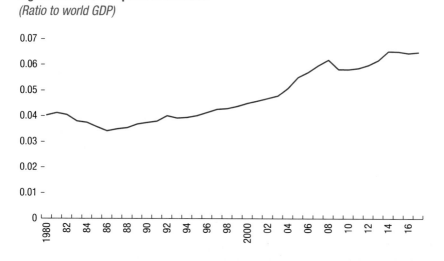

Source: Calculation by the author based on data obtained from WTO statistics (https://data.wto.org/).

Figure 4.3. World Exports of Commercial Services by Sector

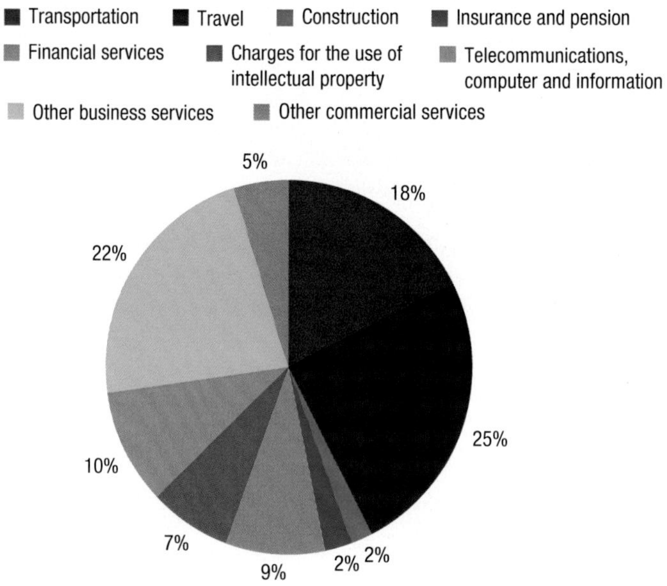

■ Transportation   ■ Travel   ■ Construction   ■ Insurance and pension

■ Financial services   ■ Charges for the use of   ■ Telecommunications,
                         intellectual property   computer and information

     ■ Other business services   ■ Other commercial services

Source: Data obtained from WTO statistics (https://data.wto.org/). Figures are for 2017.

exporter of intellectual property services (royalties on patents and trademarks), with an amount totaling $8 billion (about 2.5 percent of GDP) in 2017. China, India, and Singapore, and others, are among the important importers and exporters of commercial services in general.

Although transfer pricing rules apply to goods and services, the nature of trade in services is distinct from goods in several respects, facilitating abusive practices. For example, business services, such as management services, intellectual property, and information services, are relatively easy to be relocated across borders within the multinational group, and it is difficult to determine their market prices. In fact, compared to physical goods, it is not even straightforward to define many services. The lack of clear comparables for many services poses a challenge for many tax administrations around the world, making it inherently difficult to apply the arm's length principle. For instance, consider one affiliate of a global firm that is responsible for developing a marketing strategy for the entire group. What is the value of this function for the various subsidiaries? Typically, the affiliates will enter into a cost-sharing arrangement, but the money value of the marketing service for each subsidiary does not unambiguously have a market price. Similar difficulties occur for pricing royalties (for example, charges for the use of patents or trademarks and other forms of intellectual property) and legal services, to name two.

Figure 4.4. Intangible Capital and Value Added: The Smile Curve

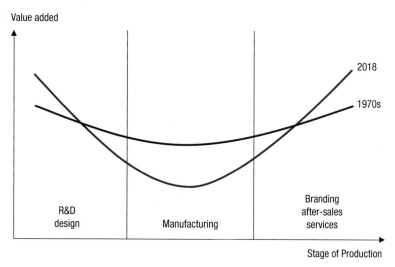

Source: WIPO (2017). Reportedly, the Smile Curve was first put forth by Stan Shih, the founder of Acer Inc.

Observation 6: The importance of intangible and intellectual property assets in the business model and cross-border trade of multinational enterprises has significantly increased.

The importance of "intangible capital"—in the form of technology, design, brand value, and managing know-how assets—has grown enormously in the last years. The World Intellectual Property Organization (2017) refers to the so-called smile curve (Figure 4.4), which illustrates the higher shares of pre- and postmanufacturing phases—such as research and development activities and branding—in production value in the 21st century compared to earlier years.

The discussion under Observation 4 explains that payments such as cross-border royalties are difficult to price, but the underlying know-how assets, per se (such as patents and trademarks), that generate royalties can also be relocated across borders. For example, an intangible asset can be sold (even before being patented) from the affiliate where it was developed to another affiliated company in another country to be patented in that country, whereby the legal ownership involves either a physical shift or just a transfer of use rights (without the need for a physical transfer to take place). The challenge is that the price of the intangible asset can be extremely difficult to determine according to the arm's length principle.

Observation 7: Multinational enterprises nowadays spend a significant amount on research and development.

At the macroeconomic and firm levels, research and development is a very instrumental policy issue, given its importance for long-term macroeconomic growth and firm growth. Currently, multinational enterprises invest significantly in research and development. Jaruzelski, Chwalik, and Goehle (2018) identify the top 1,000 innovators and report that Amazon and Apple are at the top of the list, with research and development spending reaching $22.6 and $16.2 billion, respectively. Among the top innovators are car makers and firms in the pharmaceutical and health care industries. In 2018 these 1,000 companies together spent $782 billion on research and development (this is larger than the GDP of Saudi Arabia or Switzerland).

To encourage firm innovation, many countries provide tax incentives. The economic rationale is that the social benefit from research and development is higher than the private benefit, giving Pigouvian motivation for a corrective subsidy or tax incentives to address positive externalities. Tax incentives can take two broad forms: First, research and development tax incentives can target research and development inputs, for example in the form of investment tax credits (deducting qualified investment expenses from the tax liability) or super-tax deductions of research and development input costs (from taxable income). Second, an increasing number of countries provide effective lower taxation for qualified income from intellectual property and know-how assets (regimes known as patent box regimes); that is, these incentives target the output of research and development. Incentives for research and development inputs are more efficient and effective than patent box regimes because the latter reward only successful research and development (which is also a function of inputs other than research and development) and disregard the positive externalities by research and development that does not generate immediate income (IMF 2016a; see also Chapter 6, this volume). Moreover, patent box regimes have also been used as a tool for tax competition, encouraging the relocation of (the legal ownership of) patents and know-how assets (not the underlying research and development activity) within the multinational group for tax purposes (Chapter 6).[14]

Observation 8: Low-tax jurisdictions play a disproportionate role in global trade in services and foreign direct investment.

Hebous and Johannesen (2019) show that low-tax jurisdictions play an important role in shaping the pattern of international trade in services.[15] The evidence suggests that bilateral service trade with low-tax jurisdictions is around six times larger than service trade with non-low-tax jurisdictions, whereas no such stark difference was found for goods trade. This disproportionate role in global service trade is the result of a combination of comparative advantage (specializing in specific services) and tax advantages. Low-tax jurisdictions are typically relatively small with de facto relatively low effective taxes even if the statutory corporate

---

[14] To address profit-shifting motivations, a minimum standard in the G20/OECD BEPS initiative requires linking the qualification for a lower tax on the patent income to the underlying research and development expenses on that patent.

[15] There is no widely accepted definition or a list of low-tax jurisdictions or major hubs for international tax planning. For related discussion, see Dharmapala and Hines (2009); Hebous (2018); and Hines (2010).

TABLE 4.2.

Top 10 Countries: Average Outward / Inward Foreign Direct Investment as Share of GDP (Percent), 2017

Country	Foreign Direct Investment in Percent of GDP	Share of World Foreign Direct Investment	Share of World GDP
Luxembourg	7,037	12.8	0.1
Mauritius	2,210	0.9	0.0
Malta	1,103	0.4	0.0
Cyprus	1,047	0.7	0.0
Netherlands	672	16.2	1.0
Hong Kong SAR	446	4.5	0.4
Ireland	264	2.5	0.4
Switzerland	178	3.5	0.8
Singapore	176	1.7	0.4
Hungary	159	0.6	0.2

Source: Author's calculation based on IMF Coordinated Direct Investment Survey, http://data.imf.org/cdis.

income tax rate is high (for example, because of preferential tax regimes or patent box regimes). They have emerged in the last decades as important investment hubs with very high shares of foreign direct investment to GDP—well beyond explaining foreign direct investment by the size of the domestic markets of these hubs—and in global foreign direct investment—with an astonishing share of 40 percent of global foreign direct investment being funneled through five relatively small countries: Hong Kong, Ireland, Luxembourg, the Netherlands, and Switzerland (Table 4.2), although not only tax but also nontax factors are relevant (such as benefits from specialization).

Digitalization

Observation 9: Global digital trade has been significantly growing.

According to a report by the US International Trade Commission (2017), global digital trade grew from $19.3 trillion in 2012 to $27.7 trillion in 2016. Business-to-business e-commerce—amounting to 86.3 percent of total digital trade—is six times larger than business-to-consumer e-commerce (13.7 percent of total). Top business-to-consumer e-commerce markets are China ($767 billion) and the United States ($595 billion).

The term "digital company" is vague. It has been increasingly used to refer to a handful of companies with significant social media market shares, digital advertising, or digital platforms to sell goods and services, but most companies in various industries are exhibiting increasing adaptation of their business models to digital technology (see Chapter 10).

The link between the share of subscribers (users) and the location of tangible assets (and employment) of digital companies is drastically weaker than in traditional, or last-century, business models. This challenges the link between "source" country and value creation, where source country typically refers to the country where employment and tangible assets are located. Figure 4.5 shows broad

Figure 4.5. Digital Business: Worldwide Subscribers of Selected Companies

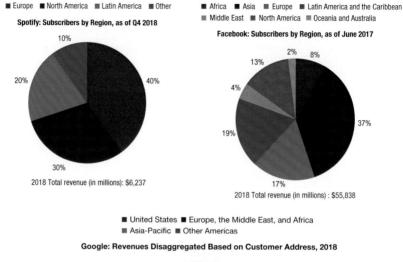

■ Europe ■ North America ■ Latin America ■ Other

Spotify: Subscribers by Region, as of Q4 2018

2018 Total revenue (in millions): $6,237

■ Africa ■ Asia ■ Europe ■ Latin America and the Caribbean
■ Middle East ■ North America ■ Oceania and Australia

Facebook: Subscribers by Region, as of June 2017

2018 Total revenue (in millions) : $55,838

■ United States ■ Europe, the Middle East, and Africa
■ Asia-Pacific ■ Other Americas

Google: Revenues Disaggregated Based on Customer Address, 2018

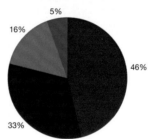

2018 Total revenue (in millions): $136,819

Sources: Spotify Technology S.A., Internet World Stats, and Alphabet Inc.
Note: Compiled by the author.

geographical distributions of users of three selected companies (Spotify, Facebook, and Google). This challenges the link between "source" country and value creation, where source country typically refers to the country where employment and tangible assets are located, and it exacerbates the limitations of the current concept of a "permanent establishment" that is ultimately requiring physical presence for the allocation of taxing rights.

From the corporate income tax standpoint, one view is to consider selling without a physical presence as exports. The question, however, apart from the large amount of profits that hypothetically could have been taxed under a traditional way of doing business, is, to what extent are users or consumers creating value? This question is at the heart of current discussions about reforming international tax, including at the OECD/G20 Inclusive Framework.

Collecting information on company users (or customers) is not new. Credit card companies and insurance companies have long collected and analyzed data about their customers. However, the new distinct feature is that revenues of "digital" companies (large amounts at stake) directly depend on information from users and consumers, and the big data they generate. It is not only that the collected data itself can be sold but also that some products, such as online advertisements, are tailored toward world customers; companies can, in turn, exploit this information and thereby generate income. In light of the weak connection between physical presence (employment and assets) and potential value creation, the discussion of value creation by users becomes crucial for determining taxing rights and understanding the motto "To tax where the value is created."

MULTINATIONAL ENTERPRISES AND MONOPOLY POWER

Observation 10: Market power in the United States has increased, implying a lower degree of competition, but this development is less obvious in developing countries.

In the United Sates, average markups (the margin of the price above the marginal cost) have risen from 21 percent in the 1980s to 61 percent in 2017 (Loeckeand Eeckhou 2017). However, estimates of level and the trend of the markup are not uncontroversial (Basu 2019). Evidence for other countries, particularly for developing countries, is rather scarce. IMF (2019b) finds that markups in a panel of advanced economies has increased by about 8 percent since 2000, but no similar significant effect can be found in emerging market economies. Moreover, results indicate that the increase in markups is concentrated among a small fraction of firms.

Many multinational enterprises have well-established positions in their monopolistic markets. For instance, in the market for online search engines, Google continuously has had a global market share of about 90 percent in the last years. Netflix user penetration rates (as a percent of digital video viewers in a country) are above 60 percent in the United States and Norway, and above 50 percent, among others, in Denmark and Sweden.

Generally, taxing monopoly rent is efficient, but the corporate income tax is a tax on normal return as well as economic rent. Other tax systems, namely cash-flow taxation or an allowance for corporate equity, tax only rent, but in practice such tax systems are rarely implemented (IMF 2016b; 2019a). Tax competition affects production decisions, including of monopolists, with efficiency implications. In this context, consideration should be given regarding the location of the rent, which should depend on the nature of the monopoly power. Location-specific rent, as in the natural resource sector, should and can be taxed at source, which would preserve revenues for the resource country. However, the source (as a location) of monopoly power of highly digitalized business, and more generally of firm-specific rent, is not clear cut, and its taxation may drive away investment. In sum, taxing rent is desirable to the extent that it raises revenues without affecting efficiency, but under current tax arrangements profit shifting and tax competition create challenges in efficiently taxing such rents.

MULTINATIONAL ENTERPRISES AND TAXATION

International Tax Arrangements Were Made with an International Company in Mind, Not a Global Firm—and Even That Is Challenging

The tax implications of current corporate income tax arrangements and possible reform options are studied in depth in this volume. The following is a brief overview focusing on the pressures associated with the evolution of multinational enterprises.

Allocation of taxing rights is an issue even in the absence of differences in taxation.

The question of how to allocate taxing rights between countries is a fundamental one even in the absence of differences in taxation. Consider a two-country world (a residence and a source country, as depicted in Figure 4.6) and the most simplistic example of a multinational enterprise that is present in two countries, loosely speaking, in the spirit of an "international company" referred to under Observation 1. Suppose both countries impose the same tax on profits. Still, the question is, how should taxing rights between countries be allocated? The country where the company is headquartered may impose a tax on worldwide profits. The country where production takes place imposes a tax on profits in that country. This leads to double taxation of profits generated in the source country.

According to current corporate income tax arrangements, in principle, source countries are typically allocated primary taxing rights to the active income—subject to finding a sufficient physical presence ("nexus") that is defined by reference to a permanent establishment in its jurisdiction—and residence countries the primary taxing rights to passive income, such as dividends, royalties, and interest income (see Chapter 3). This is governed by

Figure 4.6. A Simplistic Structure of a Multinational Enterprise

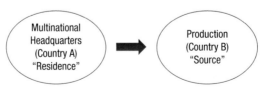

Source: Author's illustration.

domestic laws and tax treaties. The League of Nations developed first drafts of a tax treaty in 1928 following the source–residence principle.[16] A bilateral tax treaty (or a double tax agreement) between two countries allocates the taxing rights between both countries to deal with double taxation. Generally, a double tax agreement reduces the taxing rights of a source country in return for increased taxing rights of a residence country. Also, a double tax agreement, inter alia, may lower cross-border withholding tax rates on capital income (for example, dividends and interest).

Differences in taxes across countries intensify the debate about taxing rights.

Differences between countries in tax rates, and tax systems more broadly, deepen the challenges facing current taxing arrangements by generating incentives for multinational enterprises to locate profits in the low-tax jurisdictions and for countries to compete over real production and paper profits. By impacting the locations of production and profit, the allocation of taxing rights between countries (based on the source–residence principle) becomes a more pressing issue. Multinational enterprises' behavioral responses can have major revenue and macroeconomic effects.

Tax treaties open their own loopholes.

Double tax agreements can be used by multinational enterprises to minimize taxes (see Chapter 8)—mainly, but not only, by lowering cross-border withholding tax rates on royalty, interest, or dividends—by establishing "conduit" companies instead of investing directly in the final host country. A conduit company can be, for instance, a holding company (that is, a company that owns other companies but does not manage them); a management company (an entity that manages a pool of resources and provides services to, possibly offshore, related parties); a financing company (that lends to related parties); or a regional headquarters. Another example of exploiting provisions in tax treaties is to sell shares in a conduit company that derives their value from an underlying immovable asset located in another country. This offshore indirect transfer of assets can avoid capital gains taxes in the country where that asset is located.[17] Figure 4.7 depicts the growth in double tax agreement networks between 1970 and 2015. Currently, there are more than 3,000 bilateral double tax agreements with a significant increase in the number of double tax agreements in force that involve developing countries. As put in Brumby and Keen (2016), "[T]ax treaties are like a bathtub; a single leaky one is a drain on a country's revenues."[18]

---

[16] Later, the UN and the OECD built on these in developing tax treaty convention models.

[17] See the Platform for Collaboration on Tax (2020). The G20-OECD Base Erosion and Profit Shifting include minimum standards to prevent tax treaty abuse, inter alia.

[18] For studies on tax treaty shopping, see, for example, Beer and Loeprick (2018); and Riet and Lejour (2018).

Figure 4.7. Tax Treaty Networks

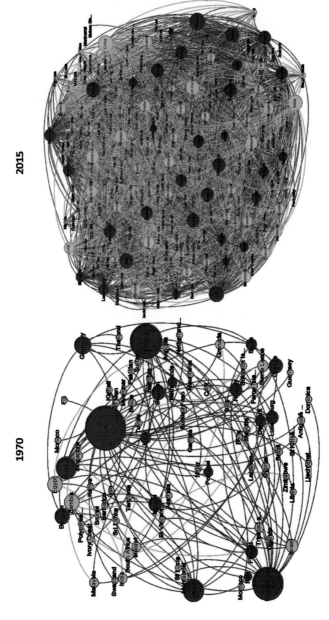

Source: Author's illustration using IBFD documents.
Note: Red nodes denote advanced economies, whereas green nodes denote developing countries. The size of a node indicates the number of treaties in a country.

The Source–Residence Principle Is Fundamentally Incompatible with The Global Firm Business Model

Keen (2017, page 10) writes: "[T]he League of Nations did not have a Facebook page. Its staff didn't Google or order online from Amazon. A century ago, foreign direct investment involved tangible things like railways and oil wells. Royalties meant charges on coal and the like, not payment for the use of brand names or patents." This quotation is a perfect summary of this discussion. The issues outlined in the preceding subsection are not new and demonstrate that even under a relatively simple form of business organization of a multinational enterprise, the arm's length principle, the source–resident principle, and distinguishing between different types of income face challenges. The global firm, however, raises these challenges to an unprecedented level. Given the existing international tax framework, as discussed in chapter 16, practices by the global firm to shift profits to low tax jurisdictions have led to the proliferation of anti-avoidance rules, especially in the last decade, which made domestic tax law systems more complex and uncertain without addressing the fundamental shortcomings of an outdated system.

Figure 4.8 illustrates a simplified structure of a typical global firm to, loosely, depict the discussion in the second section ("Multinational Enterprises Today Are Better Termed 'Global Firms'") and the observations that have been made in this chapter. The global firm does not supply the same product to fragmented national markets, but it relies on globally integrated production to supply the global market with different products. The ultimate shareholders of the global firm are typically

Figure 4.8. An Illustration of the Organizational Structure of a Global Firm

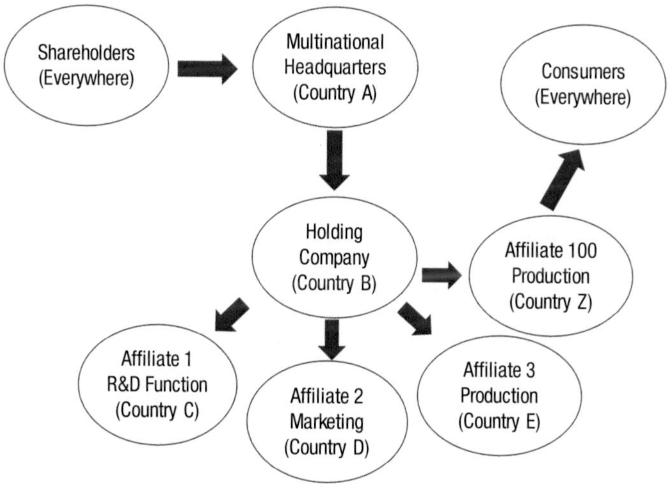

Source: Author's illustration.

residents of different countries. The global headquarters is in one country, but different foreign affiliates are tasked with different nonproduction activities for the entire group (including regional headquarters and activities such as research and development, legal services, and marketing) and production processes. In fact, many large global firms may not engage in manufacturing in the traditional sense. Typically, many of these affiliates will be owned by a holding company (often several holding companies are involved), and the concept of a management company has gained popularity. Finally, for many types of businesses, the locations of consumers do not necessarily require a (significant) physical presence of the company. Examples include, but are certainly not limited to, online retailers and advertising that is targeted to users of social media and other platforms.

- The business and the structure of the global firm (as discussed in Section 4.2) makes it difficult, if not impossible, to identify the country where the value is created. Traditionally, the location of labor and physical capital was thought to identify value creation, but this is an outdated notion for a borderless firm. First, there is an increasing value creation by intangible capital and services. Second, it can be argued, putting things together is ultimately generating value, implying that the whole is greater than the sum of its parts—that is, the value of the final product is higher than the sum of the value of marketing and the value of production, assuming these exist, and thus the location of this sum is unidentified as it is at the level of the worldwide group. Third, one can reasonably argue that consumers can generate value because of (1) the value of the data they generate and (2) their demand. That is, data collected from users generate value for many digitalized businesses, not only in terms of generating revenues through directly selling the data but also through using the data to directly tailor valuable products and services such as advertising. Moreover, the global firm does not produce where it sells, but currently the location of sales (i.e., demand) does not identify a source country under current tax arrangements. Hence, overall, it is safe to conclude that, for the global firm, the location of value creation cannot be identified by the physical presence.

- While there have always been practical concerns and questions about the economic meaning of residence–source, the distinction has become vaguer and more complex to grasp as the income of the global firm is less linked to physical capital or employment (Observations 5, 6, and 9). Decreased importance of physical presence of companies for sales significantly weakens the concept of source country. Furthermore, current arrangements do not efficiently tax economic rents (Observations 2, 3, and 10).

- The nature of research and development activities (Observation 7) has implications for profit shifting and tax competition (see Chapter 6). The global firm can locate real research and development activities in countries that provide input tax incentives (for example, tax credits) but locate the resulting patents or trademarks in countries that offer patent box regimes (where income and royalties benefit from lower taxation). Empirical evidence indicates that multinational enterprises allocate the legal ownership of know-how assets within the group for tax reasons to benefit from patent box regimes (Karkinsky and Riedel 2012). Action 5 of the G20/OECD BEPS Project on combating harmful tax practices requires, as a minimum standard, that patent box incentives be linked to the development of the patent (expenditures on the patent) in the country. As of April 2019, 126 countries have committed to this minimum standard. This may limit the scope for profit shifting using the legal location of patents but likely also intensifies competition over real research and development activities.

- The massive increase of intragroup transactions of intangibles and services, many of which do not have world market prices, have substantiality weakened the ability of the arm's length principle to determine their appropriate prices (Observations 5 and 6). For example, the value of brands or cost-sharing arrangements between affiliates poses challenges that cannot be easily solved by finding a dataset of comparables. In a way, at the current juncture, some argue that the returns of the global firm can be split into a portion that can be, to some extent, determined by the arm's length principle (routine profits) and a portion that is difficult to be subjected to the arm's length principle (residual profits).

- Many companies receive passive income (especially holding companies and management companies) that in principle should be taxed at residence. Starting in the late 1920s, some countries (largely) exempted these types of companies from taxation even though they were resident. This can be done, for example, through preferential tax regimes or tax rulings that enable specific arrangements. These become an important tax competition tool beyond the statutory tax rate (Observations 3 and 8). Moreover, distinguishing between different types of passive income and between passive and active income has become extremely difficult, in practice, due to mismatched national tax systems and different legal characterizations of similar (and rather complex) arrangements and transactions.

CONCLUSION

The owners of the global firm are all over the globe, and so are its customers. Its production is integrated across countries. Increased value creation from sources other than physical capital and employment casts doubts on the traditional way of thinking of value creation. The increased importance of intragroup trade, especially in hard-to-price services and intangibles, intensifies the challenges facing the arm's length principle. The decreased importance of maintaining a physical presence of companies for sales (and, more generally, the organizational structure of the global firm) have made guarding the borders between residence and source an extremely fragile undertaking. Distinguishing between different types of income has become more difficult and potentially prone to inconsistency across countries. The consequences are tax competition and profit shifting.

In sum, multinational enterprises have evolved with the advancement of technology and opportunities of the ever-increasingly modernized world, but international tax arrangements, with their fundamental weaknesses since their inception, could not and, as many would argue, cannot get up to speed.

REFERENCES

Antràs, Pol, and Stephen R. Yeaple. 2014. "Multinational Firms and the Structure of International Trade." In *Handbook of International Economics*, edited by Gita Gopinath, Elhanan Helpman, and Kenneth Rogoff, 4:55–130. Elsevier.

Basu, Susanto. 2019. "Are Price-Cost Markups Rising in the United States? A Discussion of the Evidence." *Journal of Economic Perspectives* 33(3): 3–22.

Beer, Sebastian, Ruud de Mooij, and Li Liu. 2020. "International Corporate Tax Avoidance: A Review of the Channels, Magnitudes, and Blind Spots." *Journal of Economic Surveys*, 34(3): 660–688.

Beer, Sebastian, and Jan Loeprick. 2018. "The Cost and Benefits of Tax Treaties with Investment Hubs: Findings from Sub-Saharan Africa." IMF Working Paper 18/227, International Monetary Fund, Washington, DC.

Bergin, Tom. 2012. "Special Report: How Starbucks Avoids UK Taxes." Special Reports. Reuters. October 15, 2012. https://www.reuters.com/article/us-britain-starbucks-tax /special-report-how-starbucks-avoids-uk-taxes-idUSBRE89E0EX20121015.

Bernard, Andrew, Bradford Jensen, Stephen Redding, and Peter Schott. "The Margins of US Trade." *American Economic Review* 99(2): 487–93.

Bernard, Andrew, Bradford Jensen, Stephen Redding, and Peter Schott. 2010. "Intrafirm Trade and Product Contractibility." *American Economic Review* 100(2): 444–48.

Bernard, Andrew, Bradford Jensen, Stephen Redding, and Peter Schott. 2018. "Global Firms." *Journal of Economic Literature* 56(2): 565–619.

Bilicka, Katarzyna Anna. 2017. How Much Tax Do Companies Pay in the UK? Evidence from UK Confidential Corporate Tax Returns. Unpublished, Oxford University, Oxford, UK.

Bilicka, Katarzyna Anna. 2019. "Comparing UK Tax Returns of Foreign Multinationals to Matched Domestic Firms." American Economic Review 109(8): 2921–2953.

Brumby, James, and Michael Keen. 2016. "Tax Treaties: Boost or Bane for Development?" IMF Blog. November 16, 2016. https://blogs.imf.org/2016/11/16/tax-treaties-boost-or-bane-for -development/.

Carr, David L., James R. Markusen, and Keith Maskus. E. 2001. Estimating the Knowledge-Capital Model of the Multinational Enterprise. *American Economic Review* 91(3): 693–708.

Cristea, Anca D., and Daniel X. Nguyen. 2016. "Transfer Pricing by Multinational Firms: New Evidence from Foreign Firm Ownerships." *American Economic Journal: Economic Policy* 8(3):170–202.

Davies, Ron, Julien Martin, Mathieu Parenti, and Farid Toubal. 2018. "Knocking on Tax Haven's Door: Multinational Firms and Transfer Pricing." *Review of Economics and Statistics* 100(1): 120–34.

De Mooij, Ruud, and Sjef Ederveen. 2008. "Corporate Tax Elasticities: A Reader's Guide to Empirical Findings." *Oxford Review of Economic Policy* 24(4): 680–97.

Devereux, Michael P., and Rachel Griffith. 1998. "Taxes and the Location of Production: Evidence from a Panel of US Multinationals." *Journal of Public Economics* 68(3): 335–67.

Dharmapala, Dhammika. 2014. "What Do We Know about Base Erosion and Profit Shifting? A Review of the Empirical Literature." *Fiscal Studies* 35(4): 421–48.

Dharmapala, Dhammika, and James Hines. 2009. "Which Countries Become Tax Havens?" *Journal of Public Economics* 93: 1058–68.

Egger, Peter, Wolfgang Eggert, and Hannes Winner. 2010. "Saving Taxes through Foreign Plant Ownership." *Journal of International Economics* 81(1): 99–108.

Egger, Peter, and Marko Köthenbürger. 2018. "Hosting Multinationals: Economic and Fiscal Implications." *Aussenwirtschaft* 67(1): 45–69.

Farrington, Anthony. 2002. *Trading Places: The East India Company and Asia, 1600–1834.* London: The British Library.

Feld, Lars, and Jost Heckemeyer. 2011. "Foreign Direct Investment and Taxation: A Meta-Study." *Journal of Economic Surveys* 25(2): 233–72.

Feld, Lars, Jost Heckemeyer, and Michael Overesch. 2013. "Capital Structure Choice and Company Taxation: A Meta-Study." *Journal of Banking and Finance* 37(8): 2850–66.

Flaaen, Aaron 2018. "The Role of Transfer Prices in Profit Shifting by U.S. Multinationals: Evidence from the 2004 Homeland Investment Act." Finance and Economics Discussion Series 2017-055. Washington: Board of Governors of the Federal Reserve System.

Freund, Caroline, and Martha Pierola. Forthcoming. "The Origins and Dynamics of Export Superstars." *World Bank Economic Review.*

Fuest, Clemens, Shafik Hebous, and Nadine Riedel. 2011. "International Debt Shifting and Multinational Firms in Developing Economies." *Economics Letters* 113(2): 135–38.

Hebous, Shafik. 2018. "Attractive Tax Jurisdictions." IEB Report 4/2018, Barcelona Institute of Economics, University of Barcelona, Barcelona, Spain.

Hebous, Shafik, and Niels Johannesen. 2019. "At Your Service! The Role of Tax Havens in International Trade with Services." CESifo Working Paper 5414, Center for Economic Studies, Munich, Germany.

Hebous, Shafik, and Alfons Weichenrieder. 2014. "What Do We Know about the Tax Planning of German-Based Multinational Firms?" *CESifo DICE Report* 12(4): 15–21.

Hebous, Shafik, Martin Ruf, and Alfons Weichenrieder. 2011. "The Effects of Taxation on the Location Decision of Multinational Firms: M&A vs. Greenfield Investments." *National Tax Journal* 64(3): 817–833.

Hines, James R. 2010. "Treasure Islands." *Journal of Economic Perspectives* 24(4): 103–26.

International Monetary Fund (IMF). 2014. "Spillovers in International Corporate Taxation.", IMF Policy Paper. Washington, DC.

International Monetary Fund (IMF). 2016a. "Acting Now, Acting Together.", Fiscal Monitor, International Monetary Fund. Washington, DC.

International Monetary Fund (IMF). 2016b. "Tax Policy, Leverage and Macroeconomic Stability." IMF Policy Paper, Washington, DC.

International Monetary Fund (IMF). 2019a. "Corporate Taxation in the Global Economy." IMF Policy Paper, Washington, DC.

International Monetary Fund (IMF). 2019b. "The Rise of Corporate Market Power and Its Macroeconomic Effects." In *World Economic Outlook*, ch. 2. Washington, DC: International Monetary Fund.

International Monetary Fund (IMF), Organization for Economic Co-operation and Development (OECD), United Nations (UN), and World Bank Group (WBG). 2020. *The Taxation of Offshore Indirect Transfers - A Toolkit.* Washington: The Platform for Collaboration on Tax (PCT).

Jaruzelski, Barry, Robert Chwalik, and Brad Goehle. 2018. "What the Top Innovators Get Right." *strategy+business* 93 (Winter). https://www.strategy-business.com/feature/What-the-Top-Innovators-Get-Right?gko=e7cf9

Keen, Michael. 2017. "False Profits." *Finance and Development* 54(3): 10–13. https://www.imf.org/external/pubs/ft/fandd/2017/09/keen.htm.

Kornhauser, Marjorie. 1990. "Corporate Regulation and the Origins of the Corporate Income Tax." *Indiana Law Journal* 66(1): 53–136.

Karkinsky, Tom, and Nadine Riedel. 2012. "Corporate Taxation and the Choice of Patent Location within Multinational Firms." *Journal of International Economics* 88(1):176–85.

Liu, Li, Tim Schmidt-Eisenlohr, and Dongxian Guo. Forthcoming. "International Transfer Pricing and Tax Avoidance: Evidence from Linked Trade-Tax Statistics in the UK." *Review of Economics and Statistics.*

Loecke, Jan, and Jan Eeckhou. 2018. "The Rise of Market Power and the Macroeconomic Implications." NBER Working Paper 23687, National Bureau of Economic Research, Cambridge, MA.

Markusen, James. 2004. *Multinational Firms and the Theory of International Trade.* Cambridge, MA: MIT Press.

Markusen, James and Keith Maskus. 2001. "Multinational Firms: Reconciling Theory and Evidence." In *Topics in Empirical International Economics: A Festschrift in Honor of Robert E. Lipsey,* edited by Magnus Blomstrom and Linda S. Goldberg, 71–98. Chicago: University of Chicago Press.

OECD, 1998, Harmful Tax Competition – An Emerging Global Issue, Paris.

Overesch, Michael, and Georg Wamser. 2009. "Who Cares about Corporate Taxation? Asymmetric Tax Effects on Outbound foreign direct investment." *World Economy* 32: 1657–84.

Palmisano, Samuel. 2006. "The Globally Integrated Enterprise." *Foreign Affairs* 85(3): 127–136.

Riet, Maarten, and Arjan Lejour. 2018. "Optimal Tax Routing: Network Analysis of foreign direct investment Diversion." *International Tax Public Finance* 25(5): 1321–71.

Tørsløv, Thomas, Ludvig S. Wier, and Gabriel Zucman. 2018. "The Missing Profits of Nations." NBER Working Paper No. 24701.

United Nations Conference on Trade and Development (UNCTAD). 2015. *World Investment Report 2015.* UNCTAD: Geneva, Switzerland.

United States International Trade Commission. 2017. *Global Digital Trade 1: Market Opportunities and Key Foreign Trade Restrictions.* Publication 4716. Washington, DC: United States International Trade Commission.

Wier, Ludvig. 2018. "Tax-Motivated Transfer Mispricing in South Africa: Direct Evidence Using Transaction Data." SA-TIED Working Paper 23, Southern Africa – Towards Inclusive Economic Development, United Nations University World Institute for Development Economics Research, Helsinki, Finland.

World Intellectual Property Organization (WIPO). 2017. *Intangible Capital in Global Value Chains.* World Intellectual Property Report 2017. Geneva, Switzerland: World Intellectual Property Organization.

World Trade Organization (WTO). 2018. *The Future of World Trade: How Digital Technologies Are Transforming Global Commerce.* World Trade Report 2018. Geneva, Switzerland: World Trade Organization.

PART II

Problems with the Current International Tax Architecture

CHAPTER 5

Difficulties in Determining and Enforcing Source-Based Taxes

Roberto Schatan*

INTRODUCTION

At the heart of the current international tax architecture, which grants primary taxing rights to source countries, is the need to determine how much profit each country can tax. This raises conceptual and enforcement issues: as discussed in Chapter 3, the geographic origin of a profit may not be clear, and as noted in Chapter 6, firms will want to shift profits toward jurisdictions with lower taxation. The standard approach to address this issue is for multinational enterprises to employ the arm's length principle when they set their transfer prices. In other words, they are supposed to charge an affiliate the same price as two independent parties would in the same transaction.

The arm's length principle is easy to apply and enforce when transfer prices are needed for standardized goods, with well-known market prices and simple measurement. With the increasingly common trade in intangible and unique products, determining the transfer price is far more challenging. In the absence of prices for comparables, the price must be backed out from a set of rules that determine how profits should be split.

Setting such rules faces both theoretical and practical problems. First, a multinational is not simply the aggregation of a number of independent domestic firms. The existence of multinationals suggests some advantage to this form of organizing business—at least in some sectors—so that its aggregate profit might exceed the sum of profits of independent firms. Second, a multinational group has many channels of control between affiliates and should strive to maximize the group's profit. The decisions on where to raise debt, where to recognize risks, and where to register patents are therefore very different from those faced by independent firms and involve much more of a choice. This chapter picks two important examples, risk and debt, to illustrate the conceptual and practical difficulties in allocating profits to source countries.

One of the features of risk is that aggregate risk is typically smaller than the sum of individual risks, given the likely offsetting shocks in different affiliates (or in

* With thanks to Narine Nersesyan for collaboration on the Annex.

statistical terms, a negative covariance). Apart from this aggregation problem, the apparent allocation of risk among affiliates can be altered by the group. The group can, for example, write contracts with an affiliate with different notional risk bearing, such as by setting prices in the currency of the country of the affiliate or of the headquarters. The group can also determine how an individual entity is funded, depending on whether its capital structure favors debt or equity. Since there are no guidelines on how to select a comparable independent capital structure, arm's length source taxation is exposed to a very significant vulnerability, ripe for profit shifting too. Countries have commonly resorted here to antiabuse measures, but how these should interact with the arm's length principle is still a gray area.

For debt there is no problem in determining the aggregate amount, which is simply the sum of all external debt. The issue here is with internal debt, which is under the control of the group and can be used to allocate profits at will, limited only by law. There are various ways to use debt to shift profits, including (1) outright internal lending, (2) choosing the interest rate for such lending, and (3) strategically choosing which affiliate issues debt. Given the artificial nature of internal debt funding, the potential revenue effects of an alternative system in which internal multinational enterprise debt is simply treated as equity for tax purposes is explored in this chapter.

RISK ANALYSIS IN TRANSFER PRICING

To determine whether a price is appropriate under the arm's length principle, both functional and comparability analyses must be done following standard guidelines, and when done correctly—the arm's length argument goes—profits are allocated among the group's affiliates according to where value is created. At the same time, the enterprise's global tax base is presumably assigned fairly among the jurisdictions where it operates.

However, transactions among independents that mimic intragroup operations are often hard to find, so—to a large extent—the art of the transfer pricing practice is determining what is comparable enough. To find the closest or most reliable market comparable, practitioners need to identify key elements defining the controlled transaction in question. The relevant elements or factors of comparability may vary depending on the nature of the transaction and on the transfer pricing method used, but the core elements are functions performed, assets used, and risk assumed by each party to the transaction; this has been the mantra since the inception of the OECD guidelines on transfer pricing (OECD 1995). Including risks in this core trio of comparability factors has the intuitive appeal that, all else equal, higher risks should attract (on average) higher returns and should thus play a material role in pricing intragroup transactions at market values. In other words, business risk is thought of as one of the key traits in a controlled transaction having a bearing on its market price or profitability.

Despite the intuitive appeal, there are some fundamental conceptual difficulties with this approach. First, the simple fact of being related typically leads to an indeterminate risk distribution among affiliates (for example, because of informal guarantees or implicit support among parties in a group, which can complicate the comparison with unrelated parties). Second, the aggregate risk of a group may be very different from the individual risks of affiliates, since there is no a priori reason for them to be closely correlated. In the absence of much guidance prior to the OECD/G20 work on base erosion and profit shifting (BEPS; see OECD 2013) on how to account for risk and its impact on profit allocation among jurisdictions, not surprisingly, risk became a popular subject in transfer pricing practice, allowing for ample room in tax planning.[1] The revised transfer pricing guidance, following the OECD/G20 discussions of BEPS, incorporated the risk factor more formally into the *OECD Transfer Pricing Guidelines* (OECD 2017b), but it is not clear if it did so in a way that makes conceptual sense or that allows for implementation.

Definition of Risk

In common parlance, risk is the possibility of incurring misfortune or loss. Modern economics equates risk to uncertainty of a future outcome, where a (subjective or objective) probability can be attached to each possible outcome.[2] Thus, investors using current resources for a future gain that is uncertain, including a potential loss, incur a risk and would expect a larger return to compensate greater risks, given the assumption that investors are commonly risk averse.

The same principle applies to all investors—shareholders or lenders—in a single business entity or a multinational enterprise. Investors assume the risk associated with the business they engage in based on the consolidated results of the enterprise, large or small. A multinational enterprise can have a more diversified portfolio, investing simultaneously in various lines of businesses and countries whose individual risks may compensate each other in differing degrees. A multinational enterprise, in a way, has the possibility of self-insuring through diversification and, as in a mutual fund, investors (and lenders) ultimately grade their returns based on the overall risk the investment implies.

The previous *OECD Transfer Pricing Guidelines* (2010) had risk as one of the key comparability factors (much in the same terms as in the 1995 *Guidelines*) and added an important discussion on risk regarding business restructuring, but the treatment of risk was vague and confusing. The *Guidelines* did not even provide a general definition of risk, and they referred to it as if it could be alternatively

---

[1] "[D]uring the 1990s and 2000s transfer pricing practice developed a perception of risk that bore virtually no relationship with economics. Risk was captured in contractual stereotypes that perfectly matched the requirements of applying TNMM [transactional net margin method] but lost connection with realities inside MNE business" (Gonnet 2016, 35).

[2] Traditionally, following Frank Knight (1921), uncertainty applied to events for which agents had no well-defined probabilities, while risk referred to events with a knowable probability distribution. However, the modern theory of choice relies on agents' subjective probability estimates, rendering the distinction irrelevant. See Leroy and Singell (1987); Hirshleifer (1970, 215); and Hirshleifer and Reiley (1992,10).

"assumed" or "allocated," a differentiation that also remained obscure.[3] There were, on the one hand, "market risks," explained by way of examples (OECD 2010, para. 1.46) and other types of risk associated with functions performed that apparently could be "allocated" by the multinational enterprise among its affiliates. There was no clarity on how these types of risk were conceptually different from one another, or whether market risk assumed could be freely reallocated within the multinational enterprise through internal contractual arrangements (some kind of self-insurance) that could easily be used for tax planning.[4] The *OECD Transfer Pricing Guidelines* (OECD 2017b), reflecting the BEPS Project agreements, attempt to solve the problem, or at least to place a significant limit to the extent that risk assumption can be divorced from functions actually performed. Nonetheless, major uncertainty remains in this regard (Collier and Andrus 2017, 205, 230).

The OECD *Transfer Pricing Guidelines* (OECD 2017b) are not clear in connecting higher risk (assumed or allocated) with higher (expected) rate of return. The causality seems to align generally with the greater scale of the business or functions performed, and thus the amounts of assets placed at risk, but not necessarily with greater business uncertainty. Conceptually, they are not the same, and one does not necessarily lead to the other, as one would define the amount of profit and the other the profit margin per unit of dollar invested (see Box 5.1).

The Arm's Length Principle and the Deconstruction of Risk

The arm's length principle requires pricing intragroup transactions as if they were carried out among independent, stand-alone entities. This implies that risk must be accounted for as if each affiliate had its own set of shareholders assuming the risk associated with its individual line of business.

One problem with this exercise is that profits of a consolidated enterprise may not match the summation of the profits of the hypothesized, risk-adjusted, single affiliates. A diversified portfolio of (uncorrelated) businesses may yield together a relatively narrow set of future income probabilities, while separately they could represent a more volatile profit stream, albeit the same on average. For risk-averse

---

[3] The *OECD Transfer Pricing Guidelines* underline that risk is an important comparability factor, which may be either assumed or allocated:

Controlled and uncontrolled transactions . . . are not comparable if there are significant differences in the risks assumed . . . Functional analysis is incomplete unless the material risks assumed by each party have been considered since the assumption or allocation of risks would influence the conditions of transactions. (OECD 2010, para.1.45)

[T]he allocation of risks assumed between the parties to the arrangement affects how profits or losses . . . are allocated at arm's length . . . Therefore, in making comparisons between controlled and uncontrolled transactions . . . it is necessary to analyse . . . which party or parties to the transaction assume these risks. (OECD 2017b, para. 1.58)

[4] The economics literature on uncertainty distinguishes exogenous and endogenous risks. The first refers to the state of nature (rain or no rain) whose probabilities individual behavior cannot change; the second instead is partially a function of individual behavior (probability of a car accident) and thus vulnerable to moral hazard.

Box 5.1. Connecting Higher Expected Returns to Greater Risks Assumed

The *OECD Transfer Pricing Guidelines* connect higher "expected returns" to higher risks as a consequence of a larger number of functions performed (and assets used) by the entity:

[W]hen a distributor takes on responsibility for marketing and advertising by risking its own resources[1] in these activities, its expected returns from the activity would usually be commensurably higher . . . from when the distributor acts merely as an agent . . . [S]imilarly, a contract manufacturer or a contract research provider that takes on no meaningful risk would usually expect only a limited return. (OECD 2010, para.1.47)

[W]here a distributor acts merely as an agent . . . [it] ordinarily would be entitled to compensation appropriate to its agency activities alone. It does not assume the risks associated with the further development of the trademark and other marketing intangibles and would therefore not be entitled to additional remuneration in that regard. (OECD 2017b, para. 6.77)

---

[1] Defining "own resources" in an intragroup setting is also problematic. There is a long-standing discussion regarding whether and up to what limit the resources made available within a group should be treated for tax purposes as equity or as a loan. (See, for example, Bulow and others 1990.)

---

investors, these income streams do not have the same value (utility), and such investors should be prepared to sacrifice some future income to obtain greater certainty to optimize their expected utility. That is to say, independent (and less diversified) businesses may imply levels of risk that would require a profit compensation on aggregate greater than the global profit of a (diversified) multinational enterprise.[5]

Further, risks may be assigned to hypothetical shareholders that no actual investor might be willing to assume. For example, vertically integrated businesses bring together activities that otherwise, if independent, could not have the capability to support the other. While investors may face a reasonable range of profit probabilities with an integrated business, investing in them separately as independent companies could represent an inordinate risk.

Inversely, separating integrated businesses may create an artificial market for insurance services; for example, hedging among affiliates of a group may make little sense for the multinational enterprise's shareholders, except for tax considerations, since the enterprise overall risk remains the same. However, such a market could very well be conceived among independent parties that individually have different attitudes toward risk. The question arises whether contractual operations in such hypothetical (intragroup) markets should be validated for tax purposes, that is, if risks can be transferred among affiliates, together with the associated expected profit stream, although they could only occur among separate and independent entities. The arm's length principle may not provide the answer to this question.

---

[5] Logically, the argument resembles the synergy benefits of multinational enterprises in self-insurance as discussed in OECD (2018).

The suggested test by the *OECD Transfer Pricing Guidelines* to distinguish a multinational enterprise's commercially legitimate transactions from those that are artificial, which serve only (or principally) as instruments for profit shifting, is to ask whether independent parties would be willing to engage in similar arrangements (OECD 2017b, para. 1.122).[6] This is a hypothetical and complicated test to apply, but it can be argued to be consistent with the arm's length principle in that it asks the question whether a transaction unique to multinational enterprises could still make sense, at least theoretically, among independents.[7] The test fails, however, in the inverse situation, that is, when it comes to a transfer of risk that is unique to independents and does not make sense for an integrated business. The arm's length principle is left here with no convincing way to draw a line between legitimate and artificial BEPS transactions.

Allocating Risks (and Profits) among Affiliates

Individualizing affiliates' business risks implies not only quantifying how risky their business transactions are, but—more importantly—understanding which party to intragroup transactions bears the risk. One way to frame the issue is to argue that the multinational enterprise faces business risks in dealing with third parties and that it can choose to allocate those risks among the entities of the group, shielding some and exposing others through controlled transactions.

Risks can be assigned by setting the contractual terms of the controlled transactions, where one party would be compensated with a fixed remuneration (for example, a profit margin within a narrow range) while the other would obtain the residual profit (see Box 5.2). Identifying the risks assumed by each party would then be quite straightforward, for they would be essentially spelled out in a contract. The main task for the tax authority would be to verify that the functions actually performed are those stipulated in that contract. Contracts can be set to locate more risk in low-tax countries, with an implicit understanding of bailouts should very negative outcomes occur. However, such bailouts would be unlikely in the event that the main profit center of the multinational enterprise were to go bankrupt. The fate of any one affiliate is ultimately linked to the risk assumed by the parent, even if the (artificial) risk allocation is supposed to protect the affiliate from a bad outcome.[8] Nonetheless, the underlying logic for transfer pricing purposes is that the assumption of risk between affiliates implies that one of them may be shielded from large business volatility.

---

[6] A related point made by the *Guidelines* is that a controlled transaction should not be rejected just because it does not take place among independents, but it is very hard to establish the commercial rationality of a transaction that is unique and occurs only within a group.

[7] A minimum condition to validate the commercial rationality of the controlled transaction from the perspective of separate and independent entities would be that, at least, it should not be expected to make any one of the parties worse off.

[8] It is conceivable that low-risk affiliates may generate profits for a period of time while the high-risk profit center is facing losses. However, systemic risk to the multinational enterprise could hardly be avoided by them.

> ## Box 5.2. Contractual Allocation of Risks among Parties to a Transaction: A Lawyer's Example
>
> There are business risks associated with engaging in any commercial relationship and, surely, diverse ways in which each party to the business bears those risks. Generally, this would be reflected in their contractual terms, fundamentally defining each party's business model. For example, a lawyer can sell his services in a wrongful termination case (or any other case litigating for damages) by any of the following methods:
>
> - Charging a fee and promising the client nothing but his best effort. The whole risk is assumed by the client, who commits to an expense in exchange for uncertain compensation.
> - Paying an upfront amount to the client, obtaining for himself (the lawyer) the right to the compensation if the case is won. The full risk is assumed by the lawyer.
> - Charging a contingent fee (percentage of the compensation) if the case is won. The risk is shared.
>
> The three scenarios involve a trade-off: a certain payment now in exchange for receiving a potentially larger but uncertain amount in the future or sharing the risks to some extent. The actual terms that independent parties will agree to in the example above depend on their respective risk aversion.

Implicit Assumption about Risk Aversion

It is understood generally that contracts among independent parties that assign the risk of the transaction to one or the other party are settled according to each party's attitude toward risk, that is, as a function of who is more or less risk averse. As in the case of an entrepreneur hiring employees, the business risk is assumed (and the uncertain profits earned) by the former, in contrast to the wage earners who prefer a fixed compensation fitting with their greater risk aversion. Similarly, a subsidiary may be a contract manufacturer to another affiliate of the group, with a guaranteed but relatively low profit margin,[9] or a full-fledged manufacturer paying a royalty to the parent company, facing market risks and expecting a higher average rate of return.

A conceptual problem here is that the arm's length principle makes no assumption about whether all "deemed" shareholders (for each contracting subsidiary or branch within the group) must have the same level of risk aversion or if they can be assumed to be different, at will. Multinational enterprises' aggressive tax planning would seem to follow tacitly the second approach, assigning the entrepreneurial (high-risk) role to the affiliate in the low-tax jurisdiction and the opposite risk profile to that in the high-tax location. Moreover, the implicit logic behind many business restructuring cases is that the attitude toward risk can also change (even suddenly), leading to a subsidiary choosing to be relieved from risk and finding refuge in another member of the group (less risk averse) that is willing to take it on (together with the residual profits).

---

[9] When the base of the profit margin is total costs and expenses of the affiliate, or some similar measure, for practical purposes the corporate income tax in that country acts almost like a payroll tax.

Strictly speaking, the multinational enterprise should be indifferent as to how to assign those roles among affiliates, except for taxes in each jurisdiction. Therefore, the central tax planner of the multinational enterprise, on behalf of actual shareholders, would have the incentive to brand each affiliate's "deemed investors" as more or less risk averse so as to minimize the tax bill of the global enterprise. The arm's length principle places few limits on this tax planning tool.

BEPS and Limiting Risk Assumption

The OECD/G20 BEPS Project made a significant effort to introduce some rules to limit the discretion of taxpayers regarding the allocation of risk among entities within a multinational enterprise, especially regarding the development of intangible property (a problem primarily faced by advanced economies). Specifically, financing research and development according to the new *OECD Transfer Pricing Guidelines* would not be a sufficient condition to argue that the risks of developing intellectual property were fully assumed by the funding entity, nor to claim, therefore, the rights to reap the full benefits from it. An additional condition must be met by the investing affiliate: it must manage or exercise control over the associated business risks. As a practical matter, this is generally hard to identify, more so in complex business environments. Ultimately, the guidance endorsed in the BEPS report relies on identifying which party to the transaction has the decision-making responsibility as an indicator of risk control regarding the related operation. Thus, risk allocation must pass this double test: the entity must have the capacity to absorb the financing risk and the control of the risk, which means making the relevant business decisions.

These limitations on the allocation of risk among affiliates would seem to work to avoid aggressive tax planning through a cash-box entity in a low-tax jurisdiction to fund cost-sharing agreements for developing intangibles. These arrangements may comply with the first condition, since financial resources can readily be transferred as equity investments by headquarters, but it is much more difficult to create the impression that the research and development carried out to develop intangible property was, in fact, run from a remote cash-rich shell office. To the extent that the rule was designed to combat such arrangements, it will probably be quite effective.

However, applying the rules to cases other than contracts through cash-box affiliates is far from straightforward. What would constitute relevant decision-making is highly subjective and certainly difficult to verify. Multinational enterprises can claim that important business decisions are made almost anywhere within the global enterprise, and it would not appear too difficult to simulate that this is the case. Also, the control of an operation can be shared between the parties to the transaction, or it can be subcontracted to a third party, so risk can be assumed without (necessarily) controlling it. The possibility of joint control among different entities of the group makes the assignment of risk for transfer pricing purposes highly challenging (Collier and Andrus 2017, 231). The managerial input may be so intricately combined with a final decision that it may make little sense to try to disentangle one from the other. Functions can be juxtaposed, and sorting out which decision relates to which functions might be very hard to show.[10] In other words, the solution developed by BEPS for making risk an intelligible factor in the application of the arm's length principle has not fully prospered, as for a large set of situations the framework is simply impracticable.

A Practitioner's Bias

Back to Basics

A key step in applying the arm's length principle is to find the comparable market match to the controlled transaction, including a matching risk profile. The general idea is briefly stated in the first *OECD Transfer Pricing Guidelines* (1995) as follows:[11]

> In order to establish the degree of actual comparability and to . . . establish arm's length conditions . . . it is necessary to compare attributes of the transaction or enterprises . . . Attributes that may be important include the characteristics of the property or services transferred, the functions performed by the parties (taking into account assets used and risks assumed), the contractual terms, the economic circumstances . . . and the business strategies pursued by the parties. (para. 1.17)

Ultimately this is an exercise in common sense: when pricing a good or service based on a comparable market transaction, it is vital to compare apples with apples; better still, compare the same type of apples, considering their distinguishing characteristics, that is, those that may affect the price. A later version of the *Guidelines* (2010) introduced an entire chapter to explain how to perform "comparability analysis."[12] This new guidance on comparability usefully clarified practical implementation issues, such as the choice of the tested party, bundling transactions, the use of commercial databases, and some specific attributes to examine[13] but said very little about how risk should be identified and compared.[14]

The current *OECD Transfer Pricing Guidelines*, however, are still short on explicit economic principles that should guide the search for comparable

---

[10] Ironically, examining the decision-making in multinational enterprise may reveal such an intricate and integrated process that, just as in the case of shared intangibles by group members, could justify the use of a profit split method rather than a one-sided transfer pricing profit method.

[11] New revised editions of the *Transfer Pricing Guidelines* were published in 2009, 2010, and 2017; the quoted paragraph was reproduced in these subsequent editions.

[12] See chapter 3 of the 2010 *OECD Transfer Pricing Guidelines*.

[13] For example, financial ratios, expenditures on research and development, possession of valuable intangibles, size of business, and number of years in business (OECD 2010, para. 3.42).

[14] The 2010 *OECD Transfer Pricing Guidelines* introduced a new chapter on business restructuring that analyzes risk in that context but does not attempt to develop general guidance on the role of risks in comparability analyses. The first comprehensive attempt is found in UN (2013).

businesses,[15] leaving the concept of risk undefined, nor do they detail how to determine that two businesses assume similar risks. They vaguely point at some risks that are inherent to the functions performed and to others that can be assigned by the multinational enterprise to any one of its related entities, as if risk were an attribute per se, separate from other functions. The latter could be understood as an implicit insurance function, where risks can be transferred or allocated across affiliates through contracts. However, as discussed earlier, this is a challenging framework, with no clear conceptual line separating artificial from legitimate transactions.

Functional Analysis: A Potentially Circular Construct

Given the weak conceptual foundation on how risks can be legitimately allocated across affiliates within a multinational enterprise, there is ample opportunity and flexibility for tax planners to set up intragroup contracts with business conditions fitting a low-risk description. Defining functions around key terms such as "strategic management," "price policy setting," "production or sales strategy," "marketing responsibilities," or any other implicit reference to business decision-making will determine a priori whether the affiliate's business is low or high risk, rather than by examining how volatile returns to functionally similar independent businesses are.

Thus, the prevalent practice establishes whether a controlled business is risky or not by examining the contractual conditions of the activity. A model contract would have one party receiving (in essence) a fee from a principal in exchange for a service, and thus—by design—branded as a low-risk activity.[16] In principle, any of the two parties could be assigned either role. Importantly, however, low risk in this context is not in absolute terms, but *relative* to the other party in the transaction, which absorbs the potential volatility of the market.

Bias in Determining Profit Margins

As a practical matter, this (a priori) approach in identifying risks assumed can bias the search for a market benchmark. In a way, it prejudges the outcome, for independent businesses with high profit margins might be disqualified as being inconsistent with (preestablished) low-risk or routine activities. More to the point, practitioners could be tempted to use ready-made sets of risk-specific (high or low profit margin) comparators. Thus, once it is established that the taxpayer's functions are low risk, a low arm's length profit ratio may be

---

[15] The *OECD Transfer Pricing Guidelines* do not discuss the general conditions under which profit rates would be expected to converge across industries or sectors, such as substitute products, low barriers to entry, or highly mobile capital.

[16] Typically, this is also the tested party, that is, the one that must be compared with the market benchmark. This means that transfer pricing documentation filed with the tax authority will show information on comparables for the low-risk entity and no information as to the residual profit that is earned by the counterparty. This information asymmetry could be resolved with access to country-by-country reporting by the parent of the multinational enterprise.

mechanically assigned to it.[17] Such an approach could miss the mark because, for one, functions performed by one party are low (or high) risk compared with the role played by its commercial counterpart and a relatively low-risk partner in a high-risk business venture may still have a high return by any other standard.

Risk and Average Returns

In practice, with the possible exception of advanced price arrangements, transfer pricing is a backward-looking exercise. The taxpayer's profit[18] in the current fiscal year is set equal to returns of comparable independent firms in prior (known) years, that is, to realized outcomes. Past returns of comparable firms are generally averaged over three to five years to estimate the arm's length current profit of the taxpayer, who does not ride the annual volatility of the market. Instead, the taxpayer is taxed on returns equal to a (moving) average without the downside of some unpredictable low-performing years. Thus, the role of risk by the mechanics of the calculation is to some extent removed from transfer pricing methods.

Different Tax Planning Concerns in Developed and Developing Countries

The concerns with tax planning through risk allocation are, for the most part, different in advanced economies as compared to developing countries. The problem in advanced economies relates more prominently to the erosion of the tax base in technology-driven sectors, rich in intangible assets. Developing countries typically face transfer pricing abuses in the natural resources sector, services, and, for many of them, in more traditional labor-intensive manufacturing export activity.

Limits on the allocation of risk might not be equally effective in combatting arbitrary allocation of risk between headquarters and traditional brick-and-mortar investments in developing countries. Headquarters will generally have a large infrastructure, will be management heavy, and will display plenty of decision-making all around. So, it would seem quite easy for a tax planner to claim that all relevant decisions are made at headquarters, depriving subsidiaries of all significant managerial and entrepreneurial initiative. This alone (for transfer pricing purposes) can transform subsidiaries in developing economies into low-risk and thus low-profit entities at the will of the multinational enterprise, without much recourse for the local tax authorities.

However, the extent to which headquarters activity diminishes the entrepreneurial significance of its subsidiaries will often be very hard to tell. Also,

---

[17] In a way, the 10 percent return on fixed assets of US-controlled foreign corporations under the global intangible low-taxed income antideferral rule (of the 2017 US Tax Cuts and Jobs Act), above which a minimum tax applies, sets a notional maximum profit margin for foreign routine activities requiring tangible assets.

[18] The taxpayer is here the entity transacting with related parties whose profit needs to be determined at arm's length.

managerial supervision from headquarters could be on behalf of shareholders, which—according to long-standing OECD transfer pricing guidance—should not be rewarded with a reallocation of intragroup profits (shareholders are rewarded with dividend distributions). However, there is little guidance on how to distinguish decision-making on behalf of shareholders from any other type of decisions. But this is what tax planners do: they arrange contracts that conveniently allocate risk assumption and provide evidence of decision-making accordingly, thereby justifying a low return to the targeted subsidiary. The BEPS test to establish if risk has been allocated on a reasonable basis seems to be no defense for this type of tax planning. On the contrary, by placing so much emphasis on decision-making it could provide ad hoc arguments to justify profit shifting.

DEBT FINANCING AND PROFIT SHIFTING

An Overview

It has been shown by economists that intragroup interest payments are a key instrument for multinational enterprises to shift profits to low-tax jurisdictions (Grubert 2003). Thus, the problems of debt bias in the corporate income tax and financial stress (De Mooij 2011; IMF 2009, 2016) are compounded by profit shifting through related (internal) loans, all of which potentially undermine a country's tax base.

Debt financing and tax base erosion by multinational enterprises might be a greater risk in low-income countries. The proportion of debt-financed foreign direct investment, on average, is substantially higher in low-income countries, as shown by data on foreign direct investment sources of funds (see Table 5.1). Revenue mobilization efforts in low-income countries therefore might be especially vulnerable to profit shifting through intragroup debt, which makes the case for those countries to adopt effective and simple policy instruments to control profit shifting through interest payments.

TABLE 5.1.

Sources of Foreign Direct Investment Funding		
(2017; average per-country level of income; percent)		
	Equity	**Debt**
Low Income	38.2	57.2
Lower-Middle Income	82.9	14.6
Upper-Middle Income	84.7	14.8
High Income	83.4	16.1
World	*83.4*	*16.0*

Source: IMF Coordinated Direct Investment Survey (CDIS).
Note: Many countries do not (directly) report shares of debt or equity foreign direct investment funding; when unavailable, data are derived from information provided by investor countries. The sum of debt and equity does not add to 100 percent of foreign direct investment because of the error of measurement in derived data. The net debt-financed foreign direct investment position for some countries is negative, reflecting subsidiaries in a lending position with the parents in the investor country. The data have been adjusted in these cases to reflect that a negative debt is equivalent to 100 percent equity funding of foreign direct investment (see Annex 5.1).

Controlling excess interest payments by applying the arm's length principle is conceptually challenging. Countries have relied mostly on (relatively) simple specific antiabuse rules, such as thin capitalization or earning stripping rules. These instruments have their own weaknesses, and how they should coexist with the arm's length principle is still a matter of debate. In July 2018, the OECD released a discussion draft[19] that attempts to clarify how the arm's length principle should apply to financial transactions, including interest payments. But this is a complex and evolving issue, especially challenging for tax authorities in low-income countries.

One simplifying approach to counter multinational enterprises' cross-border profit shifting would be to consider all internal debt as equity for tax purposes. This approach follows from the conceptual and practical difficulties in distinguishing debt from equity when the parties are related. Indeed, continual financial innovation has resulted in the development of hybrid debt instruments that have many traits of equity, making their distinction for tax purposes pretty much redundant. Often, the corporate income tax treats corporate loans to shareholders as profit distributions, so some precedent to that effect already exists. This section explores this issue.

Debt Bias in the Income Tax

Dividends are more heavily taxed than interest expenses, once at the corporate income tax rate and a second time under the personal income tax when distributed to the shareholder (the classical system). Interest instead gets taxed only once at the hands of the bondholder (Cordes 1999). This debt bias has a measurable effect. Empirical research on income taxes and corporate debt reports heterogeneous results, but De Mooij (2011) finds a "consensus estimate" of the responsiveness (elasticity) of companies to this tax bias: a 1 percentage point increase in the corporate income tax rate leads to an increase of 0.17–0.28 percentage points in their debt-to-asset ratios.

The elasticity of the debt ratio to the corporate income tax is the summation of different effects: (1) the conventional cost reduction by a legitimate substitution of equity for debt (the tax shelter effect), (2) the tax avoidance incentive to disguise equity as debt, and (3) the increase in internal debt funding to shift profits to low-tax jurisdictions. The elasticity estimation does not distinguish between these channels of tax base erosion (Buettner and Wamser 2013). An additional channel for base erosion through internal debt is mispricing the servicing of the loans (the interest rate), which is strictly a transfer pricing issue, as discussed in the section on transfer pricing.

Disguising Debt as Equity

The debt bias creates opportunities for tax avoidance. This is an old problem (King 1995), as firms prefer to compensate suppliers of capital with payments that are labeled as interest rather than dividends and have the incentive to disguise

---

[19] The discussion draft is projected to become an additional chapter in the next version of the *OECD Transfer Pricing Guidelines* (OECD 2017b).

dividends as interest payments.[20] Financial innovation since the 1980s has made it increasingly difficult to differentiate one from another (Bulow, Summers, and Summers 1990).

Firms can issue securities that function very much like equity but are treated as debt for tax purposes. These hybrid instruments can be designed in many ways: for example, debt might be issued with a very long-term maturity, paying a variable interest rate that correlates with the borrower's profitability, or it might include the right for the lender to receive some contingent payment.[21] Ultimately, taxpayers can call such financial transactions as they wish contractually, for firms can issue equity-like securities that get around statutory definitions.[22] The attempt to regulate this by defining debt and equity was deemed a failed approach in the United States by the end of the 1980s (Bulow, Summers, and Summers 1990). Twenty-five years later the situation had not changed much; as stated by the Joint Committee on Taxation (2016), there was no basic definition in the US Tax Code or Treasury regulations that could be used to determine whether participation in a corporation constituted debt or equity for tax purposes. Common law (court rulings) still is the principal source of guidance.[23] Thus, the practical difficulties in defining debt versus equity remain.

Another concern is the replacement of outstanding equity by debt. This is the case with business restructurings that involve no new investment, but the change of ownership is financed by debt and secured with the newly acquired assets. The problem is compounded by cross-border leveraged buyouts that shift profits abroad through debt pushdown transactions, where the debt contracted in the home country by the company taking over the targeted entity is ultimately transferred to the entity in the host country. The tax impact of a leveraged buyout can be severe: "Post-acquisition interest deductions can be so large as to eliminate corporate income tax payments for several years" (IMF 2009, 6). Even the threat of a leveraged buyout by a private equity fund, for example, may encourage increasing debt, since debt works as a defense against a hostile takeover: it reduces the margin for the bidder to leverage against the targeted assets.

---

[20] There will be a limit to the substitution of equity for debt among related parties, assuming that there is an increasing cost in adopting this avoidance strategy, at a minimum because it raises the probability of being challenged by the authority. Among independent parties the limit would be determined by market conditions.

[21] A hybrid instrument in the international taxation setting has a related meaning: it is a financial instrument that is treated as debt in the country of issuance but treated as equity in the other country so that it can deliver double nontaxation for the parties involved in the transaction, given the regulatory mismatch between countries, as discussed in OECD/G20 BEPS Action 2; see OECD (2015). The BEPS report on hybrids actually encourages countries to take defensive measures so that the treatment is the same for the issuer as for the holder of such instruments.

[22] It could be argued that debt bias concerns about higher financial instability and bankruptcy might be exaggerated if such debt is just equity under another name (Bulow, Summers, and Summers 1990).

[23] The 2016 US regulations targeting primarily the issuance of dividends by a US subsidiary in the case of inversion was in the process of being pared back substantively in 2019; see Internal Revenue Service, Treasury Department, *Federal Register* 84(218), November 4, 2019.

Booking Loans in Low-Tax Jurisdictions

Economic globalization since the 1990s has compounded the problem. Not only can debt financing reduce the tax burden of a corporation as a cheaper source of funds under a single tax system, but this effect can be amplified by sourcing the loan through a related party residing in a low-tax jurisdiction. In the simplest scenario, the enterprise could inject capital into an affiliate located in a low-tax jurisdiction and have that affiliate lend the funds back internally to other entities of the group in high-tax countries (Durst 2015).[24] For such a scheme to work, the lending affiliate needs to stay out of reach of the controlled foreign corporation rules that would currently tax in the home country the passive income of the foreign affiliates. Where the controlled foreign corporation rules have pertinent loopholes,[25] intragroup debt can be easily managed to shift profits of multinational enterprises from high- to low-tax countries, reducing the overall tax burden of the global enterprise. Also, intragroup loans allow to unlock profits from low-tax jurisdictions by lending them back to the parent company or to other subsidiaries of the group in third countries, which amounts to effectively repatriating profits without having to pay tax (Altshuler and Grubert 2002). Grubert (2003) shows that income shifting attributable to the two factors of industrial intangibles and the allocation of debt in low-tax jurisdictions accounts for all the observed differences in profitability between US manufacturing affiliates in high- and low-tax countries.

Transfer Pricing

The General Principle and Methods Apply

Another issue that may lead to erosion of the tax base is an excessive interest rate for servicing an intragroup loan. Formally, this is a different problem from that arising from an excessive amount of internal debt contracted among affiliates, which can lead to profit shifting even if the interest rate is the "right one." However, given that the interest rate can be a function of the amount of debt incurred, the two issues are often hard to disentangle.

Generally, the arm's length principle applies to financial transactions as it does to any other transaction among related parties. The reward for a financial service (interest rates in the case of loans) should be priced according to what independent parties would charge for a comparable transaction under similar conditions. Also, where differences with uncontrolled transactions may significantly affect the

---

[24] Or the low-tax affiliate could borrow directly from third parties and lend internally to the group, charging a fee for its intermediation services.

[25] Controlled foreign corporation rules normally grant a tax deferral to foreign sourced active income until earnings are repatriated. While this deferral does not apply to passive income, the benefit of deferral is often granted to affiliates in which at least 50 percent of their income is active, so that the other half of their income could be from financial transactions and still benefit from deferral.

price, appropriate adjustments should be made to establish the relevant (comparable) market benchmark (OECD 2017b).

The most appropriate transfer pricing method will depend on the facts and circumstances of the financial transaction. Determining the arm's length interest rate on a loan will often be established through the comparable uncontrolled price method.[26] An often-used benchmark with comparable uncontrolled price is the clearing interest rate in an organized financial market (for example, corporate bonds), not necessarily the observed rate for specific independent transactions. To select the comparable benchmark, the relevant conditions of the controlled financial transaction must be identified or delineated, such as the credit rating and solvency of the borrower, the maturity of the loan, the principal amount, currency denomination, covenants, collateral and guarantees, among other factors.[27]

The Problem of Commercial Rationality

Multinational enterprises frequently engage in controlled transactions that have no parallel in the market. The question arises as to whether it makes sense to adjust the conditions of the transactions found in the market to mimic those contracted by related parties. There might be good business reasons why agents acting under market conditions do not engage in such transactions. For example, an affiliate may loan an amount to a related party that no independent would lend to a client because of solvency issues. Legitimately, it could be a case of asymmetry of information where the affiliate has better information or can rely on an implicit guarantee (lending to itself). The case could be made in such a circumstance—although some might disagree—that adjustments to the market interest rate could recognize the material advantages of the intragroup loan as compared to a commercial operation.

However, related parties may engage in financial transactions for the principal purpose of shifting profits and lowering the tax burden of the multinational enterprise. Evidently, independent parties could not consider agreeing to such transactions since they gain no benefit in shifting profits to another party (unless colluding in a fraudulent scheme). Therefore, the transfer pricing analysis must determine or recognize whether independent parties under comparable circumstances could and would arrange for a loan on the terms agreed internally by the multinational enterprise, considering the options realistically available to them. That is, it must be established whether a transaction unique to a multinational enterprise has commercial rationality aside from tax planning, which can be a challenging and subjective exercise. Also, this analysis may be carried out by the tax administrations from each end of the intragroup loan and, ideally, they would arrive at the same conclusion about the arm's length conditions of the loan. However, in practice this might not often be the case.

---

[26] Other financial services may be priced with a cost-plus method.

[27] See OECD (2018, sections B.1 and C.1).

Recharacterizing the Financial Transaction

Adjusting market observations to match the conditions of a controlled transaction that has been structured principally to avoid tax in a way turns the arm's length principle on its head. Instead of mandating that related parties behave as if they were independents, it allows taxpayers to price their controlled transactions assuming that independents would behave like affiliates in a multinational group. For example, adjusting market operations to the conditions of a controlled financial transaction based on little equity could lead to very high interest rates that independents simply would not agree to under any conditions.

The *OECD Transfer Pricing Guidelines* (2010) allowed the authority to adjust the contractual terms of a controlled transaction when those terms did not match either the true substance of the transaction or commercial rationality. This was a sort of escape clause, deeming it appropriate and legitimate for the authority to disregard the formal structure adopted by the taxpayer. This procedure was expected to be justified only in "extraordinary circumstances" (OECD 2010, para. 1.65). This would apply, as exemplified by the *OECD Transfer Pricing Guidelines* (2010), when the taxpayer disguised equity as debt, since the transaction—as structured—would not match its substance. The tax authority in this case could recharacterize interest payments as distribution of dividends, disallowing the deduction taken by the taxpayer.

One problem in applying the arm's length principle to the underlying substance of a financing operation is the difficulty of unambiguously differentiating equity from debt. Disregarding the contractual formality does not mean that the substance can be easily reframed—the escape clause does not really solve the problem at hand, because it assumes that debt could be easily distinguished from equity, which is not the case, as pointed out in the foregoing discussion.

Too Many Unknowns

Another option, instead of recharacterizing the funding transaction as equity, is to adjust the contractual conditions of the loan to make them consistent with commercial rationality, including the principal amount. The idea is that applying transfer pricing methods should limit overindebtedness and the consequent profit shifting. But this is no less challenging. While the *OECD Transfer Pricing Guidelines* underline that the absence of parallel transactions in the market is not a sufficient reason to discard an intragroup structure, they do not explain how commercial rationality should be defined. In the case in question, the authority must determine the arm's length amount of a loan given all other conditions of the financial transaction, including the interest rate. However, by definition, the arm's length interest rate is also unknown. Thus, there is a degree of conceptual circularity about how transfer pricing methods should be used to identify simultaneously the arm's length loan amount and interest rate.

Allocating the Assumption of Risk

An additional problem in applying the arm's length principle to intragroup loans is the difficulty of ignoring the fact that the borrower is a member of a group. Third-party lenders would probably determine the interest rate they would charge to the borrower considering that there could be some degree of implicit support from the parent company. Thus, the actual market rate might not be determined as if the affiliate were an entirely independent entity, which is a critical assumption in applying the arm's length principle. Considering implicit support, and not charging for it when resulting from the passive membership in the group (as the *OECD Transfer Pricing Guidelines* indicate), is an exception to a strict interpretation of the arm's length principle that probably limits excessive rates for internal loans. However, how to value implicit support and the extent to which this can be substituted for explicit and chargeable (related) financial guarantees is a very complex exercise, subject to interpretation.

Potentially more complicated still is how the new BEPS Project guidance on risk and transfer pricing affects the analysis for determining the arm's length interest rate. A party that claims to assume the risk in a controlled transaction must have not only the resources to face the consequences (losses) of such risk, but it must also manage the risk, which means fundamentally having control of the decision-making about the assumption of such risk. Generally, identifying which party assumes the risk determines which party gets the residual profit arising from the transaction. How this rule applies to intragroup loans is not straightforward, however. Formally, the risk associated with granting a loan is assumed entirely by the lender, which is a separate risk than that assumed by the borrower in its own business, though the latter is a determinant factor in how risky the loan might be. Under transfer pricing methods this separation is no longer clear cut; whenever the lender does not have full control of the lending procedure, it may be claimed by the tax authority that it does not fully assume the risk and thus should be entitled to a lower interest rate (shifting the profits to the borrower). When the lender simply functions as an intermediating cash box for the group financing, the *OECD Transfer Pricing Guidelines*[28] suggest that a risk-free interest rate might be the arm's length reward. This is somewhat arbitrary, since such interest amount is really awarded for a loan origination–type service, not for the loan itself. However, this solution is applicable only to the pure cash-box affiliate, which arguably assumes no risk. In any other case where the lending affiliate has some substance, it is fundamentally unclear how to determine how much risk the affiliate is in fact assuming, if any, and how to calibrate accordingly the interest rate that it should charge.[29]

---

[28] Revisions to chapter 1 of the *Transfer Pricing Guidelines* under Actions 8–10 of the BEPS Action Plan limit the amount of interest payable to group companies lacking appropriate substance.

[29] The discussion draft on transfer pricing on financial transaction (OECD 2018) does not significantly reduce the uncertainty in this regard.

The sum of these methodological and practical difficulties with transfer pricing has led many countries to adopt special anti-avoidance rules to limit interest deductions. This has been, in fact, the dominant approach to profit shifting and debt bias. Despite their appeal, especially due to their simplicity, these rules have some shortcomings.

Restricting Interest Deductibility

Specific antiabuse rules against excessive debt were adopted in many countries early on, irrespective of the remedy that transfer pricing could provide.[30] The main thrust of these rules was restricting interest deductibility. The design of these rules varied quite substantially from country to country, many clearly motivated against intragroup profit shifting while others addressed the debt bias more generally.[31]

Thin Capitalization (Thin Cap) Rules

One approach is to limit the deduction of interest payments from loans above a defined ratio of debt to equity. Implicitly, the argument is that debt above the ratio should be treated as equity for tax purposes, even if the statutory cap is somewhat arbitrary or non–arm's length. Initially, a common cap for deductible interest was up to debt three times equity; this ratio was reduced over time in several countries.[32]

How to calculate the thin cap ratio and the type of interest to which it applies varies significantly from country to country. Some rules consider only related-party debt in the understanding that the problem at hand is profit shifting, while others include all debt in the ratio, with a view to address debt bias more generally. Another reason to have a broader concept of debt in the rule is that related-party debt may hide behind back-to-back loans through independent financial institutions.

Another approach is to benchmark the debt-to-equity ratio close to the multinational's global consolidated gearing ratio. This distinct antiabuse rule limits interest deductions for the local affiliate to the group's consolidated debt-to-equity ratio. This global gearing ratio, adopted early on by Australia and New Zealand, does not include related-party debt and may be a more objective (market) parameter for setting a cap for deductible interest.

---

[30] Canada adopted a thin capitalization rule in 1971; the rule that prevailed in the United States until 2017 (replaced with an earning stripping rule with the Tax Cuts and Jobs Act) was introduced in 1989. Before 1989 the IRS occasionally wielded the thin cap rule of section 385 to recharacterize debt of highly indebted companies to equity (Wynman and Wai 2018).

[31] The *OECD Transfer Pricing Guidelines* (2010) did not address thin capitalization rules, an issue that was slated for "future work" (para. 19). The chapter on safe harbors in the current edition (OECD 2017b) does not discuss provisions designed to limit deductions from excessive debt (para. 4.103). The issue is addressed separately in BEPS Action 4, but not in connection with transfer pricing analysis.

[32] For example, Canada reduced the ratio to 2:1 in 2000 and to 1.5:1 in 2012.

Thin cap rules have several limitations. Aside from having to define numerous other complex design issues such how to define debt, the treatment of the banking sector, or whether to allow carryforward of excess interest, among others, thin cap rules deal only with overindebtedness and not necessarily with excess interest expenses, which also depend on the interest rate. This is left as a separate consideration, to be dealt with by transfer pricing rules. However, there is no general criterion defining the interaction between the arm's length principle and this antiabuse rule.

Studies show that thin cap rules reduce the debt ratio among intragroup companies. But it is not as clear that they affect unrelated-party debt (Blouin and others 2014; De Mooij and Hebous 2017). This is not very surprising since most thin cap rules are designed to restrict profit shifting; that is, they only limit the deduction of interest payments to related parties. However, De Mooij and Hebous (2017) find that having a thin cap rule (or earning stripping rule) that applies to total debt marginally reduces companies' consolidated debt ratio.

However, studies also show that thin cap rules may inhibit investment and employment. Empirical studies find evidence that, by increasing the cost of capital, thin cap rules have negative economic effects, including reducing foreign direct investment, which is found to be twice as sensitive to tax rates in the presence of such rules (Buettner, Overesch, and Wamser 2014). The central message of this literature is that thin cap rules have not been very successful in limiting the effects of debt bias, while their structure is vulnerable to the same definitional problems associated with hybrids.

Earning Stripping Rules

Many countries have abandoned thin cap rules. In a landmark ruling, the European Court of Justice dismissed thin cap rules in member countries that targeted interest paid only to foreign related parties located in the European Union. It was judged contrary to the freedom of establishment. After this ruling thin cap rules in Europe were modified, dropped, or replaced. In some cases, the thin cap rule was substituted with an earning stripping rule, whereby total deduction for interest expenses were limited to a percentage of some measure of earnings. In a few cases, the thin cap rule was simply dropped in favor of transfer pricing regulation (for example, in the United Kingdom; see Dourado and de la Feria 2008).

Earning stripping rules limit the amount of total interest as a percentage of some measure of earnings.[33] Since 2008 in Germany and France that cap has been set to 30 percent of earnings before interest, taxes, depreciation, and amortization (EBITDA). This rule does not attempt to directly limit thin capitalization but puts a cap on the effects of thin capitalization. At the same time, it controls

---

[33] One design issue is how to define interest for the purposes of the rule. Multinational enterprises sometimes charge for other financial transactions to affiliates (guarantee or factoring fees, for example), which represent a deductible expense that may avoid limitations imposed on interest payments.

avoidance schemes that inflate interest rates, thereby also becoming a backstop for transfer pricing.

The BEPS Project, in one of its actions, focused on strengthening anti-avoidance rules on interest deductions (OECD 2017a). The final report on BEPS Action 4 recommended capping interest deductions with an earning stripping rule as a percentage of EBITDA (10–30 percent range). This was an influential report, as shortly after its first release (2015), the European Union[34] and the United States[35] adopted this recommendation. However, the recommendation did not break new ground, since it endorsed a practice already in place in many countries (including the global gearing ratio in Australia and New Zealand) and gaining momentum.

One of the key issues that was not addressed by BEPS Action 4 is the interaction between the anti-avoidance and the transfer pricing rules on interest payments. Fundamental questions remain about how to design a tax regime on interest:

- Should the arm's length principle apply below the earning stripping cap?
- Should the earning stripping rule be considered a transfer pricing safe harbor?
- Should such a safe harbor include an escape clause when the taxpayer can justify that an interest payment above the limit is arm's length?
- Should this clause be allowed only under an advance pricing arrangement process?
- Would a carryforward apply for interest expenses above the cap but below the arm's length level?
- Would recharacterization apply the same way? That is, should payments be considered interest even if above the cap but so long as they are below the level set by the arm's length principle?
- Would interest payments above the arm's length level be recharacterized as dividends?
- Which withholding rate would apply? Would interest payments still benefit from treaty reduced rates even if recharacterized as dividends?

In sum, while specific anti-avoidance rules restricting the deduction of interest expenses are commonplace, they are not foolproof, have some drawbacks, and do not cover all situations. Thus, the arm's length principle is still relevant to intra-group loans, so that the system has not done away with its transfer pricing complexity.

---

[34] Council Directive (EU) 2016/1164 of July 12, 2016, laying down rules against tax avoidance practices that directly affect the functioning of the internal market.

[35] Tax Cut and Jobs Act (2017). Beginning 2022 the limit to the deduction will a percentage of EBIT. The United States adopted an additional anti-avoidance rule called Base Erosion and Anti-Abuse Tax (BEAT), which is a minimum tax of 10 percent (5 percent in 2018) on corporations with more than $500 million of gross receipts that make base-eroding payments (including interest) to foreign-related parties of 3 percent or more of their deductible expenses.

Alternative Tax Systems

There is a growing current among economists who believe that the existing international tax architecture has reached its point of exhaustion. While the OECD/G20 BEPS Project has made progress, strong vulnerabilities remain, including the taxation of debt. They propose alternative directions going forward, since, in their view, the call for taxation where "value is created" has proved to be an inadequate basis for real progress (IMF 2019). Various approaches have been suggested over the years, some more narrowly seeking tax parity between interest and dividends, others with a more ambitious agenda that would fundamentally change current norms by eliminating the reliance on the arm's length principle.

Some of the main alternative approaches that have been suggested, discussed elsewhere in this book, are as follows:

- Comprehensive business income tax system
- Cash-flow base corporate income tax
- Allowance for corporate equity

Another, simpler, and more narrowly focused option would be to treat all internal multinational enterprise funding as equity participation, with no exceptions. The question has been raised: "[I]t is reasonable to ask why, in principle, any deduction at all should be given for interest paid to related parties" (IMF 2014, 31). Under the suggested policy multinational enterprises could still choose which affiliates would borrow from third parties, so some space for tax planning would remain, as well as the general debt bias, but profit shifting through internal debt would be severely curtailed. The next section explores how consequential such measure would be, especially in low-income countries.

Estimating the Impact on Tax Revenue of Debt Financing Foreign Direct Investment

The total world foreign direct investment position in 2017 was $34.6 trillion; $4.8 trillion was financed with debt.[36] This is about 14 percent of the total. However, the proportion of debt financing changes significantly depending on the country's income per capita. As shown in Table 5.1, foreign direct investment financed by debt is proportionally much larger in countries with lower rather than higher income per capita. On average, nearly 60 percent of foreign direct

---

[36] These numbers cannot be directly compared with other standard sources of data on international debt. For example, the World Bank's *International Debt Statistics* does not report intragroup debt. It reports private nonguaranteed debt from commercial banks and others for low- and middle-income countries, which presumably includes intragroup debt. For 2017 that debt from "commercial banks and others" amounted to $2.1 trillion (WB 2020,17). According to the IMF Coordinated Direct Investment Survey, middle- and low-income countries debt-funded foreign direct investment amounted to $1.1 trillion, with over 80 percent concentrated in upper-middle-income countries. The difference could be debt with commercial banks.

investment in low-income countries is financed with debt, while that share is less than 20 percent in other countries.

Intragroup debt-financed foreign direct investment can represent a potentially high tax revenue cost. Indeed, assuming a moderate annual interest rate between 5 and 7 percent,[37] servicing intragroup debt results in a sizable corporate income tax deduction for foreign investors in some countries. Table 5.2 shows the estimated impact in the 10 most affected countries,[38] different from low-tax and investment conduit jurisdictions.[39] The listed countries are mostly low income or lower-middle income, with the exception of Kazakhstan and Namibia, which are upper-middle income, and Chile, a high-income country. All ten countries have in common an economy largely dependent on the extractive sector. For other countries, the tax impact of debt-funded foreign direct investment would be a lower share of GDP (below 0.25 percent). Annex 5.1 discusses data and details of the calculation.

TABLE 5.2.

Estimated Potential Reduction in Corporate Income Tax Revenue from Servicing Intragroup Debt

(2017; percent of GDP)

	Interest Rate	
	5%	**7%**
Mozambique	3.69	5.17
Liberia	3.09	4.33
Mongolia	0.87	1.22
Zambia	0.79	1.11
Niger	0.60	0.84
Kazakhstan	0.55	0.77
Namibia	0.49	0.69
Republic of Congo	0.42	0.59
Togo	0.26	0.36
Chile	0.25	0.35

Sources: Authors' estimates, based on IMF Coordinated Direct Investment Survey (CDIS); IMF *World Economic Outlook*; KPMG. International Bureau of Fiscal Documentation (IBFD) for corporate income tax rates.
Note: The calculation assumes that negative debt positions generate an interest revenue for the host country. Recharacterizing debt as equity in such cases would mean for tax purposes replacing interest revenue for a potential stream of dividends. Conservatively, it is assumed that these would not be repatriated, implying a net tax revenue loss.

---

[37] This is the range of interest rates most common on new external private debt commitments by low-income countries, as reported by the World Bank database on debt statistics.

[38] The calculation does not consider whether the taxpayers would show a profit prior to interest expenses or if they could find other channels of deductible financing different from an intragroup loan.

[39] The countries where the measure would have the most impact on corporate income tax revenues are Andorra, Aruba, Curaçao, Gibraltar, Guam, Luxembourg, Malta, Mauritius, and Monaco. The Netherlands and Cyprus complete the list of the top 20 countries with the most significant potential tax revenue impact as a percentage of GDP. All these jurisdictions have been at one point identified as a low-tax jurisdiction or a financial center hosting a large number of special purpose entities that act as passive holding companies with very small net foreign direct investment positions. See Damgaard and Elkjaer (2017). Table 5.2 does not include this type of jurisdictions.

CONCLUSION

Investors in a multinational enterprise assume the business risk arising from the global operation of the enterprise and are indifferent as to how such risk is allocated contractually among the group's affiliates, except for its effect on the overall tax burden. Given that there is, in principle, no value creation in the reassignment of risks within the enterprise, selecting where to allocate the risk through intragroup transactions appears to be arbitrary from a transfer pricing perspective. It would seem to be simply a matter of choice by the multinational enterprise as to where to allocate the risk, with the caveat that the affiliate assuming the risk must have the financial and managerial capacity to do so. To the extent that the first condition is somewhat trivial and the second very hard to define and enforce, profit shifting through risk allocation remains wide open for tax planning.

Moreover, in practice, tax planning may not consider that contractually low-risk activities should be so labeled relative to the principal in the transaction, but not as an absolute consideration. Then, to the extent that absolute low profit margins are associated with low risk, practitioners may select comparable observations according to their profit margin level, where the profit margin becomes a key selection criterion rather than being the unknown variable that needs to be estimated resulting from a functional and comparability analysis of the tested party and independent comparators. The danger is that the analytical order of things is thus reversed. It could be argued further that the identification of a business's risk level, carried out by a tested party, should itself be dictated by an analysis of the profit volatility of functionally comparable independent businesses, rather than predefining it by an internal contract.

The choice of funding foreign direct investment either with debt or equity is also an instrument of allocating risk within a multinational enterprise; moreover, where the loan is booked is an easy instrument of tax planning. The data show that this problem might be especially concerning in low-income countries hosting large extractive industries. The application of the arm's length principle to related-party debt has been challenging, especially with regard to determining the market benchmark for the amount of debt that an independent business would rationally undersign if operating under the circumstances of an affiliate.

Thus, in practice, controlling base erosion through interest payments has been mostly delegated to specific antiabuse rules, and it is not clear how these should coexist with the notion of the arm's length principle. Indeed, it is not evident how the general rules about the assumption and control of risk apply to determine the arm's length source of funds. Prioritizing the protection of the tax base in this regard with specific antiabuse rules is in a way a tacit admission that the arm's length principle is ineffective at best to deal with the problem. Adopting a general rule that intragroup debt should be treated as equity should be further explored; it would seem to benefit low-income countries in particular.

The two examples considered in detail in this chapter show how difficult defining and enforcing source-based taxation can be, but they are certainly not the only difficulties. Many other challenges arise in determining and monitoring transfer prices under the current global corporate tax system.

ANNEX 5.1. CALCULATIONS WITH CDIS DATA

Foreign Direct Investment Threshold

The calculations in this chapter are based on direct investment position statistics, compiled under the IMF Coordinated Direct Investment Survey (CDIS). The survey includes investments made by direct investors—residents of one country who exercise control or a significant degree of influence on the management of an enterprise that is resident in another country. A "significant degree of influence" refers to instances when a direct investor owns equity to allow for 10 percent or more of the voting power in the invested enterprise.[40]

Derived Foreign Direct Investment

The CDIS includes inward and outward foreign direct investment data reported by participating countries. Additionally, the CDIS registers derived foreign direct investment data, which are estimated using the reported outward foreign direct investment data of counterpart economies. Derived data comprise a smaller amount of foreign direct investment as compared to the foreign direct investment data directly reported by host countries; the difference is larger when comparing debt-funded foreign direct investment. Thus, the calculations in this chapter use directly reported data; when directly reported data is unavailable, the chapter supplements the sample with derived foreign direct investment data.

In any case, derived foreign direct investment data show a similar pattern regarding countries' income level: the higher the income per capita, the higher the portion of foreign direct investment financed with equity, as shown in Annex Table 5.1.1.

Net Foreign Direct Investment

CDIS cross-border investment by a direct investor in an entity is *netted* against reverse investment of that entity in the direct investor's enterprise. As such, direct investment positions in the CDIS could be negative. A negative debt position means that the direct investor's debt claims in its subsidiary are less than the reverse debt claims by the subsidiary in its direct investor enterprise; that is, the subsidiary is in a lending position to the parent or investing entity. This situation lowers the overall foreign direct investment position in the host country.

Adjusted Aggregate Debt-Funded Foreign Direct Investment

When a country has negative debt funding of its (inward) foreign direct investment position with respect to another country, it can be argued that 100 percent of this foreign direct investment is equity financed, instead of over 100 percent as would arithmetically result from a negative debt. However, if the calculation of

---

[40] In many countries this represents a lower threshold than that defining related parties for tax purposes.

ANNEX TABLE 5.1.1.

Sources of Derived Foreign Direct Investment Funding *(2017; average per-country level of income; percent)*		
	Equity Financed	**Debt Financed**
Low Income	41.7	43.6
Lower-Middle Income	77.6	11.3
Upper-Middle Income	86.4	11.3
High Income	91.2	7.0

Source: IMF Coordinated Direct Investment Survey (CDIS).

the aggregate debt and equity shares of foreign direct investment is adjusted so that a net lending position is represented as zero debt, the overall shares do not change much (the proportion of debt in world foreign direct investment increases by 0.5 percentage point as compared to the unadjusted number shown in Table 5.1). The adjustment affects more notably the proportion of debt-financed foreign direct investment in high-income countries, which increases because the most significant investment conduit, low-tax jurisdictions, are high-income countries, which tend to be in a pronounced lending position. Further exploration of this issue is outside the scope of this chapter.

REFERENCES

Altshuler, Rosanne and Harry Grubert. 2002. "Repatriation taxes, repatriation strategies and multinational financial policy." *Journal of Public Economics* 87 (2002) 73–107.

Blouin, Jennifer, Harry Huizinga, Luc Laeven, and Gaetan Nicodeme. 2014. "Thin Capitalization Rules and Multinational Firm Capital Structure." IMF Working Paper 14/112, International Monetary Fund, Washington, DC.

Buettner, Thiess, Michael Overesch, and Georg Wamser. 2014. "Anti Profit-Shifting Rules and Foreign Direct Investment." CESifo Working Paper 4710, Center for Economic Studies and Ifo Institute, Munich.

Buettner, Thiess, and Georg Wamser. 2013. "Internal Debt and Multinational Profit Shifting: Empirical Evidence from Firm-Level Panel Data." *National Tax Journal* 66(1).

Bulow, I. Jeremy, Lawrence H. Summers, and Victoria P. Summers. 1990. "Distinguishing Debt from Equity in the Junk Bond Era." In *Debt, Taxes and Corporate Restructuring*, edited by John B. Shoven and others. Washington, DC: Brookings Institution.

Collier, Richard S. and Joseph L. Andrus (2017), *Transfer Pricing and the Arm's Length Principle After BEPS*, Oxford University Press.

Cordes, J. Joseph. 1999. "Dividends, Double Taxation of." In *Encyclopedia of Taxation and Tax Policy*, edited by Joseph. J. Cordes and others. Washington, DC: Urban Institute Press.

Damgaard, Jannick, and Thomas Elkjaer. 2017. "The Global Foreign Direct Investment Network: Searching for Ultimate Investors." IMF Working Paper 17/58, International Monetary Fund, Washington, DC.

De Mooij, A. Ruud. 2011. "Tax Biases to Debt Finance: Assessing the Problem, Finding Solutions." IMF Staff Discussion Note 11/11, International Monetary Fund, Washington, DC.

De Mooij, A. Ruud, and Shafik Hebous. 2017. "Curbing Corporate Debt Bias: Do Limitations to Interest Deductibility Work?" IMF Working Paper 17/22, International Monetary Fund, Washington, DC.

De la Feria, Rita and Ana Paula Dorado. 2008. "Thin capitalization Rules in the Context of the CCCTB." Working Paper 804, Oxford University Centre for Business Taxation.

Durst, Michael. 2015. "Limitation on Interest Deductions: A Suggested Perspective for Developing Countries." ICTD Working Paper 36, International Centre for Tax and Development, Brighton, UK.

Gonnet, Sebastien. 2016. Risks Redefined in Transfer Pricing Post-BEPS, in Michael Lang et al (eds), *Transfer Pricing in a Post-BEPS World*, Wolters Kluwer, The Netherlands.

Grubert, Harry. 2003. "Intangible Income, Intercompany Transactions, Income Shifting, and the Choice of Location." *National Tax Journal* 56(1), 121–42.

Hirshleifer, Jack. 1970. *Investment, Interest and Capital*, Prentice-Hall, Englewood Cliffs, N.J.

Hirshleifer, Jack and John G. Riley. 1992. *The Analytics of Uncertainty and Information*, Cambridge University Press.

International Monetary Fund (IMF). 2009. "Debt Bias and Other Distortions: Crisis-Related Issues in Tax Policy." IMF Policy Paper, Washington, DC.

International Monetary Fund (IMF). 2014. "Spillovers in International Corporate Taxation." IMF Policy Paper, Washington, DC.

International Monetary Fund (IMF). 2016. "Tax Policy, Leverage, and Macroeconomic Stability." IMF Policy Paper, Washington, DC.

International Monetary Fund (IMF). 2019. "Corporate Taxation in the Global Economy." IMF Policy Paper, Washington, DC.

King, R. John. 1995. "Debt and Equity Financing." In *Tax Policy Handbook*, edited by Parthasarathi Shome. Washington, DC: International Monetary Fund.

Knight, H. Frank. 1921. *Risk, Uncertainty and Profit*, Houghton Mifflin, Boston/New York

Leroy, F. Stephen and Larry D. Singell. 1987. Knight on Risk and Uncertainty, *Journal of Political Economy*, Vol. 95, No 2 (April).

Organisation for Economic Co-operation and Development (OECD). 1995. *Transfer Pricing Guidelines for Multinational Enterprises and Tax Administrations*. Paris: OECD Publishing.

Organisation for Economic Co-operation and Development (OECD). 2010. *Transfer Pricing Guidelines for Multinational Enterprises and Tax Administrations*. Paris: OECD Publishing.

Organisation for Economic Co-operation and Development (OECD). 2013. *Addressing Base Erosion and Profit Shifting*. Paris: OECD Publishing.

Organisation for Economic Co-operation and Development (OECD). 2015. *Aligning Transfer Pricing Outcomes with Value Creation, Actions 8-10–2015 Final Reports*, OECD/G20 BEPS Project, OECD Publishing, Paris.

Organisation for Economic Co-operation and Development (OECD). 2017a. *Limiting Base Erosion Involving Interest Deductions and Other Financial Payments, Action 4—2016 Update: Inclusive Framework on BEPS*. OECD/G20 Base Erosion and Profit Shifting Project. Paris: OECD Publishing.

Organisation for Economic Co-operation and Development (OECD). 2017b. *OECD Transfer Pricing Guidelines for Multinational Enterprises and Tax Administrations*. Paris: OECD Publishing.

Organisation for Economic Co-operation and Development (OECD). 2018. "BEPS Actions 8–10: Financial Transactions." Public Discussion Draft, OECD, Paris.

United Nations. 2013. *Practical Manual on Transfer Pricing for Developing Countries*, UN, NY.

Joint Committee on Taxation. 2016. "Overview of the Tax Treatment of Corporate Debt and Equity." Publication JCX-45-16, Joint Committee on Taxation, Congress of the United States, Washington, DC.

World Bank. 2020. *International Debt Statistics 2020*. Washington, DC: World Bank Group.

Wynman, Raymond, and Andrew Wai. 2018. "Interest Expense Limitation and the New I.R.C. § 163 (j): Not Just a Foreign Concept Anymore." Global Tax Management. https://gtmtax.com/knowledge/interest-expense-limitation-new-i-r-c-%C2%A7-163j/.

CHAPTER 6

Has Tax Competition Become Less Harmful?

Shafik Hebous

INTRODUCTION

Countries compete over productive capital and paper profits. Taxation has been one important element in the set of policy instruments regarding competition.[1] Tax instruments include, inter alia, corporate income tax rates and preferential tax regimes that offer a lower tax burden on specific types of income—typically associated with mobile activities or specific geographical areas.[2]

Tax competition has intensified in the last decades, despite international efforts to contain it. Following a relatively flat trend from 2007 to 2012, statutory corporate income tax rates continued to decline in advanced and developing economies, reaching 22.3 and 24 percent, on average, respectively (see Figure 6.1). Examples of countries that cut their corporate income tax rate in the last five years include G7 members, such as the United States (from 35 to 21 percent)[3] and France (from 34 to 25 percent); advanced small open economies, such as Belgium (from 34 to 25 percent) and Norway (from 27 to 22 percent); and developing countries, such as Tunisia (from 30 to 25 percent) and Pakistan (from 34 to 29 percent).

International initiatives opt to single out forms of tax competition that are deemed to be harmful—as defined by criteria summarized below. However, the hallmark of the OECD/G20 Base Erosion and Profit Shifting (BEPS) Project has been curbing international tax avoidance, rather than tax competition per se, mainly through strengthening anti–tax avoidance rules. Action 5 on combating

---

[1] Other policy tools include, for example, public spending and regulations. See also Schön (2005) and Sinn (1997).

[2] Generally, preferential tax regimes include also those that offer lower personal income taxes (for example, for employing foreign experts or attracting wealthy retirees). This paper predominantly focuses on corporate taxation.

[3] On top of the federal rate, there are state taxes that bring the combined corporate income tax rate in the United States to 26 percent, on average.

Figure 6.1. Trends of Statutory Corporate Income Tax Rates

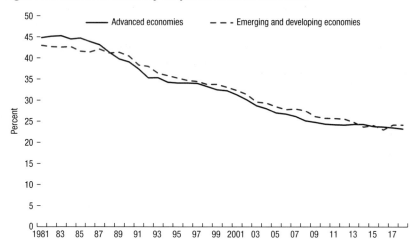

Source: Author's calculation, using the IMF Fiscal Affairs Department database.

harmful tax practices, one of the four minimum standards,[4] is concerned with constraining preferential tax regimes, in particular, insofar as they facilitate cross-border profit shifting. Other notable similar international arrangements include EU member states' obligations under state aid rules as well as their commitments under the EU Code of Conduct for Business Taxation.

Under current international corporate income tax arrangements, the tax rate and base are ultimately sovereign choices. However, recent international initiatives put limits on the design of preferential tax regimes, mainly by linking the benefits from such regimes to "substantial activity"; that is, loosely speaking, activities and their generated qualified income should be in the same country and by the same taxpayer ("nexus approach"). The level of the headline corporate income tax rate—no matter how low—thus far remains unconstrained by these initiatives. The presumption appears to be that forms of preferential tax regimes that do not establish substantiality intensify inefficiencies related to tax competition. As this chapter argues, however, this presumption is far from being clear cut in theory or in practice.

An unconstrained outcome ("equilibrium") of a tax competition game is typically welfare reducing (see "Why Does Tax Competition Lead to Inefficiently Low Tax Rates?" later in this chapter). The pressing question confronting

---

[4] The other minimum standards are regarding country-by-country reporting requirements for large multinational enterprises, tax treaty abuse, and tax treaty–related dispute resolution mechanisms. See Beer, De Mooij, and Liu (forthcoming) and Tørsløv, Wier, and Zucman (2018) for studies on profit shifting; see Chapter 4 of this volume for a discussion about the rise of multinational enterprises.

policymakers is what the outcome is of proscribing preferential tax regimes or insisting on the nexus approach? Theory provides important insights. First, in the absence of a preferential tax regime that lowers the tax on profits of mobile activities, the statutory corporate income tax rate and generally applicable tax deductions within any given country become more relevant tax policy instruments to compete for the location of corporations. This leads to lower (statutory and effective) corporate income tax rates and tax revenues from both the mobile and immobile bases, and triggers further strategic tax reactions by other countries. This outcome is possibly inferior to one with preferential tax regimes. The reason is that preferential tax regimes make it possible to restrict competition to the mobile base, thereby enabling higher tax rates on the immobile base, which in turn can be welfare improving compared to the unconstrained tax competition game. A very low tax rate, or even a zero tax per se, however, is not deemed harmful under any existing internationally agreed approaches, thus far. For example, a country with two tax rates (say, a headline rate of over 30 percent and an intellectual property box rate of 15 percent that does not fully satisfy existing criteria) can be deemed as adopting a harmful tax practice (for instance, as found in France; see OECD 2017, page 15), whereas a country that has a uniform but lower corporate income tax rate (even zero) would not.

Second, the nexus approach restrains the design of preferential tax regimes in a manner that can intensify, rather than alleviate, tax competition by expanding the scope of competition to real investment, beyond paper profits. Third, a distinct but related issue is that it remains to be seen whether BEPS Action 5 (at least indirectly) encourages an inefficient instrument—the intellectual property box regime (known as IP box or patent box)—to incentivize research and development activities and innovation, as opposed to cost-based tax incentives.

If current international corporate income tax arrangements were to be reformed, for example by introducing a (preferably internationally coordinated) minimum tax or multilateral destination-based tax (see Chapter 13), then tax competition would be alleviated or even eliminated. Tax competition, however, has not been thus far at the fore of international initiatives.

In addition to classifying tax regimes, blacklisting of jurisdictions has become a tool to pressure some countries to reform their tax systems. For example, the Global Forum on Transparency and Exchange of Information for Tax Purposes (the Forum) has adopted criteria for listing noncooperative jurisdictions focusing on compliance with tax transparency standards. Also, in December 2017, to "encourage fair competition," the European Union (EC, 2017) adopted a list of "non-cooperative jurisdictions" largely based on the implementation of OECD/G20 BEPS minimum standards, tax transparency standards, and "fair taxation" criteria (summarized in subsequent sections of this chapter). Listed countries can face "defensive measures" at the European Union and member state level. As far as tax competition is concerned, however, the achievements of this watchlist approach are not yet clear. It should be emphasized that remarkable progress has been achieved regarding tax transparency, primarily through the cross-border exchange of tax-related information, thereby significantly strengthening the fight against, inter alia, tax crimes and tax evasion.

The rest of this chapter is organized as follows: The following section briefly discusses major predictions of the theory of tax competition and empirical observations. The chapter then turns to summarizing international efforts to address harmful tax practices and then discusses whether tax competition has become less intense as a result of harmful tax practices initiatives.

WHAT IS HARMFUL IN TAX COMPETITION?

Rather than a full survey of the rich literature on tax competition,[5] the focus here is on key insights that are relevant for the discussion of harmful tax practices, abstracting from modeling details.

Strategic Tax Interactions: Main Insights

International tax competition mostly leads to suboptimal global welfare outcomes because of inefficiently low tax rates and cross-border spillovers.

Why Does Tax Competition Lead to Inefficiently Low Tax Rates?

An increase in the corporate tax rate in a country lowers its capital and increases capital employed in all other countries. A central result of a prototypical game of strategic tax setting is that in equilibrium all countries would benefit from a small increase in all tax rates. Hence, this outcome is Pareto inefficient and the low tax rates lead to underprovision of public goods. The robustness of this general result has been examined in a number of extensions and theoretical setups (Keen and Konrad 2013). Despite some model-dependent specificities, and in some cases involving conditions, the implications of this result have proved to be valid in most models.[6]

Some theoretical models predict that tax competition has a positive welfare impact in the sense that reducing the size of inefficient governments would lead to more efficient provision of public inputs. However, as mentioned in the previous paragraph, most classes of tax competition models suggest that tax rates will be too low in a Nash equilibrium, leading to underprovision of public goods. Gomes and Pouget (2008) find empirical evidence that a corporate income tax rate cut of 15 percentage points has led to a reduction in public investment in OECD countries of between 0.6 and 1.1 percent of GDP.

Regarding the distinction between competition over real investment and competition over paper profits, it is important to underscore the distinction between

---

[5] Keen and Konrad (2013) and Zodrow (2010) survey this literature.

[6] Another effect that is typically not explicitly modeled in this literature is that a lower corporate income tax rate puts downward pressure on the top personal income tax rate as the tax system struggles to avoid a disparity between the taxation of corporations and other legal forms of businesses.

effective and statutory tax rates. Effective tax rates take into account tax deductions, tax credits, and depreciation allowances in addition to the statutory corporate income tax rate. What matters for the size of the aggregate capital stock is the marginal effective tax rate—that is, the tax rate on an investment that just yields the required return to be undertaken. The average effective tax rate is important for decisions regarding location made by multinational enterprises (that is, firms with firm-specific rent). This rate is a measure of the tax burden on a profitable inframarginal investment defined as the proportion of the present value of pretax profit that would be taken in tax in a country.[7]

Paper profits react to the statutory corporate income tax rate. Lowering the statutory corporate income tax rate reduces the incentives for outbound profit shifting and lowers the tax burden on marginal investments (including by purely domestic firms). However, a cut in the statutory corporate income tax rate is more valuable for firms that generate relatively high firm-specific rents (the case for many multinational enterprises), thereby lowering the tax burden on their entire profit. Hence, a lower statutory corporate income tax rate attracts highly profitable firms. In contrast, investment allowances are more valuable for relatively low-profit activities. Thus, in competing over profitable multinational enterprises (whether their investment or their profits), the tax rate applied to profits (whether the statutory corporate income tax rate or the preferential tax regime rate) is relatively more important than tax base instruments.

Thus, overall, the tax reaction function of a country includes not only the statutory corporate income tax rate but also effective tax rates (including preferential tax regimes). The empirical evidence documented in Devereux, Lockwood, and Redoano (2008) and Leibrecht and Hochgatterer (2012) suggests that countries compete using these tax measures.

Why Spillovers?

Cross-border spillover effects from tax competition result from relocating paper profits or investments in response to a change in taxation in one country. That is, given the tax system in country i, lowering the tax burden in country j, say by cutting the corporate income tax rate or adopting a preferential tax regime, can have a negative effect on the tax base of country i. Empirical evidence suggests that spillovers from corporate income tax competition are sizable and tend to be larger for developing countries. For example, Crivelli, De Mooij, and Keen (2017), based on a large panel of countries, find that the cost of tax base spillovers from avoidance activities are larger in non-OECD countries (about 1.3 percent of GDP, on average) than in OECD countries (about 1 percent of GDP). It is

---

[7] See Devereux, Griffith, and Klemm (2002) for stylized facts about the developments of all of these rates. They argue that there are greater declines in average effective tax rates than in marginal effective tax rates, which suggests that countries have designed their tax structures to attract more profitable and mobile businesses, while becoming more distortive for less profitable, and often smaller, domestic businesses.

empirically challenging, however, to fully disentangle the investment effect from the profit reallocation effect.

How Can Preferential Tax Regimes Make Tax Competition Less Harmful?

Keen (2001) shows that deploying preferential tax regimes has positive impacts on revenues and welfare. One key factor behind this result stems from the different degrees of mobility of tax bases. In the presence of preferential tax regimes, competition between countries becomes concentrated and more intense over the mobile base, leading to a loss in revenues from this base. However, the immobile base remains to be taxed at a higher rate (using the headline corporate income tax rate) than the preferential tax regime rate for the mobile base. In contrast, repealing preferential tax regimes restricts the competition entirely to using the corporate income tax rate (applied to all bases), leading to lower tax revenues from the immobile base, which may (in Keen's model always) outweigh the gain from less intense tax competition over the mobile base. Thus, preferential tax regimes can be viewed as a mechanism of price discrimination that lowers the intensity of tax competition. Janeba and Smart (2003) show that Keen's result may not hold under some conditions, specifically if the aggregate tax base responds to a coordinated tax change.

How Does Profit Shifting Affect Tax Competition?

Somewhat similar to the logic of the foregoing discussion—but still distinct from directly discriminating tax bases based on their degrees of mobility—tightening anti–tax avoidance rules in high-tax countries may lead to more aggressive tax rate competition (see also Chapter 9). In the model of Becker and Fuest (2012), tightening anti-avoidance rules prompts low-tax jurisdictions to engage in more aggressive tax rate competition. Peralta, Wauthy, and Ypersele (2006) show that the possibility of profit shifting diverts tax competition from the location of multinational companies to their profits, while enabling countries to collect higher revenues from domestic companies (because they are subject to the corporate income tax rate and have few opportunities to avoid it). Thus, stricter anti-avoidance rules make the location choice of multinational enterprises more sensitive to international differences in tax rates. In the same vein, De Mooij and Liu (2018) find empirical evidence that affiliates of multinationals reduce their investment by over 11 percent as a result of adopting transfer pricing regulations.

Welfare Effects of Shutting Down Low-Tax and Secrecy Jurisdictions

Thus far, the discussion here has ignored differences in country characteristics, especially those regarding country size. Larger economies tend to have a larger immobile base than small countries. Hence, a tax competition game that leads to lower tax rates is costlier for larger economies (Kanbur and Keen 1993). In line with this argument, empirical evidence suggests that country size and stable governance are important determinants for being a low-tax jurisdiction (Dharmapala and Hines 2009).

"Tax havens" is a vague expression—without a universally accepted definition—broadly used in the media and by academics, among others, to refer to jurisdictions that impose low or no taxes on income, or imperfectly share (or do not share) information with other jurisdictions, thereby enabling foreigners to minimize (or escape) taxation at home or abroad (see Hebous 2018). But for welfare analysis, it is much more useful to focus explicitly on these two aspects separately: cross-border information sharing and low taxation. The OECD used the term in its work on the Forum on Harmful Tax Practices in 1998, but international organizations such as the IMF and the United Nations nowadays avoid using the term altogether.

It is tempting to conclude that in a world without low-tax jurisdictions global welfare would be unambiguously higher. Regarding the low-taxation aspect, intuitively, low-tax jurisdictions attract paper profits from high-tax jurisdictions, and hence negatively impact their revenues. Shutting down this mechanism should be welfare improving (Slemrod and Wilson 2009). However, the existence of low-tax jurisdictions can have countereffects that can offset this effect or may even lead to a net positive global welfare. Such jurisdictions may support an equilibrium with less intense tax competition between larger high-tax countries, whereby they set the same (high) tax rate and hence raise revenues (see, for example, Johannesen 2010). Another welfare channel is related to the foregoing argument that strict anti-avoidance rules can aggravate tax competition. When a firm has the possibility to shift profits, for example by borrowing from affiliates in low-tax jurisdictions, the efficiency of the firm is increased; in turn, this increases the firm's investment at home while enabling the high-tax country to apply a really high tax rate on the immobile base (Hong and Smart 2010).[8]

At a general level, in principle, cross-border exchange of information—the other aspect—has two opposing effects in a tax competition model (Keen and Konrad 2013). First, it becomes less attractive to use the low-tax jurisdiction for tax evasion. Second, to the extent that taxes in the high-tax country rise, the motives for evasion increase. It is ultimately an empirical matter to understand which effect dominates. However, there are additional mechanisms. The lack of transparency in some jurisdictions negatively impacts welfare in other jurisdictions, particularly in developing countries. This is formally shown in Hebous and Lipatov (2014), where the authors explicitly model the role of supplying secrecy services in facilitating the concealment of proceeds of corruption and firm bribery. Eliminating secrecy makes it harder to conceal corrupt officials' bribes and illegal income, which unambiguously increases the provision of public goods. Schjelderup (2016) and Torvik (2009) argue that secrecy jurisdictions reduce the costs and negative consequences of entering illegal businesses, particularly for resource-rich countries.

---

[8] Weichenrieder and Xu (2019) challenge the results of Hong and Smart (2010) in the presence of round-tripping investment (that is, domestic firms camouflaging as foreign investors) because the supply of concealment services in some jurisdictions makes it more difficult to discriminate between domestic and foreign-owned firms and therefore has a negative impact on high-tax countries' welfare. One implication of this model is that the exchange of information is welfare improving for the high-tax countries.

Overall, the literature indicates that, to the extent that enhancing tax transparency curbs tax evasion and tax crimes and strengthens the fight against corruption, it is welfare improving. Closing the business of low-tax jurisdictions, however, as long as tax competition between the rest of the countries remains unconstrained, can aggravate competition, resulting in negative welfare impacts.

Why Is Tax Coordination (Cooperation) Challenging?

Tax coordination is challenging because interests of countries widely diverge. As discussed earlier, one way to illustrate the asymmetry is to recall that a 1 percentage point cut in the tax rate in a small country to attract a foreign tax base is less costly than in a large country. Difficulties of tax coordination arise in the various reform contexts, including minimum taxes, fundamental tax reforms, and the possibility of compensating losers by agreeing on a revenue-sharing mechanism. One example illustrating this difficulty in practice is the failure to reach an agreement on a common tax base in the European Union, as proposed by the European Commission. There are, however, cases of tax coordination, such as the agreement on a minimum corporate income tax rate of 25 percent in the West African Economic and Monetary Union. A similar proposal for the European Union, put forth in 1992, failed.

The OECD/G20 Project is a partial coordination regarding specific aspects to strengthen the tax base against profit shifting, and so is the EU Anti-Tax Avoidance Directive. A question arises, however, about whether countries will compete more intensely using the uncoordinated aspects that remain outside the ambit of the OECD/G20 BEPS Project. Keen (2018) suggests that corporate income tax rates will be lower as a result of the collective reduction in tax avoidance if a lower tax rate is a strategic substitute for stricter anti–tax avoidance rules. The main lesson to be drawn in this context is that benefits from partial cooperation, for example the OECD/G20 BEPS Project, hinge on the assumption that the unconstrained tax competition instruments will not change. The point is that strategic reaction using the unconstrained instruments can to some degree offset the benefits from partial coordination.

INTERNATIONAL INITIATIVES ON HARMFUL TAX PRACTICES

OECD Initiatives—From the Forum on Harmful Tax Practices to the BEPS Project

The two major events in the OECD work on harmful tax practices are the 1998 report that established the Forum on Harmful Tax Practices, and Action 5 of the OECD/G20 BEPS Project that was adopted in 2015. Relatedly, in somewhat parallel efforts, since 2002 there has been development in the exchange of information for tax purposes. Figure 6.2 presents a timeline summarizing selected key publications and progress made since 1998.

Figure 6.2. Timeline of Major Events of the OECD Work on Harmful Tax Practices and Exchange of Information

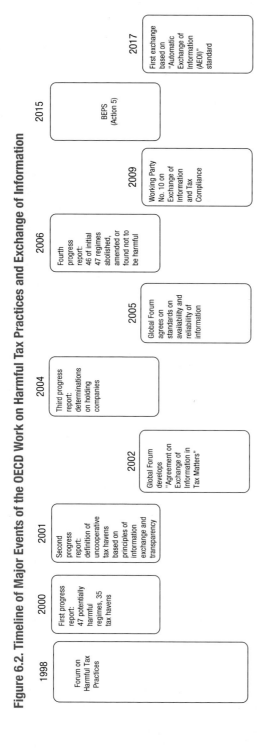

1998

Forum on Harmful Tax Practices

2000

First progress report: 47 potentially harmful regimes, 35 tax havens

2001

Second progress report: definition of uncooperative tax havens based on principles of information exchange and transparency

2002

Global Forum develops "Agreement on Exchange of Information in Tax Matters"

2004

Third progress report: determinations on holding companies

2005

Global Forum agrees on standards on availability and reliability of information

2006

Fourth progress report: 46 of initial 47 regimes abolished, amended or found not to be harmful

2009

Working Party No. 10 on Exchange of Information and Tax Compliance

2015

BEPS (Action 5)

2017

First exchange based on "Automatic Exchange of Information (AEOI)" standard

Source: Author's illustration.
Note: This timeline is not meant to give a complete summary of important events; rather, it selectively presents key progress steps.

Forum on Harmful Tax Practices

The Forum on Harmful Tax Practices was established with two primary objectives:

1. *Identify harmful tax regimes in OECD countries:* The Forum on Harmful Tax Practices had the mandate to monitor and review preferential tax regimes in OECD countries for income from geographically mobile activities. The criteria are listed in Table 6.1. The first key factor—low or zero effective tax rate on the relevant income—is a gateway criterion to determine those situations in which an analysis of the other key criteria is necessary, but zero tax per se is not deemed harmful. The main three criteria are ring fencing lack of tax transparency, and offering tax benefits in the absence of substantial activities. Eventually, in 2006, reviewing preferential tax regimes was completed, and the progress report stated, "The Committee considers that this part of the project has fully achieved its initial aims and that the mandate given by the Council on dealing with harmful preferential tax regimes in Member Countries has therefore been met" (OECD 2006, page 6).

2. *Identify non-OECD tax havens:* In 2001, the OECD analyzed 47 jurisdictions and publicly identified 35 tax havens. Eventually, as of May 2009, all jurisdictions were removed from the list.

Note that Switzerland and Luxembourg rejected the 1998 report, which stated, "As far as Switzerland is concerned, it shall not be bound in any manner by the Report or its Recommendations (page 78)," and "Luxembourg shall not be bound by the Report nor by the Recommendations to counteract harmful tax competition (page 75)."

TABLE 6.1.

Criteria for Identifying Harmful Tax Regimes	
Forum on Harmful Tax Practices: 1998 Report	**BEPS: Action 5**
Four main criteria:	Revamp and work on harmful tax practices, with
(1) No or low effective tax rates (gateway criterion)	a priority and renewed focus on two criteria:
(2) Ring-fencing of regimes	(1) Requirement of substantial activity
(3) Lack of transparency	(2) Improvement of transparency, including
(4) Lack of effective exchange of information	compulsory spontaneous exchange of
	information on ruling related to preferential
Eight other factors:	regimes
(1) Artificial definition of the tax base	
(2) Failure to adhere to international transfer pricing principles	
(3) Foreign source exempt from residence country tax	
(4) Negotiable tax rate or tax base	
(5) Existence of secrecy provisions	
(6) Access to a wide network of tax treaties	
(7) Regimes that are promoted as tax-minimization vehicles	
(8) Regimes that encourage purely tax-driven operations	

Action 5 of the BEPS Project and Current Standards on the Design of Preferential Tax Regimes

Action 5 of the OECD/G20 BEPS Project—one of the four minimum standards to which the Inclusive Framework members commit subject to peer review—requires substantial activity by the taxpayer (also known as the nexus approach) as a qualification for a preferential tax regime. As documented in Table 6.1, despite the fact that Action 5 builds on the previous work of the Forum on Harmful Tax Practices, the concept of harmful tax practices has evolved to primarily focus on the nexus approach. Preferential regimes that fail to conform to the nexus approach are deemed harmful. In November 2018 Inclusive Framework members adopted revised criteria for the substantial activities requirement for "no or only nominal tax" jurisdictions. However, this revision does not imply that the absence of a corporate income tax is harmful per se (OECD 2018a, para. 20).

It should be emphasized that Action 5 differs from the 1998 report in two important ways. First, in contrast to the 1998 report, preferential tax regimes are reviewed in non-OECD countries as long as they are members of the Inclusive Framework (137 members as of December 2019). Second, Action 5 of the BEPS initiative does not per se aim at producing a list of tax havens or noncooperative jurisdictions.

There are two broad categories of preferential tax regimes (that can be deemed harmful or not under Action 5):

1. *Intellectual Property Box regimes:* Also known as patent box regimes, these offer a reduced tax on income from intellectual property, such as patents, trademarks, and other know-how assets. The nexus approach requires a link between a taxpayer's expenditures on the intellectual property and the qualified intellectual property income. This requirement is meant to address multinational enterprises' practices of profit shifting through cross-border relocation of (hard-to-price) patents and other intangibles within the multinational group, that is, locating the *legal* ownership of the know-how asset in a low-tax jurisdiction after developing the patent in a different jurisdiction to benefit from lower taxation of royalties generated by the know-how asset (see, for example, Alstadsæter and others 2018).

2. *Non–intellectual property regimes:* The focus is on preferential tax regimes for geographically mobile activities. Examples include headquarter regimes (that is, companies that provide management services for the multinational enterprise group); preferential tax regimes for financing and leasing activities; distribution center regimes (that is, activities of purchasing from other affiliates and reselling for a percentage of profit); shipping regimes; and holding company regimes (that is, companies that hold equity participation or a variety of assets that generate royalties and other income). The nexus approach applies to non–intellectual property regimes, but the determination of qualified income is specific to each category of regimes. Generally, as stated in the OECD 2017 progress report, "Core income generating activities presuppose

having an adequate number of full-time employees with necessary qualifications and incurring an adequate amount of operating expenditures to undertake such activities" (OECD 2017, 40).

As of July 2019, 324 intellectual property and non–intellectual property regimes were reviewed by the Inclusive Framework members. Fifty-nine preferential tax regimes were found nonharmful, 53 were found nonharmful after amendment, 7 were considered "potentially" harmful, and 30 were deemed out of the scope of the review. Most of the remaining reviewed preferential tax regimes are in the process of being reviewed or abolished (OECD 2018b). Some of the abolished regimes have been reinvigorated. For example, Luxembourg, reflecting its commitmment to the BEPS project, abolished its older intellectual property box regime but introduced a new, compliant one.

Tax Transparency and Noncooperative Jurisdictions

What Is Tax Transparency?

Initiatives and measures to improve tax transparency can be broadly summarized as follows:

- *The Global Forum:* This forum, with 160 members, was established in 2000 and restructured in 2009 as a multilateral framework to carry out work on exchange of information, with the two international standards: (1) exchange of information on request; and (2) automatic exchange of financial account information in tax matters.

- *The minimum standards of OECD/G20 BEPS initiative:* Minimum standards of the BEPS initiative notably include the requirement of country-by-country reporting for multinationals and exchange of information on tax rulings under Action 5.

- *Other transparency initiatives:* These initiatives include the extractive industry transparency initiative. While these do not comprise international standards, the extractive industry transparency initiative, for instance, requests the disclosure of information along the extractive industry value chain. Standards of the Financial Action Task Force were upgraded in 2012 to include tax crimes, and they request that firms make information about beneficial ownership available to competent authorities, including tax authorities.

Noncooperative Jurisdictions for Tax Purposes

Tearing down the veil of secrecy is important for curbing tax evasion, especially by individuals, and one may argue it is an important aspect of competition over the wealth of individuals as opposed to large corporations. In any case, tax transparency is one of the three criteria endorsed in 2017 by the European Council to list noncooperative jurisdictions for tax purposes (the so-called blacklist). The other two criteria for the listing are fair tax competition, in line with the European Union's Code of Conduct or the OECD's Forum on Harmful Tax

Practices (as in Action 5, jurisdictions with a zero corporate income tax rate should implement the nexus approach), and implementing the OECD/G20 BEPS minimum standards. Selected jurisdictions that do not commit to address EU concerns are listed as noncooperative jurisdictions. As of October 2020, the list contained 12 jurisdictions. The European Council also adopts a watchlist of noncooperative jurisdictions that have agreed to modify their regimes (informally known as the grey list).

The Forum itself publishes compliance ratings for jurisdictions following a peer review. Its focus has been on tax transparency and not the effective level of the corporate income tax. A jurisdiction is identified as noncooperative if it does not meet at least two of the following three benchmarks: (1) at least a "Largely Compliant" rating with respect to exchange of information on request, (2) a commitment to implement automatic exchange of financial account information in tax matters, and (3) participation in the Multilateral Convention on Mutual Administrative Assistance on Tax Matters or a sufficiently broad exchange network permitting both exchange of information on request and automatic exchange of financial account information in tax matters. As of December 2020, only three percent of members were listed as noncompliant (OECD 2019).

HAS TAX COMPETITION BECOME LESS HARMFUL? WILL IT?

In light of this overview of international initiatives, theory, and empirics, it becomes natural to ask, Will tax competition stop or became less harmful? Without further reforms to international corporate income tax arrangements, the answer is most likely no.

A Zero or Very Low Tax Rate Is Not Less Harmful Than a Higher Rate Applied Only to Profits

As mentioned earlier, criteria for harmful tax practices do not consider a zero or very low corporate income tax rate per se as harmful,[9] and mainly focus on the nexus approach. This approach for classifying preferential tax regimes leads to suboptimal and paradoxical outcomes. As mentioned in the introduction to this chapter, a country with two relatively high corporate income tax rates could be deemed as employing a harmful tax practice, if, for example, the lower of the two rates applies in an intellectual property box that does not fully satisfy existing criteria. Another country's policy, with only one low—possibly zero—tax rate, would not be deemed harmful, even though spillovers could be significant.

---

[9] A zero corporate income tax rate is a gateway criterion for non–intellectual property regimes to be considered for the peer review.

Tax Competition in Statutory and Effective Rates Has Continued

In line with the theoretical predictions, proscribing preferential tax regimes, in some cases, has made the corporate income tax rate the most relevant tax policy instrument. For example, between 1999 and 2003 Ireland lowered its top corporate income tax rate from 32 to 12.5 percent, coinciding with abolishing a preferential rate of 10 percent under EU pressure. In 2019 Switzerland passed a reform to abolish Swiss cantonal preferential tax regimes to conform with Action 5 standards. Swiss cantons have lowered their cantonal corporate income tax rates or are expected to do so in the near future (see Hebous and Shay 2018). This decreases the average Swiss (combined federal, cantonal, and municipal) rate from about 17.3 to 14.2 percent (and to 10.86 percent taking into account the maximum allowed tax relief with the newly introduced measures, that is, intellectual property box regimes and super research and development deductions).

Providing tax deductions is also an important tool in tax competition over real investment, but as argued earlier, less important for attracting highly profitable multinationals than corporate income tax rates. Canada announced in November 2018 a provision allowing firms to immediately and fully write off the cost of machinery and equipment, referring to international tax competition as the motivation for this measure. In a statement, the Canadian Finance Department noted: "The U.S. federal tax reform has significantly reduced the overall tax advantage that Canada had built over the years, posing important challenges that, if left unaddressed, could have significant impacts on investment, jobs and the economic prospects of middle-class Canadians." The 2019 Swiss tax reform allowed cantons to offer research and development deductions and obliges them to provide intellectual property box regimes.

One measure of effective taxation that is relevant for multinational enterprises' decisions regarding discrete locations is the average effective tax rate—a measure of the tax burden on a profitable inframarginal investment defined as the proportion of the present value of pretax profit that would be taken in tax in a country. As shown in Figure 6.3, average effective tax rates have been declining, also reflecting the decline in the statutory corporate income tax rates. There have been several base-broadening and base-narrowing measures in OECD countries in the last years. Kawano and Slemrod (2016) document 331 country-year corporate tax base changes during 1980–2004 in OECD countries and report that 161 changes broadened the base, 108 narrowed the base, and 62 changes simultaneously entailed base-broadening and base-narrowing measures.

The elasticity of corporate income with respect to the corporate income tax rate appears to have increased. Beer, De Mooij, and Liu (2020) find that, on average, a 1 percentage point lower corporate tax rate will expand before-tax income by 1.5 percent.

In sum, as of 2019 there has been no indication that countries may raise the corporate income tax rate or that the downward trend in statutory or effective corporate income tax rates will end soon. Moreover, the use of intellectual property box regimes is on the rise (see Figure 6.4)—with recent adopters including

Figure 6.3. Average Effective Tax Rates

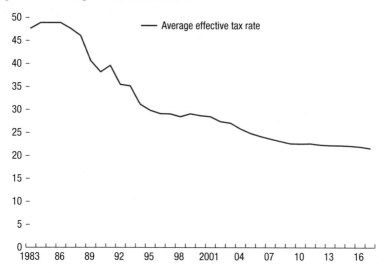

Source: Database of the Oxford University Center for Business Taxation.
Note: The sample includes 46 countries.

Figure 6.4. Selected Intellectual Property Box Tax Rates, Year of Introduction, and Statutory Corporate Income Tax Rates

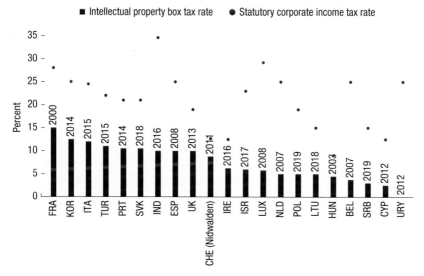

Source: Author's estimates.
Note: Above the bar is the year of introduction of an intellectual property box regime. Data labels use International Organization for Standardization (ISO) country codes.

Lithuania, Poland, and Serbia. Multinational enterprises are becoming more sensitive to international differences in taxation (see Chapter 4). Based on these observations, it is fair to say that, at least, tax competition has not stopped, and some argue it will become more intense.

The Nexus Approach Exacerbates Competition over Real Investment

A country that is found to have adopted a harmful preferential tax regime is faced with a menu of mutually nonexclusive options: (1) modify the harmful regime to comply with the nexus approach, (2) lower the statutory corporate income tax rate, or (3) introduce new tax allowances. Any combination of these responses implies a lower tax burden on real investment that will trigger strategic action by other countries. Even a modest scenario of responding by only modifying the preferential tax regime without cutting the corporate income tax rate could affect the investment location decision. For example, a compliant intellectual property box regime with a tax rate of less than 5 percent (and a nexus requirement) provides strong incentives for companies to relocate real activities. This, in turn, puts pressure on countries to also introduce intellectual property box regimes or cut the corporate income tax rate.

Shortcomings of Existing Standards

Intellectual property box regimes are inefficient and inferior to research and development tax deductions.[10] Empirical evidence suggests that one dollar spent by the government on research and development tax incentives, on average, increases domestic private research and development by one dollar, whereas one dollar spent on an intellectual property box can, at best, increase research and development by less than one dollar (IMF 2016). There are fundamental conceptual concerns with intellectual property boxes:

- The intellectual property tax relief rewards only success. Successful research and development outputs are a function of many nonrelated inputs (including management) that are not characterized with market failure. Intellectual property regimes may discriminate against potentially important research and development activities that may not be successful quickly.

- The tax relief is not connected to the level of research and development expenditure but proportional to the amount of qualifying intellectual property income. That is, two patents may generate the same income, thereby receiving the same benefits from the intellectual property regime despite having different levels of research and development inputs.

---

[10] The social benefits from research and development investments generally exceed the private benefits, which justifies governmental intervention to correct for this positive externality.

While research and development deductions do not infringe on existing commitments to international standards, as they are inherently tied to expenditure, explicitly setting standards for an inefficient policy instrument is in some respects popularizing it. Some might argue it could even make research and development deductions a less favored tool for policymakers.

Tax Incentives in Developing Countries

It is important to recognize the vast literature on tax incentives, especially those common in developing and low-income countries in the form of income tax holidays and other often ill-targeted tax breaks, to attract foreign real investment (for example, competition over hosting hotels in the Caribbean or the garment industry in the ASEAN region). These are typically found to be inefficient (for example, often covering investments that would have taken place in the absence of incentives); are in many cases poorly governed; and undermine domestic revenues (IMF 2014; Klemm and Van Parys 2012). Action 5 is not designed to address this type of incentive and form of tax competition between developing countries, which frequently appear in an environment of low tax enforcement. Action 5 will not lead to abolishing these regimes or improving their designs. Some are out of its scope (for example, in the case of special economic zones), whereas others, if reviewed with the potential to be harmful, will be amended to enact the nexus approach. In this sense, competition over real investment in developing countries will continue.

CONCLUSION

In 2006, when the Forum on Harmful Tax Practices concluded its work on harmful preferential tax regimes, the average statutory corporate income tax rate in OECD countries was 27.1 percent (with rates close to 39 percent in Germany, Japan, and the United States) and there were perhaps two or three intellectual property box regimes. In 2020 the average OECD statutory corporate income tax rate will be about 23 percent, and there will be more than 80 compliant intellectual property box regimes, including those with tax rates of 5 percent and lower. Other non–intellectual property (including headquarters and financing) regimes are still around. These simple observations do not indicate a decreasing intensity of tax competition. Going forward, while compliant intellectual property regimes and other non–intellectual property "nexus regimes" make it harder to shift profits, they incentivize shifting real activities, prompting strategic reactions in the form of lowering the corporate income tax rate or introducing such regimes elsewhere.

Fighting profit shifting per se does not mitigate tax competition, and it may even intensify it. And while acknowledging that it is still too early to evaluate recent initiatives, as long as international differences in tax rates exist, they will pay a role in investment location decisions and profit shifting will be possible—for instance, in the form of limiting the physical presence of a firm in the source country and strategic evaluation of intangibles. And as long as there are benefits for countries from lowering taxes in the form of attracting investment and profits, tax competition continues. Containing tax competition requires broad tax reforms such as minimum taxes (Chapters 11 and 12) or destination-based rent taxes (Chapter 13; Auerbach and others, 2017).

REFERENCES

Auerbach, Alan, Michael P. Devereux, Michael Keen, and John Vella. 2017. "Destination-Based Cash Flow Taxation." Oxford University Centre for Business Taxation Working Paper 17/01, Oxford University Centre for Business Taxation, Oxford, UK.

Alstadsæter, Annette, Salvador Barrios, Gaetan Nicodeme, Agnieszka Skonieczna, and Antonio Vezzani. 2018. "Patent Boxes Design, Patents Location, and Local R&D." *Economic Policy* 33(93): 131–77.

Becker, Johannes, and Clemens Fuest. 2012. "Transfer Pricing Policy and the Intensity of Tax Rate Competition." *Economics Letters* 117(1): 146–48.

Beer, Sebastian, Ruud de Mooij, and Li Liu. 2020. "International Corporate Tax Avoidance: A Review of the Channels, Magnitudes, and Blind Spots." *Journal of Economic Surveys*.

Crivelli, Ernesto, Ruud de Mooij, and Michael Keen. 2016. "Base Erosion, Profit Shifting and Developing Countries." *FinanzArchiv: Public Finance Analysis* 72: 268–301.

Devereux, Michael, Rachel Griffith, and Alexander Klemm. 2002. "Corporate Income Tax Reforms and International Tax Competition." *Economic Policy* 17: 451–95.

Devereux, Michael, Ben Lockwood, and Michela Redoano. 2008. "Do Countries Compete over Corporate Tax Rates?" *Journal of Public Economics* 92(5–6): 1210–35.

Dharmapala, Dhammika, and James Hines. 2009. "Which Countries Become Tax Havens?" *Journal of Public Economics* 93(9–10): 1058–68.

European Commission (EC). 2017. *Council Conclusions: On the Criteria for and Process Leading to the Establishment of the EU list of Non-cooperative Jurisdictions for Tax Purposes, December 2017.* Brussels, Belgium: European Commission. https://data.consilium.europa.eu/doc/document/ST-15429-2017-INIT/en/pdf.

Gomes, Pedro, and Francois Pouget. 2008. "Corporate Tax Competition and the Decline of Public Investment." ECB Working Paper Series 928, European Central Bank, Frankfurt, Germany.

Hebous, Shafik. 2018. "Attractive Tax Jurisdictions." IEB Report 4/2018, Barcelona Institute of Economics, University of Barcelona, Barcelona, Spain.

Hebous, S., and Vilen Lipatov. 2014. "A Journey from a Corruption Port to a Tax Haven." *Journal of Comparative Economics* 42: 739–54.

Hebous, Shafik, and Stephen Shay. 2018. "Taxation of Corporations in Switzerland." IMF Selected Issues Paper, Washington, DC. https://www.imf.org/en/Publications/CR/Issues/2018/06/18/Switzerland-Selected-Issues-45995.

Hong, Qing, and Michael Smart. 2010. "In Praise of Tax Havens: International Tax Planning and Foreign Direct Investment." *European Economic Review* 54(1): 82–95.

International Monetary Fund (IMF). 2014. "Spillovers in International Corporations Taxation." IMF Policy Paper, Washington, DC.

International Monetary Fund (IMF). 2016. "Fiscal Policies for Innovation and Growth." In Fiscal Monitor: Acting Now, Acting Together. Washington DC, April.

International Monetary Fund (IMF). 2019. "Corporate Taxation in the Global Economy." IMF Policy Paper 19/007, Washington, DC.

Janeba, Eckhard, and Michael Smart. 2003. "Is Targeted Tax Competition Less Harmful Than Its Remedies?" *International Tax and Public Finance* 10(3): 259–80.

Johannesen, Niels. 2010. "Imperfect Tax Competition for Profits, Asymmetric Equilibrium and Beneficial Tax Havens." *Journal of International Economics* 81(2): 253–64.

Kanbur, Ravi, and Michael Keen. 1993. "Jeux sans Frontieres: Tax Competition and Tax Coordination When Countries Differ in Size." *American Economic Review* 83: 877–92.

Keen, Michael. 2001. "Preferential Regimes Can Make Tax Competition Less Harmful." *National Tax Journal* 54(4): 757–62.

Keen, Michael. 2018. "International—Competition, Coordination and Avoidance in International Taxation." *Bulletin for International Taxation* 72(4–5). https://www.ibfd.org/IBFD-Products/Journal-Articles/Bulletin-for-International-Taxation/collections/bit/html/bit_2018_04_int_14.html

Keen, Michael, and Kai Konrad. 2013. "The Theory of International Tax Competition and Coordination." In Handbook of Public Economics, Vol. 5, edited by A.J. Auerbach, R. Chetty, M. Feldstein, and M. Saez. Amsterdam, the Netherlands and Oxford, United Kingdom: Elsevier.

Klemm, Alexander, and Stefan van Parys. 2012. "Empirical Evidence on the Effects of Tax Incentives." *International Tax and Public Finance* 19(3): 393–423.

Kawano, Laura, and Joel Slemrod. 2016. "How Do Corporate Tax Bases Change when Corporate Tax Rates Change? With Implications for the Tax Rate Elasticity of Corporate Tax Revenues." *International Tax and Public Finance* 23: 401–433.

Leibrecht, Markus, and Claudia Hochgatterer. 2012. "Tax Competition as a Cause of Falling Corporate Income Tax Rates: A Survey of Empirical Literature." *Journal of Economic Surveys* 26: 616–48.

Peralta, Susana, Xavier Wauthy, and Tanguy van Ypersele. 2006. "Should Countries Control International Profit Shifting?" *Journal of International Economics* 68(1): 24–37.

Organisation for Economic Co-operation and Development (OECD). 1998. *Harmful Tax Competition: An Emerging Global Issue.* Paris: OECD Publishing.

Organisation for Economic Co-operation and Development (OECD). 2006. *The OECD's Project on Harmful Tax Practices: 2006 Update on Progress in Member Countries.* OECD Publishing, Paris.

Organisation for Economic Co-operation and Development (OECD). 2017. *Harmful Tax Practices - 2017 Progress Report on Preferential Regimes.* OECD Publishing, Paris.

Organisation for Economic Co-operation and Development (OECD). 2018a. *Resumption of Application of Substantial Activities Factor to No or Only Nominal Tax Jurisdictions—BEPS Action 5.* OECD Publishing, Paris.

Organisation for Economic Co-operation and Development (OECD). 2018b. Harmful Tax Practices —2018 Progress Report on Preferential Regimes: Inclusive Framework on BEPS: Action 5. OECD/G20 Base Erosion and Profit Shifting Project. OECD Publishing, Paris. https://www.oecd.org/tax/beps/harmful-tax-practices-2018-progress-report-on-preferential-regimes-9789264311480-en.htm

Organisation for Economic Co-operation and Development (OECD). 2019. "Compliance Ratings for Jurisdictions on Peer Reviews on the Standard of Exchange of Information on Request." Global Forum on Transparency and Exchange of Information for Tax Purposes. OECD Publishing, Paris. https://www.oecd.org/tax/transparency/.

Schjelderup, Guttorm. 2016. "Secrecy Jurisdictions." *International Tax and Public Finance* 23: 168–89.

Schön, Wolfgang. 2005. "Playing Different Games? Regulatory Competition in Tax and Company Law Compared." *Common Market Law Review* 42: 331–65.

Sinn, Hans–Werner. 1997. "The Selection Principle and Market Failure in Systems Competition." Journal of Public Economics 66: 247–74.

Slemrod, Joel, and John Wilson. 2009. "Tax Competition with Parasitic Tax Havens." *Journal of Public Economics* 93(11–12): 1261–70.

Tørsløv, Thomas, Ludvig Wier, and Gabriel Zucman. 2018. "The Missing Profits of Nations." NBER Working Paper 24701, National Bureau of Economic Research, Cambridge, MA.

Torvik, Ragnar. 2009. "Why Are Tax Havens More Harmful to Developing Countries Than to Other Countries?" Memorandum written for the Commission to the Norwegian Government Commission on Tax Havens. https://www.regjeringen.no/en/dokumenter/nou-2009-19/id571718/sec12

Weichenrieder, Alfons, and Fangying Xu. 2019. "Are Tax Havens Good? Implications of the Crackdown on Secrecy." *Journal of Economics* 127: 147–60.

Zodrow, George. 2010. "Capital Mobility and Capital Tax Competition." *National Tax Journal* 63(4): 865–902.

CHAPTER 7

Residence-Based Taxation: A History and Current Issues

Kiyoshi Nakayama and Victoria Perry

INTRODUCTION

As discussed in previous chapters, source-based taxation faces many difficulties: it is increasingly difficult—conceptually and practically—to allocate profits to where they originate (see Chapter 5). Multinational enterprises can take advantage of such ambiguities by shifting reported profits to jurisdictions with lower tax rates. Countries then face an incentive to compete for tax bases—both reported profits and real investment (see Chapter 6). This chapter turns to residence-based taxation—the other important historical concept for corporate income taxation—to assess the difficulties that have been encountered in its implementation.

While no country relies purely on residence-based taxation, it is still instructive to think through the impact of using a pure residence-based system of corporate taxation, rather than a source-based one. Such a shift in approach would transform the problems encountered by source taxation into different ones:

- *Definition:* Once a firm's residence is determined, all problems of allocating profits to where they originate should disappear. However, determining a firm's residence is difficult, too, and can be based on various criteria, such as ownership, place of management, and main location of production, each of which could give contradictory results.

- *Tax competition and tax avoidance:* Under residence-based taxation, firms would not face incentives to shift profits and countries would not be able to use the tax system to attract real investment from existing firms. Instead, firms would have an incentive to change their place of residence, while countries would try to attract corporate headquarters.

- *Double taxation risks:* Unless taxation is limited to the country of the corporate headquarters, a company could still face double taxation risks, as a subsidiary could be considered a resident both in the country of its own incorporation and of its corporate headquarters. Apart from creating the potential for double taxation, such a scenario reintroduces the need for using transfer prices to determine the profits of the subsidiary so that it can be taxed in the country where it is located.

Hence, even a pure residence-based system would still face major challenges. In practice, however, such a system does not exist; most systems have elements of both. It is therefore important to understand the practical effects of the interactions between the two systems. When both systems apply, corporations can still take advantage of low source-based taxation by moving activities or reported profits, but the benefits of investing in countries with lower tax rates are reduced by the additional payment liability at home under the residence base. These benefits are not eliminated, though, because residence-based taxes are often easy to reduce or avoid altogether, notably as in practice they typically apply to repatriated earnings only.

This chapter first looks at the history of residence-based taxation and at some data showing where it is most relevant today. It then turns to some of the difficulties encountered with residence-based taxation, such as avoidance through deferral and manipulation of the place of residence. Finally, it examines the need for and evolution of complicated anti-avoidance rules.

HISTORICAL BACKGROUND AND CURRENT CONTEXT

History

In the early twentieth century, residence of a corporation was more easily determined than it is now. The classic multinational corporation had a national identity—through a fixed and easily identified headquarters location that generally coincided with the residence of most shareholders—and that generally was the country where the entity was formed or incorporated. These factors are largely gone now. Despite the convenient legal fiction of their existence, corporations are not human beings who are born in a country, sleep in a generally identifiable place, and hold passports. As noted in Chapter 3, most of the criteria that might logically be used to determine corporate residence tend to point in different directions now. In the inimitable words of one author, "There's a reason we call them multi-nationals" (Graetz 2001).

As discussed in Chapter 3, a corporation's income might be imposed by the country where the corporation is resident or by the country "where the income is generated"—that is, at the "source." Or some combination of the two could be used.[1] In terms of national laws, nothing would prevent a country from laying claim to tax income on either or both of these bases. But striking a compromise between residence-based taxation and source-based taxation has been a principle

---

[1] A third (at least) possibility would be for countries to impose taxes at the location where the corporation's output is used or sold; this has never been done for corporate income tax, although it is common practice for consumption-type taxes (for example, VATs), but the implications of that possibility are now under active debate, as discussed in Chapter 13. Moreover, there are other possibilities—mentioned in Chapter 12—such as identifying the corporation with the residence of its ultimate owners—which have also never been used.

of prevention of double taxation since the development of the League of Nations Model Tax Convention.[2]

The long-standing internationally agreed architecture of the corporate tax system, beginning in the early twentieth century, assigned the primary right to tax business income to the source country, but overlay that with the notion that passive income—in the form of interest payments, dividends, and the like—would be taxable by the country of residence of the recipient corporation. This was to be laid out in bilateral treaties between individual countries. At the time it was believed that this approach to taxing active and passive income would be easier to identify and enforce.

The source country of payment of passive income, nonetheless, typically imposes a withholding tax on such payments made to recipients abroad. There are then two basic mechanisms to effectuate the avoidance of double taxation and to allocate the tax base between the source country and the country of residence of the company.[3] First, most countries unilaterally provide in domestic law for the grant of a tax credit against tax paid to the source country by resident corporations on income that has been taxed by the source country. These credits are often country specific and nonrefundable; thus if the source tax exceeds the residence-based tax, there is no refund.[4] Second, the elaborate network of bilateral treaties[5] typically also provides for such tax credits, but at the same time stipulates that the source country will reduce its withholding taxes on interest and dividends paid to recipients resident in the treaty partner country thereby allocating a greater share of the tax to the residence country.

Although historically details of systems and anti-avoidance legislation have differed among countries, the most common approach involved immediately taxing profits at the source, while also levying residence-based taxes on worldwide profits. But foreign profits were typically taxed by the residence country only at the time of repatriation, and a credit for foreign tax paid was then allowed. Since the 1980s, however, there has been a strong shift toward territorial systems, in which foreign active business profits are exempt, unless captured by some anti-avoidance provision (see Chapter 3, Box 3.1).

The Role of Foreign Profits Today

As discussed in Chapter 4, the role of multinational enterprises has vastly increased in economic significance since the early twentieth century. For the present discussion about the relevance of residence-based taxation, the

---

[2] Source was an even more intuitive concept than residence, essentially referring to the geographic location of production. But now even that concept has become muddy.

[3] For a detailed discussion of determining the source of income and its allocation, including the concept of permanent establishment, see Chapters 3 and 8.

[4] A common way to overcome this limitation is to mix income from high- and low-tax jurisdictions by having a holding company in a country that does not levy residence-based taxes.

[5] See Chapter 8 for a discussion of tax treaties.

Figure 7.1. Share of Capital-Exporting Countries
(Percent)

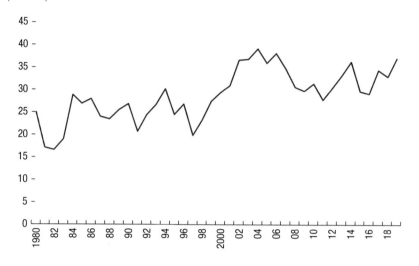

Source: IMF, Balance of Payments database.

crucial question is the importance of profits these entities earn outside their home country.

It should also be noted that the number of capital-exporting countries is increasing (Figure 7.1). This indicates that residence-based taxation is no longer an issue for advanced countries only. Companies in emerging economies have increased outbound investment considerably in recent years. Even if most emerging economies are still capital-importing countries on a net basis, they may also host capital-exporting firms, and hence securing proper residence-based taxation is becoming a key tax policy objective.

CHALLENGES OF RESIDENCE-BASED TAXATION

Avoidance through Deferral

Enforcing taxes on the foreign operations of resident companies is difficult, as the tax authority does not have access to foreign subsidiaries. For firms, compliance is also costly, as they would have to calculate their tax base both under local tax laws to satisfy their source-based liability and then again under their home country's rules to determine any residual residence-based tax. But very few countries attempt to tax foreign earnings immediately—Brazil being one example. A common simplification in worldwide tax systems is that foreign earnings of an overseas subsidiary of the resident company are not taxed until repatriated to their parent company (the resident company), a feature commonly called deferral. This was in recent years a particularly notable issue for Japan and the United States—both of which had the highest rates of corporate income taxation among the OECD (until 2014 in Japan and 2017 in the United States)—since where the statutory corporate income tax rate of a country in which a company is resident is higher than that of countries in which subsidiaries of the resident company are located, it would incentivize deferral of repatriation and thus the payment of tax on income in lower-tax jurisdictions. The resident company avoids being taxed on its foreign earnings by not distributing dividends from its overseas subsidiary to the parent company. If the foreign business is growing, this can easily be done by reinvesting all profits, but even in a mature business it can be achieved through various arrangements. In a simple example, a US-resident parent company would establish a subsidiary holding company in a low-tax jurisdiction, which in turn would own an operating subsidiary in a third country. Income would be stripped from the operating company into the holding company, by using some combination of interest payments, royalties, and dividends—which would be subject to minimal taxation in the intermediary country. Unless repatriated to the residence of the parent company—in this example, the United States—substantial taxation could be deferred essentially indefinitely.

As a result, tax revenue raised in the residence country on foreign profits is typically quite low, while the administrative and compliance costs are quite high, which could be one of the reasons behind the move from worldwide to territorial systems. Perhaps most important, though, has been the consideration of tax competition over corporate headquarters. Among advanced economies that relatively recently shifted to the territorial system, the United Kingdom, which adopted the territorial system in 2009, was indeed concerned with UK companies' competitiveness.[6] And the shift to a territorial system does not appear to have affected corporate tax revenues much (Table 7.1) Japan, which also adopted the participation exemption system in 2009, was concerned with the accumulation of foreign earnings[7] that had not been repatriated to Japan—the so-called lockout effect. For the United States (Box 7.1), there was indeed a notable increase in repatriations following the shift toward territoriality. It should be noted, though, that these repatriations, while relevant for tax purposes, do not necessarily imply any actual flows. Even when funds were kept abroad, there were various means by which they could effectively already be invested in US assets (for example, US Treasuries), while technically held by a foreign subsidiary.

---

[6] Markle (2010) indicated steep compliance costs and ineffective anti-avoidance measures under the worldwide system as motivations for the reform.

[7] Japan's Ministry of Economy, Trade, and Industry survey noted that accumulated foreign earnings in 2008 reached ¥19.6 trillion ($189 billion; ¥19.6 trillion was equivalent to 196 percent of Japan's corporate income tax revenue in 2008).

Box 7.1. Deferred Profits and the US Tax Cuts and Jobs Act of 2017—Transition Tax and Impact

Under prior law, the possibility of deferral, likely combined with the expectation of a future reduction in the tax rate applied to repatriations, resulted in US multinationals building up a substantial stock of unrepatriated earnings (in the order of $2.6 trillion by 2017). Without the expectation of such a future reduction in applicable tax, if unrepatriated funds had simply accumulated at the investor's minimum required pretax return, deferral would not have changed the present value of taxes due—and thus presumably would have been much less attractive. The expectation of a future likely reduction in tax on repatriations may have been stoked by the previous experience of a temporarily reduced rate on repatriations (for example, as part of the Homeland Investment Act of 2004) and widespread discussion at the time of the potential move to a territorial-based system—which by definition would have removed taxation on repatriation to the United States. As a transition measure associated with the move to territoriality, the Tax Cuts and Jobs Act imposed a onetime tax on the deemed repatriation of that income (no actual repatriation was needed; this was an accounting calculation). Justifying expectations of a reduced applicable rate, the rate attached, for corporate owners, was 15.5 percent for funds that were held in cash or cash-equivalent assets and 8 percent for the remainder (presumably reinvested earnings). The tax due was further reduced in present value by its payment being extended over eight years.

US-registered multinational corporations brought into tax $396.3 billion in deferred earnings from foreign affiliates in 2019. This was 53.4 percent less than in 2018, when $850.9 billion was repatriated following the introduction of the Tax Cuts and Jobs Act. But the 2019 total was still more than twice the average annual amount over the decade preceding the 2017 act, which generally eliminated taxes on future repatriated earnings. More than half of the dividends in 2019 came from affiliates in three countries: Ireland, at $85.8 billion; the Netherlands, $74.3 billion; and Bermuda, $67.9 billion. In terms of industry sectors, US multinationals in chemical manufacturing, at $99.6 billion, and computers and electronic products manufacturing, at $92.5 billion, were the largest.

Sources: Bureau of Economic Analysis (2020); and Chalk, Keen, and Perry (2018).

TABLE 7.1.

Trends in Corporate Income Tax Rates and Revenue per GDP in the United Kingdom and Japan, including Local Taxes

(Percent)

		2007	2008	2009	2010	2011	2012	2013	2014	2015	2016	2017
United Kingdom	Tax Rate	30.0	28.0	28.0	28.0	26.0	24.0	23.0	21.0	20.0	20.0	19.0
	Revenue per GDP	3.3	2.9	2.6	2.9	2.8	2.7	2.6	2.5	2.4	2.7	2.8
Japan	Tax Rate	39.5	39.5	39.5	39.5	39.5	37.0	37.0	34.6	32.1	30.0	30.0
	Revenue per GDP	4.6	3.7	2.5	3.1	3.2	3.5	3.8	3.9	3.8	3.7	3.7

Sources: IMF World Revenue Longitudinal Data; OECD Corporate Tax Statistics; Japanese Legislation.

Box 7.2. Manipulation of Irish Residency: An Example

The so-called "Double Irish" structure offers a simple example of how residency laws can be manipulated. Under this formerly available structure, one Irish subsidiary (IRL1) would be an Irish-registered company selling products to non-US locations from Ireland. A second Irish subsidiary (IRL2) would hold intangible assets and charge the IRL1 royalties, thereby shifting most profits to IRL2. IRL2 would be registered in Ireland but managed and controlled from a low- or no-tax jurisdiction. The Irish tax code considered IRL2 to be a resident of the low-tax jurisdiction (based upon the Irish "managed and controlled" test), but the US tax code considered IRL2 to be an Irish company (based on the place of incorporation or registration test). Neither jurisdiction therefore taxed the income of IRL2, as neither viewed it as legally resident within its jurisdiction. In 2015 Ireland closed this avenue of tax minimization by changing the definition of tax residence to include not only entities that are effectively managed in Ireland but also those incorporated there. However, structures already in place were grandfathered until 2020. For more than a decade, Google enjoyed an effective tax rate in the single digits on its non-US profits by using a subsidiary in the Netherlands to shift revenue from royalties earned outside the United States to Google Ireland Holdings, an affiliate based in Bermuda and not deemed resident in either the United States or Ireland.

Manipulation of Place of Residence

As noted in Chapter 3 (see examples in Table 3.1), residence criteria for corporations differ across countries, although there are two main approaches: a formal legal connection to the jurisdiction (place of incorporation or registration in the commercial register) or an economic connection (place of effective management, substantial ownership and control, or location of board of directors' meetings). A combination of these two approaches is also used.

Predictably, the discrepancies in corporate residence rules have become a fertile ground for tax avoidance and minimization schemes. Avoidance schemes can go beyond changing residence from a high- to a low-tax jurisdiction but can even lead to no significant tax accruing to any state (see Box 7.2 for one example). The late Ed Kleinbard coined the term "stateless income" to describe the results of international tax planning by US-headquartered multinational enterprises that were able to take advantage of, among other things, such lacunae in the international system for defining corporate domicile (residence): "By 'stateless income,' I mean income derived by a multinational group from business activities in a country other than the domicile (however defined) of the group's ultimate parent company, but which is subject to tax only in a jurisdiction that is not the location of the customers or the factors of production through which the income was derived, and is not the domicile of the group's parent company" (Kleinbard 2011).

One way that some multinational enterprises avoid taxation in high-tax jurisdictions is by shifting the fiscal domicile of the parent company using an approach known as inversion. A corporate inversion is a scheme that makes a resident company into a foreign company by means of a merger with a foreign company—often smaller than the resident company—or into a subsidiary of a foreign company that the resident company created. This all occurs without changing shareholders, business operations, or place of effective management. Multinationals based in a country with a worldwide tax system can lower their tax by inverting into a lower-tax jurisdiction with a territorial system. This goes beyond the tax saving of not having to pay any more residence-based taxes on existing deferred worldwide profits in the original residence jurisdiction, but also includes further gains from generating profits through increased operations abroad after the inversion.[8]

As the United States maintained a worldwide tax system in combination with one of the highest tax rates until 2017, corporate inversions of US companies became rampant. From 1982 to 2017 more than 60 US companies were reincorporated in lower-tax countries (CBO 2017). Popular destinations for inversions included Ireland and Bermuda.

ANTI-AVOIDANCE RULES

Early Efforts: The Development of Controlled Foreign Corporation Rules

To counter tax deferral under worldwide tax systems (or to bring some income into the tax net under territorial systems) an increasing number of countries have adopted controlled foreign corporation (CFC) rules that tax immediately the undistributed income of overseas subsidiaries of a resident company as income of the resident company, dependent on its share of ownership of the subsidiary as well as some other conditions. The first use of CFC rules was in the United States. The original—and current—US CFC rules (known as Subpart F rules), introduced in 1962, did not apply to all undistributed income of the overseas subsidiary, however, but only to certain categories of undistributed foreign-source income considered as passive, such as interest, dividends, rents, and royalties, and that had been subject to zero or low foreign tax rates. The original rules defined a CFC as a company that is more than 50 percent, by vote or value, owned by a US parent company or certain other US shareholders. This definition, however, proved susceptible to manipulation (Durst 2019, 42), and many changes were made to the rules.

Among the main changes introduced over the years, two exceptions, the active financing exception and look-through rules, are regarded as major factors weakening the effectiveness of the US CFC rules (Americans for Tax Fairness 2015a, 2015b). The active financing exception allows a US company to avoid the application of CFC rules on undistributed income of a CFC that is predominantly engaged in the active conduct of a banking or similar business and that conducts substantial activity with respect to such business. The CFC look-through rules

---

[8] If a country's tax law defines a resident company as one that has a place of effective management, changing a country of incorporation alone would not change the fiscal domicile. However, if the definition of a resident company is based on a place of incorporation—as in the United States—or location of a head office, a resident company can quite easily change its fiscal domicile.

allow a US company to avoid the application of CFC rules if passive income is paid to a CFC by a related CFC and that income can be traced to the active income of the payer CFC. In addition, the 1997 Treasury regulation that aimed to simplify the process of qualifying business entities as partnerships or other forms of pass-through entities for tax purposes ("check-the-box rules") undermined the operation of the CFC rules. The check-the-box rules allow US-based multinational enterprises to treat their second-tier operating subsidiaries owned by holding companies (first-tier subsidiaries of the US-based multinational enterprises in zero- or low-tax jurisdictions) not as separate companies but as unincorporated branches of the holding companies. This means payments of interest, royalties, and other kinds of passive income made by the operating companies to their parent holding companies are not legally payments, as technically they are made within a single entity. Thus, the parent holding companies in zero- or low-tax jurisdictions that are subsidiaries of US-based multinational enterprises are not treated as receiving CFC income (Durst 2019, 43). It was estimated even a decade ago that these features within the CFC rules cost the US Treasury $90 billion per year (Clausing 2011). The accumulated undistributed profit of US-based multinational enterprises reached $2.6 trillion in 2015 (Phillips and others 2017).

After the introduction of the CFC rules by the United States, other OECD member countries also introduced such rules; currently 49 countries have CFC rules (OECD 2020).[9] CFC rules in these countries are broadly similar in function to the US rules, but the design varies by country. For example, the level of the corporate income tax rate in the country of the CFC, generally a condition to apply CFC rules, ranges from 10 percent to 75 percent of the rate in the residence country.[10] Ten countries apply CFC rules only to passive income, while the rest apply the rules to all income.

In member countries of the European Economic Area,[11] CFC rules now generally apply only to operations located outside the European Economic Area. The European Court of Justice ruled in 2006 that the then-existing UK CFC rules should not apply to CFCs in Ireland controlled by the UK parent company unless the Irish subsidiaries were wholly artificial arrangements.[12] This European Court of Justice ruling was interpreted as not allowing European Economic Area countries to apply CFC rules where the subsidiary in question is an actual establishment intended to carry on genuine economic activities in the European Economic Area member state, regardless of the existence of tax motives for the establishment of the arrangements.

---

[9] Some OECD member countries without any formal CFC rules have other anti–base erosion rules that aim to achieve the same goal as CFC rules.

[10] Some countries use nominal (statutory) corporate income tax rates.

[11] The European Economic Area includes the 26 EU countries as well as Iceland, Liechtenstein, and Norway, which allows these three countries to be part of the EU's single market.

[12] Case C-196/04, Cadbury Schweppes plc and Cadbury Schweppes Overseas Limited v. Commissioner of Inland Revenue, 2006 E.C.R. 1-7995.

Recent Approaches to Strengthening Residence Taxation

Improving CFC Rules

The OECD/G20 Base Erosion and Profit Shifting (BEPS) Project, launched in 2013, aimed to close gaps in international tax rules that allowed corporate tax bases to be eroded or artificially shifted to low- or no-tax jurisdictions. The guiding principle was to "ensure that profits are taxed where economic activities take place and value is created." (OECD 2015a, p. 4) To this end, the project addressed 15 problematic areas, with the final BEPS package of 2015—endorsed by G20 leaders—including four minimum standards. Among the 15 Actions, Action 3 (*Designing Effective Controlled Foreign Company Rules*), and Action 2 (*Neutralizing the Effects of Hybrid Mismatch Arrangements*), are particularly relevant to residence-based taxation issues.[13]

The BEPS final report on Action 3 provided recommendations intended to ensure effective CFC rules, in the form of six building blocks. The OECD was not able to turn the Action 3 recommendations into minimum standards, but only recommendations, due to the lack of consensus; it explained that a one-size-fits-all approach to CFC rules might not be viable. The executive summary of the BEPS Report on Action 3 stated: "Because each country prioritises policy objectives differently, the recommendations provide flexibility to implement CFC rules that combat BEPS in a manner consistent with the policy objectives of the overall tax system and the international legal obligations of the country concerned. In particular, this report recognises that the recommendations must be sufficiently adaptable to comply with EU law, and it sets out possible design options that could be implemented by EU Member States" (OECD 2015b, p. 10).

The report acknowledged the need for "striking a balance between taxing foreign income and maintaining competitiveness" (OECD 2015b, p. 15) but also suggested that making all capital-exporting countries adopt similar CFC rules could mitigate the competitiveness concern.

Against that background, the BEPS Action 3 report set out recommendations for "jurisdictions that choose to implement them" (OECD 2015b, p. 9) for the design of effective CFC rules to prevent shifting income into foreign subsidiaries (Box 7.3).

The OECD reported that by mid-2019 almost 50 OECD/G20 Inclusive Framework countries had enacted CFC rules, with European Union member states all having CFC rules in effect since the beginning of 2019 following the adoption of Council Directive (EU) 2016/1164 (see next paragraph). This is clearly a step forward in protecting residence-based taxation—but it is not entirely clear that all choices made under these guidelines will, in fact, lead to

---

[13] Some earnings stripping techniques, which can be used to move income from source to residence countries, were also addressed—interest payments (Action 4) and general transfer pricing manipulation (Actions 8–10). However, certain important base erosion payments such as cross-border service or management fees that are used to strip income from source countries and locate them in low-tax residence countries were explicitly not addressed in the BEPS Project.

Box 7.3. The OECD Report on BEPS Action 3

The OECD report's summary of the building blocks is as follows:

Definition of a CFC – CFC rules generally apply to foreign companies that are controlled by shareholders in the parent jurisdiction. The report sets out recommendations on how to determine when shareholders have sufficient influence over a foreign company for that company to be a CFC. It also provides recommendations on how non-corporate entities and their income should be brought within CFC rules.

CFC exemptions and threshold requirements – Existing CFC rules often only apply after the application of provisions such as tax rate exemptions, anti-avoidance requirements, and de minimis thresholds. The report recommends that CFC rules only apply to controlled foreign companies that are subject to effective tax rates that are meaningfully lower than those applied in the parent jurisdiction.

Definition of income – Although some countries' existing CFC rules treat all the income of a CFC as "CFC income" that is attributed to shareholders in the parent jurisdiction, many CFC rules only apply to certain types of income. The report recommends that CFC rules include a definition of CFC income, and it sets out a non-exhaustive list of approaches or combination of approaches that CFC rules could use for such a definition.

Computation of income – The report recommends that CFC rules use the rules of the parent jurisdiction to compute the CFC income to be attributed to shareholders. It also recommends that CFC losses should only be offset against the profits of the same CFC or other CFCs in the same jurisdiction.

Attribution of income – The report recommends that, when possible, the attribution threshold should be tied to the control threshold and that the amount of income to be attributed should be calculated by reference to the proportionate ownership or influence.

Prevention and elimination of double taxation – One of the fundamental policy issues to consider when designing effective CFC rules is how to ensure that these rules do not lead to double taxation. The report therefore emphasises the importance of both preventing and eliminating double taxation, and it recommends, for example, that jurisdictions with CFC rules allow a credit for foreign taxes actually paid, including any tax assessed on intermediate parent companies under a CFC regime.

Source: OECD (2015b, 9–10).

effective taxation of the income of foreign subsidiaries—in light of the referenced policy choices and priorities of various countries who may wish to compete for the headquarters of multinationals, or even for intermediate holding companies.

Subsequent to introduction of BEPS Action 3, the European Union, addressing the use of CFC rules in the European Union, took a firmer line, requiring all European Union members to adopt certain CFC rules in their national laws by January 1, 2019, in the European Union Anti-Tax Avoidance Directive. CFC rules under Anti-Tax Avoidance Directive requirements will be triggered if the actual corporate tax paid by a subsidiary or a permanent establishment is lower than the difference between the tax that would have been paid on the same profits in the European Union member state of the parent company and the corporate tax actually paid in the source state. CFC income that will be included as income of the parent company constitutes: (1) certain predefined categories of nondistributed (passive) income of CFCs (for example, interest, royalties, dividends)—however,

CFC rules will not apply if the CFC is undertaking a substantive economic activity supported by staff, equipment, assets, and premises, as evidenced by relevant facts and circumstances (as mandated by *Cadbury Schweppes*); or (2) the nondistributed income of CFCs arises from "non-genuine arrangements that have been put in place for the essential purpose of obtaining a tax advantage." The member state can opt to adopt either option (1) or option (2). Both options in essence utilize tests that must be decided by facts and circumstances. Without uniform and detailed interpretation guidance, these CFC rules would seem to be subject to the discretion of the tax administration of each European Union member state.

Anti-inversion Rules

The US Treasury in April 2016 issued temporary and proposed regulations aimed at removing the tax benefits of inversion transactions, following on from initial measures introduced in 2014. The regulations were finalized in 2018. While the simple technique of incorporating a subsidiary in a foreign jurisdiction and having it acquire its resident parent no longer worked even before 2014, another technique, redomiciling, accomplished by merging a domestic company with a foreign-based company under certain conditions, would serve the purpose as long as, most notably, the original foreign company contributed at least 20 percent of the shares of the newly merged company. The 2014 Treasury regulations were designed to make it more difficult for newly merged companies to repatriate earnings accrued before the merger tax-free, as well as to avoid the 20 percent ownership requirement. In 2016, Treasury issued additional regulations that treated some debt transactions between related parties as equity instead of debt; this was to deter foreign-based companies from practicing income stripping, particularly in this context.

Still, inversions and avoidance of tax on deferred income still posed a problem, even though the very large rate reduction in the Tax Cuts and Jobs Act of 2017, and the shift toward territorial taxation, should have mitigated the incentives to engage in inversions. Nonetheless, as discussed in Chapter 12, the origination of much intellectual property and the location of large residual profits in the United States indicated that such incentives could well remain, and the Tax Cuts and Jobs Act therefore took additional measures against them. The transition tax rate on inverted firms' existing overseas assets was set at the full pre–Tax Cuts and Jobs Act rate of 35 percent instead of the reduced rates of 8 and 15.5 percent for other firms' assets. Under this legislation, dividends received from newly inverted firms are now taxable as ordinary income instead of at the reduced rates generally applied to qualified dividends and capital gains. If at least 80 percent of an inverted (new foreign parent) company's stock is held by former shareholders of the US company, the company is treated as a domestic corporation for US tax purposes.

Hybrid Entities

Action 2 of the BEPS Report (OECD 2105c), *Neutralising the Effects of Hybrid Mismatch Arrangements*, is, like Action 3, a set of recommendations only, not constituting minimum standards. Nonetheless, it is extremely complex (running to over 450 pages), and in the main addresses payments and instruments that may give rise to double deductions or exclusions from taxation. Chapter 7 of that report, though (the "Dual Resident Payer Rule"), explicitly identifies such double benefits in the context of dual-resident (related) entities—precisely arising in many cases because of the lacunae and overlaps in the definitions of residency used by a set of countries involved in such transactions. These problems had been identified earlier by the OECD (2012) and others and had caused increasing concern in regard to tax base erosion. To delve into the minutiae of these sophisticated tax planning arrangements, as addressed in the report on Action 2, is beyond the scope of this chapter. But the report itself provides examples of how these schemes work and how the recommendations of the Action 2 report could help to address the problem. Again, however, the main lesson is the extreme manipulability of the residence-based taxation concept in the world of modern economies and of modern tax planning.

Again, too, the European Union Anti-Tax Avoidance Directive addresses the issue of hybrid transactions in a more definitive way, mandatory for European Union and European Economic Area countries. Anti-Tax Avoidance Directive 1 was extended by Anti-Tax Avoidance Directive 2 (2017) to cover more arrangements (for example, permanent establishments of member countries, and related parties in non–European Union or non–European Economic Area countries). Notably for purposes of this chapter, among numerous transactions and arrangements covered for which double deductions, exclusions from tax, and the like could arise, Anti-Tax Avoidance Directive antihybrid provisions explicitly cover, for example, "payment[s] made by a dual resident taxpayer that is deducted under the laws of both jurisdictions where the taxpayer is resident" (Deloitte 2020, p. 2).

Exit Taxes

While many countries, including the United States, have a departure tax for individuals who cease to be tax resident, departure taxes for companies were relatively few before the European Union Anti-Tax Avoidance Directive was issued. The European Union Anti-Tax Avoidance Directive required European Union member states to introduce an exit tax by December 31, 2019. The exit tax enables a country of which a taxpayer was a resident to tax the economic value of any unrealized capital gains generated within that country until the time of exit. The tax will apply when a taxpayer transfers one or more of the following: (1) assets from its head office to a foreign permanent establishment; (2) assets from a permanent establishment in a member state to a foreign head office or permanent establishment; (3) its tax residence to another country; or (4) business carried on by a permanent establishment in a member state to another country. Where the transfer takes place within the European Union or the European Economic Area, a taxpayer can opt to defer payment of the exit tax for five years.

Canada also has a departure tax for companies that cease to be a resident of Canada.[14] When a company stops being a tax resident of Canada,[15] the company will be considered to have disposed of all its property on the day its residency ceased.[16] The 25 percent departure tax[17] will also apply to the amount by which the fair market value of a company's assets exceeds the total of its liabilities and the paid-up capital of its stock. Thus, the tax is imposed on the retained earnings and the unrealized gains that would have been subject to the Canadian tax if the company paid dividends as a resident. In contrast to the European Union's exit tax, the Canadian departure tax does not allow a taxpayer to defer this payment.

CONCLUSION

While at first sight residence-based taxation may address some of the shortfalls of source-based taxation, namely tax competition through tax rates in source countries and the need for complicated profit allocations among different source countries, a second look confirms that residence-based taxation also faces various difficulties. Still, it does provide some protection from tax avoidance, and despite the trend toward territorial taxation, residence-based elements remain in most tax systems, at least in the anti-avoidance legislation.

Some progress has been made since 2015 in closing opportunities for tax minimization using corporate residence. However, the fundamentals of the system have not been changed, and further changes are needed. Chapter 12 continues the discussion of residence-based taxation, looking at possible further-reaching approaches for reform.

REFERENCES

Americans for Tax Fairness. 2015a. "CFC Look-Through Rule Enables Profit Shifting to Offshore Tax Havens." Fact Sheet. Washington, DC.

Americans for Tax Fairness. 2015b. "Taking Exception to the 'Active Financing Exception' Corporate Tax Loophole." Fact Sheet. Washington, DC.

Bureau of Economic Analysis. 2020. "Direct Investment by Country and Industry, 2019." Press Release BEA 20–36.

Chalk, Nigel, Michael Keen, and Victoria Perry. 2018. "The Tax Cuts and Jobs Act: An Appraisal." IMF Working Paper 18/185, International Monetary Fund, Washington, DC.

---

[14] Article 219 of the Income Tax Act.

[15] While Canada adopts central management and control as one of several criteria to decide the residency of a company, the Income Tax Act deems a company incorporated in Canada as a resident of Canada. Thus, even if its central management and control is moved outside of Canada, the company remains a resident of Canada.

[16] Article 250 of the Income Tax Act.

[17] If the Canadian company became a resident of a country with which Canada has a tax treaty, a 25 percent rate will be reduced to that which would be applied to a dividend paid to a parent corporation resident in that treaty partner country (Article 219(3) of the Income Tax Act).

Clausing, Kimberly. 2011. "The Revenue Effects of Multinational Firm Income Shifting." *Tax Notes*, March 28: 1580–86.

Congressional Budget Office (CBO). 2017. "An Analysis of Corporate Inversions." Publication 53093, CBO, Congress of the United States, Washington, DC.

Deloitte. 2020. "Anti-Tax Avoidance Directive: Implementation of Measures to Counter Hybrid Mismatch Arrangements." https://www2.deloitte.com/content/dam/Deloitte/global/Documents/Tax/dttl-tax-eu-anti-tax-avoidance-directive-implementation-of-measures-to-counter-hybrid-mismatch-arrangements.pdf.

Durst, Michael C. 2019. *Taxing Multinational Business in Lower-Income Countries*. London: Institute of Development Studies, International Centre for Tax and Development.

Graetz, Michael J. 2001. "Taxing International Income: Inadequate Principles, Outdated Concepts, and Unsatisfactory Policies." *Brooklyn Journal of International Tax Law* 26(4): 1357–448.

Kleinbard, Edward. 2011. "Stateless Income." *Florida Tax Review* 11(9): 699–774.

Markle, Kevin S. 2010. "A Comparison of the Tax-Motivated Income Shifting of Multinationals in Territorial and Worldwide Countries." *Contemporary Accounting Research* 33(1): 7–43.

Organisation for Economic Co-operation and Development (OECD). 2012. *Hybrid Mismatch Arrangements: Tax Policy and Compliance Issues*. Paris: OECD Publishing.

Organisation for Economic Co-operation and Development (OECD). 2015a. *BEPS Project Explanatory Statement*. OECD/G20 Base Erosion and Profit Shifting Project. Paris: OECD Publishing.

Organisation for Economic Co-operation and Development (OECD). 2015b. *Designing Effective Controlled Foreign Company Rules, Action 3—2015 Final Report*. OECD/G20 Base Erosion and Profit Shifting Project. Paris: OECD Publishing.

Organisation for Economic Co-operation and Development (OECD). 2015c. *Neutralising the Effects of Hybrid Mismatch Arrangements, Action 2—2015 Final Report*. OECD/G20 Base Erosion and Profit Shifting Project. Paris: OECD Publishing.

Organisation for Economic Co-operation and Development (OECD). 2020. *OECD/G20 Inclusive Framework on BEPS: Progress Report July 2019–July 2020*. Paris: OECD.

Phillips, Richard, Matt Gardner, Alexandria Robins, and Michelle Surka. 2017. *Offshore Shell Games 2017: The Use of Offshore Tax Havens by Fortune 500 Companies*. Washington, DC: Institute on Taxation and Economic Policy; Denver, CO: US PIRG Education Fund.

CHAPTER 8

Are Tax Treaties Worth It for Developing Economies?

Sébastien Leduc and Geerten Michielse*

INTRODUCTION

The complex interaction—and possible overlap—between different tax jurisdictions justifies coordination efforts to avoid double taxation, which can harm international trade and investment. Originally, countries established tax jurisdiction over their own residents and over nonresidents to the extent that they receive income from domestic sources. Tax treaties allocate—and often limit—taxing rights and impose obligations on both contracting states. The core provisions of a tax treaty deal with this allocation function, while other provisions target the elimination of double taxation (for example, through credit or exemption in the residence country) and protection of treaty provisions against tax avoidance schemes. Tax treaties intend to benefit taxpayers residing in either or both contracting states; the extent to which they do ultimately depends, inter alia, on how treaty provisions compare with the domestic law of each country.

Brief History of Tax Treaties

The first tax treaty that dealt with the avoidance of double taxation dates back to 1899 and was concluded between the Austro-Hungarian Empire and Prussia. The treaty was based on the 1870 Prussian Imperial Double Taxation Law, which focused on the elimination of double taxation within the North German Confederation and provided the legal basis for Prussian taxation of foreign nationals. Although not in concept, but certainly in wording, it was the first time that taxation of land and business, and income from them, became exclusively taxable in the state of source.[1] The 1899 treaty between Austria-Hungary and Prussia laid

---

* The authors would like to express their thanks to Alice Park for the assistance she provided in preparing some of the charts for this chapter.

[1] Article 2 of the Tax Treaty between the Austro-Hungarian Empire and Prussia: "The ownership of land and buildings, and the operation of a fixed trade, as well as the income arising from these sources are only to be assessed for direct State tax in the State in which the land and buildings are situated or where a permanent establishment for the exercise of trade is maintained. Branches, factories, depots, counting houses, places of buying and selling, and other business facilities maintained for the exercise of a fixed trade by a proprietor himself, business partners, attorneys, or other permanent

the foundation and had a profound impact on the establishment of a network of ensuing similarly worded bilateral tax treaties during the first half of the 1900s.[2]

In the 1920s the League of Nations entrusted four economists to prepare a study on the economic aspects of international double taxation.[3] Their report concluded that in most cases, double taxation penalizes the existing nonresident investor and prevents nonresidents from making new investments. To address these concerns, the researchers favored, for practical reasons, allocating sole taxing rights to the country of source (method of deduction for income from abroad), as opposed to the full allocation of taxing rights to the country of residence[4] (method of deduction for income going abroad) or to the sharing of taxing rights between both states.

In 1928 the League of Nations adopted and published the *Report on Double Taxation and Tax Evasion*. A group of tax officials from various countries then drafted several bilateral conventions for the prevention of double taxation.[5] The convention on direct taxes covered both impersonal and personal taxation[6] and offered a mix of sole and shared taxing rights. It distributed the taxing rights of various incomes covered by impersonal taxes to (1) the state in which the immovable property was situated, (2) the state in which the debtor of interest income or pension was resident, (3) the state in which the real center of management of the undertaking was situated, (4) the state in which the recipients carried on their employment, and (5) the state in which the permanent establishment was situated. With respect to income subject to personal taxes, the taxing right was allocated to the state in which the recipient had its fiscal domicile (that is, normal residence). That state was also obliged to provide relief for double taxation in the form of a tax credit for taxes paid in the other contracting state.

Subsequently, the Fiscal Committee of the League of Nations worked on broadening the scope of the 1928 Convention. A regional conference held in

---

representatives are to be regarded as permanent establishments." Translation by Johann Hattingh, On the Origins of Model Tax Conventions: 19th Century German Tax Treaties and Laws concerned with the Avoidance of Double Tax, page 31.

[2] For instance, Austria-Hungary concluded treaties with Liechtenstein (1901), Saxony (1903), Württemberg (1905), Baden (1908), and Hessen (1912). Luxembourg concluded treaties with Prussia (1909) and Hessen (1913).

[3] The *Report on Double Taxation* (1923) was authored by Professors Bruins (Commercial University of Rotterdam), Einaudi (Turin University), Seligman (Columbia University, New York), and Sir Josiah Stamp, KBE (London University).

[4] This was the researchers' preferred option from a conceptual perspective.

[5] A Bilateral Convention for the Prevention of Double Taxation in the Special Matter of Direct Taxes, a Bilateral Convention for the Prevention of Double Taxation in the Special Matter of Succession Duties, a Bilateral Convention on Administrative Assistance in Matters of Taxation, and a Bilateral Convention on (Judicial) Assistance in the Collection of Taxes.

[6] Commentary on Bilateral Conventions for the Prevention of Double Taxation in the Special Matter of Direct Taxes (League of Nations, 1928): ". . . that impersonal taxes are in most cases levied on all kinds of income at the source, irrespective of the personal circumstances of the taxpayer (nationality, domicile, civil status, family responsibilities, etc.) thus differing from personal taxes which rather concern individuals and their aggregate income."

1943 in Mexico City with representatives of countries in North and South America adopted a new draft tax treaty model. The significant feature about that draft was its underlying premise: the primary taxing jurisdiction was to be the state of source of the income, a position advantageous to developing countries. This, however, proved to be short lived. During the London meeting of the Fiscal Committee in 1946, the primary taxing jurisdiction shifted back in favor of the state of residence of a taxpayer.

The Mexico and London Models laid the foundation for treaty negotiations up until the late 1950s. During that period, over 70 new bilateral tax treaties were signed. However, these treaties had several gaps and consequently were not fully accepted or unanimously followed. In 1945 the United Nations (UN) succeeded the League of Nations, but it took until 1956 for the Fiscal Committee of the Organisation for European Economic Cooperation (OEEC), later transformed into the Organisation for Economic Co-operation and Development (OECD), to take over the review and further development of the League's London Model. The committee produced four reports on the elimination of double taxation, which were published in 1963 and embodied into the *Draft Double Taxation Convention on Income and on Capital*.

The 1963 *Draft Double Taxation Convention* was built to account for the interests of the OECD membership and thus allocated considerable taxing rights to residence countries. As international fiscal relations increased, tax systems became more complicated, and new business sectors and organizations were emerging, it became apparent in the early 1970s that the 1963 draft model required updating. A final version of the first *OECD Model Double Taxation Convention on Income and on Capital* (OECD Model) was published in 1977 and became the standard for bilateral treaty negotiations for years to come (mainly between developed countries). Since the 1990s the OECD Committee on Fiscal Affairs regularly reviews and updates the model.

In parallel, the UN developed its own Treaty Model, which it first published in 1980. Given the premise upon which the OECD Model is written, and the interests of the members of the OECD whom the model serves, it is not unexpected that developing countries (being capital-importing countries) did not feel that it represented a reasonable sharing of taxing rights. The response of the developing countries was recourse to the UN to develop a model tax treaty that better reflected their interests. The Ad Hoc Group of Experts on Tax Treaties between Developed and Developing Countries[7] finalized the 1980 *UN Model Double Taxation Convention between Developed and Developing Countries* (UN Model), whose aim was to promote the conclusion of treaties between developed and developing countries, acceptable to both parties. In that sense, the UN Model provides a benchmark for a compromise treaty that better balances residence and source taxation. To a large

---

[7] This ad hoc group was renamed the Ad Hoc Group of Experts on International Cooperation in Tax Matters in 1980; in 2005 it was renamed the Committee on International Cooperation in Tax Matters.

extent, the UN Model followed the 1977 OECD Model. However, it did grant greater taxing rights to source states, that is, the capital importing and developing countries. The UN Model has been, and continues to be, widely embraced by most developing countries (see Wijnen and Magenta 1997).

Influence of the OECD and UN Models

The success of the OECD Model and (although to a lesser extent) the UN Model has been astounding. Since World War II, the number of tax treaties concluded has rapidly increased to over 3,000 treaties (Figure 8.1), and the overwhelming majority of these treaties follow provisions that are in either or both the OECD and UN Models. Their wide acceptance and the resulting standardization of many international tax rules has been an important factor in reducing international double taxation in recent years. Although the economy has fundamentally changed since the 1920s from a brick-and-mortar economy into a globalized, integrated, and increasingly digitalized economy, both models are still to a large extent based on the underlying premise that the primary taxing jurisdiction is the state of residence of the taxpayer, whereas the state of source should limit or forgo its taxing jurisdiction.

The structure and key provisions in bilateral tax treaties based on either the OECD or UN Model tend to be very similar. Chapter 1 identifies the persons whose tax obligations are affected by the treaty, generally residents of either or both contracting states, and describes the taxes covered by the treaty, generally taxes on income and capital (that is, wealth) imposed by the contracting states and their political subdivisions. Chapter II provides definitions of important terms used in the treaty.[8] Chapter III contains what are often referred to as the distributive or allocative rules of the treaty: a set of provisions dealing with various types of income derived by a resident of one or both of the contracting states. In general, these provisions determine whether there are shared or exclusive taxing rights. In the case of shared taxing rights, a priority is given to source taxing rights by Article 23, which deals with the elimination of double taxation. Chapter IV deals with the taxation of capital (not income from capital). Chapter V provides two alternative methods for eliminating double taxation: the exemption method and the credit method. Chapter VI contains special provisions providing protection against various forms of discriminatory taxation by the source and residence countries, administrative cooperation between the contracting states in relation to assistance in collection and exchange of information, and a mutual agreement procedure to resolve disputes concerning the application of the treaty. Finally, Chapter VII provides rules to govern the entry into force and termination of the treaty.

The OECD Model favors capital-exporting countries over capital-importing countries. Often, its proposed solution to eliminate or mitigate double taxation is to have the source country forfeit some or all its taxing rights on certain categories

---

[8] Including general definitions in Article 3, a definition of the term "resident" in Article 4, and "permanent establishment" in Article 5. Other definitions are also found elsewhere, such as "immovable property" under Article 6, "dividends" under Article 10, "interest" under Article 11, and "royalties" under Article 12.

Figure 8.1. Development of Worldwide Tax Treaty Network
Number of Tax Treaties

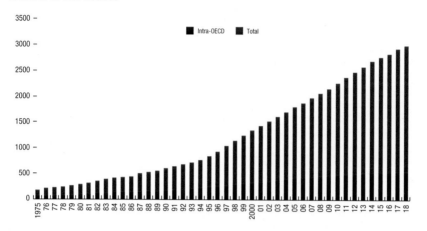

Source: IMF staff based on IBFD data.

of income. Good examples of this are Article 12 on royalty payments and Article 13 on capital gains related to dispositions of shares, for which the OECD Model Tax Treaty proposes exclusive taxing rights to the residence country. The UN Model imposes much fewer restrictions on source-country taxing rights (Box 8.1).

Legal Considerations

In general, tax treaties do not impose tax. Instead, that is the role of domestic legislation, while tax treaties are primarily relieving in nature in the sense that they can constrain the reach of domestic legislation. In other words, tax treaties limit the taxes otherwise imposed by a country but cannot extend a country's right to tax income where such taxing rights are not provided for under domestic law. Considering this fundamental principle, it is usually appropriate before applying the treaty provisions to determine whether the income in question is subject to domestic tax. It is also worth keeping in mind that domestic legislation can be changed freely and frequently (subject to the legislature's approval), whereas the provisions negotiated in tax treaties tend to remain in place for many years, even decades.[9] Extreme prudence should thus be exercised in negotiating a tax treaty.

---

[9] Article VI of the US Constitution states: ". . . laws of the United States which shall be made in pursuance thereof: and all treaties made, or which shall be made, under the authority of the United States, shall be the supreme law of the land . . ." The US Supreme Court has held as its interpretation that as treaties and domestic law are equal (that is, the Constitution does not imply a hierarchy between them), the principle of *lex posterior* should prevail (most recent law is that which is applicable). As such, the general US rule is that any statute that is later in time than a treaty, and that conflicts with it in some way, is a treaty override. For additional background, see Avi-Yonah and Wells (2018). This is contrary to the domestic law of most other countries.

Box 8.1. Main Differences between OECD and UN Models

Business Income (Articles 5 and 7)

The UN Model uses a permanent establishment definition allowing source countries to more easily establish a sufficient economic linkage to trigger a permanent establishment designation; this is achieved by more restrictive duration tests for building and construction permanent establishments, by defining a permanent establishment for service activities not set forth in the OECD Model, and by creating a permanent establishment for collecting premiums or insuring risks. The UN Model is also more source-country friendly when it comes to allocating profits to the permanent establishment; it includes a limited force-of-attraction rule that extends a source country's right to tax business income to activities undertaken therein by a nonresident if these activities are identical or similar to those carried out by the permanent establishment.

Investment Income (Articles 10, 11, and 12)

The most important difference between the two models regarding treatment of investment income is that the UN Model maintains source-country taxing rights over royalties, whereas the OECD Model provides exclusive taxing rights to the residence country. Further, the UN Model retains source-country withholding tax rights over equipment rental fees and radio or television broadcasting royalties, whereas the OECD Model considers them business income (Article 7). Finally, the OECD Model explicitly suggests withholding tax rates (5 percent for direct dividends, 15 percent for portfolio dividends, and 10 percent for interest), whereas the UN Model leaves them up to negotiation.

Service and Management Fees (Article 12A)

Since 2017, the UN Model has proposed that source countries retain the right to impose a withholding tax on gross payments to nonresidents in relation to services of a managerial, technical, or consultancy nature, even if the service provider has no physical presence in the source country.

Capital Gains (Article 13)

The UN Model provides for source-country taxation of shares if a holding is over an agreed threshold (substantial shareholdings).

Mutual Agreement Procedure (Article 25)

The OECD Model proposes that countries include a clause that provides for mandatory binding arbitration for cases that remain unresolved after two years. In contrast, the UN Model provides two alternatives. The first option is for contracting states to agree to have mandatory binding arbitration if cases remain unresolved after three years (Article 25B). In this case, and unlike for the OECD, arbitration is triggered by either of the contracting states (and not the taxpayer). The second option is to forgo arbitration and simply have contracting states endeavor to revolve any issues related to the application of the tax treaty (Article 25A).

The interpretation of tax treaties is a task that must be undertaken by taxpayers, tax authorities, and domestic courts alike. In filing their tax returns, taxpayers must claim treaty protection. Decisions made by tax authorities against a taxpayer's views are (ultimately) subject to judicial recourse. From a simplistic perspective, tax treaties can be interpreted broadly to give effect to their perceived purposes or narrowly to adhere strictly to their literal wording. In that sense, the interpretation of tax treaties bears certain similarities to that of domestic tax legislation. There are, however, several important differences between the legal interpretation of treaties and that of domestic tax legislation:

- Because two contracting states are involved in every treaty, questions of interpretation should be resolved by reference to the mutual intentions and expectations of both contracting states.

- Treaties are addressed to a broader audience than domestic legislation, namely, to both the governments and taxpayers of each country.

- Treaties are often not drafted using the same terms as domestic legislation.

- Treaties are, as previously discussed, primarily relieving in nature.

- The OECD and UN Models (and their commentaries, which serve as interpretive guidance) have no counterparts in the context of domestic tax legislation.

As tax treaties are international agreements, the Vienna Convention also governs their interpretation. The basic rule of interpretation in Article 31(1) of the Vienna Convention provides that "[a] treaty shall be interpreted in good faith in accordance with the ordinary meaning to be given to the terms of the treaty in their context and in light of its object and purpose." The context includes the text of the treaty and any agreements between the parties made in connection with the conclusion of the treaty and any instrument made by one of the parties and accepted by the other party. Under Article 32 of the Vienna Convention, other elements, referred to as supplementary means of interpretation, which include the preparatory work of the treaty and the circumstances of its conclusion, are only to be considered to confirm the meaning established pursuant to Article 31, or to establish the meaning if Article 31 produces an ambiguous, obscure, absurd, or unreasonable result. In treaty cases from virtually all countries, the courts usually give the OECD and UN Models and their commentaries substantial weight. To this end, developing countries that agree to include verbatim provisions found in either model should be very familiar with the related commentary and, if they disagree with the suggested interpretation, either amend the language of the article or formally reject the interpretation by way of a technical note.

In addition to the provisions of the Vienna Convention, tax treaties based on the OECD or UN Model contain an internal rule of interpretation. Article 3(2) (general definitions) provides that any undefined terms used in a treaty should be given the meaning that they have under the domestic law of the country applying the treaty unless the context requires otherwise. However, the determination of the meaning of a term under domestic law also may be difficult.[10] Another

---

[10] For instance, some definitions in tax treaties are inclusive, meaning that the term has its ordinary meaning in addition to items that are specifically mentioned. Furthermore, definitions in the treaty often contain terms that are undefined in domestic legislation or have more than one meaning in the domestic legislation, depending on the context in which they are used.

important and controversial issue of interpretation in connection with Article 3(2) of the OECD and UN Models is whether a term has its meaning under domestic law at the time that the treaty was entered into (static approach) or its meaning under the domestic law as amended from time to time (ambulatory approach). As a matter of principle, international tax law experts are generally averse to the idea of an ambulatory approach (see, for example, Avery Jones 2002; Land and Brugger 2008; and Ward 2006). This reluctance seems tied to their understanding of the theoretical framework of the applicable international law, which is exclusively governed by the Vienna Convention.

RECENT DEVELOPMENTS: BEPS AND 2017 MODEL TREATIES

As part of its agenda to counter base erosion and profit shifting (BEPS), the OECD and G20 also looked into treaty-related tax avoidance strategies (see OECD 2013a; 2013b). The most preeminent treaty issue discussed and agreed to as part of the BEPS Project relates to the need for countries to better protect the integrity of their treaty network from potential abuses such as treaty shopping (see "Treaty Shopping," later in this chapter, for a fuller discussion). A consensus emerged out of this work for countries to include in treaties a "principal purpose test" provision, or a limitation of benefits clause restricting access to treaty benefits, or a combination of the two (Action 6), as evidenced by the retention of this measure as a "BEPS minimum standard." Another BEPS minimum standard that links with tax treaties is provided under Action 14 and aims at making dispute resolution mechanisms more effective by requiring countries to commit to resolving treaty-related disputes in a timely, effective, and efficient manner. The BEPS Project also resulted in several other non-minimum standard recommendations that would assist countries in strengthening the integrity of their tax treaties, including changes to the permanent establishment definition and provisions intended to address hybrid mismatch arrangements, among others.

The BEPS Project also brought forward an innovative instrument for countries to promptly amend their tax treaties. On June 7, 2017, the so-called multilateral instrument—often known as MLI—was signed by 67 countries and jurisdictions, including G20 members except Brazil, Saudi Arabia, and the United States.[11] The multilateral instrument implements the BEPS outcomes—both minimum standards and others[12]—in as far as it requires amendment of existing tax treaties (see Table 8.1). Signatories are required to identify those treaties that they wish to cover by the multilateral instrument: so-called covered

---

[11] As of December 21, 2020, 95 jurisdictions had signed the multilateral instrument and four countries had indicated their intention of becoming signatories in the short term.

[12] Further, the multilateral instrument also provides an option for countries to include in their tax treaties Article 13(4), which provides for source-country taxation on capital gains realized on indirect transfers of immovable property, which is not a BEPS-related measure.

TABLE 8.1.

Content of the Multilateral Instrument	
Multilateral Instrument Article(s)	**Content**
1	Scope Modifies all covered tax agreements
2	Interpretation of Terms Identifies—among other things—which tax treaties are covered
3–5	Hybrid Mismatches • Incorporates a new provision in which transparent entities will be taxed according to the treatment applicable in the country of residence of its participants • Amends the tie-breaker rule that determines in what country an entity has its treaty residence by using the mutual agreement procedure, and provides that treaty benefits will be denied if such agreement is not reached • Eliminates double taxation as a result of the application of primary and defensive domestic rules
6	Purpose of a Covered Tax Agreement Changes the preamble language to add after the intention to eliminate double taxation "without creating opportunities for non-taxation or reduced taxation through tax evasion or avoidance"
7	Prevention of Treaty Abuse Includes a general anti-abuse rule based on the principal purpose of transactions or arrangements; may be supplemented by a simplified limitation-on-benefit provision
8–11	Other Anti-abuse Rules • Introduces a minimum holding period to obtain preferred source taxation on dividends (8) • Allows source-country taxation in cases of indirect sales of immovable property (9) • Denies tax treaty benefits to any item of income on which the tax rate in the third jurisdiction in which an exempt permanent establishment is located is taxed below 60 percent of the tax that would be imposed in the residence country of the enterprise (10) • Provides a so-called "saving clause" that preserves the right of a contracting state to tax its own residents (11)
12–15	Avoidance of Permanent Establishment Status • Redefines the definition of an "independent agent" to mitigate commissionaire arrangements (12) • Addresses situations in which the specific activity exemptions give rise to BEPS concerns (13) • Nullifies the splitting up of contracts for the avoidance of permanent establishment status (for example, construction sites) (14)
16	Mutual Agreement Procedures • Modifies the wording of Article 25 of the OECD Model to allow a taxpayer to present a case to the competent authority of either contracting state within a limited period not less than three years • Requires that signatories implement any mutual agreement reached, notwithstanding the statute of limitation under domestic law
17	Corresponding Adjustments Extends the mutual agreement procedure to transfer pricing disputes, unless a tax treaty contains Article 9(2) of the OECD Model

(continued)

TABLE 8.1. *(continued)*

Content of the Multilateral Instrument	
Multilateral Instrument Article(s)	**Content**
18–25	Mandatory Binding Arbitration (optional) Provides that, where the competent authorities are unable to reach an agreement on a case pursuant to the mutual agreement procedure within a period of two years, unresolved issues will, at the request of the person who presented the case, be submitted to arbitration; further provides that the arbitration decision shall be binding on both contracting states (limited exceptions) and implemented through the mutual agreement procedure
26–39	Final (Procedural) Provisions Deals with, for instance, the ratification and notification procedures, interpretation and implementation, the date this convention shall have effect with respect to covered tax agreements, and the possibility and effects of withdrawal from this convention

Source: IMF staff.

tax agreements. Subsequently, they must choose from the options for the minimum standards related to addressing treaty shopping (see following discussion) and can make reservations to provisions other than those relating to the minimum standards. From a legal perspective, the multilateral instrument will not change the text of existing tax treaties, but it will be applied alongside such treaties, modifying their application to implement the BEPS measures.

Out of some 3,000 tax treaties that are currently in force, over 1,500 treaties will be covered by the multilateral instrument. Thus, the multilateral instrument marks unprecedented progress in international tax cooperation. Reservations and options have nonetheless resulted in a complex matrix in which it is not immediately clear how individual tax treaties have been or will be amended. The multilateral instrument will only revise those articles of the covered tax agreements that both signatories do not reserve (other than those regarding the minimum standards) or that both signatories do not consider contain a provision described in the multilateral instrument. Thus, even if a signatory intends to apply all provisions of the multilateral instrument, the provisions that will be revised by the multilateral instrument will be limited to those agreed to by other contracting states. To this end, due to the widespread use by signatories of reservations on nonminimum standard provisions, the actual extent to which the multilateral instrument will revise individual treaty provisions may be quite limited in practice.

The treaty-related outcomes from the BEPS project are now reflected in 2017 updates to the OECD and UN Models. The main changes include amendments to the title and preamble of both models, the introduction of a new article about entitlement to benefits to protect against treaty shopping, modifications of the definition of permanent establishment, and amendments to the mutual agreement procedure. In addition to these BEPS-related changes, the OECD update also includes changes to the commentary on residency by clarifying the meaning of "permanent home available" and "habitual abode," and explicitly noting that registration for the purpose of VAT is, by itself, irrelevant for the purpose of the application and interpretation of the permanent establishment definition.

The update of the UN Model includes a more substantive change that extends beyond BEPS-related outcomes and is specifically intended to address developing countries' concerns over base-eroding payments in relation to services rendered by nonresidents. The 2017 UN Model includes a new Article 12A, which allows source countries to apply a final withholding tax on gross payments for technical services. All cross-border payments for technical services, irrespective of whether those services were performed inside or outside the tax jurisdiction of the source country, can be taxed in that state. As discussed later in this chapter (see "Key Allocative Provisions"), this is a major extension of the taxation right of low- and middle-income countries and establishes a better protection against erosion of their tax base.

TAX TREATIES AND DEVELOPING COUNTRIES

Tax Treaties and Developing Countries: Recent Trends and Stylized Facts

There are currently about 3,000 comprehensive bilateral income tax treaties in effect. As depicted in Figure 8.2, high-income countries have concluded substantially more tax treaties than any other income group category, while low-income countries tend to have the narrowest treaty networks. This has important

Figure 8.2. Total Number of Tax Treaties in Force by Country Income Group

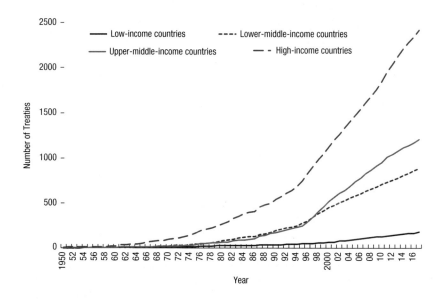

Source: IMF staff based on IBFD data.
Note: Cumulative number of tax treaties concluded where at least one of the contracting states is part of a given country income group. There is, therefore, duplication of treaties where contracting states are part of different income groups.

Figure 8.3. Average Number of New Treaties Each Year by Decade

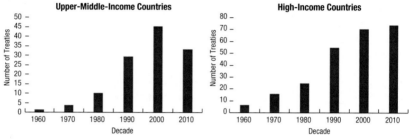

Source: IMF staff based on IBFD data.

implications for tax treaty negotiations between countries in these two income groups, as the former will typically have greater experience and better institutional and technical knowledge than the latter in terms of treaty negotiations.

The pace at which countries have concluded tax treaties has significantly increased starting in the mid-1990s (Figure 8.2). In the 1950s tax treaties played a marginal role in defining the international tax policy of countries in all income groups. Starting in the early 1960s high-income countries began concluding an increasing number of treaties mostly among themselves, while developing countries[13] continued to refrain from enacting tax treaties. This all changed in the early 1970s, when the pace of concluding tax treaties increased across all country income groups (although to a lesser extent for low-income countries). Another defining point occurred in the mid-1990s, when high-income, upper-middle-income, and lower-middle-income countries all experienced a further increase in the number of tax treaties being concluded and enacted. While less apparent in Figure 8.2 due to scaling, low-income countries experienced a similar increase: the number of tax treaties concluded by countries in this category increased from an average of about one per year in the 1960s, 1970s, and 1980s to three per year in the 1990s and six per year in the 2000s and 2010s. This is shown in Figure 8.3.

---

[13] Developing countries are taken as those that are low-income, lower-middle-income and upper-middle-income countries as per World Bank classification.

Figure 8.4. Tax Treaties in Force, by Counterpart Country Income Group

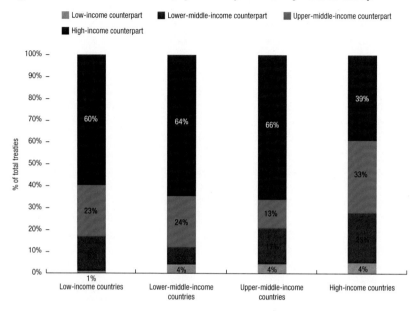

Source: IMF staff based on IBFD data.

Most tax treaties that are concluded by developing countries are with a high-income country (Figure 8.4). The share of low-income countries' tax treaties that are concluded with high-income countries sits at about 60 percent. Of the remaining share, 23 percent are concluded with upper-middle-income countries and 16 percent with lower-middle-income countries, and only 1 percent is concluded between two low-income countries. Similarly, lower-middle-income and upper-middle-income countries also tend to have close to two-thirds of their treaties concluded with high-income countries. This has notable implications for developing countries in terms of analytical capacity and experience in negotiating tax treaties, and especially in terms of the economic implications of tax treaties. For low-income countries these are dictated by mostly unilateral flows of trade and investment from more economically developed countries.

Assessing the Reciprocity Argument

It is often argued or assumed that tax treaties are reciprocal in light of the fact that the exact same provisions will generally apply to residents of both contracting states. However, assessing de jure reciprocity provides an incomplete picture of what is truly at stake for different contracting states. Taking withholding tax as an example, de jure reciprocity means that if the negotiated withholding tax on interest is 8 percent, as in the Mozambique–Mauritius treaty, this same rate applies to payments received and beneficially owned by residents of both states. Is that a sufficient condition to assess the treaty provision as being effectively de facto reciprocal? One may argue, for instance, that reciprocity ought also to be assessed in terms of magnitude of the benefits that this provision confers to residents of both contracting states, and hence in terms of the cost the provisions, imposes to contracting states in terms of revenue forgone. As will be further discussed, this will depend, inter alia, on the degree to which the provisions in the tax treaty depart from applicable domestic legislation. To illustrate this point, consider that the applicable domestic legislations in Mozambique and Mauritius currently provide for, respectively, 20 percent and 0 percent withholding tax interest paid to nonresidents.[14] Hence, as the cost of the negotiated 8 percent withholding tax rate under the Mozambique–Mauritius treaty is effectively only binding for Mozambique, it is hardly conceivable to assert that this provision is truly reciprocal.[15] It is thus of critical importance to bear in mind the domestic legislations of both contracting states when engaging in treaty negotiations and assessing the desirability and reciprocity of the treaty and its provisions.

Further, and perhaps more fundamentally important for developing countries, is the fact that reciprocity also needs to be assessed in the context of the existing and prospective economic relationships. The investment flows between the two contracting states will to a large extent dictate who will bear the cost of different treaty provisions. As most tax treaty provisions will impose various constraints on source-country taxation, while providing few limitations on residence countries beyond those already contemplated under prevailing domestic legislation,[16] the costs of entering into a tax treaty will generally be greater for net capital importers. This is particularly relevant for developing countries, given that investment flows make developing countries typically net capital importers.

Figures 8.5 to 8.8 illustrate the trend in inward and outward foreign direct investment stocks relative to GDP across four different country income groups, as well as the trend in the inward-to-outward foreign direct investment ratio.[17] A clear picture emerges from this analysis: low-income countries and lower-middle-income countries remain large net capital importers.[18] The unidirectional flow of foreign direct investment into low-income countries is in fact more pronounced today than it was in 1997, as evidenced by the fact that the inward-to-outward

---

[14] Mauritius's 0 percent withholding tax rate on interest payments to nonresidents is subject to holding a category 1 or category 2 global business license or a banking license.

[15] From the perspective of reciprocity in terms of benefits to taxpayers and costs to contracting states, reciprocity would be better achieved by having the treaty stipulate an agreed reduction over the applicable statutory withholding tax rate. This, of course, runs into difficulties where one country, like Mauritius, adopts a 0 percent withholding tax rate domestically (unless a subsidy scheme is then contemplated).

[16] Indeed, most capital-exporting countries have nowadays legislated foreign tax credit provisions or foreign income exemptions in their domestic legislation such that the requirement under the tax treaty to eliminate double taxation (Article 23) does not typically go beyond domestic law.

[17] This ratio shows the balance between inward and outward investment flows. A ratio about 1 shows a balance in importing and exporting capital from and to international markets, while a high ratio is indicative of a net capital importer.

[18] IMF Coordinated Portfolio Investment Survey data reveal a similar pattern for portfolio holdings.

Figure 8.5. Low-Income Countries

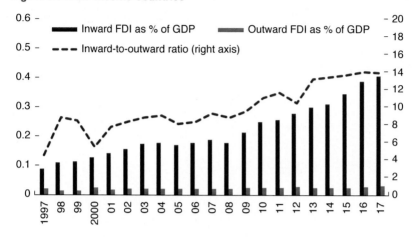

Figure 8.6. Lower-Middle-Income Countries

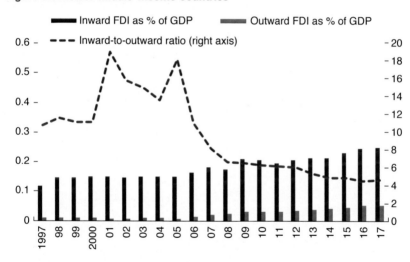

Source: IMF staff using UNCTAD data[1] and World Bank country classifications.
Note: FDI = foreign direct investment.

[1] UNCTAD (United Nations Conference on Trade and Development), *Bilateral FDI Statistics, United Nations Conference on Trade and Development.*

Figure 8.7. Upper-Middle-Income Countries

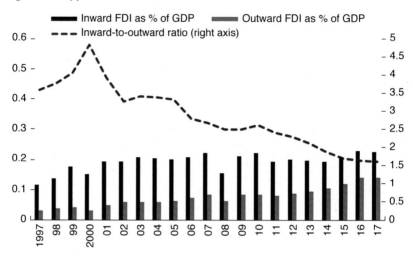

Figure 8.8. High-Income Countries

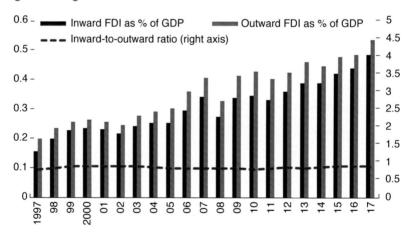

Source: IMF staff using UNCTAD data[1] and World Bank country classifications.
Note: FDI = foreign direct investment.

---

[1] UNCTAD (United Nations Conference on Trade and Development), *Bilateral FDI Statistics, United Nations Conference on Trade and Development,* https://unctad.org/en/Pages/DIAE/FDI%20Statistics /FDI-Statistics-Bilateral.aspx.

ratio now approaches 14. The total value of inward foreign direct investment represents 40 percent of low-income countries' GDP, whereas outward foreign direct investment accounts for approximately 2.9 percent. Lower-middle-income countries' ratio has declined in recent years, although inward foreign direct investment (approximately 25 percent of GDP) is still significantly higher than outward foreign direct investment (5.4 percent).

Upper-middle-income countries have in recent years increasingly exported capital, such that the outward foreign direct investment reached 14 percent of the group's aggregate GDP. With inward foreign direct investment having seemed to stabilize at about 20 percent of GDP, the inward-to-outward foreign direct investment ratio has thus declined to about 1.6. As for high-income countries, they remain capital exporters at the margin, although the ratio has been relatively stable since 1997 at just under 1. As illustrated by these figures, the challenges posed by the limitation on source-country taxation in tax treaties may thus be particularly pronounced for the poorest countries, although such limitations remain important for high-income countries in the context of their economic relationships with other high-income countries (as illustrated, for example, by the ongoing discussions regarding appropriate nexus and profit allocation rules for companies operating in the digital economy).

BENEFITS AND COSTS OF TAX TREATIES

Proclaimed Benefits of Tax Treaties

The traditional motivation for concluding a tax treaty is to promote and reduce barriers to international trade and investment.[19] Tax treaties may help achieve this objective through a number of different channels. First and foremost is the elimination of double taxation, which, if it exists, can indeed be harmful to investment, trade, and economic growth. Double taxation can take several forms. One of them is economic double taxation, which refers to the taxation of the same income in the hands of different taxpayers. Treaties mitigate against risks of economic double taxation through the adoption of a common understanding on the adoption of the arm's length principle to determine appropriate pricing of transactions between associated enterprises, as stipulated under Article 9 of both the OECD and UN Models.[20] Dispute resolution under the mutual agreement pro-

---

[19] This section focuses on tax treaties in developing countries. Developed countries may have other objectives when entering into treaty negotiations, such as the facilitation of outbound investment by residents (see United Nations 2016).

[20] In particular, paragraph 9(2) provides that contracting states shall make appropriate corresponding transfer pricing adjustments (a "correlative adjustment"). Paragraph 6 of the commentaries to Article 9 note, however, that this correlative adjustment is contingent on the other contracting state agreeing that the adjustment appropriately reflects an arm's length position. Since 1999, the UN Model has included a new paragraph 3 in Article 9, which provides that there is no obligation to provide a correlative adjustment where the juridical, administrative, or other legal proceedings have resulted in a final ruling that, by actions giving rise to an adjustment of profits under 9(1), one of the enterprises is liable to penalty with respect to fraud, gross negligence, or willful default.

cedure (Article 25) is also aimed at providing a framework for resolving cases of double taxation,[21] including for instances regarding correlative adjustment under paragraph 9(2) in response to a primary transfer pricing adjustment by one of the contracting states.

Another, and arguably the most prevalent, type of double taxation that tax treaties aim at addressing is juridical double taxation, which arises when the same income is taxable in the hands of the same person in more than one country. Three separate cases of juridical double taxation exist: residence-residence, source-source, and source-residence. Residence-residence double taxation arises when both contracting states' domestic laws provide that a given taxpayer has tax residence in their jurisdiction.[22] In principle, such residence-residence double taxation is addressed through the tie-breaker rules in Article 4. Source-source double taxation arises when two countries, through their domestic legislation, adopt different sourcing rules, the result of which is that a single payment is then simultaneously sourced in two countries.[23] Tax treaties may eliminate some of these situations by providing sourcing rules (for example, for interest under Article 11 and royalties under Article 12), although not all source-source double taxation is necessarily resolved by treaties.[24] Source-residence double taxation arises when one state exercises jurisdiction to tax on the basis of residency while another jurisdiction exercises its jurisdiction to tax income based on its domestic source. Source-residence double taxation is addressed through the allocative provisions in tax treaties (Articles 6–22), which allow for either exclusive or shared taxation rights, and the provisions for the elimination of double taxation under Article 23.

A second channel through which tax treaties could potentially promote trade and investments is by reducing source-country taxation (through limitations on withholding taxes, for example). Assuming that the residence country adopts a territorial system for active business income earned by foreign subsidiaries of domestic multinational enterprises (as is nowadays the international norm), then reducing source-country taxation could be expected to increase investment, as it will lower the pretax rate of return required by investors to make a project viable on a posttax basis. As will be discussed, the empirical validity of this effect of tax treaties (and source-country tax incentives more generally, especially in developing countries) on investment is, at best, mixed.

---

[21] And, more generally, inappropriate application of the treaty by one of the contracting states.

[22] For example, a country may use place of incorporation to establish corporate tax residency, whereas another country may use a place of effective management test, giving rise to the possibility of dual residence for companies that are incorporated in the former country with an effective place of management in the latter.

[23] For example, a country may source services where they are actually performed, while another country may source services based on the tax residency of the payor.

[24] For example, where services are being provided in a contracting state (which sources services based on the location of the provision) by a resident in a third country for the benefit of a resident in the other contracting state (which sources services based on where they are being utilized or consumed), the tax treaty will not be helpful, as the issue does not arise with respect to a resident of a contracting state, and therefore who is not a covered person pursuant to Article 1.

Tax treaties may also promote trade and investment by increasing predictability and stability in source-country tax systems. For example, tax treaties are, by their very nature, less prone to change than domestic law. Further, tax treaties may signal to the international community a source country's willingness to adhere to international standards developed by the OECD (whose membership comprises of large capital exporters to developing countries), most notably in terms of key issues such as permanent establishments (Article 5), transfer pricing (Article 9), and nondiscrimination (Article 24).

Beyond its possible effect on trade and investment, tax treaties offer administrative benefits that can assist countries in monitoring and enforcing tax compliance. Of particular relevance are Article 26 (exchange of information) and Article 27 (assistance in collection). Article 26 offers a legal basis for contracting states to undertake automatic, spontaneous, or on-request exchange of information, while Article 27 provides a commitment—which can be supported by a separate memorandum of understanding—for contracting states to help each other in the collection of revenue claims. This has led some to suggest that the prevention of tax evasion and avoidance and of double nontaxation is an important operational objective of tax treaties (see, for example, Arnold 2015). As argued in the following subsection, "Assessment of the Proclaimed Benefits," we dismiss this argument, as tax treaties have in practice been more likely to create—rather than eliminate—opportunities for tax avoidance and as other, arguably more effective, instruments exist to achieve these objectives that do not entail forfeiting taxing rights.

Last, but not least, tax treaties have at times been used support or further diplomatic relationships between states. It is, for instance, not uncommon for negotiations to be either recommended or even initiated by foreign affairs ministries rather than by ministries of finance, where as tax policy ought to be designed in support of other fiscal policy matters.

Assessment of the Proclaimed Benefits

The preceding discussion indicated that the benefits of tax treaties can be broken down into three main categories: tax treaties can stimulate cross-border trade and investment, support tax administration functions, and further international relations. Various channels have been argued to establish first—the linkage between tax treaties and trade and investments—including, most notably, the mitigation of double taxation and the reduction in source-country taxation.

To what extent is double taxation preventing cross-border trade and investment? A long tradition of legal scholars argue that capital-exporting countries already relieve the bulk of any possible double taxation unilaterally, such that treaties' benefit on investment through relief from double taxation is essentially a myth (Hearson and Kangave 2016).

When tax treaties were first being negotiated, most countries adopted a worldwide corporate income tax system. The possibility for double taxation was consequently much more pronounced, and tax treaties might, in these circumstances, have been quite useful in ensuring proper relief from double taxation, thereby encouraging trade and investment. Nowadays, however, most capital-exporting countries have shifted toward territorial tax systems where foreign-source active business income of controlled foreign corporations of domestic multinationals is fully exempt, meaning that tax treaties' role in relieving source-residence double taxation is at best questionable. Further, where capital-exporting countries do tax foreign-source profits (for example, for some countries in the case of a foreign branch or passive income), they typically will provide unilateral relief from double taxation (either through an exemption or a foreign tax credit) through provisions in their domestic tax law.

This is not to say that double taxation no longer exists. There may, for instance, still be cases where dual residence arises or where double taxation remains given that the residence country offers an income tax deduction, as opposed to an income tax credit. That said, those cases are relatively rare. The key message is thus that policy shifts in recent decades have certainly reduced the prevalence of double taxation, to a point where it is worth questioning whether it remains a sufficiently important issue to justify the presence of tax treaties. If multinationals have been so agile in exploiting the current framework to find opportunities for double nontaxation (for example, stateless income, hybrid mismatches), then one would expect that they would also be able to avoid double taxation.[25]

If double taxation no longer appears to be a significant barrier to trade and investment, can source countries still benefit from tax treaties by reducing source-country taxation? Three major reasons point to a negative answer to this question:

- Empirical evidence on the impact of tax treaties on foreign direct investment is inconclusive. One of the key challenges is addressing possible endogeneity: should an increase in investment be attributed to the presence of a tax treaty, or did investors' desire to undertake investment result in the conclusion of a tax treaty with a given country? Studies have used bilateral country-level data or microdata to assess the impact of treaties (as a binary variable) and withholding tax rates on investment, with some showing positive impacts (for example, Barthel, Busse, and Neumayer 2010; Di Giovanni 2005; Millimet and Kumas 2007; Neumayer 2007), while others find no or even negative impacts (for example, Blonigen and Davis 2004, 2005; Egger and others 2006; Louie and Rousslang 2008).[26]

---

[25] Ultimately, the possibility of double taxation needs to be assessed on a case-by-case basis at a bilateral level. For example, the case for residence-residence double taxation of individuals may be more pronounced for neighboring countries. Should this prove problematic, consultations among country officials to find national solutions could prove desirable over concluding a tax treaty based on such a premise.

[26] For a more extensive overview of current literature, see IMF (2014, appendix 5).

- More generally, while tax incentives—including, for instance, reduced with-holding taxes under a tax treaty—may have a positive effect on investment in developing countries, the effect tends to be smaller than in developed countries (Abbas and Klemm 2013; De Mooij and Ederveen 2008; Van Parys and James 2009). In many cases, however, tax incentives have been found to be highly redundant,[27] as was the case, for example, in Rwanda (98 percent), Uganda (93 percent), Guinea (92 percent), Tanzania (91 percent), and elsewhere (James 2014). Further, tax incentives have generally scored low in investor surveys in terms of decisional factors: a 2010 United Nations Industrial Development Organization (UNIDO) survey covering 7,000 companies in 19 sub-Saharan Africa suggests that tax incentive packages ranked 11th out of 12 factors.[28]

- Finally, the optimal policy response would not in any case be to sign a bilateral tax treaty. Indeed, if one believes—contrary to much evidence—that source-country tax incentives bring about an important inflow of foreign direct investment and increase other social benefits such as employment and knowledge and technology spillovers, then the optimal policy would seemingly be to adopt this reduction unilaterally under domestic statutes (by legislating moderate-to-low statutory withholding tax rates, for example).[29]

Tax treaties should not be entered into for the sole or primary purpose of pursuing either administrative or political motives. Historically, developing countries have very seldom availed themselves of exchange-of-information or assistance-in-collection clauses to better monitor and enforce compliance. And, in any case, these provisions are more widely accessible under Articles 4–7 and 11 of the Multilateral Convention on Mutual Administrative Assistance in Tax Matters, which now has 125 participating jurisdictions.[30] As for the international relations argument, there are surely better ways of making friends or soliciting development aid than by sending them a blank check.

Costs of Tax Treaties

There are two main costs associated with tax treaties (Hearson and Kangave 2016): first, the deliberate—although sometimes unexpectedly excessive—cost resulting from the restrictions that the treaty imposes on the developing country's taxing rights; second, the unintended cost resulting from the abuse of certain tax

---

[27] In this context, "redundant" refers to the offering of a tax incentive to an investor who, by his own admitting, would have invested even in the absence of the incentive.

[28] See UNIDO (2011) for the investor survey, and IMF, OECD, WB, and UN (2015) for a more general assessment of the use of tax incentives for investment in low-income countries.

[29] Canada, for instance, eliminated withholding tax on interest paid or credited to arm's length nonresidents, effective January 1, 2008, in an effort to provide increased access to foreign capital for Canadian businesses.

[30] As of July 2018.

treaty provisions through tax-planning schemes, mostly in the form of treaty shopping.

As large capital importers, developing countries will bear direct costs when tax treaty provisions restrict source-country taxation. The most important provisions in this regard are generally those related to the taxation of business profits (Articles 5 and 7), services (Articles 5 and 12A of the 2017 UN Model), withholding taxes on dividends, interest and royalties (Articles 10, 11 and 12, respectively), and capital gains (Article 13).[31] The revenue forgone as a result of these provisions can be large, albeit challenging to quantify due to data-availability constraints.

It is possible to obtain rough estimates of source countries' revenue losses that originate from lower withholding taxes on dividend and interest payments. This can be done using a simple revenue forgone approach,[32] along with some assumptions that are inevitable due to the lack of available data. Table 8.2 illustrates results from a select set of tax treaties for 2016. The methodology is a simple one that relies on IMF Coordinated Direct Investment Survey (CDIS) bilateral foreign direct investment positions, treaty and statutory withholding tax rates, and assumed returns on equity and debt investments.[33] It is thus estimated in Table 8.2 that Mongolia may lose as much as 0.2 percent of its GDP in tax revenues annually due to low withholding taxes in its treaty with Canada.[34]

Other studies have also used similar approaches to quantify revenue forgone due to dividend and interest withholding tax provisions in tax treaties, including in Janský and Šedivý (2018)[35] and McGauran (2013). The latter study focuses on

---

[31] These provisions are only referenced here, as they are discussed in greater detail in the following section.

[32] The revenue forgone approach is an ex-post estimation that measures the reduction in tax revenue that is caused by the introduction of a tax preference, assuming no changes in taxpayers' behaviors. This is the most popular method for calculating tax expenditures. However, if any increase in investment occurred the revenue forgone would be reduced.

[33] Our methodology assumes a 6 percent yield on equity and 4 percent yield on debt, which we view as being relatively conservative. Ratios generated from interacting IMF balance of payment (flows of dividend and interest payments) and IMF CDIS (stock of equity and debt foreign direct investment) data in relation to investments in developing countries suggest an average expected yield on foreign direct investment equity of 10 percent and an expected yield on foreign direct investment debt of 4.4 percent.

[34] It should be kept in mind that the revenue forgone as a result of low withholding tax rates in a tax treaty is a function of the domestic withholding tax rates, which set up a benchmark against which treaty rates are to be assessed. Given that the underlying objective here is to give an appreciation of the possible costs of tax treaties, the authors have purposely not included countries where treaty rates are near or above domestic statutory rates. An unknown portion of the revenue forgone estimated here is likely attributable to indirect costs such as treaty shopping.

[35] Janský and Šedivý (2018) estimate dividend and interest payments on a bilateral level by multiplying balance of payment flows by the share of a given country's foreign direct investment to total foreign direct investment (not distinguishing equity from debt foreign direct investment). They find the greatest potential aggregate revenue loss (that is, across all estimated treaties) to be about 0.2 percent of GDP for Mongolia and the Philippines. Of the country pairs presented in Table 8.1,

TABLE 8.2.

Dividend and Interest Withholding Tax: Estimated Revenue Forgone of Select Tax Treaties

	Statutory Rates		Treaty Rates		Foreign Direct Investment Stock (Source)		Revenue Forgone (est.)
	Dividends	Interest	Dividends	Interest	Debt	Equity	(% of GDP)
Uganda / Netherlands	15%	15%	0%	10%	3,722	177	**0.1%**
Mozambique / Mauritius	20%	20%	8%	8%	1,402	1,001	**0.1%**
Mongolia / Canada	20%	20%	5%	10%	733	3,115	**0.2%**
Republic of Congo / France	15%	20%	15%	0%	2,902	1,694	**0.2%**

Sources: IMF CDIS, World Economic Outlook, and International Bureau of Fiscal Documentation.[1]
Note: Foreign direct investment in US$ in millions. Dividend rate is for qualified dividends. Assumed yield of 6 percent on equity and 4 percent on debt.

---

[1] IMF Coordinated Direct Investment Survey (CDIS), http://data.imf.org/?sk=40313609-F037-48C1-84B1-E1F1CE54D6D5 &sId=1482331048410.

tax treaties concluded by the Netherlands and finds revenue losses as high as 0.1 percent of GDP for treaties between the Netherlands and both Kazakhstan and Venezuela. While different methodologies will inevitably yield different outcomes, these estimates appear quite significant considering that McGuaran's study reflects only two provisions in tax treaties and already accounts for millions in dollars of revenue forgone.

Indirect costs of tax treaties are even more opaque than their direct costs. Indirect costs essentially refer to treaty shopping, which are arrangements by which investors residing in third states attempt to avail themselves of favorable tax provisions negotiated between two other contracting states by setting in one of those states an intermediary (or conduit) structure through which investment in the other contracting state will be channeled (see following discussion).

Anecdotal evidence tends to support the claim that treaty shopping has historically been a major problem worldwide. To address the risks associated with a wide treaty network with heterogenous tax provisions, the United States has for many decades insisted on including limitations on benefits provisions in its tax treaties. More recently, broad international consensus over the high prevalence of treaty

---

only the Mongolia–Canada treaty can be estimated using Janský and Šedivý's methodology, given data requirements and availability. We are unable to reconstruct Janský and Šedivý's estimate for the Mongolia–Canada treaty, as the value of Canadian foreign direct investment stock for 2015, which we obtain from the IMF CDIS ($7,733 million), differs significantly from that used by Janský and Šedivý ($403 million). Consequently, this leads to our estimate being much larger.

shopping and the important risks this poses to government revenue has led the G20 and OECD to agree on a so-called minimum standard to address treaty abuse as part of the BEPS Project.[36] Some anecdotal evidence may also be inferred from bilateral foreign direct investment data patterns, which can be suggestive of strong linkages between favorable tax treaties and inward foreign direct investment into developing countries.[37] A few examples will serve to illustrate this point:[38]

- At the end of 2016, about 20 percent (or $73.6 billion) of all inward foreign direct investment stocks into India came from—or transited through— Mauritius. The India–Mauritius treaty, which was signed in 1982, provides an exemption from source-country capital gains.[39]

- The United Arab Emirates holds the largest stock of foreign direct investment into Mozambique at just over $9 billion, which accounts for about a quarter of the country's total inward foreign direct investment. The UAE–Mozambique treaty has several favorable provisions, including 0 percent withholding tax on interest and dividends and a 5 percent withholding tax on royalties.

- About 45 percent of all inward investment into Uganda originates from—or transits through—the Netherlands, with a dollar value estimated at just under $4 billion. As previously noted, the Uganda–Netherlands treaty (which is currently under renegotiation) conveniently offers investors a 0 percent withholding tax on qualified dividends.

There are many other such examples, although the presence of a tax treaty does not always appear to be a necessary condition for investors to channel investments in developing countries through conduit countries.[40]

Empirical evidence also tends to support the importance of treaty shopping (see the sixth section) and its effect on foreign direct investment flows. For example, Beer and Loeprick (2018) find that treaty shopping drives nominal investment flows into sub-Saharan Africa and that revenue losses for countries having concluded a treaty with at least one investment hub are on average 15 percent of corporate income tax revenues. Other studies, including those of Petkova, Stasio, and Zagler (2018); Weichenrieder and Mintz (2008); and Weyzig (2013), also find evidence suggesting that treaty conclusion with conduit countries leads to a rerouting of investment (that is, treaty shopping).

---

[36] Treaty shopping and the minimum standards agreed to under the BEPS project to address this issue are discussed in the sixth section, "Treaty Shopping."

[37] Similar patterns are also observed across developed countries. For instance, Luxembourg, the Netherlands, and Switzerland collectively account for over 43 percent of total non-US foreign direct investment into Canada in 2017.

[38] Foreign direct investment statistics referenced here are drawn from the IMF CDIS.

[39] A recent protocol to the India–Mauritius Treaty was announced on May 10, 2016. The protocol provides for the phasing out of the capital gains tax exemption from 2017 to 2019, with grandfathering for shares acquired before April 1, 2017.

[40] For example, there is over $3.3 billion in investment into the Democratic Republic of Congo (DRC) originating from Mauritius, and there is no tax treaty between the DRC and Mauritius.

Other costs should not be neglected. This includes the time spent on preparing for and negotiating tax treaties, which inevitably entails an opportunity cost that is particularly pronounced in the context of tax administrations with limited capacities or resources (as is most often the case in developing countries). Once in force, treaties then entail administrative costs, including for the processing of withholding tax refund claims and for the monitoring of the adequacy of treaty provisions in light of changes to domestic legislation. Yet another cost is the loss of flexibility within the tax policy framework—tax treaties tend to be in effect for a long period of time and may be difficult to renegotiate.

KEY ALLOCATIVE PROVISIONS

Four provisions play a key role in determining the extent to which source countries may forfeit taxing rights under a tax treaty. These provisions relate to permanent establishments, withholding taxes, service fees, and capital gains.

Taxation of Business Income and Permanent Establishments

In the current international tax architecture, income from business activities is typically taxable in the jurisdiction in which these activities take place. However, where these business activities are undertaken by a nonresident entity, source-based taxation is usually limited to situations in which the business activities exceed a qualitative threshold referred to as a permanent establishment. The implementation of this concept in domestic legislation is often based on administrative ease: it is hard for tax administrations to identify and determine taxable profit for each separate business transaction of a nonresident. For instance, it would be quite impractical for a country to assert tax jurisdiction over a portion of the business profits of nonresidents' entities that merely export into its territory. Having a de minimis threshold allows the tax administration to forgo incidental transactions and concentrate on the more important taxpayers.

The notion of permanent establishment is one of the most important issues in treaty-based international fiscal law. The permanent establishment concept determines both the tax jurisdiction (or "right to tax") and the tax base for business profits of a nonresident enterprise (Reimer 2015). It was historically founded on the basis that the nonresident needed sufficient physical presence and engagement in core activities in the source state to justify the allocation of taxation rights to the source state (Skaar 1991). It essentially contemplated that a nonresident entity needed labor or physical capital to undertake production, distribution, or retail operations in the source country to trigger source-country rights to tax business profits, and that mere exports would in turn not give rise to source-country taxing rights.

Article 5(1) of the 2017 OECD and UN Models provides for a qualitative definition of a permanent establishment. The general principle of a permanent establishment is "a fixed place of business through which the business of an enterprise is wholly or partly carried on." "Fixed" refers to a link between the place of business and a specific geographical point, as well as a degree of permanence with respect to time. In other words, to be fixed, the activities need to be at a given place for a sufficient amount of time. A "place of business" refers to some facilities used by an enterprise for carrying out its business, and the premises must be at the disposal of the enterprise (either owned or rented). Finally, the "business of the enterprise" must be carried on wholly or partly at the fixed place. Paragraph 2 of Article 5 of the OECD and UN Models contains an illustrative list of what should be considered beyond doubt as constituting a permanent establishment, while paragraph 4 lists a number of cases that should not be considered permanent establishments even if they are indeed carried out through a fixed place of business.[41]

In addition, most tax treaties contain special rules with respect to construction sites. Under those treaties, a building site or construction or installation project constitutes a permanent establishment only if a given project lasts more than a specified length of time, which is typically from 3 months to 12 months (Table 8.3). The 2017 OECD Model suggests a period of more than 12 months, whereas the 2017 UN Model chooses a period of 6 months. The latter also includes all the related supervisory activities in determining whether the minimum period has been met.

Beginning with its 2011 revision, the UN Model has also contained a special rule regarding the provision of services. If an enterprise, through its employees or other personnel engaged by it, continues to furnish services within a contracting state for more than 183 days in any 12-month period, that enterprise is deemed to have a permanent establishment in that state. The issue is taken up in the following subsection ("Technical Services") as part of a broader discussion on the taxation of cross-border services.

In addition, both models provide that the activities of a dependent agent may give rise to a permanent establishment for the principal. Specifically, where a person acts on behalf of an enterprise and habitually concludes contracts, or plays the principal role leading to the conclusion of contracts that are routinely concluded without material modification by the enterprises, that enterprise will be deemed to have a permanent establishment in the country in which this person operates if the contracts are (1) in the name of the enterprise; (2) for the transfer of the ownership of, or right to use, property; or (3) for the provision of services.[42] Brokers, general

---

[41] This list includes business activities that are deemed not to constitute a permanent establishment given that they share the common feature of being merely preparatory or auxiliary activities in nature. A key difference between the OECD and UN Models is that the UN does not consider delivery services as being preparatory or auxiliary in nature, whereas the OECD Model does characterize such activities as such (meaning that they are deemed to give rise to a permanent establishment even in the presence of a fixed place of business under paragraph 5(1)).

[42] It should be noted that the UN Model's agency permanent establishment test is somewhat broader in scope than the OECD's. Indeed, Article 5 of the UN Model includes a subparagraph (b) providing that a foreign enterprise will be deemed to have a permanent establishment if a person habitually maintains a stock of goods or merchandise from which it regularly delivers goods or merchandise on

TABLE 8.3.

Construction Permanent Establishment Thresholds in Tax Treaties

	Two Non-OECD	OECD and Non-OECD	Two OECD
No threshold	1	1	0
3 months	26	13	0
4 months	2	1	0
5 months	1	1	0
6 months	391	337	57
7 months	1	0	0
8 months	7	2	0
9 months	131	130	14
10 months	0	1	1
12 months	190	328	150
15 months	0	1	0
18 months	9	5	0
24 months	1	0	2

Source: IMF staff based on Wijnen and De Goede (2014).
Note: Covers 1,811 tax treaties concluded between April 1997 and January 2013.

commission agents, and other independent agents are explicitly excluded from becoming a permanent establishment if such persons are acting in the ordinary course of their business.[43] The agency–permanent establishment concept was justifiably tightened as part of the BEPS Project; the previous agency–permanent establishment definition required that the agent have "authority to conclude contracts in the name of the enterprise," which resulted in the common use of commissionaire arrangements[44] and other tax-planning techniques to avoid meeting this test. Although these structures have been subject to significant litigation by various tax authorities, the tax administrations' arguments have been rejected in most cases. Another outcome from the BEPS Project was the tightening of the definition of an independent agent, which no longer includes independent agents that exclusively or almost exclusively act on behalf of one or more enterprises to which they are closely related. However, these modifications may be insufficient: as long as the foreign enterprise can perform functions beyond the mere rubber-stamping of contracts concluded by an agent (that is, to ensure that contracts are not "routinely adopted without material modification"), the enterprise may still be in a position to avoid having a permanent establishment.

---

behalf of the enterprise, notwithstanding whether the person habitually concludes contracts or plays the principal role leading to the conclusion of such contracts.

[43] Article 5(6) of the 2017 OECD Model and Article 5(7) of the 2017 UN Model.

[44] A commissionaire arrangement may be loosely defined as an arrangement through which a person sells products in a country in his own name but on behalf of a foreign enterprise that is the owner of these products. Through such an arrangement, a foreign enterprise sells its products in that country without technically having a permanent establishment to which such sales may be attributed and without, therefore, being taxable in that country on the profits derived from such sales. Since the person that concludes the sales does not own the products that it sells, that person cannot be taxed on the profits derived from such sales and may only be taxed on the remuneration that it receives for its services (usually a commission). See OECD (2015).

Once a country recognizes a permanent establishment of a foreign enterprise within its jurisdiction, profits of that enterprise must be allocated to the permanent establishment. This raises practical difficulties, as both the foreign enterprise and permanent establishment are the same legal entity. The basic profit allocation rule provided for under Article 7 is that profits attributable to the permanent establishment are those that it would be expected to make "if it were a separate and independent enterprise engaged in the same or similar activities under the same or similar conditions, taking into account the functions performed, assets used and risks assumed by the enterprise through the [permanent establishment] and through the other parts of the enterprise."[45] This brings in the full transfer pricing issues that are discussed in Chapter 5. In addition, the 2017 UN Model explicitly notes that certain payments made by the permanent establishment to its headquarters "by way of royalties, fees or other similar payments in return for the use of patents or other rights, or by way of commission, for specific services performed or for management, or, except for a banking enterprise, by way of interest on moneys lent to the permanent establishment" shall not be allowed as deductible expenses.[46] In other words, internal charging to the permanent establishment by the headquarters in this form is not taken at face value and is rather subjected to the general arm's length test described earlier. The omission of rental fees from this list is enigmatic, as it may open the door to tax planning. Executive and general administrative expenses—whether made in the permanent establishment country or elsewhere—are for their part explicitly allowed as tax deductions. A final note on allocation is that, unlike the OECD Model, the UN Model provides that income from sales and other business undertaken by the nonresident enterprise in the source country that are similar or identical to the activities of the permanent establishment can be attributed to the permanent establishment. This so-called limited force-of-attraction rule is contained in subparagraphs 7(1)(b) and (c), which developing countries should seek to include in their tax treaties. While the limited force-of-attraction rule may be successful in preventing some form of abusive tax-planning schemes, it is by no means bulletproof. For instance, it does not capture the activities of all related nonresident entities that are part of the group, which could be added to a force-of-attraction rule to increase its effectiveness.

The overall relevance and applicability of the permanent establishment threshold as currently formulated has clearly reached its limits. While there appears to be growing consensus toward this conclusion, including as part of the ongoing debate regarding the taxation of the digital economy, efforts to date have for the most part focused on incremental changes to the permanent establishment concept, as illustrated, for example, by the outcomes under Action 7 of the BEPS Project (see OECD 2015). Fundamental reforms, such as the abandonment of the permanent establishment concept in favor of formulary apportionment, could address the issue but raise challenges on their own, including questions regarding

---

[45] Article 7(2) of the 2017 OECD Model.

[46] Article 7(3) of the 2017 UN Model.

international coordination, political feasibility, and transition to this new architecture of the international tax system.

There may, however, be a more pragmatic and shorter-term solution to addressing permanent establishment–related issues: the use of a quantitative threshold as a backstop deeming rule. If the underlying motivation for the permanent establishment threshold is to require that there be sufficient economic nexus between the activities of a multinational enterprise and a given source country to allow this country to tax part of the multinational enterprise's profits, there appears to be little better proxy to measuring that economic integration than a simple—and objective—turnover-based test in which nonresidents' enterprises whose sales exceed a given threshold would be deemed to have a permanent establishment, notwithstanding the fact that it may not operate through a fixed place of business.

Withholding Taxes

Withholding taxes are final taxes levied at source on gross payments to nonresidents.[47] They hence matter greatly to capital-importing countries. It is helpful to divide the discussion on withholding taxes between withholding on deductible expenses and withholding on dividends, as they raise very different conceptual challenges.

Tax treaties typically provide limits on source-country withholding on two types of deductible expenses: interest payments (Article 11) and royalties (Article 12).[48] There are essentially two conflicting policy objectives that can influence policymakers' determination of what constitutes a reasonable or desirable withholding tax rate on these payments:

- On the one hand, developing countries, and capital-importing countries more generally, may want to promote economic development by facilitating access to credit and foreign technologies and know-how, as discussed at length above. This weighs in the favor of adopting low withholding taxes so as to reduce the cost of capital to stimulate investment and encourage the transfer of technologies to support productivity growth.

- On the other hand, the deductible nature of these expenses poses a risk to the integrity of corporate income tax revenues. More than ever, cross-border trade and investment is dominated by multinationals.[49] These commonly use deductible intragroup payments, such as interest charges and royalties, to engage in tax planning with a view to maximizing the after-tax return on their investments. In the context of porous interest limitation rules and weak administrative capacity to safeguard the domestic corporate income tax base

---

[47] Withholding taxes may also be used domestically, for example, as final or nonfinal withholding on employees' wages.

[48] Some treaties also provide for withholding on technical services. This is not taken up here, as it is subject to a separate discussion in the following subsection.

[49] The UNCTAD estimates that 80 percent of trade takes place in value chains linked to multinational enterprises.

against abusive transfer pricing, withholding taxes can serve as an important backstop that reduces—but does not eliminate[50]—intragroup base erosion incentives and hence protects the integrity of corporate income tax revenues.

Policymakers need to carefully consider and balance these two considerations to determine an appropriate nonresident withholding tax policy for interest and royalties. While there is no one-size-fits-all solution, experience from the IMF's technical assistance in tax policy overwhelmingly points to the need for developing countries to better safeguard corporate income tax revenues from international tax avoidance. As such, the retention of meaningful withholding tax rates on interest and royalties would in most cases be expected to outweigh any possible benefits stemming from the adoption of low withholding tax rates (Table 8.4 offers summary statistics on withholding taxes in sub-Saharan Africa). This sharply contrasts with the OECD Model's suggestion to rely on a 0 percent withholding tax rate for royalties.[51]

While the preceding discussion has focused on the withholding tax rate, another important consideration relates to the definition of the payments to be covered by these provisions. Developing countries should generally aim to have as broad a scope as possible in order to maximize source-country taxing rights,[52] simplify administration, and limit avoidance opportunities.[53]

Source-country withholding tax limitations on dividends, as provided for under Article 10, raise a different set of considerations. In theory, dividends are distributions of a company's after-tax profits to its shareholders. As the distributing company has in theory already paid corporate income tax on the underlying profits, any additional taxation in the form of a withholding tax on dividends paid to its nonresident parent typically leads to economic double taxation. Further, the total tax burden faced by the multinational group will then depend on its organizational structure (that is, how many tiers it has), such that the tax system loses some of its desired neutrality. From this perspective, it would appear sensible for policymakers to consider adopting low (or no) withholding taxes on intracompany cross-border dividend distributions. Recognizing that the risk of double (or multiple) taxation is more significant in the context of closely held

---

[50] As the corporate income tax rate will typically exceed the withholding tax rate by multiple percentage points, base-erosion incentives will not be completely eliminated even if a relatively high withholding tax is retained. This outcome is nonetheless justifiable on the basis that the withholding tax acts as a tax on the nonresident's gross income, without regard to any related expenses.

[51] The OECD Model suggest a more reasonable rate for interest (10 percent). However, this rate needs to be assessed in the context of OECD countries' interest-stripping limitations, which are typically much more robust than those observed in developing countries, and of OECD countries' statutory corporate income tax rates, which are generally lower than those used by low-income countries.

[52] For instance, the UN Model Tax Treaty's definition of royalties is broader than that in the OECD Model Tax Treaty, and includes payments related to broadcasting and equipment rental.

[53] Nonresidents earning income not covered under Articles 11 and 12 will be assessed against the standard permanent establishment threshold in Article 5 to determine their taxable status in the source country.

TABLE 8.4.

Summary Statistics on Withholding Taxes in Sub-Saharan Africa
(Percent)

	Interest	Royalties	Dividends	Portfolio Dividends
Average Statutory	15	16	11	13
Average Treaty Withholding Tax	9	9	8	11
Maximum Treaty Withholding Tax	25	20	25	25
Minimum Treaty Withholding Tax	0	0	0	0
Share of Countries with at Least One Treaty with 0% Withholding Tax	36%	36%	39%	31%
Share of countries with at least one treaty with 5% WHT or less	47	58	61	47

Source: IMF staff using IBFD data.
Note: Includes 38 sub-Saharan Africa countries.

entities operating as part of a multinational group, both the UN and OECD Models contemplate the use of a lower withholding tax for direct dividends than for portfolio dividends. [54]

In practice, however, it is far from given that the distributing company will have fully paid corporate income tax in the developing country in which it is operating. For one, profit manipulation—which can be attributed to either or both standard tax planning and aggressive tax avoidance—may drive a wedge between "true" and "reported" taxable income,[55] with the former being unknown and hardly detectable by the tax authorities. This would consequently argue in favor of a higher withholding rate, including for direct dividends, given that the risks for profit shifting are higher in the case of subsidiaries of multinationals.[56]

Developing countries will once again need to consider and balance these considerations. While country-specific circumstances will to a large extent dictate what is deemed to be a reasonable dividend withholding tax policy, a zero rate should in most cases be avoided. It will also be important to assess whether the conceptual appeal of distinguishing between direct and portfolio dividends

---

[54] The 2017 OECD Model Tax Treaty proposes 5 percent for direct dividends and 15 percent for portfolio dividends, with a 25 percent ownership test defining the nature of these dividends. The UN Model also contemplates the use of a dual rate at a 25 percent threshold but does not propose specific rates.

[55] Although such conflicts should be primarily solved by domestic legislation, treaties might be used as an additional line of defense.

[56] Another possible justification for using a higher withholding tax rate would be to make domestic reinvestment of retained earnings domestically more attractive compared to repatriating the income overseas. However, such high withholding taxes would likely be factored in by multinational enterprises in making their investment decisions. For instance, it could either entice taxpayers into using tax-planning arrangements (for example, transfer pricing, service fees, interest payments, and so forth) to circumvent the withholding or discourage investment altogether.

warrants the additional administrative cost this dual approach would create. If a dual-rate approach is indeed retained, the minimum 365-day holding period introduced in the updated 2017 UN and OECD Models should in all cases be included to avoid tax avoidance opportunities.

Technical Services

Intragroup cross-border services pose important profit-shifting risks for developing countries. The high concentration of economic activity arising from subsidiaries of multinationals, coupled with often outdated anti-abuse provisions and difficulties in assessing arm's length prices, make developing countries particularly vulnerable to the erosion of the domestic corporate income tax base through deductible charges for intragroup services.[57] This is an issue that has not been addressed holistically as part of the G20/OECD BEPS Project, but was rather touched upon indirectly under various action items including Action 1 (Digital Economy), Action 5 (Permanent Establishment), and Action 10 (Transfer Pricing—Other High-Risk Transactions).

However, the predominant approach to dealing with services under tax treaties is to simply ignore the specific challenges that these activities pose vis-à-vis the standard permanent establishment concept. This means that contracting states provide identical treatment for business income earned either through the furnishing of services or through the sale of goods. This approach is promoted by the OECD Model, whose commentary argues that services should generally be treated the same way as other business activities with the same permanent establishment threshold test determining source-country taxing rights.[58]

Such a view seems to derive either from an archaic view of international commerce or from an understanding that capital exporters' best interests lie in minimizing source-country taxation. Many have recognized that the permanent establishment concept is ill suited to address the challenges raised by the service industry, particularly in the case of developing countries. Nowadays, in large part thanks to advances in information and communication technologies, it is much easier for nonresident service providers to fully participate in the economic life of a source country without having a physical presence akin to production, distribution, or retail facilities, as would be the case for the trading of goods.

Following the UN Model, some countries are attempting to bridge this gap by including a permanent establishment test that is specific to services. The so-called

---

[57] The motive for multinationals to set up service centers may in some cases predominantly arise out of efficiency gains derived from economies of scale. Nonetheless, a secondary motivation, or at least an ancillary benefit, of service centers is that they offer a convenient mechanism for conducting tax optimization strategies. Typically, these services will fall into the broad categories of human resources, finance, information technology, legal, and marketing support.

[58] Other than international transportation and government services, which are dealt with in Articles 8 and 17, respectively. See paragraph 132 of the commentary to Article 5 in the 2017 OECD Model Tax Treaty.

"service permanent establishment" provision is found under Article 5(3)(b) and provides that nonresident service providers may be deemed to have a permanent establishment even in the absence of a fixed place of business under Article 5(1). More specifically, the service permanent establishment provision triggers a deemed permanent establishment where the nonresident service provider is physically present in the source country to provide services for a sufficient amount of time. Article 5(3)(b) of the 2017 UN Model defines a permanent establishment as including "[t]he furnishing of services, including consultancy services, by an enterprise through employees or other personnel engaged by the enterprise for such purpose, but only if activities of that nature continue within a Contracting State for a period or periods aggregating more than 183 days in any 12-month period commencing or ending in the fiscal year concerned."

The OECD Model does not suggest the use of a service permanent establishment clause; however, its commentary has provided elective wording for such a provision since 2008.[59] The OECD's elective service permanent establishment provision contemplates two alternative tests: the first is similar to the UN provision but would require that the 183-day threshold be met in respect of the "same or for connected projects,"[60] while the second requires that more than 50 percent of the nonresident's active business income be derived from services performed in the source country and that services be performed in the source country through an individual who is present for more than 183 days. As one can appreciate, the OECD's elective service permanent establishment provisions place a higher threshold for the triggering of a deemed service permanent establishment as compared to the UN's provision.

Of the 1,811 tax treaties concluded between 1997 and 2013 that were analyzed by Arnold (2014), 42 percent contained a service permanent establishment provision. Unsurprisingly, this provision was most prevalent in treaties between two non-OECD countries (58 percent), and least prevalent in countries between two OECD countries (17 percent).

While service permanent establishment provisions attempt to address specific problems related to the application of the standard permanent establishment test to service providers, several factors limit their practical usefulness:

- Most treaties rely on the UN's previous service permanent establishment language, which applies the threshold on a project-by-project basis. This creates important administrative implications for developing countries that may be challenged in detecting and addressing avoidance schemes aimed at circumventing the test.[61]

---

[59] See paragraph 144 of Article 5 of the 2017 OECD Model Tax Treaty.

[60] This language was also used in previous UN Model Tax Treaties (up to 2011 inclusively).

[61] Including, most notably, multinationals' fragmentation of intragroup activities.

Figure 8.9. Frequency of Time Thresholds for Service Permanent Establishment Provisions
(In months)

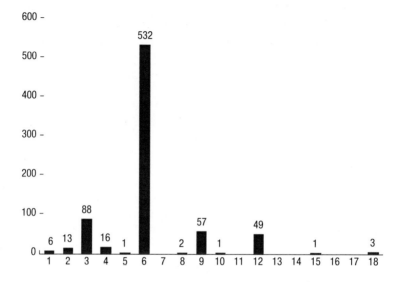

Source: Arnold (2014).

- As made clear by the OECD Model[62] and, although less explicitly, by the UN Model,[63] the threshold applies only in respect of "working days," which considerably narrows the application of the provision. As illustrated in Figure 8.9, the six-month test is the most common threshold.

- While this may appear prima facie as setting a half-year test, a nonresident's presence extends from January 1 well into September if no services are being performed during weekends (as they are not working days). The working day concept is unique to the service permanent establishment provision and is not used for other duration-based tests such as the construction permanent establishment, independent personal services, or dependent personal services.[64,]

---

[62] See paragraph 163 of the commentary to Article 5 of the 2017 OECD Model Tax Treaty.

[63] See paragraph 12 of the commentary to Article 5 of the 2017 UN Model Tax Treaty.

[64] The construction permanent establishment provision relies on the length of the project from start to finish, while the independent personal services provision under Article 14 of the UN model uses a presence test. The dependent personal services or income from employment provisions under Article 15 also contemplate a presence test.

An interesting approach targeted at higher-risk transactions that conveniently circumvent the limitations posed by the application of a working-day-based test is that used by India in its treaties with Switzerland and Australia, in which the time threshold is made much shorter in the case of related-party services.

- A related issue concerns the difficulties in administering a working-day-based threshold, as it is more challenging to monitor working days than it is to monitor presence days since the latter conveniently leaves behind immigration documentation.

- Finally—and perhaps more fundamentally—it is not at all clear that a working day test (or a duration test more generally) is a good proxy for assessing the degree of economic integration between a nonresident service provider and the economic life of the source country. Services may lead to both high profits for the nonresident enterprise and significant base-eroding corporate income tax deductions in the source country without necessitating significant or extended physical presence. Although not seen in practice, other thresholds based on the economic activity generated by the nonresident (as could be measured by turnover, for example), would appear to offer a much better proxy of the extent of the enterprise's economic integration with the source country.

The insufficiencies of service permanent establishment provisions in meaningfully addressing the challenges posed by cross-border services has motivated a push toward finding alternatives, primarily in the form of withholding.[65] Such a provision is found under the domestic legislation of several countries but has yet to translate broadly into tax treaties. According to Wijnen, de Goede, and Alessi (2012), only 134 of some 1,600 bilateral tax treaties concluded in the period 1997–2011 contained an autonomous withholding tax provision dealing with managerial, technical, and consulting services. The low prevalence of "service fee" withholding in tax treaties can in part be attributed to the historical absence of such provisions from both the OECD and UN Models. That is, until recently.

The UN Committee of Experts has been working since 2008 on provisions dealing with the taxation of services, although work picked up in 2011 when the committee decided to make the taxation of services fees a priority. In 2013 the committee formally endorsed the addition of a new article to the UN Model to deal with fees for technical services, and a majority supported proposing a broad provision applicable to services performed inside and outside the source country, without a threshold for source-country taxation and taxation on a gross basis.[66] This new provision is now included as Article 12A of the 2017 UN Model. The UN's decision to promote the use of final withholding at source on gross payments in relation to managerial, technical, and consultancy services[67] arguably constitutes the most

---

[65] Other policy responses include the institution of caps on the deductibility of service payments (for example, to a specified percentage of turnover).

[66] The two other options contemplated were as follows: (1) to adopt a provision applicable only to services rendered in the source country with no threshold and taxation on a gross basis at a limited rate; or (2) to adopt a narrow provision restricted to services performed in the source country with a time threshold for source-country tax and taxation on a net basis.

[67] These terms are not defined under Article 12A and will hence take the meaning attributed under the domestic law of contracting states.

substantive divergence between the OECD and UN Models to date and is hence telling of the extent to which it poses specific problems for developing countries.

As previously discussed, even in the presence of a service permanent establishment clause, Article 5 does not offer a sufficiently robust solution to source-country taxation of services. The digitalization of the economy means that physical presence is not always needed and that more and more services can be "exported" without any sort (or at least very limited) physical presence (this also offers scope for profit-sifting within a multinational group). Further, and perhaps more fundamentally, developing countries are considerably challenged to assess the presence and proper registration of permanent establishments, the ensuing challenge of determining a proper allocation of profits based on the assets used, risks assumed, and functions performed where such permanent establishments are found to exist, and the application of robust arm's length principle–based transfer pricing legislation to assess the market value of intragroup services if such permanent establishments are not found to exist. The service fee provision is precisely aimed at addressing developing countries' challenges in adequately protecting their domestic tax bases from profit shifting by multinationals through intragroup service charges and can thus be viewed as an anti-avoidance provision.

Service fee provisions may be desirable for developing countries. The key advantage of such provisions is that they conveniently transform the traditional determination of whether a nonresident service provider will or will not be liable for source-country taxation based on whether a permanent establishment is found to exist into a determination of whether the nonresident will pay tax on a net or gross basis.[68] Importantly, the resident will consequently inevitably be paying taxes in the source country. Opportunities for arbitrage between gross and net taxation may still exist, however, and will depend on the calibration of the withholding tax rate to the corporate income tax rate, bearing in mind companies' profit margin and ability to minimize this margin by manipulating the allocation of income and expenses to the permanent establishment (Box 8.2). Hence, service fee provisions can be useful to mitigate risks related to source-country taxation of nonresident service providers but are not a panacea.

Although the desirability of service fee provisions for low-capacity developing countries is strong,[69] there is considerable opposition. OECD countries—which overwhelmingly take the role of residence countries in their economic relations with developing countries—are reluctant to accept service fee withholding as an acceptable solution to the problem. Some refuse to acknowledge that services constitute a specific challenge that justifies the use of a final withholding at source, which they argue as being an excessively blunt instrument. Turnover taxes provide an imperfect assessment of one's ability to pay, as they disregard the costs

---

[68] It is thus conceptually similar to domestic tax provisions under which companies pay tax on a net basis under the corporate income tax, but small traders are, for administrative and compliance purposes, often rather charged tax on a presumptive basis as a percentage of their turnover.

[69] That said, the question of the incidence of the withholding tax on technical services remains an open debate that extends beyond the scope of this chapter.

Box 8.2. Stylized Illustration of Service Permanent Establishment and Service Fee Provisions

The table below depicts the possible application of, and interaction between, the service permanent establishment and service fee provisions. The table illustrates how the overall tax burden varies for different non-resident service providers located in Country X and performing services in Country Z. As can be seen, the effective tax rate remains constant at 30% (the assumed corporate income tax rate) under profit-based taxation in the case of a permanent establishment, but will vary greatly for service fee withholdings depending on the service provider's profit margin, since the tax is levied on turnover and not profits.

	Medium Profit Margin		Low Profit Margin		High Profit Margin	
	Service Fee	PE	Service Fee	PE	Service Fee	PE
Residency	Country X	Country X	Country X	Country X	Country X	Country X
Physical presence in Country Z	Intermittent	Sustained	Intermittent	Sustained	Intermittent	Sustained
PE tax rate	n/a	30%	n/a	30%	n/a	30%
Withholding rate	15%	n/a	15%	n/a	15%	n/a
Income from services in Country Z	$100	$100	$100	$100	$100	$100
Deductible expenses	($50)	($50)	($70)	($70)	($30)	($30)
Pre-tax profits	$50	$50	$30	$30	$70	$70
Tax payable	$15	$15	$15	$9	$15	$21
Effective tax rate	30%	30%	50%	30%	21%	30%

involved in earning the income. Even if the withholding tax rate is carefully calibrated and provides for a sensible outcome on the aggregate, it will inevitably provide for a very heterogenous treatment of different taxpayers whose profit margins are likely to vary considerably across sectors and through time. From this perspective, there is a risk that service fee provisions could in some instances prove punitive, especially if levied at excessive rates.

Service fee provisions also conflict with the view of some countries that services should be taxed where they are provided. By disregarding the location of service provision and instead relying on a sourcing rule that relies on the fact that there is a tax-resident payor or permanent establishment (or fixed base) that bears the fees,[70] the UN's service fee provision is thus perceived by some as constituting

---

[70] The sourcing rule is provided by Article 12A(6) of the 2017 UN Model Tax Treaty.

an overreach of the source country's taxing rights. Another source of discomfort with service fee provisions lies in the fact that it departs from the long-standing principle that nonresidents should exceed a given threshold before being taxed by the source country on income earned therein.[71] As far as tax treaties are concerned, service fee provisions may simply be too significant a departure from previous norms.[72] That said, source-country withholding on service fees is simply an extension of the widely accepted practice of applying final withholding at source on dividends, interest, and royalties, which primarily constitute passive investment income but may also constitute income from an active business (for example in the case of banks or investment funds).

The inclusion of a service fee provision in the 2017 UN Model certainly adds legitimacy to the request of developing countries for such provisions in their treaty negotiations. However, at the other end of the spectrum, the OECD Model dismisses altogether the need to provide tailored solutions to address the specific challenges raised by the service industry. Unsurprisingly, developing countries are thus facing an uphill battle when attempting to include service permanent establishment and, more meaningfully, service fee provisions in their tax treaty network. In the meantime, however, developing countries should review their domestic legislation and consider what additional safeguards—including service fee provisions—are needed to deal with the risks posed by cross-border intragroup services. In most cases, the introduction of withholding on service fees at a moderate rate would seem desirable for developing countries.

Capital Gains

In general, capital gains are taxable in the country in which the seller (the recipient of the proceeds) is resident. There are some exceptions to this general rule. The taxing rights of business assets belonging to a permanent establishment are given to the country in which the enterprise holds a permanent establishment. In the case of immovable property, the country in which this immovable property is situated is given unconstrained taxing rights over the capital gain under Article 13(1) of both the OECD and UN Models. Further, the taxing right on capital gains from the alienation of ships or aircrafts used in international transportation typically remains in the country in which the place of effective management of the enterprise is located. Finally, a special allocation rule also applies to shares.

Capital gains on shares are generally taxable only in the country in which the shareholder is a resident unless targeted tests are included in the tax treaty. As provided for in Article 13(5) of the 2017 UN Model, one of those tests relates to capital gains on substantial shareholdings, which may be taxed in the country in

---

[71] This principle is embodied in Articles 5 and 7, which contemplate that that nonresident enterprises should have sufficient economic nexus in the source country for this country to exercise any taxing rights over the business profits earned by this enterprise.

[72] A risk that should not be underestimated is that of precedence—once a country agrees to include service fee provisions, it becomes increasingly challenging to defend against its propagation in the country's treaty network.

which the company that issued the shares is a resident. This reflects the fact that some countries are of the view that they should be able to tax a gain on the alienation of shares of a company resident in that country whether the alienation occurs within or outside that country, but concede that for administrative reasons that right to tax should be limited to alienations of substantial shareholdings. A substantial shareholding is typically measured by a minimum participation (most often 25 percent of the share value or voting rights) at any time during the 365-day period preceding the alienation of the shares. There seems to be very little take-up of this provision in tax treaties: of the 1,811 treaties concluded between 1997 and 2013 analyzed by Wijnen and De Goede (2014), only 17 percent included this provision. This outcome is somewhat surprising if we consider the potential arbitrage opportunities that may arise from different tax treatment of dividends and capital gains.[73] However, the low take-up may to a great extent be influenced by the omission of this provision from the OECD Model, as well as the provision's somewhat narrow scope (it only applies if the alienator of the share is resident in one of the contracting states).

Article 13(4) of both the 2017 OECD and UN Models contains a provision that is intended to deal with transactions often referred to as offshore indirect transfers. The models state that capital gains on shares "derived by a resident of a Contracting State . . . may be taxed in the other Contracting State if . . . these shares . . . derived more than 50 percent of their value directly or indirectly from immovable property . . . situated in that other State." This provision is especially important for developing countries with substantial natural resources. Taking a mining project as an example, there are in principle two main ways that an interest in this project can be realized. First, a domestic licensee company can sell its interest in tangible and intangible assets (including its interest in the mining license) relating to the mining operations. If the tangible and intangible assets are transferred, the tax consequences apply at the level of the domestic company holding the license, thereby ensuring taxation by the country in which the resources are located. Second, as depicted in Figure 8.10, the direct (Company B) or indirect (parent company) owner of the shares in the domestic licensee company (Company A) can sell the shares it owns, thereby giving the buyer indirect possession of the underlying license. There may be several tiers of companies (sometimes located in low-tax jurisdictions or countries with beneficial tax treaties) between the parent company and the licensee. If the parent company sells its shares in the licensee company (or an intermediary company), the tax consequences apply at the level of the parent company (or the intermediary company), as it may realize a gain (or loss) on its disposal of the shares. This is where Article 13, paragraph 4 of the 2017 OECD and UN Models comes into play; if the shares of this mining company are sold or transferred and more than 50 percent of the underlying value is attributable to the mining license, the source country

---

[73] For example, undistributed income may be held in retained earnings, which increases the fair market value of the shares and may be accessed by the shareholder upon alienation.

Figure 8.10. Illustration of an Offshore Indirect Transfer Structure

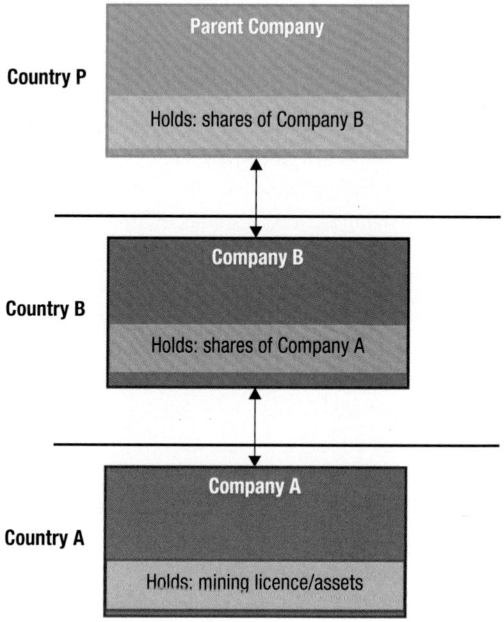

Source: IMF staff.

(here Country A) may tax the gain on the shares. It is of concern, however, that only around 35 percent of all tax treaties worldwide contain this provision, and that it is less likely to be found when one party is a low-income, resource-rich country (Platform for Collaboration on Tax 2017).[74]

While Article 13(4) is effective in ensuring that the source country does not forfeit its right to tax such sales, its ability to effectively tax these gains will also depend on its domestic legislation and specifically the formulation of its source rule. The domestic rule to enable taxation of offshore indirect transfers can be designed in two different ways: (1) by deeming a direct sale by a resident or (2) by taxing the nonresident seller. The first approach seeks to tax the domestic company that directly owns the asset by treating that company as disposing of, and reacquiring, its assets for their market value where a change of control occurs (for example, because of the offshore indirect transfer).[75] The second approach seeks to tax the nonresident seller of the relevant shares via a source of income rule providing that the gain is sourced in the country when the value of the interest disposed of is derived, directly or indirectly,

---

[74] Article 9 of the MLI provides signatories with the option to insert this provision in their covered tax treaties. However, with this not being a minimum standard from the BEPS project, a majority of countries have opted out of it through a reservation.

[75] This approach has, for example, been adopted by Ghana, Nepal, and Tanzania.

principally from immovable property located in that country.[76] The source of income rule may also provides that taxation of offshore indirect transfers will only apply to disposals of substantial interests (for example, where a 10 percent shareholding is met) to exclude from the scope of the rule the disposal of portfolio investments. The rule can also prescribe whether the entire gain will be subject to tax when the value of the indirect interest is less than wholly derived from local immovable property or, alternatively, whether the gain will be subject to tax on a pro rata basis. Both approaches, however, require backup measures to ensure enforcement.

TREATY SHOPPING

By concluding its first tax treaty, a country immediately opens up the option for taxpayers to plan their international activities in such a manner as to take advantage of the treaty benefits. In other words, as the tax treaty applies to residents of either or both contracting states, residents located in third states can avail themselves of treaty benefits by establishing residence in either contracting states (that is, treaty shopping). However, restructuring in itself does not automatically constitute an abuse, as taxpayers are typically allowed to structure their businesses in the most cost-effective manner. It can be abusive, however, if the restructuring lacks economic substance.

Treaty Shopping as Treaty Abuse

It is accepted that treaty shopping is an instrument of international tax planning, either as part of bona fide commercial arrangements or as part of wholly artificial arrangements that are considered to be abusive in nature. However, it is never easy to distinguish between abusive tax avoidance and legitimate tax planning, as it will always be a matter of facts and circumstances. The term "treaty shopping" generally refers to abusive arrangements and encompasses, for example, structures in which an intermediary company acts as a pure conduit with no economic substance whatsoever, completely owned and controlled by a parent company located in a third country and based in a low-tax jurisdiction. Treaty shopping by using conduit arrangements is overwhelmingly viewed as constituting an abuse of tax treaties.[77] In contrast, where the intermediary has some degree of substance in one of the contracting states (for example, it conducts its own trading activities), the structure is generally not perceived as being abusive.

Treaty shopping raises several concerns:

- Treaty shopping breaches the principle of reciprocity of a treaty and alters the balance of concessions attained therein between the two contracting states.[78] It results in the granting of treaty benefits to a resident whose country does not participate in the treaty and will not reciprocate with corresponding benefits.

---

[76] This approach is most commonly used (the tax liability remains with the person that receives the proceeds of the transfer).

[77] See the OECD Model Tax Convention on Income and on Capital (Full Version) 2017, OECD, Paris, Commentary on Article 1.

[78] OECD (1987), paragraph 7, letter (a).

- It has been argued that the conduit country gains revenue power, absent any (substantial) claim to economic allegiance in the case of treaty shopping (Rosenbloom and Langbein 1981). An international tax premise is that the tax base is attributable to the jurisdiction in which it is thought to owe its economic existence. In typical conduit arrangements, such economic substance is lacking for the interposed conduit company. It is a matter of interpretation as to what kind of nexus is required for the duty of economic allegiance to be generated in favor of a jurisdiction. Various countries apply different and highly variable interpretations of what is considered sufficient economic substance.[79]

- Treaty shopping often results in a (undesired and unforeseen) revenue loss for developing countries. Tax treaties are based on a perceived balance of actual and potential income and capital flows between the contracting states. When the benefits of a given treaty are abused, this balance is distorted. As is now commonly recognized, a generous tax treaty with one trading partner runs the risk of becoming a treaty with the world, with the consequence being a potentially large revenue loss for source countries.

Conduit Structures

A conduit company is typically regarded as a wholly owned entity located in a state for the sole or primary purpose of claiming the benefits of the tax treaty in its own name. Such benefits can generally only be denied if the entity used as a conduit is not recognized as a legal person or is not liable to tax in the state of conduit based on its place of effective management or the assets that give rise to dividends, interest, and royalties and does not enjoy freedom over the use of such assets. In practice, however, it is often not easy to verify that such specific circumstances are present.

The essence of conduit arrangements is the reduction of source-based taxation in the source country (State S) by interposing between the payer of the income and the ultimate recipient of such income a company that is entitled to more favorable treatment given the presence of a tax treaty with the source country. These arrangements are only effective if the interposed company is not subject to significant taxation in the country whose treaty network is used (State R). This entails both the residence-based corporate income taxation and the withholding tax on the income paid to the treaty "shopper" (investor). The two main forms of treaty shopping using conduit companies are via direct conduits or stepping-stone conduits (OECD 1987), described in Box 8.3.

---

[79] The Netherlands, for instance, applies very lax substance requirements. The main requirements (regarding the place of residence of at least half of its directors; the place where board decisions are made, the principal bank account is held, and bookkeeping takes place; annual salary cost of at least €100,000; and maintenance of a business address in the Netherlands for at least 24 months) can be achieved by a trust office. The requirement that the company runs an economic risk is covered by Section 8c of the Corporate Income Tax Act 1969, which assumes, for instance, minimum equity for interest conduit companies of the lesser of 1 percent of the outstanding loans or EUR 2 million.

Box 8.3. Direct and Stepping-Stone Conduits

Direct Conduits

A company resident of State R, owned by an investor (resident of State P), receives dividends, interest, or royalties from State S. Under the tax treaty between States R and S, the company claims it is fully or partially exempted from the withholding tax of State S. The investor, resident in State P, is not entitled to the benefit of the treaty between States R and S. The structure has been created with a view to taking advantage of the treaty's benefits, and for this purpose the assets and rights giving rise to the dividends, interest, or royalties are transferred to the company in State R. The income is tax exempt in State R, for example in the case of dividends, by virtue of a parent–subsidiary regime provided for under the domestic laws of State R, or in the treaty between States R and S.

Stepping-Stone Conduits

The basic structure is identical to that of direct conduits, except that a second, related conduit company is necessary to erode the tax base in State R. The company resident of State R is fully subject to tax in that country (for example, on its interest and royalty receivables). It pays high interest, commissions, service fees, and similar expenses to a second, related conduit company set up in State B. These payments are deductible in State R and tax exempt in State B, where the company enjoys a special tax regime.

Source: OECD (1987, 88–89).

Beneficial Ownership

Both the OECD and UN Models have traditionally, but unsuccessfully, attempted to deal with conduit structures by denying access to lower withholding taxes on dividends, interest, and royalties if the recipient is not the so-called beneficial owner. The OECD commentary on Articles 10, 11, and 12 states that an agent or nominee would normally not qualify as a beneficial owner. A reference is also made to the Conduit Companies report (OECD 1987), which concludes that conduit companies are also less likely to be beneficial owners. Neither the OECD nor the UN Model includes a definition of beneficial owner. Undefined terms are typically interpreted according to the domestic law of the state applying the bilateral tax treaty, unless the context requires otherwise (OECD 1987). Two issues may, however, support a more international meaning: (1) most countries have not identified the term in their domestic legislation; and (2) if they have defined it, these definitions can differ widely from one country to another.

Several cases that deal with the concept of beneficial ownership have been decided under domestic jurisdictions. Although the concept remains vague and largely based on facts and circumstances, in general, two different types of tests are used to determine whether beneficial ownership is present: a technical test and a substance-over-form test:

- *Technical test:* The technical test examines whether restrictions apply to the ownership of the income. In other words, it examines who enjoys the fruits of the ownership or can dispose of it for his own benefit. As case law shows, the difficulty is that it is hard to prove whether a person or entity has limited capability to use the income as he pleases. For instance, in the *Prévost* case,[80] the UK partner in a Canadian joint venture held through a Dutch holding company requested dividend payment to alleviate its financial distress. It applied the reduced withholding tax on dividends paid by the Canadian company under the Canadian–Dutch treaty, which was denied by the Canadian tax authorities. The Tax Court of Canada ruled differently, even though one of the partners was requesting the dividend distribution; the relationship between the partners in the joint venture was structured to grant the Dutch intermediary company at least some discretion as to the use or application of funds put through it. Under other circumstances (for example, the existence of a legal binding obligation to "push through" dividends), the judge might have decided differently. One can conclude that the technical test is highly dependent on the facts and circumstances of the situation involved.

- *Substance-over-form test:* The substance-over-form test requires one to look through the legal form to the economic reality. Substance over form draws the line between legitimate tax planning and abusive tax avoidance. When this line is crossed, recharacterization of transactions is necessary to properly tax these transactions. This test was applied in the *Bank of Scotland* case,[81] where the Bank of Scotland acquired usufruct rights on preference shares from a US company that entitled the Bank of Scotland to receive dividends from a French subsidiary of the US company. The Bank of Scotland requested the benefits under the UK–French tax treaty.[82] The French Supreme Court denied the treaty benefits, as it argued that in fact the usufruct right was a concealed loan to be repaid by the French subsidiary and that this transaction was primarily based on fiscal motives (that is, receiving the *avoir fiscal* credit).

The result of the legal interpretation of beneficial ownership is not encouraging as to its effectiveness. The technical test relies heavily on the facts and circumstances of the case, while the substance-over-form test is heavily based on the intention of the taxpayer when entering into the arrangement, the residual taxable income remaining in the conduit, or the economic reality of the arrangement.

Limitation-on-Benefits Provision

The US anti-treaty-shopping efforts that have been undertaken since *Aiken Industries, Inc.*[83] in 1971 are very confusing, incongruent, and heterogeneous. No

---

[80] Tax Court of Canada on April 22, 2008 (Prévost Car Inc. v. The Queen, 2008 TCC 231).

[81] French Supreme Court (Conseil d'Etat, December 20, 2006, no. 283314).

[82] In this case a reduction of the French withholding tax to 15 percent and a refund of the *avoir fiscal* (a credit for the French corporate income tax). The latter was not available under the US–French tax treaty.

[83] Aiken Industries, 56 TC 925 (1971).

general rule or principle could be clearly drawn from the US cases,[84] and the judicial doctrines such as substance-over-form and step-transaction were sometimes denied, and sometimes accepted, by the courts. In this context, the United States started to develop limitation-on-benefits provisions in its tax treaties.

The United States first introduced a limitation-on-benefits article in its US 1996 Model Treaty[85] and refined this limitation-on-benefits article in its 2006 Model Treaty. The technical explanation to the US 2006 Model Treaty provides a detailed interpretation for applying the limitation-on-benefits articles. Currently, limitation-on-benefits articles can be found in several tax treaties and are no longer only a US international tax policy. In 2003 the OECD added an example of a limitation-on-benefits article—like the US version—to its commentary on Article 1 of the OECD Model. In addition, the OECD BEPS Action 6 report provides for a more advanced version than that in the commentary, but still to a large extent based on the US version.

The limitation-on-benefits article is premised on the view that a resident of a contracting state must have some further connection to that country in order to benefit from that contracting state's tax treaties. Thus, the limitation-on-benefits article limits the ability of third-country residents to engage in treaty shopping by establishing legal entities in either contracting state. Each limitation-on-benefits article sets forth several objective tests, and a resident of a contracting state that satisfies any of those tests generally is entitled to the treaty benefits, even if such resident was arguably formed or availed of for purposes of tax avoidance based on a subjective assessment of the facts and circumstances. The common objective tests include the following:

- *Public company test*: In this test, a corporation that satisfies certain public trading requirements—typically a minimum shareholding—qualifies for treaty benefits. The test reflects that treaty negotiators are relatively unconcerned about the risk that a public company might be used for treaty shopping purposes.

- *Ownership and base-erosion test:* This test generally requires that more than 50 percent of the voting power and value of the company's shares be owned, directly or indirectly, by residents of the same country as the company (ownership). The second requirement is that less than 50 percent of the company's gross income is accrued or paid, directly or indirectly, to persons who are not residents of the same country as the company (base erosion).

- *Active trade or business test:* This test requires that the company be engaged in an active trade or business in its country of residence, that its activities in that country be substantial in relation to its activities in the other contracting state, and that the income be derived in connection with or incidental to that trade or business.

---

[84] See, for example, Northern Indiana Public Service Co. v. Commissioner, 105 TC 341, *aff'd*, 115 F.3d 506 (7th Cir. 1997); SDI Netherlands B.V. v. Commissioner, 107 TC 161 (1996); and Del Commercial Properties, Inc. v. Commissioner, 251 F.3d 210, 213 (DC Cir. 2001).

[85] US Model Tax Convention on Income (September 20, 1996).

Principal Purpose Test Provision

Since 2017, and consistent with the outcomes from the BEPS Project, the OECD and UN Models have included a more general anti-abuse rule based on the principal purposes of transactions or arrangements: the principal purposes test. Under that rule, treaty benefits should not be available where one of the principal purposes of certain transactions or arrangements is to secure those benefits. Obtaining such benefits in these circumstances would be contrary to the object and purpose of the relevant provisions of the tax treaty. An additional treaty provision allows countries to address cases of improper use of tax treaties even if their domestic law does not allow them to do so (that is, due to the absence of a domestic general anti-abuse rule); it also confirms the application of these principles for countries whose domestic law already allows them to address such cases.

Whether one of the principal purposes of any person concerned with an arrangement or transaction is to obtain treaty benefits depends on an assessment of the all the facts and circumstances. It is sufficient that at least one of the principal purposes was to obtain that benefit. A purpose will not be a principal purpose when it is reasonable to conclude that obtaining the benefit was not a principal consideration and the arrangement or transaction giving rise to the benefit would have been entered without the treaty considerations (for example, where an arrangement is inextricably linked to a core commercial activity and its form has not been driven by considerations of obtaining a benefit).

The commentary on the principal purposes provision suggests that—as in the case of domestic general anti-avoidance rules—tax authorities may establish some form of (administrative) approval process. In some cases, the process provides for an internal acceleration of disputes to senior officials in the administration. In other cases, the process allows for advisory panels to provide their views to the administration on the application of the rule. This reflects the serious nature of disputes in this area and promotes overall consistency in the application of the rule.

Although the principal purposes test is presented as something close to a more general anti-avoidance rule on the treaty level, it faces similar problems as the beneficial ownership concept. It requires a legal judgment of the arrangement based on facts and circumstances on a case-by-case basis, so that the source country can reasonably conclude that the intention of the taxpayer was to obtain the benefits of the tax treaty. In developing countries with less or no experience in applying general anti-abuse concepts, a principal purposes test would most likely not be very helpful to combat treaty shopping.

BEPS Solution

BEPS Action 6 requires, as a default option for addressing treaty abuse, the introduction of a principal purposes test provision in existing tax treaties, with the option either to add a simplified limitation-on-benefits provision or to replace the principal purposes test provision with a full limitation-on-benefits provision. In capturing the broad spectrum of treaty shopping arrangements, such a full limitation-on-benefits provision is necessarily highly complex in terms of the language used, which reduces its predictability and practicability. This often results in costly litigation and uncertainty for taxpayers. On the other hand, a simplified limitation-on-benefits provision may not cover all potential treaty abuse situations, but its objective tests will be easier to apply. Developing countries may have difficulties applying a principal purposes test provision as they face issues in assessing facts and circumstances that often even occur outside their jurisdiction (for example, the intention to set up a conduit company typically occurs in the country of the ultimate investor rather than in the country of source). However, a good option would appear to apply a simplified limitation-on-benefits provision and protect its integrity with a complementary general anti-avoidance approach, such as the principal purposes test, as a backstop. Although given as an option in BEPS, this option is not the default and requires that both contracting states opt for it. Based on the current multilateral instrument matrix, this is the exception, if it at all has materialized.

CONCLUSION

Developing countries face specific challenges with regard to treaty policy. One of those challenges is the lack of technical experience and expertise, which generally applies to international tax issues more broadly. Two possible causes are the lack of an adequate institutional framework for undertaking tax policy analysis and the lack of experience in negotiating tax treaties. On the institutional front, many developing countries still do not have a dedicated tax policy unit, such that all policy-related matters are undertaken by the tax administration or agency.[86] Further, the relatively low number of tax treaties in developing countries may render difficult the allocation of scarce resources to this specialized topic and accelerate the erosion of any prior institutional knowledge. Developing countries are consequently forced to play catch-up when approached to enter into treaty negotiations, which makes them particularly vulnerable to concluding bad treaties.

All countries—but developing countries in particular—should critically assess the extent to which a given tax treaty is truly reciprocal. Such an analysis should extend well beyond a de jure look at a tax treaty's provisions and consider the domestic legislations of, and economic relationship between, contracting states. If the investment flows are largely unidirectional, as is the case for most low-income and lower-middle-income countries, the costs of forfeiting source-country taxing rights may be borne unilaterally by these countries.

---

[86] Consequently, responsibility for tax policy design thus falls over and above other tasks, such that it inevitably does not receive the attention it deserves. In additional, policy recommendations by tax administrations may inadvertently give disproportionate weight to administrative considerations.

A careful analysis of the benefits and costs of tax treaties is needed to assess whether it is justified to enter into a particular negotiation. Developing countries will inevitably incur possibly large costs when agreeing to tax treaties, the size of which is mostly unknown, which is worrisome. However, tax treaties may also bring about potential benefits, although that should not be taken as a given. Historically, few developing countries have systematically conducted benefit-cost analyses to guide their choice of prospective treaty partners[87] or to assess the merits of different tax treaties. Initiating such studies appears as a logical step in the way of guiding developing countries into adopting sound international tax policies. Ultimately, however, developing economies should be skeptical as to whether benefits of tax treaties outweigh their costs, and should view any one treaty as a treaty with the world, given the challenges in detecting and addressing treaty shopping.

Four provisions play a key role in distinguishing good from bad tax treaties. While historically broadly accepted, the permanent establishment concept seems outdated and ill suited to determine the true degree of economic integration between a nonresident enterprise and a given source country. A quantitative threshold based on the total volume of sales would appear justified as a complementary test to objectively establish permanent establishment status. On withholding taxes, different considerations arise for tax-deductible payments, such as interest and royalties, and for dividends, which are paid out of after-tax income. In any case, trade-offs exist between encouraging investment by reducing the cost of capital and ensuring proper source-country taxation, which generally points to the need to maintain withholding taxes, albeit at moderate levels. Taxation of cross-border services has proven problematic, in part due to the inappropriateness of the traditional permanent establishment test, and also due to the insufficiencies of the service permanent establishment provision proposed under the UN Model. Low-income countries would be well advised to retain the right to levy a final withholding tax on cross-border service fees as contemplated in the 2017 UN Model. Last, a specific challenge for resource-rich countries relates to indirect transfers of immovable property through the sale of shares in foreign entities, which may not be taxed in the country where the underlying property is located. This is inconsistent with the principles laid out under Article 6 of both models, to the effect that the strong linkage between immovable property and its location should give source countries unlimited taxing rights over the associated income or capital gain. Inclusion of paragraph 13(4) of the OECD and UN Models is thus important to safeguard source-country taxing rights, and so, too, is the inclusion of adequate sourcing and collection provisions under domestic law.

---

[87] In the vast majority of cases involving a developed-developing country relationship, treaty negotiations are initiated by developed countries.

REFERENCES

Abbas, Ali, and Alexander Klemm. 2013. "A Partial Race to the Bottom: Corporate Tax Developments in Emerging and Developing Economies." *International Tax and Public Finance* 20 (August): 596–617.

Arnold, Brian. 2015. "An Introduction to Tax Treaties." available at http://www.un.org/esa /ffd////wpcontent/uploads/2015/10/TT_Introduction_Eng.pdf

Avery Jones, John. 2002. "The Effect of Changes in the OECD Commentaries after a Treaty Is Concluded." *Bulletin for International Taxation* Volume 56, No. 3: pages 102–109.

Avi-Yonah, Reuven S., and Brett Wells. 2018. "The BEAT and Treaty Overrides: A Brief Response to Rosenbloom and Shaheen." Law & Economics Working Papers 157, University of Michigan Law School Repository, University of Michigan, Ann Arbor, MI.

Barthel, Fabian, Matthias Busse, and Eric Neumayer. 2010. "The Impact of Double Taxation Treaties on Foreign Direct Investment: Evidence from Large Dyadic Panel Data." *Contemporary Economic Policy* 28(3): 366–77.

Beer, Sebastian, and Jan Loeprick. 2018. "The Cost and Benefits of Tax Treaties with Investment Hubs: Findings from Sub-Saharan Africa." IMF Working Paper 18/227, International Monetary Fund, Washington, DC.

Blonigen, Bruce, and Ronald Davies. 2004. "The Effects of Bilateral Tax Treaties on U.S. Foreign Direct Investment Activity." *International Tax and Public Finance* 11(5): 601–22.

Blonigen, Bruce, and Ronald Davies. 2005. "Do Bilateral tax Treaties Promote Foreign Direct Investment?" In *Economic and Legal Analyses of Trade Policy and Institutions*, 526–46. Vol. 2 of *Handbook of International Trade*, edited by Eun Kwan Choi and James Hartigan. London: Blackwell.

De Mooij, Ruud. A., and Sjef Ederveen. 2008. "Corporate Tax Elasticities: A Reader's Guide to Empirical Findings, Oxford Review of Economic Policy." 24(4): 680–97.

Di Giovanni, Julian. 2005. "What Drives Capital Flows? The Case of Cross-Border M&A Activity and Financial Deepening." *Journal of International Economics* 65(1): 127–49.

Egger, Peter, Simon Loretz, Michael Pfaffermayr, and Hannes Winner. 2006. "Corporate Taxation and Multinational Activity." CESifo Working Paper 1773, Center for Economic Studies, Munich, Germany.

Hearson, Martin, and Jalia Kangave. 2016. "A Review of Uganda's Tax Treaties and Recommendations for Action." Working Paper 50, Institute of Development Studies, International Centre for Tax and Development, London, UK.

International Monetary Fund (IMF). 2014. "Spillovers in International Corporate Taxation." IMF Policy Paper, Washington, DC.

International Monetary Fund (IMF), Organisation for Economic Co-operation and Development (OECD), World Bank (WB), and United Nations (UN). 2015. "Options for Low-Income Countries' Effective and Efficient Use of Tax Incentives for Investment." Report to the G-20 Development Working Group, Washington, DC.

Janský, Petr, and M. Šedivý. 2018. "Estimating the Revenue Cost of Tax Treaties in Developing Countries." Working Papers IES 2018/19, Faculty of Social Sciences, Institute of Economic Studies, Charles University, Prague, Czech Republic.

James, Sebastian. 2014. "Tax and Non-Tax Incentives and Investments: Evidence and Policy Implications". Investment Climate Advisory Services. World Bank Group.

Lang, Michael, and Florian Brugger. 2008. "The Role of the OECD Commentaries in Tax Treaty Interpretation." *Australian Tax Forum* 23: 95–108.

League of Nations. 1923. *Report on Double Taxation*. Document E.F.S.73. F.19. Geneva, Switzerland: League of Nations.

League of Nations. 1928. *Report on Double Taxation and Tax Evasion*. Document C.562. M.178. 1928.II. Geneva, Switzerland: League of Nations.

Louie, Henry, and Donald Rousslang. 2008. "Host-Country Governance, Tax Treaties and U.S. Direct Investment Abroad." *International Tax and Public Finance* 15(3): 256–73.

McGauran, Katrin. 2013. *Should the Netherlands Sign Tax Treaties with Developing Countries?* Amsterdam: Center for Research on Multinational Corporations (SOMO).

Millimet, Daniel, and Abdullah Kumas. 2007. *Reassessing the Effects of Bilateral Tax Treaties on U.S. foreign direct investment Activity.* Dallas: Southern Methodist University.

Neumayer, Eric. 2007. "Do Double Taxation Treaties Increase Foreign Direct Investment to Developing Countries?" *Journal of Development Studies* 43(8): 1501–19.

Organisation for Economic Co-operation and Development (OECD). 1977. *Model Tax Convention on Income and on Capital.* Paris: OECD.

Organisation for Economic Co-operation and Development (OECD). 1987. *International Tax Avoidance and Evasion: Four Related Studies.* Issues in International Taxation1. Paris: OECD.

Organisation for Economic Co-operation and Development (OECD). 2013a. *Action Plan on Base Erosion and Profit Shifting.* Paris: OECD Publishing.

Organisation for Economic Co-operation and Development (OECD). 2013b. *Addressing Base Erosion and Profit Shifting.* Paris: OECD.

Organisation for Economic Co-operation and Development (OECD). 2015. *Preventing the Granting of Treaty Benefits in Inappropriate Circumstances: Action 6 – 2015 Final Report*, OECD/G20 Base Erosion and Profit Shifting Project. Paris: OECD Publishing.

Organisation for Economic Co-operation and Development (OECD). 2015. *Preventing the Artificial Avoidance of Permanent Establishment Status: Action 7 – 2015 Final Report*, OECD/G20 Base Erosion and Profit Shifting Project. Paris: OECD Publishing.

Organisation for Economic Co-operation and Development (OECD). 2016. *Multilateral Convention to Implement Tax Treaty Related Measures to Prevent BEPS.* Paris: OECD Publishing.

Organisation for Economic Co-operation and Development (OECD). 2017. *Model Tax Convention on Income and on Capital.* Paris: OECD Publishing.

Platform for Collaboration on Tax. 2017. *Discussion Draft: The Taxation of Offshore Indirect Transfers—A Toolkit.* https://www.oecd.org/ctp/PCT-offshore-indirect-transfers-draft-toolkit -version-2.pdf.

Petkova, Kunka, Andrej Stasio, and Martin Zagler. 2018. "On the Relevance of Double Tax Treaties." WU International Taxation Research Paper Series 2018-05, Vienna University of Economics and Business, Vienna, Austria.

Reimer, Ekkehart. 2015. "Permanent Establishment." In *Klaus Vogel on Double Taxation Conventions*, 4th ed., edited by Ekkehart Reimer and Alexander Rust, Chapter 5. Wolters Kluwer.

Rosenbloom, David, and Stanley Langbein. 1981. "United States Tax Treaty Policy: An Overview." *Columbia Journal of Transnational Law* 19: 397–98.

Skaar, Arvid A. 1991. *Permanent Establishment: Erosion of a Tax Treaty Principle.* Series on International taxation: No. 13, Kluwer Law and Taxation Publishers, London, The Hague, Boston.

United Nations. 1980. *Model Double Taxation Convention between Developed and Developing Countries.* New York: United Nations.

United Nations. 1999. *Model Double Taxation Convention between Developed and Developing Countries.* New York: United Nations.

United Nations. 2016. *Manual for the Negotiation of Bilateral Tax Treaties between Developed and Developing Countries.* New York: United Nations.

United Nations. 2017. *Model Double Taxation Convention between Developed and Developing Countries.* New York: United Nations.

United Nations Industrial Development Organization (UNIDO). 2011. *Africa Investor Report: Towards Evidence-Based Investment Promotion Strategies.* UNIDO Publication, UNIDO.

Van Parys, Stefan, and Sebastian James. 2009. "Why Tax Incentives May Be an Ineffective Tool to Encouraging Investment?—The Role of Investment Climate." Unpublished, World Bank, Washington, DC.

Ward, David. 2006. "The Role of Commentaries on the OECD Model in the Tax Treaty Interpretation Process." *Bulletin for International Taxation* Volume 60 No. 3: 97–102.

Weichenrieder, Alfons, and Jack Mintz. 2008. "What Determines the Use of Holding Companies and Ownership Chains?" Working Paper 08/03, Oxford University Centre for Business Taxation, Oxford, UK.

Weyzig, Francis. 2013. "Tax Treaty Shopping: Structural Determinants of Foreign Direct Investment Routed through the Netherlands." *International Tax and Public Finance* 20(6): 910–37.

Wijnen, Wim F.G., and Jan de Goede. 2014. "The UN Model in Practice 1997–2013." *Bulletin for International Taxation* 68(3), 118–146.

Wijnen, Wim F.G., Jan de Goede, and Andrea Alessi. 2012. "The Treatment of Services in Tax Treaties." *Bulletin for International Taxation* 66(1): 27–38.

Wijnen, Wim F.G., and Marco Magenta. 1997. "The UN Model in Practice." *Bulletin for International Fiscal Documentation* 51(12): 574–585.

CHAPTER 9

The Impact of Profit Shifting on Economic Activity and Tax Competition

Alexander Klemm and Li Liu

INTRODUCTION

Multinational corporations can often reduce their global tax liabilities through profit-shifting activities (Chapter 5). Typical examples include transfer price manipulation, intracompany debt, and the strategic location of intangible assets, such as intellectual property. There is plenty of empirical evidence that reported profits by multinationals indeed respond to international tax differentials. A recent survey article (Beer, de Mooij, and Liu 2020) estimates the consensus value of the semi-elasticity of reported profits with respect to international tax differential to be 1.5. That is, a 1 percentage point reduction in the statutory corporate income tax rate in a certain location is expected to raise reported profits by multinationals in that location by 1.5 percent, all else equal.

The size of tax revenue at stake is also substantial. For the United States alone, tax avoidance cost about between one-quarter and one-third of total corporate tax revenue in 2012 (Clausing 2016). Losses elsewhere could be much larger and possibly amount to several points of GDP, especially in lower-income countries with weak enforcement capacity. Revenue losses are of particular concern for developing countries, which derive a higher share of their total revenue from corporate taxes and have fewer alternative revenue sources to fall back on (Keen 2017).

During the last few decades, many countries have adopted a variety of anti-avoidance regulations to mitigate international corporate tax avoidance (Chapter 11). These include, for example, the adoption of increasingly detailed transfer pricing regulations, thin capitalization rules, controlled foreign corporations rules, or a general anti-avoidance rule. In recent years, these efforts have been elevated to supranational levels in light of the G20/OECD Base Erosion and Profit Shifting (BEPS) initiative. The project aims to address major tax avoidance opportunities arising under the current international tax framework in a coordinated manner (OECD 2015). For instance, countries participating under what is now called the inclusive framework on BEPS commit to four minimum standards (for example, on treaty abuse) and adhere to the common approaches to adopt anti-avoidance legislation.

Profit shifting and potential solutions are discussed in other chapters of this volume as well as other publications. The focus here is on the impact of profit shifting and its countermeasures on real investment and tax competition. Our analysis shows the following:

- Real investment can be affected by profit shifting in various ways. Most obviously, investment in high-tax countries may be higher if investors know that they are able to avoid some of the tax through profit shifting. More subtly, investors may also invest more in low-tax jurisdictions, because having capital there may facilitate shifting profits into those jurisdictions.

- Tax competition is the process of lowering taxes to attract capital investment. A permissive attitude toward profit shifting could be a component of such competition, as governments can reduce effective tax levels by tolerating such behavior. In turn, if profit shifting is limited through international coordination, governments may face stronger pressure to reduce tax levels directly, for example by cutting statutory tax rates.

This chapter discusses these two channels and their policy implications. It is structured as follows: The first section discusses the theoretical impact of profit shifting on investment and tax competition when there is only one type of capital. This capital is internationally mobile—or more precisely—allows profit shifting at some cost. Further interesting issues arise when capital is heterogenous with only some capital internationally mobile. The implications of this, and the similarities of profit shifting with preferential tax regimes, are discussed in the third section. The fourth section discusses related empirical evidence. The final section draws overall conclusions.

THE EFFECTS OF PROFIT SHIFTING WHEN CAPITAL IS MOBILE

Conceptual Framework

Tax-motivated profit shifting changes the effective tax rates paid by multinational corporations. For example, in the extreme case of costless profit shifting, multinational corporations could entirely avoid corporate income tax by shifting all profits into a country with no (or minimal) corporate income tax. Then its effective corporate income tax rate for investment becomes zero—even in the high-tax country. Its cost of capital—or using the expression coined by Grubert and Slemrod (1998, p. 372), its "income shifting adjusted cost of capital"—is reduced to the normal rate of return. This reduction in the cost of capital would boost investment compared to the case of no profit shifting.

More realistically, profit shifting is not without limits. Legal profit shifting is restricted by a range of laws and regulations. As these laws are not very precise—for example, determining the transfer prices of intangibles is not an exact science—shifting small amounts of profits is relatively inexpensive. Shifting larger amounts will, however, require setting up complicated structures (for example, companies that hold intellectual property assets) or relocation of at least some real activity. Any profit shifting through tax avoidance additionally carries a risk of detection and penalties, which is likely to rise with the amount of tax avoided.

In a simple model that follows, we illustrate the exact role of profit shifting in affecting the cost of capital where profit shifting is costly. The model is based on the frameworks described in Grubert and Slemrod (1998) and Hines and Rice (1994). A similar approach is also described in Suárez Serrato (2018) and Desai, Foley, and Hines (2006), who allow firms to invest in low-tax jurisdictions so as to obtain access to profit-shifting opportunities. A somewhat different model, which also leads to a tradeoff between profit shifting controls and tax cuts, is described in Peralta, Wauthy, and van Ypersele (2006). Specifically, they assume a monopolist can locate production in either of two countries, from which both will then be served and between which profits can be shifted. Governments set the tax rate and decide on whether to allow profit shifting. Lenient transfer price control can be used as a substitute for tax cuts and can reduce competition over rates.[1]

Consider a multinational corporation locating in n countries. Assuming a territorial system of taxation,[2] after-tax profits for the multinational corporation are given by the following:

$$\sum_j \left(1 - t_j\right) f_j\left(K_j\right) - r \sum_j K_j,\tag{1}$$

where $f_i(\cdot)$ is a firm's production function in country i, which is assumed to be increasing in capital $(f_i'(K_i) > 0)$ and exhibits decreasing returns to investment $(f_i''(K_i) < 0)$, and r is the required rate of return.

The firm undertakes two sequential decisions.[3] First, it decides how much capital to invest in each country. In the second period, it chooses the optimal profit-shifting strategy. Specifically, a firm engages in profit shifting by reporting some profitability π_i instead of its true profitability $(f_i(K_i)/(K_i))$. The cost of reporting a profit that is different from true profit is modeled as proportional to local investment and rising quadratically in the degree of profit shifting:

$$c\left(\pi_i, K_i\right) = \frac{K_i}{2a}\left(\pi_i - \frac{f_i\left(K_i\right)}{K_i}\right)^2.\tag{2}$$

---

[1] Another related paper is Johannesen (2012), which considers the implications of withholding taxes on international interest payments as a means of limiting profit shifting through thin capitalization.

[2] If we wish to distinguish between the county of the parent p and other countries, this can be rewritten as $\left(1 - t_p\right) f_p\left(K_p\right) + \sum_{j \neq p}\left(1 - t_j\right) f_j\left(K_j\right) - r\left(\sum_j K_j\right)$. A complication arises in case of countries with worldwide taxation: the tax rate in countries other than p will reflect both source and residence-based taxation (in case of full worldwide taxation on an accruals bases, t_i would equal t_p for all countries with rates below the parent country and there would be no incentives to shift profits out of country p).

[3] In an alternative model in Harper and Liu (2019), the firm decides jointly on the size of investment and the scale of profit shifting, whereas the cost function is modeled as increasing in the proportion of profit shifted. The key conclusions remain the same.

The parameter a measures the extent of costs from reporting local profits different from true profits, with high values of a implying lower profit-shifting costs. In particular, stricter anti-avoidance regulations (or stronger administrative capacity) increase the cost of profit shifting or lower the value of a. The shape of the cost function is crucial. If profit shifting were independent of capital stocks, for example, if it depended only on the absolute amount of profit shifted, very different results would be obtained, and certainly real investment would not be linked to profit shifting. For many profit-shifting scenarios, though, a link to capital is likely: the more actual activity there is in a country, the more profit can be shifted by a small transfer price change. Moreover, profits that are very out of line with the size of operations would likely attract the attention of tax authorities.

The firm's optimization problem can be solved starting from the second period. Given a capital allocation $\{K_j\}$, the firm solves the following tax-planning problem:

$$max_{\{\pi_j\}} \sum_j K_j \left[\left(1 - t_j\right)\pi_j - r - \frac{\left(\pi_j - \frac{f_i(K_i)}{K_i}\right)^2}{2a} \right], s.t. \sum_j f_j\left(K_j\right) = \sum_j \pi_j K_j.$$

(3)

The constraint implies that the firm must report total profits truthfully but may shift the location of its profits to minimize taxes. Optimal reported profitability, by solving the first-order conditions of Equation (3), is:

$$\pi_i = \frac{f_i(K_i)}{K_i} + a\left(\tilde{t} - t_i\right),$$

(4)

where $\tilde{t}$ is the capital-weighted-average tax rate $\left(\sum_j t_j K_j / \sum_j K_j \right)$.

The relationship in Equation (4) summarizes three simple and intuitive results. First, the direction of profit shifting depends on the relative statutory tax rates, that is, the difference between the host country statutory tax rate and the capital-weighted average tax rates. The firm underreports profits in countries where the corporate tax rate is above the capital-weighted average tax rate, and overreports in countries with a lower corporate tax. This result reproduces the Hines and Rice (1994) prediction that a firm's reported profitability is negatively correlated with the country's tax rate. Second, the magnitude of reported profitability is positively correlated with economic profitability. Third, optimal reported profitability is inversely related to profit-shifting costs; that is, increasing concealments costs dampen the extent of profit reallocation.

In the first period, the firm foresees its profit-shifting strategies and invests across countries to maximize a combination of economic and profit-shifting incentives. Substituting the optimal reported profitability into the objective function, and rearranging, we get:

$$max_{\{K_j\}} \sum_j \left[\left(1 - t_j\right) f_j\left(K_j\right) - rK_j \right] + a \sum_j K_j \left[\left(1 - t_j\right)\left(\tilde{t} - t_j\right) - \frac{\left(\tilde{t} - t_j\right)^2}{2} \right].$$

(5)

Maximizing with respect to K_i gives the user cost of capital:

$$f_i'\left(K_i\right) = \frac{1}{1 - t_i}\left[r - \frac{a}{2}\left(\tilde{t} - t_i\right)^2 \right].$$

(6)

Impact on Real Investment

The reduction in the cost of capital can be expected to raise real investment. As shown in Equation (6), the income-shifting-adjusted user cost of capital is reduced by the net marginal benefit from profit shifting. One particularly interesting aspect is that profit-shifting opportunities reduce the cost of capital both in countries whose tax rates exceed and undercut the weighted average. The reduction in the cost of capital thanks to profit shifting is largest in countries with (1) tax rates that are most different from the average, (2) higher tax rates, and (3) less stringent anti-avoidance rules (which is reflected in a higher value of a).

Impact on Government Behavior

Governments that engage in strategic tax setting, such as tax competition, have more than one instrument at their disposal. Most importantly, they can (1) reduce the statutory corporate tax rate, (2) introduce preferential tax regimes, (3) loosen anti-avoidance regulations, or (4) signal lax enforcement. In terms of Equation (6), the first two instruments are reflected in a lower value of t_i, while the latter are reflected in a higher value of a. In this model, lower corporate tax rates and lax anti-avoidance measures are substitutes in reducing the profit-shifting-adjusted user cost of capital.

To understand the choice between two instruments better, we consider the revenue implications of adjusting either.[4] Assuming that firms choose the optimal capital stock K^* determined by equation (6), revenue (R) in each country is given by:

$$R_i = t_i f\left(K_i^*\right) + at_i\left(\tilde{t}^* - t_i\right)K_i^* = t_i f\left(K_i^*\right) + at_i\left(\frac{\sum_j K_j^*\left(t_j - t_i\right)}{\sum_j K_j^*}\right)K_i^*.$$

(7)

---

[4] An analytically more demanding approach, left for future research, would involve defining a government objective function, capturing revenue in addition to other objectives, such as output.

The difficulty in assessing equation (7) is that the optimal capital stock is a function of the tax rate and the cost of profit shifting. However, the impact can be gauged by imposing some simplifying assumptions. Specifically, if we focus on a two-country case (labelled 1 and 2) and impose a specific production function of $f(K) = K^{\alpha}$, we can illustrate the trade-offs. In this case we obtain:

$$K_1 = \left(\frac{\alpha(1 - t_1)}{r - \dfrac{a\left(K_2(t_2 - t_1)\right)^2}{2\left(K_1 + K_2\right)^2}} \right)^{\frac{1}{1-\alpha}}. \tag{8}$$

By symmetry the same applies to the other country. While this is still difficult to solve analytically, a solution can be computed iteratively.

Costs of Profit Shifting

Consider first the cost of profit shifting. Assume that Country 1 is in relative terms a high-tax country with a tax rate of 30 percent, while Country 2 has a lower tax rate of 20 percent. The calculations assume a world-required rate of return of 10 percent and a production function with $\alpha = 1/3$. Qualitatively similar results are obtained with any other reasonable assumptions (that is, both figures above zero and below 1). The left panel of Figure 9.1 shows how the capital stock in each country changes as a function of the ease of profit shifting (that is, parameter a). As expected, the low-tax country has a higher-capital stock, and in both countries

Figure 9.1. Capital Stock and Tax Revenue in Two-Country Case
$(r = 10\%, \alpha = 1/3)$

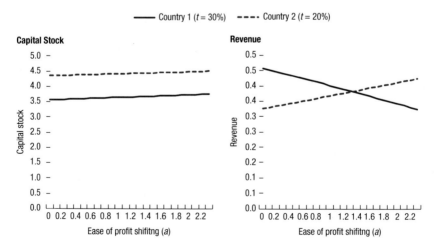

Source: Authors' simulation.

the stock rises as profit shifting becomes less costly. The right panel shows that revenues rise in the low-tax country and fall in the high-tax country, the easier it is to shift profits. This means that—at least in this simple model—taxes on the additional real capital that is drawn in as a result of profit shifting is not enough to undo the lost reported tax base. For high-tax countries there is therefore a trade-off: implementing measures to protect tax bases from profit shifting reduces the capital stock but raises revenue. For low-tax countries, there is no trade-off, and relaxing profit-shifting rules boosts both capital stocks and revenues.

The Tax Rate

To illustrate the impact of the tax rate, we fix the cost parameter of profit shifting ($a = 0.2$), keeping the same required rate of return production function parameter as in the previous subsection. Country 2 is assumed to maintain a tax rate of 20 percent as before. Country 1, however, is now allowed to vary its tax rate. Figure 9.2 shows the impact of the choice of Country 1's tax rate on revenues. The right panel shows, for comparison, the results if there is no profit shifting. The left panel reveals very clearly how raising the tax rate is much less effective in increasing revenues. The spillovers on the other country are, as expected, positive for any tax rate above 20 percent and negative otherwise. The presence of profit-shifting opportunities therefore has an ambiguous impact on tax competition: it reduces the benefit in terms of revenues when raising rates, but it reduces the costs in terms of lost investment. To the extent that raising revenues is weighed highly

Figure 9.2. Tax Revenues as Function of the Tax Rate in Two-Country Case
($r = 10\%$, $\alpha = 1/3$)

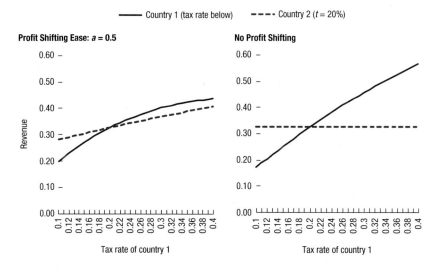

Source: Authors' simulation.

in the government's objective function, the assumption would be that profit shifting leads to downward pressure on tax rates, at least based on this simple model.

A different argument for why tightening profit-shifting rules may intensify tax competition is made in Becker and Fuest (2012). In their model, allowing profit shifting to low-tax jurisdictions encourages them to levy a higher tax rate. If rules are tightened, low-tax jurisdictions may react by cutting rates to save some of their tax base.

PROFIT SHIFTING WITH HETEROGENEOUS CAPITAL

Even though the simple model just described already leads to ambiguous effects of profit shifting on welfare, it still overlooks a very important aspect in practice. Notably, not all capital is equally mobile.

A few theoretical papers analyze the interaction between profit shifting, the tax rate, and investment allowing for such heterogeneous capital. Hong and Smart (2010), for example, find that profit shifting within certain limits can benefit even the countries that lose tax bases, because of an increase in investment (as discussed), but also because this allows countries to raise the statutory tax rate without driving away mobile capital. The result is ambiguous, however, and depends on tax rates not being too high and tax avoidance activities not being excessive. Haufler and Runkel (2012) consider the choice between profit shifting through thin capitalization and the tax rate. They find—in line with the tax competition literature—that in an uncoordinated equilibrium, countries choose tax rates that are inefficiently low. Moreover, they also choose inefficiently lenient thin capitalization rules. If countries coordinate on tightening thin capitalization, this benefits both countries, despite resulting in more intense competition over tax rates. As the global capital stock is fixed in their model, it is not clear whether this result holds more generally.

A related literature on preferential tax regimes (Janeba and Smart 2003; Keen 2001) has shown that offering a lower tax rate to the more mobile capital can be welfare enhancing. The intuitive explanation is that offering a special regime allows countries to restrict competition to the mobile base (K^M), without giving up as much of the revenues from the immobile base (K^I).

If the mobile tax base is also the base that has access to profit shifting, then there is a clear link between this literature and the issue considered here. Specifically, if only mobile firms have access to profit shifting (or face a naturally much lower cost), then profit shifting permits a differentiation in effective tax levels between such firms. Hence, the discussion of the usefulness of global measures to make it harder to shift profits is very similar to the benefits and harms of preferential tax regimes. Table 9.1 summarizes the comparison between both issues. The last row shows the likely policies of countries that act without coordination: because of the greater elasticity of mobile capital, the maximizing tax rate is lower, which can be achieved either by tolerating some profit shifting or by offering a special regime.

TABLE 9.1.

Duality between Profit Shifting and Preferential Tax Regimes

	Differentiation by Tax Regime	Differentiation by Profit-Shifting Opportunities
Immobile capital, K^I	Standard regime	No profit shifting
Mobile capital, K^M ($\varepsilon^M > \varepsilon^I$)	Preferential regime	Profit shifting
Uncoordinated tax policy	t determined by ε^I Special regime by ε^M	t determined by ε^I BEPS measures by ε^M
Possible coordination	Restrict rate differential	Agree on measures to curb profit shifting

Source: Authors' assessment.

Janeba and Smart (2003) discuss the conditions under which international coordination to restrict special regimes can be beneficial. Their approach considers two tax bases with different elasticities. The innovative aspect of their analysis is to consider both the elasticity of a tax base in response to a tax rate change by one country only ($\varepsilon_i^a = -\dfrac{t_i}{x_i(t_i,T_i)}\dfrac{\partial x_i(t_i,T_i)}{\partial t_i}$),[5] and the elasticity in response to a change by both countries ($\varepsilon_i^b = -\dfrac{t_i}{x_i(t_i,T_i)}\left(\dfrac{\partial x_i(t_i,T_i)}{\partial t_i} + \dfrac{\partial x_i(t_i,T_i)}{\partial T_i}\right)$). As the latter elasticity keeps relative tax rates constant, it abstracts from any impact on capital mobility, and instead reveals the closed-economy equivalent relationship between the tax rate and the capital stock, or equivalently the responsiveness of the global capital stock to a global change in the tax rate (in Keen 2001 this is assumed to be zero, that is, the global capital stock is fixed). They then label a tax base as mobile if the difference ($\varepsilon_i^c = \varepsilon_i^a - \varepsilon_i^b$) is large, that is, if most of the change in the tax base is the result of capital mobility. They conclude that restricting rate differences is generally revenue raising if the mobile base is also the more elastic one, but is revenue losing if the mobile base is less elastic.

Based on the duality with the profit-shifting channel, this suggests that international agreements to curb profit shifting, such as the OECD/G20 BEPS initiative may or may not increase revenues—even abstracting from possibilities of uneven implementation.

The duality is not perfect, however. One advantage of profit shifting over preferential regimes is that it allows self-selection of firms. Preferential regimes imply a lot of costs and risks, including for compliance and administration and the scope for corruption.[6] To the extent that the link between mobility and access to profit shifting is indeed strong, a method based on self-selection can reduce these costs and risks. A disadvantage of profit shifting is that it incurs a deadweight cost, both in the model described in this section and most likely also in

---

[5] Notation: x is the tax base, of which there are two indicated by i, t is own tax rate, and T is the other country's tax rate.

[6] For an overview of the benefits, costs, and risks of tax incentives, see, for example, Klemm (2010).

practice as firms have to bear the costs of setting up structures with no productive use (for example, subsidiaries in low-tax jurisdictions with no actual activity).

EMPIRICAL EVIDENCE

The existing empirical literature has paid relatively little attention to the interaction between profit shifting and the allocation of real activities by multinational corporations. Most existing research has focused largely on either quantifying the scale of profit shifting and its revenue impact at national or global level, or instead on quantifying the impact of taxes on the location of foreign direct investment. There are, however, a number of recent papers that come closer to the interaction of interest here.

In terms of the simple model set forth in the previous section, the link between real investment and profit shifting operates both through the tax differential and the cost of profit shifting (Equation (6)). While we are not aware of any paper analyzing both channels simultaneously, the literature has considered both of them separately. Table 9.2 classifies the literature by the channel studied, and the following two subsections discuss selected papers and their findings.

Evidence on the Investment Effect of Tax Differences

Overesch (2009) uses panel data on German inbound investment and shows that real investment increases by 0.971 percent with each percentage point increase in the tax rate difference between Germany and the investor's country. This can be interpreted as indirect evidence of real investment being responsive to the profit-shifting opportunities. Goldbach and others (2019), also using German data, find that multinationals increase their investment in Germany following investment abroad. They find that this effect is stronger the greater the tax differential, suggesting that profit-shifting opportunities indeed raise investment even in the high tax country. Desai, Foley, and Hines (2006) consider regional investment of

TABLE 9.2.

Empirical Literature Related to Profit Shifting and Real Investment		
Channel		**Papers**
Changes in $(\tilde{t} - t_i)$		Desai, Foley, and Hines (2006) Overesch (2009)
Changes in a	Firm-specific proxies	Grubert and Slemrod (1998)
	Transfer pricing regulations	De Mooij and Liu (2020) Buettner, Overesch, and Wamser (2018)
	Thin capitalization rules	Buettner, Overesch, and Wamser (2018) De Mooij and Liu (2021) Weichenrieder and Windischbauer (2008)
	Controlled foreign company rules	Egger and Wamser (2015) Albertus (2018)

Source: Authors' compilation.

multinationals and find a positive relationship between the use of a low-tax jurisdiction and real investment in the same region. Specifically, if the likelihood of establishing a low-tax jurisdiction affiliate rises by 1 percent, then sales and investment in the region, but outside the low-tax jurisdiction, grow by 0.5–0.7 percent.

Becker and Riedel (2012) consider a somewhat different model, where investment in a host country depends on parent-country taxes not only through profit shifting, but also because investment in both locations is interdependent. They find a semi-elasticity of host-country investment with respect to the home-country tax rate of –0.56, which they argue is due to negative investment spillovers. This finding is not directly comparable, though, because an increase in parent-country tax rate could increase or reduce the difference with host country.

Evidence on the Investment Effect of Profit Shifting Costs

Grubert and Slemrod (1998) show that investment by Puerto Rican affiliates of US multinational corporations responds significantly to firm-level proxies for cost of shifting. Moreover, simulation results suggest that nearly half of all US firms in Puerto Rico are there solely for the profit shifting benefits. A later paper by Suárez Serrato (2018) further shows that limiting profit shifting for US multinationals by removing the tax advantage of shifting profits to Puerto Rico reduced the domestic investment of affected US multinationals by 38 percent and their domestic employment by one million jobs.

Another related paper is Mintz and Smart (2004), which is mostly dedicated to estimating income-shifting elasticities, but also presents one result of the impact of profit-shifting opportunities on real investment choices. Specifically, the paper uses Canadian data to split firms into those that have limited and those that have ample possibilities for intraprovincial profit shifting. They find that that firms with access to shifting are more sensitive to tax rates—which is not in line with their model or our expectations.

A small, but growing, literature analyzes the effect of anti-avoidance rules on investment. If anti-avoidance rules reduce the scope for profit shifting, then there should be a negative impact on real investment, based on the considerations discussed above.

Transfer pricing regulation: De Mooij and Liu (2020) study the impact of introducing or tightening transfer pricing regulations using European data. They find that such regulations have a negative and significant effect on multinational corporation investment in fixed assets, with the introduction of such regulations reducing multinational corporation fixed investment by 15 percent, compared to investment by domestic companies. Buettner, Overesch, and Wamser (2018) also consider transfer pricing regulations using data for German multinational corporation affiliates, but they find no significant impact.

Thin capitalization rules: In addition to discussing transfer pricing regulations, Buettner, Overesch, and Wamser (2018) also analyze thin capitalization rules. They find a negative effect of thin capitalization rules on investment and employment. De Mooij and Liu (2021) confirm the result of a negative impact of thin capitalization on investment using a panel dataset of multinational affiliates in 32 countries. Moreover, they show that the negative investment effect of thin capitalization rules is more pronounced for highly leveraged affiliates with tighter safe-haven ratios. Weichenrieder and Windischbauer (2008), on the other hand, find no impact of thin capitalization rules on real investment using German data, which they argue can be explained by firms being able to use a loophole to avoid the rules (a preference to holding companies). Ruf and Schindler (2015) discuss the experience of thin capitalization rules in Germany and the related literature.

Controlled foreign corporation rules: Egger and Wamser (2015) study the impact of controlled foreign corporation rules and find that the German controlled foreign corporation rule decreased foreign subsidiaries' real investments by about €7 million per subsidiary in a regression discontinuity design. Albertus (2018) study of foreign multinational corporations in the United States found that when a US subsidiary is subject to a controlled foreign corporation law, the subsidiary's US investment decreases by around 12 percent.

Another related paper is Nicolay, Nusser, and Pfeiffer (2017), which studies the interaction between different measures to restrict profit shifting. Analyzing a French reform, the paper finds that tightening transfer pricing rules not only reduces profit shifting, but also causes substitution toward more debt shifting and vice versa. Moreover, the substitution is stronger for firms with high shares of intangible profits, and hence presumably more opportunities to shift profits.

CONCLUSION

This paper has considered the link between profit shifting and real investment. One of the strong insights from the analysis is that profit-shifting opportunities unambiguously reduce the cost of capital in all countries—irrespective of whether they charge higher or lower taxes than the global average (for countries charging exactly the global average rate, there is no impact). Hence, profit shifting raises global capital stocks by effectively reducing the tax burden. That does not necessarily imply that it is also efficient, as it creates a distortion between the purely domestic and international parts of the economy, leading to a shift of capital from purely domestic to multinational firms.[7] The impact on welfare and optimal behavior by governments is ambiguous, however. While jurisdictions with relatively low taxes are likely to gain revenues and capital, high-tax countries are likely to gain capital but lose revenue.

Considering that tax bases may differ in the degree of mobility—or their access to profit-shifting opportunities—reveals a mechanism through which curbing profit shifting will have an ambiguous impact on tax revenues and welfare, similar to the ambiguous results about the benefits of permitting special regimes for mobile capital.

---

[7] This could be mitigated by positive spillovers from the multinational to domestic investment.

Given the ambiguity of many of the findings, the recent strength of international efforts at curbing profit shifting may appear surprising. Of course, there are many important aspects that are beyond simple models. For example, allowing effectively lower taxation of mobile activities may put local businesses at a competitive disadvantage, creating incentives for mergers with firms that have global activities, even without a business reason. Politically, it could also be costly to charge lower effective taxes to mobile businesses that often are particularly profitable.

The illustrative use of the simple model also revealed the difficulty in assessing separately the impact of changes to tax rates or the ease of profit shifting on investment and revenues. If this is complicated already in a very simple model, it must be much more so in practice, where many further channels and interactions exist. So, while countries may indeed have more than one instrument at their hand to react to competitive pressures, it is not easy for them to determine the optimal strategy.[8]

REFERENCES

Albertus, James F. 2018. "The Real Effects of U.S. Tax Arbitrage by Foreign Multinational Firms." SSRN Working Paper.

Becker, Johannes, and Clemens Fuest. 2012. "Transfer Pricing Policy and the Intensity of Tax Rate Competition." *Economics Letters* 117(1): 146–48.

Becker, Johannes and Nadine Riedel. 2012. "Cross-Border Tax Effects on Affiliate Investment—Evidence from European Multinationals." *European Economic Review* 56(3): 436–50.

Beer, Sebastian, Ruud de Mooij, and Li Liu. 2020. "International Corporate Tax Avoidance: A Review of the Channels, Effect Sizes and Blind Spots." *Journal of Economic Surveys* 34: 660–88.

Beer, Sebastian, Alexander Klemm, and Thornton Matheson. 2018. "Tax Spillovers from U.S. Corporate Income Tax Reform." IMF Working Paper 18/166, International Monetary Fund, Washington, DC.

Buettner, Thiess, Michael Overesch, and Georg Wamser. 2018. "Anti Profit-Shifting Rules and Foreign Direct Investment." *International Tax and Public Finance* 25(3): 553–80.

Clausing, Kimberly. 2016. "The Effect of Profit Shifting on the Corporate Tax Base in the United States and Beyond." *National Tax Journal* 69(4): 905–34.

De Mooij, Ruud, and Li Liu. 2018. "At a Cost: The Real Effects of Thin Capitalization Rules." IMF Working Paper, forthcoming, International Monetary Fund.

De Mooij, Ruud, and Li Liu. 2020. "At a Cost: The Real Effects of Transfer Pricing Regulations." *IMF Economic Review*, 68, pages 268–306

---

[8] The December 2017 US tax reform, for example, includes various—in some case counteracting—measures (for its international spillovers, see Beer, Klemm, and Matheson 2018). The US corporate income tax rate is reduced by 14 percentage points (and more if profits qualify for treatment as Foreign Derived Intangible Income). Profit shifting was made easier through the move to territoriality, but at the same time harder through global intangible low-taxed income and the base erosion and anti-abuse tax provisions, with the exact impact depending on a firm's circumstances. Interestingly, global intangible low-taxed income discourages profit shifting only for high returns on tangible assets. In terms of the model as in equation (2), this means that the cost of profit shifting (a), becomes a function of the capital stock (K).

Desai, Mihir, C. Fritz Foley, and James Hines, Jr. 2006. "Do Tax Havens Divert Economic Activity?" *Economics Letters* 90: 219–24.

Egger, Peter, and Georg Wamser. 2015. "The Impact of Controlled Foreign Company Legislation on Real Investments Abroad. A Multi-dimensional Regression Discontinuity Design." *Journal of Public Economics* 129: 77–91.

Goldbach, Stefan, Arne Nagengast, Elias Steinmüller, and Georg Wamser. 2019. "The Effect of Investing Abroad on Investment at Home: On the Role of Technology, Tax Savings, and Internal Capital Markets." *Journal of International Economics* 116: 58–73.

Grubert, Harry, and Joel Slemrod. 1998. "The Effect of Taxes on Investment and Income Shifting to Puerto Rico." *Review of Economics and Statistics* 80(3): 365–73.

Harper, Andrew, and Li Liu. 2019. "UK Accelerated Depreciation Policy in an International Context." *British Tax Review* (3):257–64.

Haufler, Andreas, and Marco Runkel. 2012. "Firms' Financial Choices and Thin Capitalization Rules under Corporate Tax Competition." *European Economic Review* 56(6): 1087–103.

Hines Jr., James, and Eric Rice. 1994. "Fiscal Paradise: Foreign Tax Havens and American Business." *Quarterly Journal of Economics* 109(1): 149–82.

Hong, Qing, and Michael Smart. 2010. "In Praise of Tax Havens: International Tax Planning and Foreign Direct Investment." *European Economic Review* 54(1): 82–95.

Janeba, Eckhard, and Michael Smart. 2003. "Is Targeted Tax Competition Less Harmful Than Its Remedies?" *International Tax and Public Finance* 10(3): 259–80.

Johannesen, Niels 2012. "Optimal Fiscal Barriers to International Economic Integration in the Presence of Tax Havens." *Journal of Public Economics* 96(3): 400–16.

Keen, Michael. 2001. "Preferential Regimes Can Make Tax Competition Less Harmful." *National Tax Journal* 54(4): 757–62.

Keen, Michael. 2017. "False Profits." *Finance and Development* 54(3): 10–13.

Klemm, Alexander. 2010. "Causes, Benefits, and Risks of Business Tax Incentives." *International Tax and Public Finance* 17(3): 315–36.

Mintz, Jack, and Michael Smart. 2004. "Income Shifting, Investment, and Tax Competition: Theory and Evidence from Provincial Taxation in Canada." *Journal of Public Economics* 88(6): 1149–168.

Nicolay, Katharina, Hannah Nusser, and Olena Pfeiffer. 2017. "On the Interdependency of Profit Shifting Channels and the Effectiveness of Anti-avoidance Legislation." ZEW Discussion Papers 17-066, ZEW – Leibniz Centre for European Economic Research, Mannheim, Germany.

Organisation for Economic Co-operation and Development (OECD). 2015. *Explanatory Statement*, OECD/G20 Base Erosion and Profit Shifting Project. Paris: OECD Publishing.

Overesch, Michael. 2009. "The Effects of Multinationals' Profit Shifting Activities on Real Investments." *National Tax Journal* 62(1): 5–23.

Peralta, Susana, Xavier Wauthy, and Tanguy van Ypersele. 2006. "Should Countries Control International Profit Shifting?" *Journal of International Economics* 68(1): 24–37.

Ruf, Martin, and Dirk Schindler. 2015. "Debt Shifting and Thin-Capitalization Rules— German Experience and Alternative Approaches." *Nordic Tax Journal* 2015(1): 17–33.

Suárez Serrato, Juan Carlos. 2018. "Unintended Consequences of Eliminating Tax Havens." NBER Working Paper 24850, National Bureau of Economic Research, Cambridge, MA.

Weichenrieder, Alfons, and Helen Windischbauer. 2008. "Thin-Capitalization Rules and Company Responses Experience from German Legislation." CESifo Working Paper 2456, Center for Economic Studies, Munich, Germany.

CHAPTER 10

Taxing the Digital Economy

Aqib Aslam and Alpa Shah

INTRODUCTION

Technology is being harnessed to redefine traditional business models and provide new ways for buyers and sellers to interact both locally and globally. The result has been the emergence of a handful of firms—the so-called tech giants—that are capitalizing on first mover advantages and network externalities to boost profitability, capture market share, and turn themselves into the world's most highly valued companies. They have inevitably captured the attention of policymakers, and in the realm of international taxation, the debate has coalesced around a number of issues that are driving the debate over whether and how countries should be able to tax the returns to highly digitalized multinational businesses (IMF 2014, 2019). More generally, an increasing number of firms are digitalizing, leading to several issues that raise or intensify challenges for the international tax system.

The first issue relates to the increasingly sophisticated information and communications technology systems—including the internet—that have facilitated a surge in remote cross-jurisdictional sales, decoupling economic and physical presence. Moreover, with this ability to market and sell goods and services remotely, online retailers are also challenging and displacing traditional physical stores (of all sizes). For example, in the United States, the share of e-commerce in retail sales has tripled to almost 10 percent compared to a decade ago. This has strained the traditional concept of permanent establishment, which relies on a fixed physical presence as a precondition for governments to exercise their right to tax.

The second issue is that intangible assets have a greater role than ever before, with modern multinational enterprises deriving a larger share of their value from intellectual property that is both easy to shift across borders and hard to value for transfer pricing purposes due to lack of comparables. This has frustrated the arm's length principle and exacerbated opportunities for profit shifting.

A third issue—and an important focus of this chapter—is that the online customer or user is now considered by many as being a critical driving force behind the value of digital services. Digitalization has allowed businesses to harvest data and information about their users at an unprecedented scale. Users provide data on their preferences, be it through their online search, purchase of goods and services, or through their interactions with others over social media platforms. However, user participation is not recognized under the existing international tax framework as a source of taxable value. As a result, the blurred line between their role in both supply (production) and demand (sales) has—for better or for worse—opened the door to an important conversation about the concepts of source, destination, taxable presence, and profit attribution.

Seeing the largest digitalized businesses paying minimal tax in the jurisdictions where they provide services, policymakers are raising questions about the adequacy of the current tax system in both generating a sufficient level of taxation from such highly digitalized businesses and appropriately distributing that taxation across countries.[1] Resolving these issues is now becoming increasingly important as almost all businesses are steadily moving toward what might be termed a digital asymptote.

A number of policy proposals have been put forward which seek to limit the scope of tax avoidance and tax competition, by attempting to pre-determine a distribution of taxable profits across countries. Many are predicated—implicitly or explicitly—on the idea that the user has a role to play in value creation, justifying the designation of source-based taxing rights to the jurisdiction in which they are located (see, for example, European Commission 2018; HM Treasury 2017). Most prominent among these are the proposals for pure formulary apportionment, or a hybrid residual profit allocation alternative, both of which include some measure of user value as an allocation key. Another related proposal is the allocation of profit to market jurisdictions based on marketing intangibles, also justified by the notion that soliciting the sustained engagement and active participation of users is a critical component of value creation. In the interim, a number of countries have begun to implement user-based turnover taxes, targeting specific digitalized industries and activities.

Many of these proposals have tended to restrict the scope of special tax treatment, singling out particular activities or business models that are seen as particularly data intensive. Yet, as noted in IMF (2019), the collection and use of potentially monetizable information is so pervasive in today's economy that drawing a line between cases in which users are and are not material contributors is inevitably fraught. It would seem that if user data is indeed being exploited at a scale large and wide enough for it to be both recognized as an economic input to production and protected on behalf of the user, it should be recognized for all businesses.

This chapter attempts to understand more comprehensively the role that user-generated value can or should play in determining the structure of the future corporate tax system. It starts by setting out the contentious issue of the role of the user in digitalized business models, and then explores the way in which

---

[1] For example, see the Institute on Taxation and Economic Policy (ITEP) report: https://itep .org/amazon-in-its-prime-doubles-profits-pays-0-in-federal-income-taxes/.

recognition of the user as a source of profits might alter the allocation of taxing rights and the apportionment of profits, respectively. The chapter then turns to a discussion of alternative instruments for taxing the returns to user participation, drawing on lessons from the taxation of location-specific rents in the extractive industries, before concluding.

UNDERSTANDING USER-GENERATED VALUE

In this section, the focus is on the exchange between users and a digitalized business, and the question of whether the former generate "value" for the latter.

The internet—including the decreasing fixed costs of accessing it—and increasing global connectivity have provided the opportunity for e-commerce transactions to grow substantially, vastly increasing the potential number of users and the scale and scope of their digital activities.

Users are claimed to create value in two ways. The first is the provision—or allowing for the collection—of personal data and the creation of digital content, which can then be monetized by the business. The increasing digitization of everyday activities means that individuals produce trails of information almost continuously as they consume goods and services. The data being generated and harvested from these users is not only vast but also an integral part of the business models of the most highly digitalized businesses, allowing the services offered to be better refined for new and existing users. The second is the role that users play in building a network, which is also critical to the viability of many of these digital business models.

The User

The user of the good or service is typically identified as the buyer or consumer of a good or service, regardless of whether the transaction takes place physically (in person) or virtually (online). Below are some specific examples of how users interact with digitalized businesses (and one another) to help clarify the types of individuals we are considering in this paper:

- A user can purchase a good or service online. In doing so, the user also reveals information about their preferences, which are recorded by the business for future use and monetization.[2] During this transaction the user is exchanging not only a financial payment for the underlying good or service, but also data about themselves in exchange for the use of the online marketplace. Where a third-party digitalized platform intermediates transactions between a buyer and a seller (two-sided markets), both parties are considered users of the service.

---

[2] While the value of business-to-business e-commerce transactions is larger, business-to-consumer e-commerce transactions are the primary focus in the current debate.

- A user can browse the internet using a "free" search engine service or mobile application, without ever financially transacting. In this case, the user is sharing and revealing information about themselves and their interests as they do so, in exchange for accessing search (and match) services.

- A user can interact with other individuals over social media platforms. They can post information and generate digital content (for example, educational material, experiences, photos, videos, views about and reactions to events), or promote certain goods and services in the role of social influencer. In doing so, again the user is revealing information about themselves as they use the platform, trading it in return for the ability to interact with their community.

- A user can operate a device that is connected to the internet and through which the manufacturer collects data on its users. This is increasingly common with the internet of things—the networking of everyday physical objects or "things" embedded with sensors to send and receive data (for example, thermostats, vacuum cleaners, toothbrushes, and cars).

The more exchanges that take place, the greater the flow of data from the user to the business and the larger the information set about the user collected—that is, the stock of data about the user increases. And while previously personal data might have been restricted to discrete facts (such as name, age, income, address, health, and education history) in a computer database, the data collected by digital service providers consists of vast real-time flows of unstructured information on individuals' web browsing activity and use of web applications.

Common to all of these interactions is the so-called digital barter: users exchange—knowingly or otherwise—data on their preferences and activity, which can then be used and monetized by the business for a free or underpriced digital service. While recent highly publicized data breaches have raised awareness about the corporate practice of personal data collection and trading, it seems fair to say that a large majority of users have been unaware of the extent to which they are passively generating personal data that is being harvested and monetized. When signing up for a service, users typically consent—without fully realizing—to this monitoring of their digital activity, with little or no option to maintain privacy. Some companies are even able to follow a user's activity when they are no longer using their platform, through the use of tracking cookies. Similarly, a number of web applications have access to a user's location even when they are not actively using the application. In these cases, data is observed by the business and collection is carried out with the user's formal consent—for example, by accepting terms of service—but without their direct involvement, active transmission, or complete understanding.

Some observers distinguish between this type of passive data generation, provided unconsciously while consuming digital services, and active user contributions on social media platforms. In the case of passive data collection, where the user's role is limited to their prior consent, it has been argued that it is the business and not the user who really "produces" the raw input data (Becker and

Englisch 2019). As such, mere acquiescence to being observed should not be deemed as cocreation of value by users. These observers argue that only when user data is actively solicited or provided—for instance, in the form of survey or complaint—should users be regarded as creating value.[3] However, in practice, the line between active and passive data provision is not only difficult to draw, but more importantly is irrelevant as long as both types of data have value and can be monetized.

User Data

Once collected, this data is used by the companies in a number of different ways. For example,

- Businesses can use the data to refine existing products and services or develop new ones, similar to the way in which customer focus groups are used.[4] Large consumer data sets are now also being used for the development of data-intensive machine learning and artificial intelligence technology.

- Companies can analyze data to discern behavioral trends and preferences for marketing purposes—for example, to create more targeted advertisements, either for their own products and services or to provide advertising services to third parties.

- Data can be used by digital platforms to customize and improve search and matching functions. An example of the former are recommendation engines, which suggest goods and services a user might enjoy based on matching their preferences with those of other users deemed similar.

- Data can be sold in its raw or processed form to other businesses, which can then refine it further for use or sell it on again. An industry of data mining and brokerage firms has emerged that specializes in the collection and sale of consumer data sets. These companies harvest data using multiple access points across a range of internet-based activities and then package it for sale to retailers and advertisers.[5]

Given the different ways that digitalized businesses can benefit from user data, they have often invested heavily in honing techniques to collect and analyze it. As

---

[3] Other examples of valuable user contributions include those that (1) are only temporary in nature, such as product and service feedback that eventually expires; (2) are already compensated, such as paid social media influencers; or (3) deliberately eschew remuneration to (altruistically) improve noncommercialized goods, such as pro bono open source collaboration.

[4] On some platforms, users are unwittingly even training business algorithms (for example, to recognize faces, by observing how users tag photos on social media platforms, and to identify traffic patterns and optimal routes by tracking driver movements on navigation applications).

[5] The industry includes not only the large technology companies but also entities such as credit rating agencies (for example, Experian) and data analytics firms (for example, Axiom and Oracle). In cases where data is mined and gathered by such firms, rather than via the provision of digital services, users are left uncompensated and unaware of the use of their personal data. Regulations around such web scraping or mining are only now emerging.

such, consumer data has now become a strategic asset for most retail businesses, many of which rely on data acquired to maintain a competitive advantage by way of knowledge-based product improvements or services.

While the collection of personal data by companies has raised a number of issues around the right to data privacy and the appropriate use of such data, at the heart of taxation debate, and the focus of this chapter, is the issue of compensation for the use of this commercially valuable data. Given the information asymmetry between the user and the company with respect to data collection and use, as well as the lack of options to maintain privacy, is it clear that the user is currently being adequately compensated for their data in the digital barter? And if they are not, should they be remunerated directly, and then taxed under the personal income tax schedule with that remuneration deducted at corporate level? Or should the government tax a portion of the profits of digitalized businesses on their behalf? In other words, should user-generated value establish source-based taxing rights for the country in which the users reside? And if so, how would such a system operate?

A number of observers have proclaimed data to be the "oil" of the twenty-first century (Gupta and others 2017). Indeed, increased data collection and processing capabilities have driven a large amount of new economic activity. And just as natural resource companies explore for and then extract crude oil from designated national deposits using exploration and extraction technology, user data is collected from individuals during the digital barter. In the same way that resource companies process and refine the commodity into various oil-based products for onward sale, data is either traded among brokers or processed to facilitate the provision of revenue-generating data-intensive services. And in both cases, the underlying assets, the users, as with natural resource assets, are immobile, or unique to a particular location, giving rise to the possibility of "location-specific rents" (Cui 2018).

The analogy with natural resources is not exact: unlike information, oil is a rival good. Varian, Farrell, and Shapiro (2005) note that rather than data "ownership," the more appropriate concept for data is "access," on the basis that data is not usually "sold" in the manner that private goods are; rather, it is (or at least should be) licensed for specific uses. Given that the resource is never "depleted" in the same way that physical commodities would be, the access to an underlying data pool or asset may be the more appropriate terminology. And while in the resource sectors the scarcity of the nonrenewable resource leads to the generation of large economic rents when extracted, in the case of personal data, the source of large-scale rents, if they arise, are not due to the scarcity of the resource, but rather to the natural monopoly effects described in Aslam and Shah (2020).

Despite these differences, as we will explore further in this chapter, the analogy with natural resources may provide valuable comparative insights for the tax treatment of user-generated data. First, the case for allocating taxing rights over resource rents to the host country is widely accepted, and legal provisions to create such taxing rights are well established. Second, as data becomes increasingly standardized and commoditized, valuation methods for natural resources could prove useful, as well as the institutional and regulatory frameworks that would be necessary to achieve this. Third, international practice in tax policy toward the extractive industries may provide insights into how best to design a fiscal regime to appropriately tax large potential economic rents from data extraction.

The Value of User Data

Determining the value of user data will be an important ingredient for some of the methods for apportioning and attributing company profits to countries where users are located, which we cover later in the chapter.

Does Data Even Have Any Value?

This determination requires some common acceptance that raw data, before any processing by the company, does in fact have some inherent value. This would seem logical, just as any primary commodity has some value before it is processed and transformed into a final product (for example, crude oil, which has value in its raw form upon extraction).[6]

Many digitalized businesses have, however, claimed that such data is only valuable once it has been analyzed and processed—that is, the real value comes from the intangible assets, such as algorithms and coding, which are used to interpret data and provide the revenue-generating service. The latter reasoning has been used to undermine the assertion that user-generated value can be attributed to users, and to instead claim that all value creation is done at the level of the firm that manipulates the data. While it may be the case that a large portion of the value realized from data is generated in the processing stages, it may equally be argued that without any user data to process there would be no value realized at all.

Moreover, user data is a nonrival but excludable "club" good—similar to other inputs such as "know-how" or "ideas" that feature in endogenous growth models (Romer 1990)—which benefits only those businesses that collect, buy, trade, and process it. The company would not be incentivized to collect user data—by providing services for free—unless there were some value in doing so, and the fact that companies have proprietorship over the data they collect on their users is one facet that allows companies to secure market power and extract rents. If all user data was to be made publicly available, the value derived from the excludability property would disappear. [7]

---

[6] Varian (2019) describes a data pyramid to depict the relationship among data, information, and knowledge. A system must be designed to first collect the data, and subsequently organize and analyze that data in order to turn it into information that can be understood by humans, the insights from which can be turned into knowledge.

[7] Businesses could still charge users or governments for collecting, storing, and processing public data. But companies would have to rely to a far greater extent on their algorithms, intellectual property, and other intangible assets to derive rents from digital interactions with users without ownership and control over user data. It is likely competition would increase then, driving down rents.

Determinants of Data Value

From the perspective of the firm, user data is a very heterogeneous good, and it—and therefore its value—is likely to depend on the type of digital service being provided, as well as the characteristics of the data, such as quality, utility, and the availability of substitutes. Indeed, the value of user data to a firm can be affected by a wide range of variables, including the following:

- The value of user data will depend on its vintage, quality, and sensitivity (for example, data value may change over time in response to security issues, litigation, or legal regulations, which affects how it can be used).

- The value of user data will vary from one individual to another based on their economic profile—for example, their affluence (purchasing power), propensity to spend, and consumption habits—and therefore the extent to which their engagement with a platform can be monetized (HM Treasury 2018). In this way, the average value of data will also vary by country based on the distribution of its users and its economic size, and so on.

- The value of user data can change around key life events, such as marriage or childbearing.

- The value of user data can depend on the intensity of a user's engagement with a service. Some users are much more active and generate significantly larger data volumes than others—increasingly accurate user profiles may make them more or less valuable to a company.

- The more users a business has, the more valuable will be the aggregate data set collected for the purposes of inferring trends and preferences. The value of data is likely to increase more than proportionately with the volume collected; this nonlinearity is driven by network externalities that are discussed later in this chapter. The value of data to a particular firm will also depend on its productivity and the amount of data already in the firm's possession.

As we can see, given that users generate data of differing quantity and quality, valuing data can be complex and highly context dependent. Moreover, since data is not widely traded on markets but often stays within the firm that has produced it, it is hard to value, because its economic usefulness depends on the individual capacity of the acquiring firm to distill relevant information from it using algorithms, aggregation, and other tools, and subsequently to use this information to meet customer needs. Companies can also combine publicly available and proprietary data to create unique data sets for sale or use.

Conversely, from the perspective of the user, how they value their data will depend on the individual's preferences regarding data privacy, as well as the value they place on the service they are trading their data for—both the initial service as well as the customization of that service, which may depend on user activity. Just as for firms, these values will vary by individual, and will depend on the degree of trust in the firm's integrity regarding data usage. For those that value privacy highly, the net benefit of using digital services will be lower. In addition, the perceived profits accruing to the businesses that harness this data could factor into the user's willingness to engage in the digital barter.

Imputing the Value of Data

Data brokerage business sell information, but little is known about the value of such sales. It is, however, possible to get some idea of the value of user data—much like other intangibles—from past mergers and acquisitions, as well as bankruptcies. Examples include the sale of RadioShack's data in following its 2015 bankruptcy; Microsoft's 2016 acquisition of LinkedIn ($260 per user), and Facebook's purchases of Instagram in 2012 ($20 per user) and WhatsApp in 2014 ($42 per user).

Small-scale efforts have emerged to create a user-centric personal data economy that empowers individuals to retain control over their data and in some cases monetize it themselves (for example, Datacoup and Meeco). The converse approach is the pay-for-privacy model, where consumers pay an additional fee to prevent their data from being collected and mined for advertising purposes (Elvy 2017). Although not yet widely used, these efforts also provide some initial indications of how users value their own personal data.

The issue at hand is how to value a commodity for which there are no market prices or established benchmarks. Open and transparent markets in which standardized units of user data can be traded have failed to develop so far, preventing businesses and governments from quantifying data inputs to production. Institutions, regulations, and transparency are therefore needed to build economy-wide (minimum) rules for benchmark values for different types of data. Then, just as for oil, country-specific adjustments can be made to determine country-specific values for user data.

In the absence of such benchmarks, policymakers might look to more observable proxies of user data value. Some proposals have looked to the final revenues of companies from certain activities. However, unlike natural resources, data is not a physical commodity that can be traced from the point of extraction to a specific point of consumption. Rather, it will likely be blended, processed, and analyzed for use in delivering a wide range of goods and services in a range of different countries. The nonlinear value of data poses an additional challenge in establishing a method to netback from these final revenues to the initial information used as inputs to digital services.

One exception may be the case of advertising, where data is used as an input in determining the placement of person-specific (and, therefore, location-specific) advertisements.[8] In principle, each advertisement viewed by a particular user has

---

[8] Advertising services provided by large multinational enterprises such as Google or Facebook are typically priced using instantaneous sealed-bid auctions, which take place every time someone searches on Google or visits a site that shows AdWords advertisements. Companies can specify the target audience of their advertisement, as well as minimum and maximum bid parameters. Bids are typically based on a cost per click; a cost per viewable impression (that is, number of times an ad shows in a viewable position); or a cost per acquisition (that is, when people take a specific action on a website after clicking the advertisement, such as a purchase or sign-up). Advertising revenues are therefore made up of this variable component, along with fixed minimum payments and service fees.

an associated value, determined by auction according to the willingness to pay by online retailers, and would presumably correlate closely with the relative value of the initial data provided by that user. However, the blending of data from different sources, possibly across different countries, when determining how to best target advertisements would mean that the value of the advertisement is only a proxy for that value of that particular user's data.[9]

More generally, if revenues are used to derive a proxy for user value, what would be necessary, then, is an agreement on the size and scope of netback deductions to determine the value of the initial information used as inputs to these services. In the case of extractive industries, countries often use the net smelter return concept, taking the international market price of the final refined metal product as a benchmark and making deductions for treatment and refining costs to derive the value of the mineral at the point of extraction. We will return to this analogy in more detail later.

User Value from Network Externalities

Beyond the use of personal data in production, the other much-cited source of user-generated value is the role that users play in creating valuable networks for digitalized businesses. The success of digital platforms relies on the interaction between both buyers and sellers, which gives rise to strong complementarities—notably, network and information externalities—where the value in transactions increases for both groups as the numbers on each side increase (Armstrong 2006; Caillaud and Jullien 2003; Ellison and Fudenberg 2003; Evans 2003; Rochet and Tirole 2003; Rysman 2009).

Of course, such network effects have existed well before digitalization (Katz and Shapiro 1985, 1994; Liebowitz and Margolis 1994). For example, the underlying idea of a ride-sharing app is that each individual user adds to the pool of users that make up the network and thereby increases the overall value of the service. This concept applies to a number of both digital and nondigital networks. In a nondigital setting, a farmer's market is more valuable to buyers and sellers if there are more farmers and more shoppers participating. Newspapers and television networks are another widely referenced example where network externalities exist between the market of readers and advertisers. Collier (2018) and Collier and Venables (2018) also highlight how the externalities associated with urban agglomeration produce rents that accrue to a small group of individuals and businesses (the "urban surplus").[10]

Digitalization has exponentially increased both the scale and the speed with which network effects ratchet up. Users posting on social media provide

---

[9] It is likely that the advertisement displayed on a user's screen may not be a simple function of their own data but may rather be derived from a large pool of data from other similar users, particularly if a retailer is entering a new market or the user is new to the platform.

[10] Henry George was the original proponent, in 1879, of a tax on the value of land to capture some of the benefits of land appreciation in urban areas.

content that can quickly attract other subscribers, and the more users engage with one another on the platform, the more content they create, and so on (OECD 2018). And the more users there are on the platform, the more the firm will invest in its development. There are also information externalities: users on retail platforms provide feedback through reviews that influence other users of the platform in their consumption choices. While users might be acting in their own interest, their actions both attract other users and continue to reveal more and more commercially valuable information about themselves, creating increasingly valuable opportunities for marketing and product improvement. Other digitalized markets also display such scale effects, such as in the financial services sector (for example, for credit card services) and in the insurance market, where liquidity and heterogeneity of participants is particularly important.

Given the existence of network externalities in both digital and nondigital marketplaces, they would not appear to justify ring-fencing digitalized services and taxing them differently. However, some governments feel that they are a source of rents for the businesses that capture growing user bases. Cui (2018) also notes the location specificity of network effects (both direct and indirect) as the source of location-specific rents. Moreover, the policy implications are unclear. On the one hand, the network externalities highlighted so far also appear to be positive—they generate increasing value for users that are part of the network. From the perspective of optimal taxation, a positive externality in a one-sided market would, in fact, lead to the underprovision of the good or service, so the government should instead subsidize it to increase its production. On the other hand, for two-sided markets, Kind, Köthenbürger and Schjelderup (2008, 2010) show instead that increasing (ad valorem) tax rates—rather than using subsidies—would increase output and improve welfare.

Even if policymakers could rationalize the taxation of rents, the network externalities that generate them can be just as challenging as user data to evaluate. Cui (2018) provides a theoretical description of how user value (encompassing both data provision and network effects) could be measured. Such a method requires measurement of the demand curves for a range of products and services and measurement of the changes in such demand curves upon the introduction of online reviews and customized advertising, from which one can calculate the increase in producer surplus arising from such changes. As we proceed to examine how a system that allows countries to tax user-generated value might operate, we leave aside the notion of user-generated network externalities, and instead focus on value generated from user data.

Taxation or Regulation?

More generally, one might question whether tax is the right tool to address the issue of seemingly excessive rents being generated through network externalities. Markets where these network effects exist without any interoperability between providers typically tend toward monopoly, in the absence of any intervention.[11] As a result, there has been a rapid consolidation of power among certain digitalized businesses—such as internet search and social media firms—which have been able to develop some of the largest user bases thanks to positively reinforcing network effects. Facebook, for example, has over 2 billion users as of 2019, which is about 70 percent of the world's population that has access to internet.[12] This market concentration has reinforced the ability of only a handful of digital platforms to monopolize the aggregation and analysis of large amounts of personal data.

Indeed, where a market tends to natural monopoly, taxation is not typically the optimal policy response—regulation is typically the first best. The approaches can vary from breaking up monopolies into smaller units (for example, AT&T's Bell system in 1982) to price regulation. At present, few of the recent wave of digitalized businesses have been subject to any form of antitrust regulation in the United States. The previous notable case was that of Microsoft in 2001, in which it was asserted that the company was using its control over the personal computer market to force out competing operating systems and browsers. Google could be considered a potentially similar case, given its dominance of search and, therefore, advertising services—notably, the European Commission has already fined it for manipulated search results (EUR 2.42 billion in 2017) and for bundling activities (EUR 4.34 billion in 2018).

In the case of Amazon, some have argued that the company has become a utility—given its distribution infrastructure, which is used by many other businesses—and is engaging in anticompetitive actions by pricing below cost to eliminate competitors or force their acquisition by sale (Khan 2017). While this has not triggered reaction thus far, as the impact is admittedly to the benefit of the consumer, this "antitrust paradox" is reducing competition across the retail sector. Price regulation could be a natural response by regulators to such tactics.

What is ultimately important to note is that the economic features of platform-based digitalized businesses can incentivize rapid growth over profits in the short term to secure market dominance (Aslam and Shah 2020). This tends to make anticompetitive behavior, such as predatory pricing and the large-scale acquisition of competitors, a rational strategy. Furthermore, for those sorts of digital platforms where network effects lead to substantial market share through access to user data, and where breaking up companies into smaller (more regional) units does not necessarily solve the problem, price controls—where applicable—are the more efficient tool. Ultimately what works for one type of digitalized business might not be appropriate for others, making a business-by-business (or sector-by-sector) approach necessary. For example, specific regulation bills—akin to the

---

[11] Grinberg (2018) noted that while the fax machine network displayed network effects, the interoperability of fax machines made by different manufacturers and the further interoperability between various telephone providers meant that the network effect did not lead to a monopolistic result.

[12] About 40 percent of the world population has an internet connection today. In 1995, it was less than 1 percent. The number of internet users has increased tenfold from 1999 to 2013. The first billion was reached in 2005, the second billion in 2010, and the third billion in 2014.

US 1996 Telecommunications Act—that govern a wide range of activities, from data collection and privacy to ethical content, might be necessary for those companies that provide certain types of universal services, such as messaging and social media.

As Grinberg (2018) observes, the nature of these markets suggest that tax and regulation need to be appropriately distinguished in the digital economy debate. With ever-increasing market share, rents from monopoly power over information are likely to increase. By resorting to taxation as a means for sharing and redistributing the rents being generated by user-derived network externalities, the question is whether tax policy is being used to treat a symptom, whereas regulation might be more appropriate to address the underlying cause.

THE USER AS THE BASIS FOR THE RIGHT TO TAX AND ALLOCATE PROFITS

As noted, the nature of digital service provision sees the user play a dual role in their exchange with the service provider: the user is a producer of valuable information (while also generating network externalities) and a consumer of digital services. It is the potential difference between the values of these two legs of the exchange that many governments implicitly contest. They see users in their countries being insufficiently compensated for the inputs they supply in return for a service that has a marginal near-zero cost to provide (Aslam and Shah 2020). The uncompensated value accrues to the firm exploiting the information, boosting their rents, which on most occasions lies beyond the legal reach of the government.

In order to remedy the inadequate compensation of users for valuable inputs, some governments claim that the location of users—that is, where they consume digital services and thus where the valuable data input is generated—should confer both the right to tax and a share of profits. Indeed, one of the hallmarks of digitalization is the decoupling of market (or user) presence and the physical presence of companies. As such, existing nexus and profit allocation rules are ineffective should countries wish to exert taxing rights under the source principle.

If we accept the premise that users contribute value, the first step is to establish a legal basis for taxation in the countries in which users are located. One related question is whether "user countries" should have supply-side source-based rights—with users as factors of production—or demand-side destination-based rights. The second step is to determine how users can be part of any profit allocation strategy. In other words, establishing taxing rights is a necessary but not sufficient condition for allocating profits. These are the issues and questions we turn to in this section.

Designating Taxing Rights

The Production and Ownership of User Data

Establishing a right to tax the income derived from user-generated value relies on carefully disentangling the relationships between the user, the digitalized business, and the data being traded between them. Typically, under rights conferred through national legislation, and by contractual agreement, the owner of any factor of production is directly remunerated by the business for its use, and that income is then subject to tax in the jurisdiction in which the factor is located. However, with largely undefined property rights over personal data, and in the absence of legislation governing the collection of or access to data, ownership over the user data is implicitly vested in the companies that collect it, with no legal obligation to compensate the individuals that have generated this data—beyond the digital service for which this data may have been exchanged. Many companies also feel justified in owning the data as it is their intellectual know-how and technology that enabled its collection, storage, and processing in the first instance. Furthermore, nonrival user data can be used repeatedly by the business and even sold to other businesses, which means that without any rights or control, users are unable to extract the full return on their data.

Ultimately, there is a dilemma over who should have ownership or control over user data, either explicitly through legal property rights or implicitly through compensation for its use. Does the data belong to the user or the firm that collected it? Should user data be owned by the government on behalf of its citizens? If these issues can be defined more clearly, it might then be possible to determine the basis on which the user (or government) can be compensated. Recent reforms have gone in this direction, with greater attention paid to regulating the privacy of and control over personal data, the stringency of which has implications for both ownership and value, and, therefore, the possibility for compensation of users. [13]

If we take the view that the underlying subject of the data, the user, is entitled to compensation for its use, then the nature of such compensation will depend on the ownership or control of the data once it has been collected. If the data is owned by the company, then the relationship between user and business could be analogous to that of an employee and employer, where the former has been actively engaged by the latter and whose time and inputs should be contracted and compensated, but who do not own their work product—in this case, user data.[14] The level of compensation could in this case reflect the present value of the data, which may, of course, be used repeatedly by the firm over time. Alternatively, if the ownership or control over data remains with the user, then there would need to be mechanisms in place to allow businesses to access and remunerate users accordingly, perhaps either on a per-use basis or over a certain time period. From a taxation perspective, if the user is compensated directly for primary collection or sale of their data, this remuneration would be deducted at the corporate level, and the user would simply be taxed under the personal income tax schedule—in a manner similar to a self-employed business that declares its earned income.

---

[13] New data privacy requirements (for example, the EU's General Data Protection Regulation 2016/679) apply to a wide range of companies and activities, including search engine, social media, online retailers.

[14] There are numerous practical, legal, and administrative issues with treating users—both regular and casual, numbering for many digitalized businesses in the millions—as employees, leaving this notion as a loose but instructive analogy at best.

A related issue is whether users should be individually compensated or whether the government should be compensated on their behalf. Indeed, the nonstandard and person-specific nature of data—together with the ability of individuals to move location, change nationality, and so on—might suggest that individuals should directly be compensated for access to or collection of their data. Unlike a subsurface natural resource that is generally acknowledged to be a collective national asset (though not in the United States, where subsurface rights belong to the landowner), it could be argued that user data is an inherently personal asset that lends itself more readily to the notion of individual sovereignty.

However, for individuals to be able to exercise and enforce these rights requires not only a strong legal system, but also additional shifts in technology. For example, for users to have full ownership and control over their data, they would need to be able to take it with them between digital platforms, retrieving and sharing their data as they move from one digital service provider to another, or at least monitoring its use. Therefore, the nature of system and software interoperability and data portability would need to evolve.

Moreover, the nature of the exchange of user data for digital services might raise practical questions regarding the feasibility of compensating each user for their data or access to the data. As noted earlier, digital barters are not large, infrequent transactions between businesses but instead are small, high-frequency microtransactions between businesses and consumers across multiple separate online platforms. For example, social media platforms and search engines record billions of "likes" and queries each day, and trillions of queries every year. The value of the data being traded in these microbarters is likely to vary significantly, and the current lack of a transparent market or an agreed standardized measure for the value of such data further exacerbates the difficulty in determining and reporting a verifiable person-specific financial value for each exchange.

A more practicable alternative might be achieved if custody over citizens' data were assigned to the government as a proxy. For example, in the case of natural resources, governments typically hold the resources in trust on behalf of their citizens and collect payment for extraction in the form of government revenues. In the case of digital services, data on the behavior and preferences of a country's citizens would be seen as a collective national asset with compensation for its use payable to the government. Indeed, a government is better placed to exert collective power on behalf of individuals who cannot capture their rents by levying a tariff (for example, an export tax) on the extraction of data by foreign digital service providers (Hufbauer and Lu, 2018; IMF, 2019). This arrangement would apply whether data ownership is transferred to the company upon collection or retained by the government, although the arrangement chosen (that is, time-bound access or indefinite ownership) would have implications for the level of compensation. And indeed, while user data is intrinsically tied to an individual, the nature of data collection, and the fact that the nonlinearly increasing value from user data is often derived not only from aggregating data related to a large number of individuals but also from multiple points in time, suggests the practical need to centralize ownership so as to coordinate access and compensation.

If such an arrangement were developed, companies that wish to collect user information would then need to compensate the jurisdiction in which the information was collected in accordance with agreed rules, through the corporate income tax system or through other tax instruments, such as a payment of a royalty. Such an arrangement still does not obviate the need for clear valuation rules around the data collected but does allow for the possibility of using country-level proxies or formulary methods for determining user value, which will be explored further in this section.

Reappraising the Permanent Establishment Concept

For governments to have the right to tax the returns associated with user data through the corporate income tax system, there needs to be an explicit basis on which to recognize the economic activity of data collection in the local jurisdiction. As noted in Chapter 3, the traditional basis for a government exerting income taxing rights over a foreign multinational enterprise doing business and deriving profits from their activity in their jurisdiction is the presence of a "permanent establishment." The following discussion considers how this concept might be amended to facilitate source-based taxing rights over value generated from user data (see Chapter 11 for a more general examination of the concept).

The collection of data from users—regardless of whether it is in exchange for a digital service or not—is typically conducted remotely by the business without any physical presence in the country of the user and therefore does not create a permanent establishment under current definitions. Even when online retailers operate storage and distribution centers in market jurisdictions, these are typically exempted in treaty definitions of permanent establishment (OECD 2017b, Article 5, para. 4). Local affiliates are also commonly structured to have no ownership interest in intangible assets, perform no development, enhancement, maintenance, protection, and exploitation functions, and do not assume any risks. Accordingly, only a modest return may be allocated to these limited-risk distributors.

While activities such as local data collection or warehousing were previously considered to be of a merely auxiliary nature—typically contributing only marginally to business profits and therefore neglected for the purposes of profit allocation or justifying only low profit attributions—they now form core elements of digitalized business models. In other words, previously simple routine functions for which it was generally acceptable to allocate only a small share of the overall business profits have arguably become key activities for many firms, with a pivotal role for data analytics.

However, this surge in cross-border business-to-consumer sales as a result of digitalization has taken us into a gray area. Traditional exporters of goods and services have never been subject to permanent establishment for tax purposes in importing countries. This could be due to the fact that the majority of exports were typically from business to business, especially in the case of intermediate goods. However, the scale of growth of peer-to-peer exports, as well as exports of retail and intermediation services by highly-digitalized businesses is straining the traditional permanent establishment concept. As businesses increasingly digitalize, the user in the importing country generates valuable inputs for an increasing number of exporters. By ignoring these issues, a consequence of a tax system that relies on physical presence to assert taxing rights is to create variation in the cost of capital between those businesses exporting to or producing domestically for the same market.

Any solution that calls for a different allocation of profits beyond what the current system enables will need to be supported by new or expanded taxing right. As has also been acknowledged under the OECD's (2019) Pillar One proposal (the "Unified Approach"), the current definition of permanent establishment would need to be modified to establish the right for user jurisdictions to tax multinational enterprises that collect data on their citizens. Until then, a multinational enterprise can sidestep the nexus issue by operating remotely, or establishing local affiliates that are not entitled to an appropriate share of the group's profit.

Many have already put forward ways to modify the permanent establishment concept. For example, online retailers, warehouses, and distribution networks developed to cater to users (buyers and sellers) were previously excluded from the definition of the permanent establishment in the existing version of the OECD Model Treaty (OECD 2017b). However, Action 7 of the OECD/G20 Base Erosion and Profit Shifting (BEPS) Project and Article 12 of the Multilateral Instrument provide a basis for an extensive application of the permanent establishment concept to account for the fact that these functions are no longer merely auxiliary but instead form a strategically decisive component of the business model. Some countries have also already taken steps to change the permanent establishment threshold tests in domestic legislation, including India, Israel, Slovakia, and the United Kingdom.

User-Based Approaches

In proposing options to extend the permanent establishment concept to include the location of the user and their data, a number of approaches focus on characteristics of the market. OECD (2018) sets out options for modifying and expanding the permanent establishment definition to include a range of quantitative and qualitative benchmarks, such as the number of registered users, the number of active users, the amount of revenue earned within a market, the level of expenditure, or the existence of a local domain, a dedicated local digital platform and local payment options. Hongler and Pistone (2015) suggest establishing a new permanent establishment nexus by appealing to the idea that users enhance the value of digital services.

Recent legislative developments have also provided glimpses into the way that users can qualify as a form of nexus. In the landmark South Dakota vs. Wayfair, Inc. case, the United States Supreme Court ruled in June 2018 that physical presence should not be required for a state to compel out-of-state sellers to collect state sales tax on sales to customers in a state, thereby overturning its own precedent dating back to 1992.[15] In other words, a company can now be obliged to collect sales tax from the consumer for the jurisdiction in which that consumer is located, even if the seller has no physical presence there.

Specifically, the wording of the majority opinion noted that "a business may be present in a State in a meaningful way without that presence being physical in the traditional sense of the term." The opinion goes on to say that "[i]t is not clear why a single employee or a single warehouse should create a substantial nexus while 'physical' aspects of pervasive modern technology should not. For example, a company with a website accessible in South Dakota may be said to have a physical presence in the State via the customers' computers. A website may leave cookies saved to the customers' hard-drives, or customers may download the company's app on to their phones. Or a company may lease data storage that is permanently, or even occasionally, located in South Dakota."[16]

The idea that virtual access to a catalogue of people (for example, Facebook); products (for example, Amazon or eBay); services (for example, Airbnb or Uber); or other websites (for example, Google) could be equivalent to an individual visiting a physical shop—in this case corresponding to social clubs, department stores, letting agents and taxi services, or public libraries—and browsing these items in person is a powerful notion. The devices that provide users with mobile market access and the opportunity to browse goods and services from any location—computers or mobile phones—could therefore form the basis for location-specific permanent establishment based on the location where the user is when they use a service. In a number of countries, servers already give rise to a permanent establishment even if the business has no other presence. In February 2012 India's Authority for Advance Rulings ruled that a foreign company's server constitutes a permanent establishment for tax purposes, and the profits arising from it are taxable—so including devices would be an extension of that existing concept. This was also later clarified in the commentary to the updated UN and OECD Model Tax Conventions, at least in cases where multinational enterprises own or lease a whole server, although not in cases where they rent a space on another entity's server (OECD 2017b).

Even before the Supreme Court case, US states had already attempted to use novel interpretations of "physical presence" to establish nexus and impose sales tax collection obligations on out-of-state retailers: the so-called Amazon laws. For example, in September 2017 Massachusetts adopted a "cookie nexus" law, under which out-of-state sellers are deemed to have a physical presence with the state

---

[15] The ruling is in respect to South Dakota's law, but has implications for all US states.

[16] In the end, the case upheld the nexus rules of the South Dakota sales tax, that is, on a yearly basis delivering more than $100,000 of goods and services into the state or engaging in 200 or more separate transactions for the delivery of goods or services into the state. By taking this broader approach to nexus, the Supreme Court sidestepped questions such as whether cookies, apps, and so forth can amount to physical presence, as this would have "embroil[ed] courts in technical and arbitrary disputes about what counts as physical presence." (South Dakota v. Wayfair, Inc., 585 U.S. ___ (2018)).

simply by placing a cookie on the computer or device of an in-state purchaser.[17] Ohio followed suit with a similar law, under which nexus is presumed to exist when a vendor uses "in-state software" to sell taxable goods or services to local customers. As early as 2008 some states had already enacted so-called click-through nexus statutes, which define nexus to include out-of-state sellers that reward in-state residents who refer potential customers through links on a website.

However, even cookie nexus, while a novel approach, can run into familiar threshold questions as to whether a cookie can be considered a significant physical presence. It can be argued that the electronic data that comprises a cookie is intangible and therefore incapable of creating a physical presence. A cookie, after all, cannot physically be held, weighed, or touched on its own. But the idea of what can be considered tangible is expanding in many contexts.

Investment- or Asset-Based Approaches

Other approaches focus on the company's investments to access a market and develop its customer base. For example, Schön (2018) contends that if it can be shown that a digitalized business has invested capital in a specific market in order to access a specific customer base, this investment can give rise to taxing rights in the respective market country, not simply because there is a market with customers ordering goods or services, but because the company has invested into that market and expects a return on this investment.

However, to contain the proliferation of small permanent establishments around the world, one would have to introduce a meaningful qualitative and quantitative threshold on that investment, such as singling out specific digital elements of that investment or setting a minimum level of investment to bring forward the right to tax. It would also require carving out the part of the firm's investment that is of a general nature and the part that is devoted to individual markets. For example, for firms which process user-generated content, like Facebook, Instagram, Snapchat, Twitter, or YouTube, this would require identifying how much has been invested in providing "free" communication services to these customers in order to create market access for the profit-generating advertising business run by these firms. Likewise, Google invests in a local market by providing search functions to local customers, which enables them to sell advertising slots to business clients.

While this approach is fully in line with basic legal and economic assumptions about the corporate income tax, it is clearly not related to the "benefit principle"

---

[17] The regulation provides that a vendor has physical presence to the extent that (among other requirements) it has "property interests in and/or the use of in-state software (for example, 'apps') and ancillary data (for example, 'cookies') which are distributed to or stored on the computers or other physical communications devices of a vendor's in-state customers, and may enable the vendor's use of such physical devices." The collection requirement is only imposed to the extent that the vendor's annual sales total at least $500,000 or 100 individual transactions (http://www.mass.gov/dor/businesses /help-and-resources/legal-library/regulations/64h-00-sales-and-use-tax/830-cmr-64h-1-7.html).

in its classical spatial form. This is because these "country-specific" investments may be targeted at a local customer base, but they are not dependent on any spatial relationship to the market country or any specific public goods provided by the market country. Taxing the returns on these "sunk" investments could be justified in economic terms as far as these profits may typically represent location-specific rents that are immune to erosion by tax competition.

Along the same lines, an alternative proposal for establishing physical presence and allowing market jurisdictions a basis for claiming more taxable income—albeit only to a limited extent—focuses on "marketing intangibles." These are broadly defined assets that can include brands, goodwill, and trademarks, as well as user data (OECD 2017a).[18] Advocates for this option acknowledge that the value of marketing intangibles is linked to the market in which sales to users take place, potentially meaning that the market country is the source of value for the marketing intangible. Once rights have been assigned, a formula would be required to allocate profits to the various newly empowered jurisdictions.

Overall, this proposal aims to prevent unnecessary ring-fencing while also helping to preserve the existing arm's length principle. However, many companies—notably in the pharmaceuticals industry—contend that by using marketing intangibles to extend taxing rights, a disproportionate share of profits would be moved away from research and development toward populous end markets. Should marketing intangibles form the basis of a new approach, there is a risk that policymakers may limit its application to only those business-to-consumer businesses for which such intangibles are sizeable; that is, certain types of businesses end up being targeted and ring-fenced.

Moreover, distinguishing marketing intangibles from other types of intellectual property is a difficult exercise. Just as with user data, the subjectivity of the value of marketing intangibles remains an issue that could lead either to disputes between territories or to an arbitrary formula that is not based on any core principles, meaning it could change at any time as political consensus shifts.

A related proposal has been put forward by Becker and Englisch (2019), who define the concept of a "sustained user relationship" built on the repeated provision of online services over time. This concept can serve as a proxy for the potential to legally collect certain types of data from a user continuously and on a large scale, and to exploit them commercially. This sustained user relationship—defined over some threshold—could be used to establish nexus for the allocation of taxing

---

[18] A "marketing intangible" is defined in the 2017 *OECD Transfer Pricing Guidelines for Multinational Enterprises and Tax Administrations* as "an intangible . . . that relates to marketing activities, aids in the commercial exploitation of a product or service and/or has an important promotional value for the product concerned. Depending on the context, marketing intangibles may include, for example, trademarks, trade names, customer lists, customer relationships, and proprietary market and customer data that is used or aids in marketing and selling goods or services to customers." (OECD 2017a, p.27). In its March 2019 comments to the OECD, Johnson & Johnson proposed a formula for profit attribution, starting with a fixed percentage of global operating profits, and adjusting it based on overall group profitability and business marketing expenditure across countries, subject to a ceiling and floor.

rights. As the authors themselves note, this nexus criterion does not differ markedly from an approach that emphasizes user participation. But for the purpose of profit allocation, the significance of the user relationship and the corresponding access to data could be more helpful for granting permanent establishment rather than assessing the value of uncompensated (user) labor.

Hence, one could treat the sustained user relationship as an intangible asset of the business that maintains it and can rely on it to systematically milk the relevant user data. This intangible also clearly would have a positive monetary value, in the same way previous corporate acquisitions have seen large amounts exchanged for user databases. Yet the valuation of this intangible remains as fraught as valuing the individual data. In this case, certain attributes of the data might be more relevant, such as the quality and strength of a typical relationship over time.

Allocating Profits

Even if the presence of a taxing right were to be agreed and resolved comprehensively, there are still some steps left before profits can be taxed. This includes determining (1) the level of profits attributable to each country, and (2) how profits should be taxed. The second step remains under the sovereign purview of the country once it has secured the right to tax profits. It is likely to consist of the application of the domestic corporate income tax to this new tax base. However, the first issue is more involved and relates back to the measurement of user value and the overall identification of business functions and factors that could determine how profits should be distributed.

Separate Accounting

As noted in Chapter 3, the current system is based on separate accounting, with each part of a multinational enterprise treated as a separate entity, with taxes determined on separately calculated profits, and with transfer prices required to be set under the arm's length principle. Under this current framework, the choices that multinational enterprises make as to how they internally organize themselves across multiple jurisdictions—between branches, holding companies, parent companies, subsidiaries, and so on, have important tax consequences.

Chapter 5 spelled out various difficulties of separate accounting under the arm's length principle, notably the technical difficulties in obtaining prices for hard-to-value goods and services, and the incentive created for profit shifting. The problems are particularly acute for highly digitalized companies. Their transactions involve unique and intangible goods and services, which are genuinely hard to value. And they often earn high rents from these assets, which can be shifted with relative ease to low-tax jurisdictions or tax-favored vehicles, such as intellectual property boxes. In the case of user data collection, using the arm's length principle approach would involve establishing the associated income and costs for the multinational enterprise, as if the collection agency were a separate enterprise. However, as digitalization leads to countries becoming increasingly integrated economically, it is impractical to use a separate accounting system to determine how much of a multinational enterprise's income is earned by an affiliate in one country and how much by an affiliate in another.

In sum, the application of arm's length principle is not only increasingly difficult but unrealistic as intellectual property and intangibles come to dominate company activity and value. The irony is that multinational enterprises arose precisely to avoid the inefficiencies that arise when unrelated companies must transact with one another at arm's length. The convergence of these frustrations with the existing arm's length principle and the increasingly digitalized economy, which has exacerbated the limitations of the current nexus requirement of a permanent establishment, has intensified the debate surrounding the fair allocation of taxing rights and the need for fundamental reform.

Formulary Apportionment for Highly Digitalized Businesses

An alternative to the separate accounting approach—discussed in detail in Chapter 14—would be to disregard all of these legal distinctions and simply look at a company as a large, single unit and allocate its profits by formula. In this chapter, the focus is not on the general pros and cons of formulary apportionment but rather on the question of whether formulary apportionment could effectively account for value created by digitalized businesses from user data, and if so, what it would look like.

There are a number of strengths of applying a formulary apportionment system to accommodate increasing digitalization:

- As the nature of business changes, the formula can be augmented (or reduced) to account for those factors that are most critical for determining a business's connection to a location—and the base for its tax liability. Formulae often vary by sector, such as in Canada, where special factors and weights apply to insurance, banking, and transportation, and in the United States,[19] where Alaska uses an origin-based sales factor for extractive industries (De Mooij, Liu, and Prihardini 2019).

- Formulary apportionment does not need to apply to all profits. To the extent that certain countries demand that a certain portion of profits must remain within their jurisdiction, apportionment can then be applied to residual profits (see next section). Again, in the case where market countries demand a share of profits given the contributions of their users, profits can be first split, with only a certain fraction available for apportionment using some sort of user-based factor.

The specification of the formula can have important implications for a number of reasons. For example, the inclusion of certain factors, such as assets and employment, creates an implicit tax on them, discouraging their accumulation in high-tax locations. Furthermore, not all of these factors might be relevant for

---

[19] The United States already uses formulary apportionment domestically to determine the taxable share of US-source corporate profits across states.

gradually digitalizing businesses. Payroll is one such case, which might find itself increasingly irrelevant: given the ability to sell remotely, there can be virtually zero labor presence in certain markets and therefore zero apportionment.

The principle that taxes should be applied "where value is created" fails to provide guidance on relevant factors (Devereux and Vella 2018). As discussed, there are many activities that create value on the demand or supply side. The chosen formula can therefore potentially combine a number of location-specific factors from both sides of the market. If measurable, these could include, for example, the following:

- *From the demand side:* sales, population (total or by age), mobile phone and internet penetration (as a proxy for usage of digital services)
- *From the supply side:* assets (total, tangible, intangible), employees (or payroll), users (volume, value of data they provide)

To the extent that user data is essential to digitalized businesses and can be valued, it can potentially feature in the formula. The latest draft proposal for the EU-wide Common Consolidated Corporate Tax Base includes a fourth data factor that reflects the collection and use of personal data of online platforms and services users.[20]

One proxy for user value is the volume of users, which can be measured in many ways. For example, a country's population could represent the potential maximum volume of users in each jurisdiction; alternatively, we could consider volume as that part of the population that has access to mobile telephony and the internet. However, it is unclear that the volume of users would be sufficient.

First, the population of a country is not static—it can change over the course of the year for many reasons. And a country's user population will include foreigners that are resident in the country as well as its own citizens. In other words, migration flows alter the population of a country throughout the year, especially in the case of seasonal flows from activities such as tourism, which can in many cases swell the numbers in a country at any one time—think small island tourist destinations.

Second, even with accurate statistics that can be used to gauge the flows and stock of users in each country, what will also matter for apportionment is intensity. It is not necessarily the case that each user is equally valuable both within and across countries. In April 2019, India proposed assigning different weights to different categories of digital businesses depending on the level of user intensity—namely, 10 percent to the users for those business models involving low or medium user intensity and 20 percent to those business models involving high user intensity. However, the determination of intensity remains undefined.[21]

---

[20] "Amendment 10 of European Parliament Legislative Resolution of 15 March 2018 on the Proposal for a Council Directive on a Common Consolidated Corporate Tax Base" (EC 2018).

[21] See India's Central Board of Direct Taxes, "Public Consultation on the Proposal for Amendment of Rules of Profit Attribution to permanent establishment-reg," April 18, 2019. (https://www.incometaxindia.gov.in/News/Public_consultation_Notice_18_4_19.pdf).

Moreover, it is not necessarily the case that each user is equally valuable both within and across countries. Certain income and demographic profiles would matter more for some businesses than others. For example, users from countries with higher per capita incomes would be more valuable for retail businesses, which therefore suggests that those economies should have a larger apportionment of profits.

The choice of factors can have important implications for the distribution of profits (see Figure 10.1). Large, populous economies that are both large-source and destination economies, such as the United States and China, would secure a larger share of profits under formulary apportionment with greater sensitivity to users (proxied by the size of the population). However, other destination countries with large markets would also gain substantially, while small-source countries would lose. To the extent that formulary apportionment is applied universally, tradable sectors with global supply chains would be affected disproportionately.

In addition, longer-term demographic trends that mean that the share of the youngest in the population—that is, those that typically use technology and digital services more frequently and intensively—is set to expand in certain parts of

Figure 10.1. Distribution of Alternative (User-Related) Factors for 20 Most Populous Economies

(2018; multiples of USA quantities; USA=1)

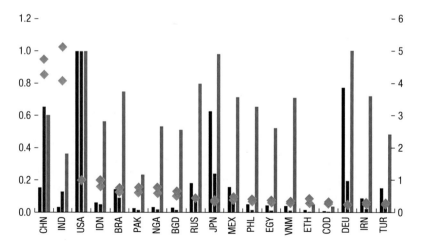

Sources: IMF, World Economic Outlook database; International Telecommunications Union; UN Department for Economic and Social Affairs, Population Division; authors' calculations.
Note: Data labels use International Organization for Standardization (ISO) country codes.
RHS = right-hand side.

the world while contracting in others. In this case, user-based factors would imply a gradual reallocation profits to these economies—notably in Africa and Asia—where demand for digital services is likely to be greater.

Residual Profit Allocation

Alternative forms of apportionment have also been proposed that allocate only residual profit by formula (Chapter 14). Such forms require distinguishing between routine and nonroutine returns to investment. The routine return can be calculated in a number of ways: for example, it could be associated with the economic concept of normal profits, calculated as some markup on costs or a fixed return on tangible assets. In doing so, it can also still allow for partial use of the existing arm's length principle approach.

The key notion is that residual profits are those that are harder to attribute to specific jurisdictions, that is, the profits of a business after the activities of service providers have been awarded a normal return. Once calculated, these profits can be allocated using an agreed-upon formula. This allocation of residual profits, while arguably adding a new layer of complexity, eliminates the existing complexity in measuring and valuing intangible assets. While still administratively complex, such a hybrid solution may be more politically palatable and expedient than comprehensive formulary apportionment, as it more closely resembles the current system.

One application of this method in a digital setting—though not part of the current OECD proposal for a unified approach—would be to attribute these profits to the value created by the activities of users, through quantitative or qualitative information, or through a simple percentage. This portion of profits could then be allocated between the jurisdictions in which the business has users, based on another agreed allocation factor, as discussed above.

ALTERNATIVE APPROACHES TO TAXING USER VALUE

We already introduced the analogy between user data and natural resources. In this section, we consider how other revenue-raising instruments could be used to compensate countries for the use of their citizens' personal data, drawing on experiences from the extractive industries. Moreover, we show that under certain conditions, even in the absence of agreement over the approach, the widespread implementation of unilateral user-based tax measures by governments would tend in the limit to the outcome under a user-based apportionment of global profits.

Royalties on User-Generated Value

Taxing User Value: Lessons from the Extractive Industries

The approach to taxation in the extractive sectors has evolved over time, in line with a shifting balance of power between host governments and investors. Hogan and Goldsworthy (2010) note that, prior to World War II, governments typically granted concessions to investors to explore for and extract natural resources in exchange for a relatively low burden of initial bonuses, royalties, and land rental fees. Decolonization after World War II and establishment of the permanent sovereignty principle[22] drove the desire of a number of resource-rich countries to receive a larger share of the resource rents, at which point fiscal regimes began to involve the increased use of state participation, income taxes, ad-valorem royalties, and other revenue instruments.[23]

One might conclude that similar trends are emerging with respect to the "extraction" of personal data. With largely undefined property rights and legislation over personal data, its collection and use have gone largely uncompensated, except indirectly through the taxation, if any, of overall returns under the current corporate tax system. However, governments are now exerting greater sovereignty over their citizens' data, and seeking a "fairer" global distribution of tax revenues, both through the corporate tax system and through the application of new instruments, as will be discussed in this section.

The key objective of extractive industry fiscal regimes is to maximize compensation to host governments, while maintaining the investor's incentives to undertake exploration and extraction, given their respective risk profiles. While an objectively "fair" division of resource rents remains contentious, international norms have developed over time. Regimes typically comprise a combination of production and profit-based instruments[24] to make up a combined "resource charge", and thus involve an inherent trade-off between the efficiency and neutrality of the regime, as well as the timing and risk associated with revenues.

One could conceive of a similar approach to the taxation of value from user data. The design of any data-specific fiscal regime or resource charge (perhaps an "access charge", depending on whether the individual or government retains data ownership) must appropriately balance a sufficient return to the investor with the need for a "fair" level of government revenue as compensation for extraction or access to the national data asset. Given the range of companies involved in the

---

[22] The United Nations adopted resolution 1803 (XVII) on the "Permanent Sovereignty over Natural Resources" on 14 December 1962. This resolution provides that States and international organizations shall strictly and conscientiously respect the sovereignty of peoples and nations over their natural wealth and resources in accordance with the Charter of the United Nations and the principles contained in the resolution. These principles are set out in eight articles concerning issues such as the exploration, development and disposition of natural resources, nationalization and expropriation, foreign investment, and the sharing of profits.

[23] In the developing world, a number of contractual schemes were developed in the mid-1960s, such as the production sharing contract, and fee-for-service contracts in the context of fully nationalized industries.

[24] Production-based instruments, such as royalties, despite their regressivity, are often used by governments to secure revenues from the outset of production and to protect against profit shifting. And recognizing the larger rents generated by the resource industries, the overall level of taxation in the extractive industries is often higher than for other sectors, with a component of progressivity, through a resource rent tax instrument, to allow the capture of a larger share of rents from more profitable projects.

data economy and the variability in their profitability, a degree of progressivity may be desirable, in order to capture large rents if they arise. It may also be desirable to ensure a minimum charge for all data collection activity regardless of rents, which governments would need to moderate to avoid deterring the development and growth of data-intensive companies—like natural resource companies, a high degree of risk typically characterizes the initial start-up phase, particularly given the high fixed (and sunk) costs incurred for data collection and the development of analytical capabilities.

While there are many possible alternative tax instruments—or combinations of instruments—that can compensate countries for the collection and use of personal data, the focus here will be on the design of a production-based instrument, that is, a royalty on data collection.

Designing a Royalty on User-Generated Value

Royalties are payments that companies must make to governments for permission to engage in certain activities. They are commonly charged for the right to use intellectual property, such as copyrights, patents, and trademarks, and in the extractive industries for the extraction of natural resources, and typically complement corporate income taxes. Royalties are also a useful—if nonetheless imperfect—substitute when direct taxation of rents is difficult, particularly for sectors heavily reliant on hard-to-value assets, where administrative capacity is weak, and where rent taxation is therefore vulnerable to cost-based profit shifting (Boadway and Keen 2015). Furthermore, by relying on revenues, they are simpler to administer than profit-based taxes, reducing the need to monitor costs. Finally, royalties sidestep the practical legal challenges associated with adjusting direct income taxes, since they do not require modification of existing permanent establishment rules or changes to income tax treaties.

Their application as a charge for the use of consumer data is therefore logical if not also somewhat ironic, since intra-company royalties are already used by multinational enterprises themselves to shift profits across jurisdictions. In the natural resource sectors, they have proven attractive to governments on the grounds that they secure some revenues as soon as production begins. Indeed, IMF advice to resource-rich member countries, particularly low-income countries, has been to charge a modest royalty alongside the statutory corporate income tax, with an additional rent-capture mechanism for particularly profitable projects (IMF 2012).

In terms of design, a broadly-applicable royalty is likely to be desirable given the wide range of digitalized businesses collecting personal data. As the range of digital services continues to expand, it is important to prevent the proliferation of multiple royalty rates and bases across countries and activities which can generate both inefficiency and non-neutrality. This will also simplify administration and limit the scope for (purposefully) misclassifying taxable activities. Moreover, as we will show later in this section, under certain simplifying conditions, if all countries apply a consistent approach to determining user-based royalties, this would be broadly equivalent—in revenue terms—to a system of user-based formulary apportionment of profits.

There are a number of options for the design of the royalty base. A simple ad valorem royalty based on the value of the flow of data collected from a country and used by a company in a given year would be the ideal design—this is the most common specification used in the extractives sector. Alternatively, if the firm retains ownership over the data, rather than accessing it on a use basis, countries may wish to tax the stock of data held on a periodic basis, justified by the fact that companies are repeatedly generating value from this data.[25] However, both methods require either standardized data valuation methods or the establishment of a spot market for data.

In the absence of clear valuation methods, as long as the volume of data (stock or flow) collected from a country can be measured, a simpler approach would be to charge a specific royalty on this base. This can take the form of a defined volume-based charge on a unit of data collection, such as a pre-specified monetary charge per terabyte. This approach is often used for bulk, low-value minerals such as aggregate and sand. However, it would require some careful design and monitoring by governments to ensure that the tax is periodically adjusted to reflect evolving data compression technologies.

Without valuation methods and volume measurement capabilities, an alternative two-step approximation for user-generated value can be considered. The first step would be to estimate the portion of a company's final revenues from digital services that were generated by a particular country's users. Once these country-specific revenues have been determined, the second step is to allow for a (standardized) netback deduction from these country-specific revenues, to account for value added from post-data collection processing and analysis.[26] These steps provide a proxy for the value of a country's user data, which can then serve as the base of the royalty. Indeed, in the extractive industries, countries often simplify valuation by using internationally-quoted benchmark prices for finished minerals, restricting netback costs to those that are easy to measure, or standardizing allowable deductions in contracts or legislation.

The first step requires a method for apportioning a company's user-generated revenues by location to approximate the relative value of the user base in different countries. However, this can be difficult because as discussed before, data is unlike other physical commodities, which can be traced from their point of extraction to their point of use. Moreover, its nonrival nature means that the same portion of data may be blended, processed, and used simultaneously in the production of multiple goods and services—in some cases even many years after it has been collected. The previous section reviewed some of the country characteristics that

[25] The stock of user data could also then be reported as a special sub-category of intangible assets on firm's balance sheets in the same way that petroleum and mineral reserves are measured, valued, and "booked".

[26] For those businesses which also engage in other "less digital" activities, it would be necessary to determine the portion of overall revenues that are attributable to their digital activities.

can be used to inform such apportionment, for example, population, purchasing power, and sales revenue (in the case of online retailers).

Without coordination amongst countries, there is a risk that revenue attribution methods may vary within and across both countries and the digital services being targeted, introducing the opportunity for multiple (inconsistent) approaches. For example, the apportionment method for advertising revenues may differ from that used for user data sales, online sales of goods, and intermediation revenues. Even within certain activities, different keys could be used by different countries (for example, value-based versus volume-based keys). Further complications might arise from competing claims over the revenues from cross-border transactions and sales of multinational data sets.

For the second step, the netback deduction would serve as an approximation to derive a value for the underlying personal data. This could be defined company-by-company—given different data refinement processes and cost structures—or in legislation at broader (sub)industry levels to ease administration. A case could be made for standardization of this netback across countries, assuming that multinationals are collecting data of similar quality from users worldwide and centralizing their processing operations, implying a common cost structure.

Alongside the royalty base, the choice of the rate is also important. The netback deduction and royalty rate are two sides of the same coin, since a country can calibrate the effective tax burden by adjusting either the netback or the rate of the royalty. In the extractive industries, for example, some countries disregard costs altogether in defining their royalty base, instead valuing output at the benchmark price for its mineral content and lowering the royalty rate to compensate.

Rates should be set at an appropriately modest level, as they are applied to revenues rather than profits.[27] Where royalties are charged on a gross—rather than a net—basis, they no longer only tax pure economic rents and can distort the activities they are targeting.[28] This is analogous to the disincentive effects of royalties on exploration activity in the extractive industries. Thus, those countries with lower value consumer markets (for example, with fewer active users or lower purchasing power) might set rates lower so as not to disincentivize data extraction by nonresident digitalized businesses or deter market entry altogether.

In setting the rate, policymakers should also be sensitive to the risks of excessive pass-through to consumers. While the location-specific nature of the asset

---

[27] For example, a royalty of 4 percent is the equivalent to 20 percent corporate income tax rate assuming a 20 percent average profit margin across all businesses, but the effective income tax burden increases as the profit margin declines. Using average profit margins means that royalties might be too high for low-profit or loss-making businesses.

[28] A tax on pure economic rents does not distort the mix of inputs used in production. At the margin, firms employ factors of production (capital, labor, etc.) until the marginal return on the additional unit equals its marginal cost. In economic terms, rents are zero at the margin, negative if production is too great, and positive if too little. A pure rent-based tax, therefore, neither discourages nor encourages investment or production, as it will not influence production decisions at the margin (Mintz and Chen, 2010).

means that companies cannot themselves relocate to avoid payment of the tax, their relative market power may allow them to pass the tax on to consumers. This is likely much easier than in the resource sectors where for most countries commodity prices in export markets are exogenously determined.

At the same time, this risk should not be overstated. If the marginal cost of providing the taxed service is low, then the royalty acts like a tax on the firm's quasi-rents: rents that are exclusive of costs sunk in establishing the business (IMF, 2019). The primary impact may therefore not be on current pricing but on future investment. However, if the digital service is itself used as a business input, then the royalty may introduce production inefficiencies. This would reduce profitability for businesses and may raise prices for consumers, though the magnitude of such inefficiencies are unclear.

Cui and Hashimzade (2019) show that when the marginal cost is non-zero, the incidence of a tax on platform revenue will fall on both the platform and the advertisers/producers, but the effect on consumers is ambiguous. Moreover, as the authors argue, countries may well view some cost-passthrough to domestic users as a reasonable price to pay for capturing some of the platform rent. However, incidence effects are complex in two-sided markets. Firms may aim to shift some burden to the untaxed side: a tax on advertising creates an incentive to raise the price charged (or reduce the subsidy provided) to users; the price of advertising services may even fall. On tax incidence in two sided-markets, see Bourreau, Caillaud, and De Nijs (2016) and Kind, Köthenbürger and Schjelderup (2008 and 2010).

Businesses at different points in their life cycle might require different tax treatment. For this reason, a case could be made to introduce thresholds and rates that vary by the size of a business. Safe harbor rules could also be used to protect small or loss-making companies. However, such provisions might quickly become nonbinding even for small, digitalized businesses given the nature of their cost structure (Aslam and Shah 2020). With low (or falling) marginal costs, average variable costs will also be low, allowing small businesses to scale up operations profitably and quickly.[29]

Royalties are a powerful fiscal instrument with a long history of application in a sector that shares a number of characteristics with data-intensive digitalized business models. However, they should be carefully approached so as not to generate other economic distortions. If royalties are intended as a substitute rather than a complement to the corporate income tax, then a lack of multilateral consensus risks unwanted international double taxation if they are not creditable against corporate income tax payable in home jurisdictions. If applied unilaterally such tax measures may also risk retaliation, especially if these measures end up being de facto targeted on firms from a few countries (Hufbauer and Lu, 2018).

---

[29] Indeed, as noted by Cui (2018), the variable costs of data capture through the operation of a search engine or a social media network and its subsequent storage and maintenance would seem largely negligible.

The Implications of Moving Toward a Royalty on User-Based Revenues

In the absence of multilateral consensus, Box 10.1 explores—in a highly stylized setting—what the noncooperative outcome could be if all countries were to impose user-based royalties on the revenues from digital services. It illustrates that, ceteris paribus, countries will be indifferent (in terms of tax revenues)[30] between a user-apportioned profit tax and a royalty on user-based revenues, if the ratio of the royalty rate and the profit tax rate applicable to the multinational enterprise is set in proportion to the company's global average profit margin. This result holds irrespective of the global distribution of profits or revenues—and, by implication, the global distribution of costs.

While this is a very simplified result, which abstracts from some important real-world considerations and complexities, we can get a sense that should several countries move to implement such (short-term) royalties on user-based sales, then under the specified condition, the system would gradually come close to a system under which global profits are apportioned by the same user-based sales. This result should be familiar as it is the same logic that is commonly applied for calibrating standard turnover taxes for simplified small business regimes. In these systems, tax rates on turnover are typically set to ensure that the liability for the average small business would be the same as that under the application of the corporate income tax on profits. Just as in the small business setting, a turnover tax calibrated using average profit margins would be too high for low-profit or loss-making digitalized businesses (and vice versa), disincentivizing investment.

As this section has discussed, there are several reasons why policymakers should not preclude the use of a user-based royalty tax instrument as a complementary measure or as part of a globally cooperative approach to tax data-intensive services. Firstly, royalty payments are common between private parties for the right to use intellectual property and other intangible assets, such as copyrights, patents, and trademarks. This sets a natural precedent for governments to charge similar payments for the use of a national (intangible) asset—such as a user data—by digitalized businesses. Secondly, as noted earlier, royalty taxes are often a necessary substitute when the direct taxation of rents is difficult, for example, in the resource sectors. Indeed, a royalty instrument is less vulnerable to profit shifting, particularly in a sector heavily reliant on hard-to-value intangibles. Thirdly, given the clear practical and political challenges of reforming income taxes to account for user value, well-designed user-based royalty instruments—which can also allow for some sort of netback to account for data processing—may provide a feasible and more realistic option. If designed and applied comprehensively and coherently to all services that use data as an input (that is, little or no ring fencing around specific digital services), they could provide a valuable alternative or complement to the corporate income tax.

---

[30] Such indifference does not hold for individual firms as the distribution of the tax burden can be markedly different; there is also no indifference in terms of distortions.

Box 10. 1. Digital User-based Royalties as a First Step on the Way to Formulary Apportionment

This box explores the outcome should all countries apply some sort of unilateral royalty on user-based revenues. In a static setting, we can consider the implications for two countries, A and B, which can either (i) unilaterally tax user-based revenues earned by a nonresident multinational enterprise for the provision of digital services, or (ii) apply a single corporate income tax rate to an agreed upon allocation—in this case based on user-based sales—of the multinational enterprise's globally consolidated profits. We want to derive the conditions under which tax revenues from the two systems will be the same for a country such that they will be indifferent between them.

We start with the following expressions for tax revenues in a country i from the application of a user-based royalty:

$$\tau_i' R_i,$$

where τ_i' is the royalty rate in country i applied to user-based revenues, R_i, earned by the nonresident highly-digitalized multinational enterprise in return for services provided to domestic users in country i.

Under user-based formulary apportionment of global profits, each country is assigned:

$$\tau_i^c \alpha_i \pi_G,$$

where $\alpha_i = \dfrac{R_i}{R_G}$ is country i's share of total global user-derived revenues, and $\sum_{i \in \{A,B\}} \alpha_i = 1$; $R_G = \sum_{i \in \{A,B\}} R_i$; τ_i^c is the corporate income tax rate for country i; and $\pi_G = \sum_{i \in \{A,B\}} \pi_i$ is the multinational's globally consolidated profits and $\pi_i = R_i - C_i$ is the profit generated in country i (but not necessarily booked there).

For each country we get the following under revenue neutrality of both tax systems:

$$\tau_i^c \alpha_i \pi_G = \tau_i' R_i,$$

which, after substituting in for α_i, reduces to the following expression:

$$\frac{\tau_i'}{\tau_i^c} = \frac{\pi_G}{R_G}.$$

What this highly stylized model shows is that for the two systems to deliver equal tax revenues for each country, the ratio of the two tax rates for each country i must equal the ratio of global profits to global revenues, that is, the global average profit margin. In other words, assuming all countries have introduced user-based royalties, a country can earn the same revenues as if all countries had agreed on a user-based split of the multinational enterprise's globally consolidated profits, if and only if the ratio of the corporate income tax rate to the royalty rate is the same for all countries.

Some recent proposals for turnover taxes on digital services already take on the flavor of a user-based royalty. These include the digital services tax proposed by the European Commission, and variants subsequently proposed or enacted unilaterally by individual member states. This formulation of digital services tax should be distinguished from non-user-based equalization levies on payments for digital advertising services. This type of levy was introduced by India in 2016 taking the form of a withholding tax on payments to nonresidents for certain digital services. It has subsequently been expanded in scope in 2020 to a user-based turnover tax targeted only at nonresident businesses. Both types of tax attempt to target digital services provided by businesses operating remotely within a jurisdiction. They have also been formulated to sidestep income tax treaty issues by basing taxes on gross income (that is, sales/turnover) rather than net income (that is, profits)—for instance, as an excise tax on the supply of digital services or a tariff to protect domestic service providers.[31]

The Dangers of Ring Fencing

Regardless of the fiscal instrument selected, this chapter has consistently pointed out the importance of its general application to all types of businesses in the economy, with little or no ring fencing. With digitalization pervasive across the entire economy, it is both impractical and economically undesirable to single out more digital or less digital businesses or identify a so-called digital economy. As such, attempts to design policies specific to a so-called digital economy are potentially flawed—it is generally better for policy makers to ignore the distinction and take a holistic approach, particularly when it comes to areas such as international taxation. This was the view put forward in the 2014 report from the expert group on taxation of the digital economy convened by the European Commission (European Commission 2014), which noted that there should be no special tax regime for more digitalized companies. Rather, general rules should be applied or adapted so that there is equal treatment for all businesses. The OECD (2015) also suggested that countries should not attempt to ring-fence particular companies or business models for special tax treatment, noting that "the digital economy is increasingly becoming the economy itself."

Nevertheless, as noted above, a more targeted and discriminatory approach has gained significant traction in recent years and is set to be implemented unilaterally by some members of the European Union. These measures not only target digitalized businesses, but also isolate both a particular size of business and subset of digital activities. A case could be made that some degree of early ringfencing could be helpful in the (very) short run as tax measures are tested and adapted. However, more generally, from the point of view of efficiency and neutrality, establishing a parallel tax regime for digital services and other digitalized business models would drive an inefficient wedge between the digital and the non-digital sectors of the overall economy. Moreover, poorly-designed and uncoordinated measures run the risk of becoming entrenched.

---

[31] The OECD in its 2018 Interim Report provides guidance on the legal design of an excise tax on e-services, to ensure that they do not fall within the scope of income tax treaties. The case would be stronger where such an excise is (i) levied on the supply of a certain defined category or categories of e-services and imposed on the parties to the supply without reference to the particular economic or tax position of the supplier; (ii) charged at a fixed rate, calculated by reference to the consideration paid for those services (without reference to the net income of the supplier or the income from the supply); and (iii) not creditable or eligible for any other type of relief against income tax imposed on the same payment.

CONCLUSION

Digitalization—as a general-purpose technology—has unlocked the ability for businesses to collect vast amounts of data about agents in the economy from all manner of business-to-business and business-to-consumer transactions, including the so-called digital barter. By combining it with other nonrival, excludable intangible goods—such as intellectual property and knowhow—businesses have been able to design and remotely provide new and existing products and services at low marginal costs, fostering the emergence of large near-monopolistic and oligopolistic markets.

As businesses in almost every sector take advantage of the benefits of digitalization, the need to address the shortcomings and unresolved issues within the international corporate income tax system has become that much more urgent. The current system of arm's length pricing and the growing importance of near-impossible-to-value intangibles—including user data—has allowed opportunities for corporate income tax avoidance to proliferate. As a result, many countries are seeing profits shifted out of their reach by companies using transfer pricing tactics, while those without any permanent establishment-based taxing rights are missing out on the opportunity to tax these companies altogether.

As a result, the contribution of user data to the profitability of highly-digitalized businesses has become a rallying point for governments seeking to redress the perception of an unfair distribution of profits and taxing rights. A number of policy proposals have been put forward which seek to limit the scope of tax avoidance and tax competition, by attempting to pre-determine a distribution of taxable profits across countries. Many of these proposed rules for splitting income are predicated, whether implicitly or explicitly, on the idea that the user of a digital service has a role to play in value creation and which, if necessary, cede source-based taxing rights to the jurisdictions where they are located.

And indeed, as this chapter has argued, a plausible case can be made to tax this value generated by users under the corporate income tax. It seems reasonable to acknowledge that raw user data must have some underlying value prior to processing, just as any primary commodity has some value before it is transformed into a final product, for example, crude oil or timber. However, governments remain divided over its importance and the resulting implications for the distribution of profits worldwide. Should governments eventually recognise and agree on the importance of user data—and if the valuation of such data can become standardized along certain key dimensions/uses— its role in providing a basis for corporate taxation could help to remedy some of the shortcomings of the international tax system.

In practical terms, the first obstacle to overcome is the assignment of taxing rights to data-producing (user/market) countries through revised nexus rules (for example, a new permanent establishment concept). The second challenge is to design revised profit allocation rules which reflect user contribution. Most notably, there are no available market-based prices or established benchmarks to guide how user data should be measured and valued, preventing governments from being able to quantify the importance of user data to production. In other words, the issue of user data has added to the scale of the existing valuation issues posed by intangible assets, while also expanding the potential number of countries claiming the right to tax. Both issues are heavily politicized and influenced by countries jockeying for position.

One of the cleaner solutions is rooted in the idea of formulary apportionment which reflects the user as a factor. Cleaner because it helps diminish the opportunities for profit shifting that exist under the current system of arm's length pricing. However, while some countries could gain—for example, large populous economies and those with greater purchasing power—others could lose in this shift toward a sales-based system. The formula can also be modified to accommodate (original) source economies, where these multinational enterprises—digitalized or otherwise—developed. Of course, international agreement on any formula is also likely to be fraught.

There are a number of possible solutions that fall between the old and the new. The new family of solutions go halfway toward full-blown formulary apportionment, while retaining elements of the existing arm's length pricing. Two such related proposals gaining traction are those of marketing intangibles and residual profit allocation. Both approaches acknowledge the rights of—and reallocation of income to—market jurisdictions, while preserving the rights and tax bases of current source-based jurisdictions.

Other instruments are available to governments seeking compensation for the use of their citizens' personal data. Such measures can either substitute (in the short term) or complement existing taxes, such as the corporate income tax. One example is a royalty on the value of user data, proxied by revenues from digital services until a market for data develops. These revenues could also be adjusted to account for a highly-digitalized business' value added from the processing of data using some form of netback deduction. Indeed, while multilateral consensus should remain the endgame, this chapter has also highlighted that under simplifying assumptions, where all countries calibrate their tax systems to global profit margins, unilateral adoption of user-based royalties could lead to an outcome where countries are indifferent (in terms of revenue) between these taxes or user-based formulary apportionment. In other words, under these specific circumstances, the gradual and sequential implementation of user-based royalties could eventually bring the world toward a corporate taxation system apportioned by user-derived sales.

However, these measures are not without their potential pitfalls, particularly if uncoordinated. Possible drawbacks include the creation of undesirable disincentives for investment, and the proliferation of double taxation and excessive tax burdens due to multiple royalty rates and bases, administrative complexity, and the risk of misclassified activities. The resulting variation in effective tax rates across jurisdictions could have a tangible impact on global resource allocation—all in return for potentially very little tax revenue. There may also be political economy costs from retaliation.

The absence of international consensus and a lack of clear data valuation methods have already pushed many countries to impose targeted turnover-based measures on varying subsets of digital services. In some cases, indirect proxies for user value are used as the tax base, for example, revenues from online advertising or from remote selling through online platforms, where the transaction value is observable. Other governments have side-stepped the valuation issue by basing their taxes on directly observable indicators, such as the volume of users. While these are all practical solutions, the risk remains that they do not sufficiently address the issue of taxing profits from value created—in this case by users. Furthermore, such an inconsistent approach could leave countries with a patchwork of overlapping measures that create more problems than they solve.

Moreover, with digitalization permeating all sectors of the economy, user data is being exploited at a scale large enough to be recognized as an economic input to production. It should therefore be recognized for all businesses that do so—even if with varying degrees of intensity and relevance—with little or no ring-fencing of specific digital activities. Empirical data also does not conclusively suggest that highly-digitalized companies are particularly different (in terms of profitability, intangible assets, and effective tax rates) from other large businesses—though it is important to note that the data is insufficient to definitively identify differences between companies and sectors.

What this chapter attempts to highlight is not only the value of the user to highly-digitalized businesses but also that the user is likely to become increasingly important for all businesses going forward. Therefore, it is important to consider their role in providing a basis for taxing rights and the attribution of profits. For this reason, shifts in the international tax system to reflect their worth not only seem inevitable but also tec(h)tonic.

REFERENCES

Armstrong, Mark. 2006. "Competition in Two-Sided Markets." *RAND Journal of Economics* 37(3): 668–91.

Aslam, Aqib, and Alpa Shah. 2017. "Taxation and the Peer-to-Peer Economy." IMF Working Paper 17/187, International Monetary Fund, Washington, DC.

Aslam, Aqib, and Alpa Shah. 2020. "Tec(h)tonic Shifts: Taxing the 'Digital Economy.'" IMF Working Paper 20/76, International Monetary Fund, Washington, DC.

Becker, Johannes, and Joachim Englisch. 2019. "Taxing Where Value Is Created: What's 'User Involvement' Got to Do with It?" *Intertax* 47(2): 161–71.

Boadway, Robin, and Michael Keen. 2015. "Rent Taxes and Royalties in Designing Fiscal Regimes for Non-Renewable Resources." in David Layton and Robert Halvorsen (eds), *Handbook on the Economics of Natural Resources*. Cheltenham: Edward Elgar.

Bourreau, Marc, Bernard Caillaud, and Romain De Nijs. 2016. "Digital Platforms, Advertising and Taxation." *Journal of Public Economic Theory*. Special issue on Taxation in the Digital Economy 20(1): 40–51.

Caillaud, Bernard, and Bruno Jullien. 2003. "Chicken and Egg: Competition among Intermediation Service Providers." *RAND Journal of Economics* 34: 309–28.

Collier, Paul. 2018. *The Future of Capitalism: Facing the New Anxieties*. London: Allen Lane.

Collier, Paul, and Anthony J. Venables. 2018. "Who Gets the Urban Surplus?" *Journal of Economic Geography* 18(3): 523–38.

Cui, Wei. 2018. "The Digital Services Tax: A Conceptual Defense." Unpublished manuscript, Allard School of Law, University of British Columbia, Vancouver, British Columbia.

Cui, Wei, and Nigar Hashimzade. 2019. "The Digital Services Tax as a Tax on Location-Specific Rent." CESifo Working Paper 7737, Center for Economic Studies, Munich.

De Mooij, Ruud, Li Liu, and Dinar Prihardhini. 2019. "An Assessment of Global Formula Apportionment." IMF Working Paper 19/213, International Monetary Fund, Washington, DC.

Devereux, Michael P., and John Vella. 2018. "Value Creation As the Fundamental Principle of the International Corporate Tax System." European Tax Policy Forum Policy Paper.

Ellison, Glenn, and Drew Fudenberg. 2003. "Knife-Edge or Plateau: When Do Market Models Tip?" *Quarterly Journal of Economics* 118(4): 1249–78.

Elvy, Stacy-Ann. 2017. "Paying for Privacy and the Personal Data Economy." *Columbia Law Review* 117(6): 1369–1454.

Evans, David S. 2003. "The Antitrust Economics of Two-Sided Markets." *Yale Journal of Regulation* 20: 325–81.

European Commission (EC). 2014. "Report of the Commission Expert Group on Taxation of the Digital Economy." Directorate-General for Taxation and Customs Union, European Commission, Brussels, https://ec.europa.eu/taxation_customs/sites/taxation/files/resources /documents/taxation/gen_info/good_governance_matters/digital/report_digital_economy .pdf.

European Commission (EC). 2018. "Proposal for a Council Directive on the Common System of a Digital Services Tax on Revenues Resulting from the Provision of Certain Digital Services." Procedure 2018/0073/CNS. European Commission, Brussels, https://ec.europa .eu/taxation_customs/sites/taxation/files/proposal_common_system_digital_services_tax _21032018_en.pdf

Grinberg, Itai. 2018. "User Participation in Value Creation." *Georgetown Law Faculty Publications and Other Works*. 2102.

Gupta, Sanjeev, Michael Keen, Alpa Shah, and Genevieve Verdier, editors. 2017. *Digital Revolutions in Public Finance*. Washington, DC: International Monetary Fund.

HM Treasury. 2017. *Corporate Tax and the Digital Economy: Position Paper*. HM Treasury: London.

HM Treasury. 2018. *Corporate Tax and the Digital Economy: Position Paper Update*. HM Treasury: London.

Hogan, Lindsay and Brenton Goldsworthy. 2010. "International Mineral Taxation: Experience and Issues" in Daniel, Philip, Michael Keen, and Charles McPherson (Eds.), *The Taxation of Petroleum and Minerals: Principles, Problems and Practice*. Oxford: Routledge.

Hongler, Peter, and Pasquale Pistone. 2015. "Blueprints for a New PE Nexus to Tax Business Income in the Era of the Digital Economy." IBFD Working Paper, International Bureau of Fiscal Documentation, the Netherlands.

Hufbauer, Gary Clyde, and Zhiyao (Lucy) Lu. 2018. "The European Union's Proposed Digital Services Tax: A de Facto Tariff." PIIE Policy Brief PB18-15, Peterson Institute for International Economics, Washington, DC.

International Monetary Fund (IMF). 2012. "Fiscal Regimes for Extractive Industries—Design and Implementation." IMF Policy Paper, Washington, DC.

International Monetary Fund (IMF). 2014. "Spillovers in International Corporate Taxation." IMF Policy Paper, Washington, DC.

International Monetary Fund (IMF). 2019. "Corporate Taxation in the Global Economy." IMF Policy Paper, Washington, DC.

Katz, Michael L., and Carl Shapiro. 1985. "Network Externalities, Competition, and Compatibility." *American Economic Review* 75(3): 424–40.

Katz, Michael L., and Carl Shapiro. 1994. "Systems Competition and Network Effects." *Journal of Economic Perspectives* 8(2): 93–115.

Khan, Lina M. 2017. "Amazon's Antitrust Paradox." *Yale Law Journal* 126(3): 710–805.

Kind, Hans J., Marko Köthenbürger, and Guttorm Schjelderup. 2008. "Efficiency Enhancing Taxation in Two-Sided Markets." *Journal of Public Economics* 92(5–6): 1531–39.

Kind, Hans J., Marko Köthenbürger, and Guttorm Schjelderup. 2010. "Tax Responses in Platform Industries." *Oxford Economic Papers* 62(4): 764–83.

Liebowitz, Stan J., and Stephen E. Margolis. 1994. "Network Externality: An Uncommon Tragedy." *Journal of Economic Perspectives* 8(2): 133–50.

Organisation of Economic Co-operation and Development (OECD). 2015. *Addressing the Tax Challenges of the Digital Economy, Action 1 – 2015 Final Report.* Paris: OECD Publishing.

Organisation for Economic Co-operation and Development (OECD). 2017a. *OECD Transfer Pricing Guidelines for Multinational Enterprises and Tax Administrations.* Paris: OECD Publishing

Organisation for Economic Co-operation and Development (OECD). 2017b. *The 2017 Update to the OECD Model Tax Convention.* Paris: OECD Publishing.

Organisation for Economic Co-operation and Development (OECD). 2018. *Tax Challenges Arising from Digitalisation—Interim Report 2018: Inclusive Framework on BEPS.* OECD/G20 Base Erosion and Profit Shifting Project. Paris: OECD Publishing.

Organisation for Economic Co-operation and Development (OECD). 2019. *Programme of Work to Develop a Consensus Solution to the Tax Challenges Arising from the Digitalisation of the Economy. OECD/G20 Inclusive Framework on BEPS.* OECD, Paris.

Rochet, Jean-Claude, and Jean Tirole. 2003. "Platform Competition in Two-Sided Markets." *Journal of the European Economic Association* 1(4): 990–1024.

Romer, Paul M. 1990. "Endogenous Technological Change." *Journal of Political Economy* 98(5): S71–S102.

Rysman, Marc. 2009. "The Economics of Two-Sided Markets." *Journal of Economic Perspectives* 23(3): 125–43.

Schön, Wolfgang. 2018. "Ten Questions about Why and How to Tax the Digitalized Economy." *Bulletin for International Taxation* 72(4–5): 278.

Varian, Hal. 2019. "Artificial Intelligence, Economics, and Industrial Organization." In *The Economics of Artificial Intelligence: An Agenda*, edited by Ajay Agrawal, Joshua Gans, and Avi Goldfarb, 399–419. Chicago: University of Chicago Press.

Varian, Hal, Joseph Farrell, and Carl Shapiro. 2005. *Economics of Information Technology.* Cambridge, UK: Cambridge University Press.

PART III

Potential Solutions

CHAPTER 11

Strengthening Source-Based Taxation

Sebastian Beer and Geerten Michielse

INTRODUCTION

Source-based taxation lies at the heart of the current international tax architecture (see Chapter 3), and its importance has further risen with the abolition of worldwide taxation of active business income by essentially all of the major capital exporting economies, including now the United States, the United Kingdom, and Japan.[1] Notwithstanding its importance, defining the source of income is increasingly problematic, as discussed in Chapter 5. It has been made more difficult by the increasing importance of intrafirm cross-border trade and complex production chains, the increasing contribution of hard-to-value and easily mobile intangible assets to value added, and the increasing digitalization of the economy—and this increasing digitalization means that the old idea of physical presence as the main criterion for source is outmoded (see Chapter 10).

To sustain a tax system that taxes profits where they originate thus requires addressing three fundamental challenges of source-based taxation. First, the legal definitions of what constitutes domestically sourced income are out of line with today's economic realities. Traditionally, source refers to the place where investments are made and where production takes place, which has been determined by the physical presence of labor and capital. Today, many of the most valuable companies provide electronic services, and the most valuable assets are intangible in nature and by their nature easily "moved." Still, countries typically tax nonresidents only if certain thresholds of physical presence—known as permanent establishments—are met.

Second, source-based taxation requires allocating a multinational enterprise's consolidated profit among its affiliates and between jurisdictions. Typically, countries' laws aim at achieving an allocation of income within a group by requiring the subsidiaries of a multinational group to engage in arm's length transactions, that is, to charge prices on internally provided goods and services at the same

---

[1] Residence-based taxation is also an important, but typically secondary or additional component, of tax systems. Strengthening residence-based taxation—which in turn strengthens source-based taxation, given the interaction between the principles—is covered in Chapter 12.

prices that unrelated parties would. However, multinational enterprises are integrated entities that benefit from economies of scope and scale. The productive activity of any one affiliate has positive spillovers on other group entities, making unrelated-party transactions and prices a poor proxy for the true profitability of the component parts of the multinational enterprise. The allocation of risk is a particularly strong example of this difficulty (see Chapter 5). Moreover, verification of whether internal prices are at arm's length requires data from unrelated-party transactions. This information may be available for routine functions that bear limited risk and where profit margins do not vary widely. However, multinational enterprises are increasingly generating supernormal returns linked to unique intangible assets, such as patents or trademarks (see IMF, 2019). For transactions involving these assets, comparable data are often nonexistent and compliance with the arm's length standard thus hard to verify. Multinational enterprises frequently exploit these ambiguities and shift taxable income to locations where the tax will be lowest (see Beer, De Mooij, and Liu 2019).[2]

Third, countries face pressures from tax competition (see Chapter 6). Governments have long provided preferential tax terms to attract internationally mobile investments that would be taxed at source, that is, in their jurisdiction. Tax competition between source countries is apparent in the massive declines in statutory corporate income tax rates over the past 40 years, in the spread of preferential regimes targeting specific income types, and in the continued reliance on special economic zones or tax holidays in many developing countries. Moreover, tax competition is likely to intensify in the future for three reasons: First, technological progress means that the production of goods and services is increasingly separated from the location of consumers; as a result, the tax base that is internationally mobile will increase and, with it, governments' returns to offering preferential terms. Second, multilateral initiatives aimed at curbing harmful tax regimes[3] will reduce governments' options for providing tailored tax incentives and may put downward pressure on general tax rates, with negative effects on revenue generation (see Keen 2001). Third, the increasing spread of anti-avoidance measures reduces multinational enterprises' ability to shift taxable profits between countries without commensurate adjustments in real production decisions. Actual investment decisions will thus become more sensitive to taxation, which in turn increases countries' marginal returns to engage in tax competition.

This chapter discusses strategies to strengthen source-based taxation by addressing these three challenges. The next section recaps current approaches to taxing nonresidents in source countries and lays out options for expanding definitions of source income. This is followed by a section providing an overview of

---

[2] For example, Tørsløv, Wier, and Zucman (2018) estimate that roughly 40 percent of global profits end up in low-tax jurisdictions annually.

[3] The OECD/G20 Base Erosion and Profit Shifting (BEPS) Project's Action 5, which is one of the four minimum standards, targets harmful tax regimes to limit negative spillovers between countries' tax bases. The preferential regimes of all members of the Inclusive Framework are subject to peer review.

strategies that can strengthen the allocation of profits between tax jurisdictions, reducing ambiguities and the scope for profit shifting of multinational enterprises. The discussion then turns to strategies to address tax competition.

EXPANDING THE DEFINITION OF SOURCE-BASED TAXATION

Current Situation

Source-based taxation allows countries to tax the income of both resident and nonresident taxpayers, with the profits of nonresident taxpayers[4] only taxed if there is sufficient "nexus" with the jurisdiction. Broadly, three types of income have historically met this requirement:

- *Profits (including capital gains on the sale of business assets) of permanent establishments:* Since taxing one-off business transactions is administratively burdensome, countries have generally self-imposed a threshold only above which business activities will trigger the source country's tax jurisdiction. Finding a permanent establishment typically requires that the activity is conducted through a fixed place of business.

- *Passive income payments (dividend, interest, and royalties) representing domestically sourced profits paid from resident to nonresident entities:* These types of cross-border payments represent income generated in the source country, and the rights to tax them, in whole or in part, are typically exercised through withholding taxation.[5]

- *Capital gains from the sale of domestic immovable property located in the source country, and related rights.* While capital gains on immovable property are typically taxed in the country where the property is located (the source country), capital gains on movable property, such as on shares, are typically taxed in the country where the owner is located (residence country). However, the distinction between movable and immovable property is not always clear-cut, effectively allowing taxpayers to choose where certain capital gains are taxed.

The increasing digitalization of the economy has challenged traditional definitions of what constitutes a source. Multinational enterprises benefit from customers or users in countries where they do not have a physical presence. Under

---

[4] Note that subsidiaries of foreign multinational enterprises are incorporated businesses and hence are normally residents in the jurisdiction where they are incorporated.

[5] The residence country, if it imposes tax on its residents on a worldwide basis, also would have the right to tax this income. Though in most cases either unilaterally or under tax treaties, the residence country would grant a credit for taxes paid in the source country. Importantly, though, under the standard international tax architecture using bilateral double taxation treaties, the source country would lower its withholding rates, in some cases to zero, in favor of leaving some or all taxing rights with the country of residence of the recipient person or entity.

current rules, these countries are not allocated a share of profits. By enacting or threatening to enact new taxes on these profits[6]—often referred to as digital service taxes—several countries have put pressure on the international community to find a solution (see Chapter 10).

Expanding the Definition of Nexus

As noted, countries typically tax the income earned by nonresidents on a net basis, with expenses reducing the taxable base, if the activity is carried out through a fixed place of business.[7] For instance, a building site or a construction and installation project usually constitutes a permanent establishment only if it lasts for more than a specified length of time—often 183 days in a calendar year. In addition, the activities of a dependent agent, which includes employees or other persons under the control of the principal, may give rise to a permanent establishment for the principal. However, many activities are explicitly excluded from the permanent establishment concept under typical treaties.[8]

Strengthening the jurisdiction over business income of nonresidents requires broader domestic permanent establishment definitions, which could be achieved incrementally or through more substantial deviations from current definitions. For instance, at the simplest level, source countries could refrain from granting typical exclusions for activities—such as those having an auxiliary and/or a preparatory character even where conducted through a fixed place of business. Similarly, countries could shorten the length of time required to recognize a construction- or project-based permanent establishment or to define a permanent establishment based upon the physical presence of service providers—so-called "service-permanent establishments." A still more pragmatic and simpler—though also far more radical—solution could be the introduction of a quantitative threshold as a backstop: a nonresident would become subject to profit taxation in the source country if, for instance, total annual turnover that source country exceeded a certain threshold. The "force of attraction" principle provides that when an enterprise sets up a permanent establishment in the source country that country can tax all profits that the foreign enterprise derives there, irrespective of whether the business transactions are related to the permanent establishment—thus expanding the source tax base. For instance, if the head office provides goods or services directly to customers in the source country in which it operates a permanent establishment and the permanent establishment is also involved in the same line of activity, the profits earned by the head office directly could be taxed as profits attributable to

---

[6] India was the first to tax multinational enterprises without a physical presence by enacting its equalization levy.

[7] Most countries use a permanent establishment definition that is similar to that of the OECD and UN Model treaties. See Article 5(1) of the OECD and UN Models.

[8] Most importantly, activities of independent agents, ancillary and preparatory activities, the use of storage facilities, the maintenance of stock and goods solely for processing, and purchasing or information gathering activities typically do not trigger a permanent establishment. See Article 5(4) of the OECD and UN Models.

the permanent establishment. Some countries, and some treaties, permit such a force of attraction doctrine, but others do not.[9]

However, to secure source-based profits of nonresidents that do not have any physical presence will require more fundamental changes to current definitions, as referenced above. For instance, Action 7 of the OECD/G20 Base Erosion and Profit Shifting (BEPS) Project focuses on redefinitions of the permanent establishment concept to capture so-called "commissionaire arrangements," which are loosely defined as arrangements through which a person sells products in a host country in their own name but on behalf of a foreign enterprise that is the owner of these products. The commissionaire does not take title to the products and hence traditionally does not establish a permanent establishment for the principal in the host country. BEPS has expanded the agency permanent establishment on this point. A dependent agent would now apply to anyone who "habitually concludes the contracts, or habitually plays the principal role leading to the conclusion of contracts that are routinely concluded without material modification."[10]

Various countries have introduced the concept of a "digital permanent establishment," defined, for example, by the presence of a certain number of digital sales or by a website directed at their markets (see Chapter 10). Related variants were also discussed at the Taskforce on the Digital Economy under the OECD's Inclusive Framework (OECD 2019a). While now superseded by the unified approach (OECD 2019b), their underlying principles remain part of the debate, and while primarily designed to address challenges of the digital economy, these principles are potentially applicable to a much broader group. First, the "marketing intangibles" proposal is based on the idea that marketing efforts establish country-specific intangible assets based on which that country would have some taxing rights. Second, the "user value" proposal suggests that in modern business models, users create value—just as do capital and labor—as they share digital information that the multinational enterprise may then monetize.

Expanding Withholding Taxes

Most source countries tax cross-border passive income payments, which include dividends, interest, and royalty payments, on a gross basis using withholding taxes. Withholding taxation is an important backstop to base erosion as it allows taxing payments that are often deductible from the domestic corporate tax base and otherwise hard to capture.

Strengthening source-based taxation of cross-border payments can take the form either of a rate increase or of broadening the definition of which payments are domestically sourced (and thus taxable via withholding). For example, unless a rental activity forms a business—in which case the permanent establishment rules apply—rental income is difficult to reach where it flows out of the country.

---

[9] Article 7.1 of the UN Model explicitly allows source countries to apply a "force of attraction" rule.

[10] Article 5, paragraph 5 OECD Model 2017; See also the discussion of the diverted profits tax in the following section, "Strengthening the Allocation of Profits."

Withholding can be a solution to administer a tax on rental income of nonresidents. A few countries have introduced a withholding tax on intragroup cross-border (re-)insurance premiums for coverage of risks in their country (partly as an anti-avoidance device), as well as some other types of withholding, such as on management fees paid to a parent company abroad.

Finally, source countries may introduce a branch profit tax to afford equal tax treatment to income generated by a domestic company controlled by a foreign shareholder and to income generated by a permanent establishment of a nonresident. The idea is that the total tax burden on permanent establishment profit should equal that of profit realized by a subsidiary of a foreign parent company. Although this is normally the case for corporate income tax imposed on domestic profits, remittances by a permanent establishment to its foreign headquarters will not be subject to withholding tax, as are dividends distributed by the subsidiary to its foreign shareholder(s), unless this is specifically made the case by a branch profits tax provision.

Capital Gains

Most countries tax capital gains on the domestic sale of business assets, securities, and real property. However, capital gains on business assets sold by a nonresident will typically be subject to tax only if they can be attributed to a permanent establishment in the jurisdiction. Shares and other securities in most cases are not taxable (sourced) in the country in which the issuing company is located, but rather are subject to tax in the jurisdiction of the seller (only). A few countries have, however, extended their jurisdiction to tax capital gains on the alienation of shares representing a substantial shareholding in a resident company, typically defined by a minimum number or value of shares and holding period.[11]

Nonresidents owning real (immovable) property in the host country are typically subject to tax on the sale of those immovable assets. Source countries may use a withholding tax to ensure that capital gains on the sale of real property owned by nonresidents are effectively collected.[12] However, there has been quite widespread concern among developing countries—especially those with substantial mineral resource deposits—that indirect transfers farther up the chain of ownership can be used to avoid capital gains on natural resources themselves, or on mining or exploitation licenses.[13] The reason is that capital gains on the alienation of shares held in resident companies are typically exempt in a cross-border situation. Capital gains on immovable property can thus be avoided by selling the immovable asset indirectly, by incorporating a company that holds the assets and

---

[11] Capital gains on other movable assets is very hard to tax and therefore often not attempted by jurisdictions at all.

[12] The United States, for instance, withholds a 15 percent tax on the sales proceeds from real property owned by nonresidents. If the nonresident subsequently files a proper tax return and is assessed, this withholding tax is creditable against the capital gain tax due.

[13] For more detailed approaches to address these indirect transfers, see *The Taxation of Offshore Indirect Transfers—A Toolkit* (Platform for Collaboration on Tax 2018).

then selling shares in the company abroad ("indirect transfer"). To close this loophole, most source countries attempt to tax the capital gain on shares of a nonresident company if the value of its shares is derived principally from an asset located in the source country.[14] This rule is, for example, embodied in Article 13.4 of the UN Model Treaty, regardless of whether the assets are held through a domestic company or a company resident in a third country.[15]

It is important to note that the above measures to extend the sourced-based taxation of nonresidents have most effect if double taxation treaties are not limiting the right to tax of the host country or the host country has not concluded any double taxation treaties, which typically restrict taxing rights of those countries. If a country extends its geographic source rules, it may have to amend its double taxation treaties to ensure that those extended rules are not restricted by the international agreements (see further discussion in Chapter 8).

STRENGTHENING THE ALLOCATION OF PROFITS

Market forces are not fully at play in transactions between related parties, providing multinational enterprises with much room to relocate profits to wherever they are taxed the least. Profit shifting is not limited to cross-border transactions. Developing countries often provide a preferential tax treatment to selected companies in special economic zones, and many countries apply higher statutory tax rates on the profits in the natural resource sector. These statutory tax rate differentials, irrespective of whether they arise between countries or within one jurisdiction, are factored into the internal pricing strategies and structures of multinational enterprises and used to reduce their overall tax burden.

Many countries have adopted transfer pricing rules to limit multinational enterprises' tax avoidance. These rules require that the price used in internal transactions aligns with the prices that unrelated parties would charge in similar circumstances (the "arm's length standard"). However, verification of the arm's length standard builds on a comprehensive analysis of the transaction and requires reference to data from uncontrolled transactions. This information is frequently not available, and many tax administrations lack the expertise necessary to verify whether prices were at arm's length.[16]

---

[14] "Principally" is often defined as a minimum value of assets (for example, $10 million) or as a minimum percentage ("more than 50 percent"), and some source countries decide that taxation on indirect transfers will only be triggered if there is a minimum change of control.

[15] Recently, countries confronted with dilution of the proportion of the value of shares that is derived from immovable property have added that "at any time during the 365 days preceding the alienation" the value should be derived more than 50 percent directly or indirectly from such property.

[16] Implementation of the arm's length standard in the extractive industries, which constitute a critical revenue source for many developing countries, can be particularly challenging, given the high importance of hard-to-price intangible assets, highly specialized services, and vertically integrated production processes (see Chapter 15, this volume; Beer and Loeprick 2015).

While profit shifting often involves the mispricing of internal transactions, multinational enterprises can avoid taxes at arm's length prices too.[17] For instance, multinational enterprises can exploit the tax deductibility of interest payments by providing loans from affiliates in low-tax jurisdictions to related parties in high-tax jurisdictions—where these loans trigger tax-deductible interest payments. With these internal loans, multinational enterprises can increase the group's consolidated after-tax profit while leaving pretax profits and their overall debt exposure unaffected.

More generally, multinational enterprises use multiple techniques to avoid corporate income taxation and withholding taxes, which are the primary taxes employed to capture source-based income, including the following:

- Exploiting the deductibility of operating expenses, such as of interest and royalty payments, to reduce the group's corporate income tax liability
- Exploiting a country's double taxation treaty network to reduce withholding taxes
- Using artificial structures to avoid the status of a permanent establishment (see previous section)

Countries have responded to these strategies by implementing diverse anti-avoidance measures. While the specificities of these measures differ, a common feature is that many disregard expenses that are normally deductible for corporate tax. In a way, antiabuse measures increase the importance of a firm's turnover in assessing the tax liability, thus discouraging production at a theoretically efficient level. However, reducing production efficiency might be justified in situations where tax avoidance is pervasive. For instance, Beer and Loeprick (2018) show that a revenue-maximizing withholding tax policy effectively disallows the deductibility of interest payments as treaty shopping becomes excessive.[18] This finding resembles an earlier result by Best and others (2015), showing that tax avoidance justifies the taxation on a gross rather than on a net basis to support revenue efficiency.

The following subsection lays out options to strengthen the arm's length standard and presents the most important anti-avoidance measures.

Strengthening the Arm's Length Principle[19]

Over 120 countries have implemented transfer pricing legislation, but with widely varying approaches: while some countries require multinational enterprises to submit granular information, including on the group structure, financial

---

[17] Notably, the arm's length principle is broader than arm's length pricing. For example, while the price of a specific transaction could be in line with general market prices, it is possible that this transaction would not occur between unrelated parties due to the specifics of the situation. In this case, the transaction would not be at arm's length even though the prices used may seem to be.

[18] The intuition for this result is that lower withholding tax rates may facilitate base erosion through treaty shopping while reducing the cost of capital, with positive effects on investment. As the costs of abusing double tax treaty networks decreases, the (revenue) costs associated with reduced withholding tax rates increases and there is less justification to apply reduced rates.

[19] For a comprehensive discussion of the arm's length principle and its implementation in developing countries, see Cooper and others (2016), which this section heavily draws on. See also Chapter 5.

Figure 11.1. Worldwide Transfer Pricing Rules

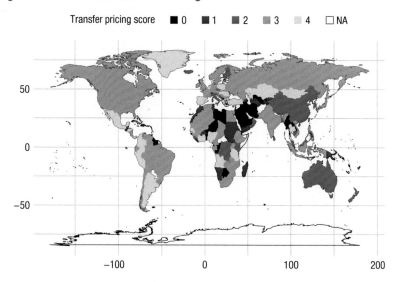

Sources: Deloitte; Ernst and Young; PricewaterhouseCoopers; and authors' calculations.
Note: Graph illustrates transfer pricing practices globally, with a lower score indicating less strict rules.
Transfer pricing score is 0 when a country does not adopt transfer pricing regulation; a score of 4
indicates that the country adopts transfer pricing regulation, including all three of the following features:
(1) documentation requirements for cross-border transactions, (2) documentation requirements for
domestic transactions, and (3) penalties for inappropriate documentation.

positions in each country, and transfer pricing strategies adopted, other countries
have implemented the arm's length principle but do not require companies to
submit any information at all (see Figure 11.1).

At its core, the arm's length principle requires that the transaction taking place
between related parties is comparable, in both its structure and its terms, to a
transaction between unrelated parties. Verifying comparability requires an understanding of the key features of the transaction, including the market structure, the
risk borne by each party, the functions performed, the assets provided, and the
business strategies pursued. These characteristics determine which of the available
methods is most suited to determine the price that unrelated parties would charge.

However, limited access to financial data and limited capacity is a distinctive
characteristic of many developing countries, making implementation of the arm's
length standard difficult.[20] The ORBIS database, commercially offered by the
Bureau van Dijk, is one of most comprehensive data sets available for conducting
comparability analyses outside North America. The information recorded in this

---

[20] See Platform for Collaboration on Tax. 2017. A Toolkit for Adressing Addressing Difficulties
in Accessing Comparables Data for Transfer Pricing Analyses, https://www.oecd.org/tax/toolkit-on
-comparability-and-mineral-pricing.pdf

Figure 11.2. Profit and Loss Data from Independent Firms

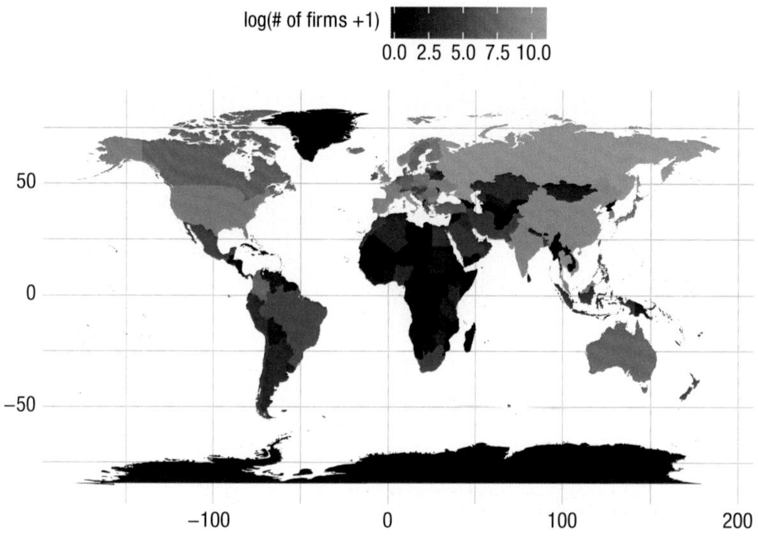

Source: Authors' calculation, based on ORBIS.
Note: Figure illustrates ORBIS coverage of independent firms in July 2019. The selection criteria were that selected companies need to (1) be active, (2) have a known value for turnover and profit before taxation, and (3) have no shareholder owning more than 25 percent.

database includes detailed accounting and ownership information, as well as independence indicators. ORBIS has also recently made it possible for tax administrations to access more detailed price information, including on interest and royalty rates used in independent transactions. The database records information on turnover and profit and loss before taxation for around 300,000 independent and active firms, allowing users to compute simple profitability margins. Figure 11.2 illustrates the distribution of these firms globally. Most firms are located in Europe, Russia, and some Asian countries. However, there is less data available for South America and hardly any data for African countries.

Several options could increase data availability. For instance, the information collected by tax administrations through tax filings or at customs provides a valuable data source for verifying multinational enterprises' pricing strategies. However, this information is often covered by tax secrecy rules and not available to taxpayers. Countries have taken different approaches to the use of such so-called secret comparables, ranging from provisions allowing the explicit use of such information in China to a strong opposition to their use in Austria and the United States. In cases where the use of secret comparables is not allowed, profitability margins observed elsewhere need to be adjusted to reflect potential differences in the accounting standards, market risks, or other factors that might drive a wedge in the profitability margins achieved. However, there exists no universally

---

Box 11.1. Country-by-Country Reporting

The *G20/BEPS Action 13 Report* (OECD, 2015) provides for multinational enterprises to report annually and for each tax jurisdiction in which they do business specific information set out in a country-by-country report. The report contains the following key elements:

- Model legislation that requires the ultimate parent company of a multinational enterprise to file the country-by-country report in its country of residence
- Three model competent authority agreements that could facilitate the exchange of country-by-country reports (these three models are based on existing international agreements such as the Multilateral Convention on Administrative Assistance in Tax Matters, bilateral double tax treaties, and tax information exchange agreements)

Although the information received through the exchange of country-by-country reports cannot directly be used to make a transfer pricing adjustment, the receiving authority may use it to initiate further transfer pricing audits. A common criticism of country-by-country reports is the high threshold of €750 million to require multinational enterprises to file the reports. Many multinational enterprises located in developing countries may not exceed this threshold and are thus not required to file a report. The other criticism is that developing countries cannot use the information provided in the country-by-country report for transfer pricing adjustments, even though it might be their best comparable. Finally, concluding a competent authority agreement is not always easy for developing countries due to the high standards-of-secrecy rules that OECD member states require before being willing to exchange country-by-country reports.

---

accepted adjustment method nor agreement on the reliability of different comparability adjustment methods.

A key information source for verifying whether transactions have been priced at arm's length is documentation submitted by multinational enterprises.[21] Transfer pricing documentation can take different forms: simple transfer pricing returns or country-by-country reports, which are part of the BEPS minimum standards but not necessarily available to all tax administrations and contain high-level information on related-party transactions, such as on the turnover achieved with related parties and with independent entities (see Box 11.1). This type of information can support effective risk assessments and audit selection, thus increasing the efficiency of scarce administrative capacity. Local or master files contain more detailed information, such as the business purpose of a specific transaction, the transfer pricing method applied, and a comparability analysis of the price chosen. This type of information can support verifying implementation of the arm's length standard during an audit. Moreover, many countries have made the filing of documentation a mandatory requirement, which is commonly assumed to have strong signaling effect that enhances taxpayer compliance (see Beer and Loeprick 2015).

While comprehensive documentation should provide tax administrations with better information to target its efforts, thus also reducing taxpayer compliance costs arising from unfocused or misdirected audits, the preparation of such reports can be costly, and finding the right balance between the tax authorities'

---

[21] See Platform for Collaboration on Tax (2019) and OECD (2017), chapter 5, "Documentation."

needs and avoiding excessive compliance costs is not always an easy task. Moreover, the increasing implementation of transfer pricing rules with widely varying approaches to documentation has also raised multinational enterprises' compliance costs and limited governments' ability to effectively exchange information. While there are several multilateral initiatives aimed at unifying documentation approaches, no internationally agreed format of documentation has been developed to date.[22] In designing documentation requirements,[23] countries should ensure they meet the following criteria:

- Requirements must be sufficiently clear, so that taxpayers know how to document their transfer pricing calculations.

- Requirements should be comprehensive enough to provide the tax administration with all relevant information needed before and during an audit.

- Requirements should be sufficiently balanced to avoid an excessive documentation burden on multinational enterprises.[24]

- Critically, requirements should be linked with a penalty if multinational enterprises fail to comply—which can take the form of late, incomplete, or incorrect filing.

Increased data availability is a prerequisite for an accurate implementation of the arm's length principle. However, governments can also aim to implement approximate arm's length results. With prescriptive approaches, such as safe harbors or fixed margins, transactions are considered to be at arm's length if the applied price (or margin) falls within a prespecified range. For instance, Australia provides a safe harbor for intragroup financing arrangements: in-bound loans are considered to be at arm's length if the interest rate applied to the loan does not exceed a specific indicator lending rate of the Reserve Bank of Australia.[25]

---

[22] For instance, the OECD/G20 BEPS initiative outlined a standardized approach to documentation in its BEPS Action 13, consisting of three elements: (1) a master file, which contains information on the overall group level; (2) a local file, containing specific information on the local enterprise and relevant related-party transactions; and (3) a country-by-country report, which describes the financial and economic position of the overall multinational group. Another example is the Code of Conduct on Transfer Pricing Documentation for Associated Enterprises in the European Union, which suggests a common master file as well as standardized country-specific documentation. However, application of the Code of Conduct was optional for taxpayers. To date, only country-by-country reporting has become part of the minimum standards that all members of the Inclusive Framework pledged to implement.

[23] See also Practical Toolkit to Support the Successful Implementation by Developing Countries of Effective Transfer Pricing Documentation Requirements (Platform for Collaboration on Tax 2019).

[24] For instance, many countries have restricted comprehensive documentation requirements to their largest taxpayers to avoid disproportionate compliance costs.

[25] In addition, the following conditions need to be met: (1) the combined cross-border loan balance must be less than AUD 50 million at all times during the year, (2) the funds provided and the interest paid must be denominated in Australian dollars, (3) the taxpayer should have no sustained losses, (4) the taxpayer should have no related-party dealings with affiliates in specified countries, and (5) the entity must be in compliance with general transfer pricing rules.

Prescriptive approaches are most appropriate in situations where one-sided transfer pricing methods, such as the comparable uncontrolled price method or cost-plus method, would also work. By eliminating the need to conduct a full comparability analysis, these approaches reduce the costs of both taxpayers and tax administrations. However, to effectively approximate arm's length results, prescriptive approaches require a careful design that would also need to be based on some type of comparability analysis. If the specified profit margin is too low, countries may forgo tax revenue, while too high a margin would imply an excessive tax burden to firms and potentially deter investments. Moreover, differences in rules across countries can lead to double taxation or undertaxation of some part of profits.

Anti-avoidance Rules

Thin Capitalization Rules

Tax avoidance using related-party loans is one of the most pervasive forms of tax avoidance, ranking second after the mispricing of internal transactions (see, for instance, Beer, De Mooij, and Liu 2019; Heckemeyer and Overesch 2017). By exploiting differences in statutory tax rates across countries, multinational enterprises reduce their overall tax bill without increasing the group's debt exposure or bankruptcy risk. Empirical studies show that tax differentials explain the internal debt decisions of multinational enterprises in Germany (for instance, Buettner and Wamser 2013; Schindler and others 2013); in Europe more generally (for instance, Huizinga, Laeven, and Nicodème 2008); or in the United States (for instance, Desai and others 2004). On average, a one percentage point higher corporate income tax rate increases the debt-to-asset ratio by between 0.17 and 0.28 (see De Mooij 2011).

To counter tax avoidance via related-party loans, many countries have introduced thin capitalization rules that limit the deductibility of interest payments in specific situations. These rules generally operate in one of two ways:

- *Ratio approaches:* These operate by specifying the maximum amount of debt on which deductible interest payments are available. Often the maximum is expressed in terms of the firm's equity.

- *Earning stripping approaches:* Earning stripping rules, on the other hand, specify the maximum amount of deductible interest payments, rather than debt, by reference to some other variable, such as the firm's profit.

Figure 11.3 illustrates the global spread of thin capitalization rules in 2017. In many African economies, thin capitalization rules are not yet implemented, and if they do exist, ratio approaches are more common. For instance, Kenya disallows the deductibility of interest payments on any debt that exceeds three times a firm's equity; Ghana disallows the deductibility of interest payments once the debt-to-equity ratio exceeds 2:1. In contrast, advanced economies typically rely on earning stripping approaches. For instance, the United States introduced an earning stripping rule that caps deductibility of interest payments at 30 percent of earnings before interest, tax, depreciation, and amortization (EBITDA). Beginning in 2022 this limit will become more binding as it will apply to earnings before

Figure 11.3. Global Thin Cap Rules

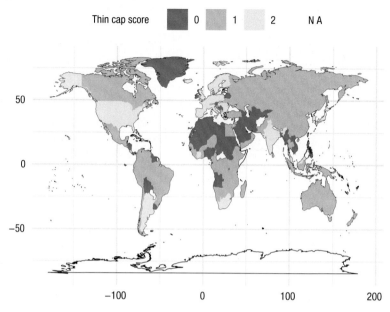

Source: Deloitte; Ernst and Young; PricewaterhouseCoopers; and authors' calculations.
Note: Map illustrates spread of thin cap rules globally in 2017. A thin cap score of 0 indicates that no thin cap rule is implemented; a score of 1 indicates reliance on a ratio approach; a thin cap score of 2 indicates reliance on an earning stripping approach.

interest and tax (EBIT). Similarly, as of 2019, the European Union's Anti-Tax Avoidance Directive limits the deductibility of interest payments at 30 percent of an affiliate's EBITDA in all EU member states.

A common concern with ratio approaches is that the line between debt and equity is difficult to draw. To avoid loopholes exploiting this ambiguity, equity should be defined in a broad sense and include share capital, retained earnings, capital contributions, interest-free loans, or revaluation reserves. Debt, in turn, should encompass anything that is substantively a loan, such as finance leases, financial derivatives, or debt factoring arrangements. A simple indirect definition is that the thin cap rule regards as debt anything that triggers tax-deductible payments. Moreover, ratio approaches differ in whether they limit total or related-party debt. While the latter approach appears more targeted at tax avoidance, multinational enterprises can circumvent such rules by using back-to-back arrangements, where internal loans would appear as originating from a third-party lender (such as a bank) through shareholder or related-party guarantees. To avoid situations where multinational enterprises strategically reduce the amount of debt just before compliance with the ratio is verified, such as at the year's end, many countries have opted to specify the debt limit as an average or a maximum over a reporting period. However, even modest loans can erode a country's tax base if they are linked with excessive interest rates. Ratio approaches thus need to be complemented with effective transfer pricing legislation to curb profit shifting.

Earning stripping approaches, on the other hand, protect the domestic tax base more directly by specifying limits to the tax deductibility of interest payments. Many countries include de minimis thresholds where the rule is only applicable if net interest payments exceed a specific amount. For instance, the threshold is set to €3 million in the European Union's Anti-Tax Avoidance Directive. One challenge of earning stripping approaches is that the limitation is affected by the economic cycle. With the denominator of earning stripping ratios decreasing during downturns, the restrictions become more binding and increase the costs of capital in times when additional spending would be most needed.[26] Most countries that rely on earning stripping approaches thus define exceptions to the general deductibility limit in so-called escape clauses. For instance, the European Union's Anti-Tax Avoidance Directive allows taxpayers to fully deduct its net interest payments if their ratio of equity to total assets is equal or above the group's equity ratio. However, the application of escape clauses is not always straightforward: the reference to a group's equity ratio typically requires adjustments to account for potential differences in accounting standards between the group's affiliates. Moreover, local balance sheets need to be adjusted for any claims against, or shares in, foreign group entities to ensure a fair basis of comparison.

More General Deductibility Limits

Related-party loans are just one of many assets used within a multinational enterprise that can erode a country's corporate income tax base. More generally, structures that facilitate tax avoidance are often created in two steps: First, multinational enterprises transfer valuable assets, such as financial or intangible assets, into jurisdictions that tax the return to these assets at low rates. Second, the assets are provided to other group affiliates where they erode the tax base by triggering tax deductible payments, such as interest, royalty, or service-fee payments. These payments increase profits in the low-tax jurisdiction where the asset is located. Tax avoidance that combines such structures with transfer mispricing is more effective but not necessary to reduce the multinational enterprise's global tax bill.

Two important examples of assets that are easy to relocate and whose value is difficult to determine are intangible assets and internal services. Hebous and Johanesson (2015) provide evidence for the importance of tax avoidance using internal service fees related to captive insurance companies or entities providing headquarter functions, such as advertising or management. Several empirical studies highlight the importance of intangible assets in international tax avoidance, either by mispricing royalty payments (see, for instance, Desai, Foley, and Hines 2006; Grubert 2003) or by the strategic location of intangible assets in low-tax jurisdictions (see, for instance, Dischinger and Riedel 2011; Griffith, Miller, and

---

[26] This is somewhat mitigated by the any decline interest rates during downturns.

O'Donnell 2014). While governments have long relied on thin capitalization rules, restrictions to the deductibility of other payments have spread more recently. For instance, restrictions on the deductibility of royalty payments have been introduced in Austria in 2014, in Germany in 2017, and in Poland in 2018. The Polish rule caps deductibility at 5 percent of EBITDA, while the Austrian and German rules disallow any deduction if the royalty income is taxed lightly abroad.[27]

Alternative minimum taxes are blunter instruments, targeting all types of related-party payments. Corporations generally pay the greater of their regular tax liability and the minimum tax liability. For instance, the United States introduced an alternative minimum tax, the Base Erosion Anti-Abuse Tax (BEAT), as part of the Tax Cuts and Jobs Act. The measure targets corporations with gross receipts exceeding $500 million per year on average over the last three years that make more than 3 percent of their deductible payments to foreign base related parties. In calculating the tax base, the Base Erosion Anti-Abuse Tax disregards most related-party payments—except those for intermediate goods—and applies a lower rate on this base.[28] African economies often rely on simpler and less targeted alternative minimum taxes that are calculated as a small share, often 1 to 2 percent, of a corporation's turnover and that apply also domestically.

India chose a different approach and introduced a so-called equalization levy in 2016, applicable to payments for online advertising. The equalization levy is imposed at the rate of 6 percent of the gross amount paid to a nonresident for online advertising services. It is collected by withholding from the payer and applies only to payments made by businesses. While imposed as a separate levy, it is, in substance, an extension of the withholding tax on technical fees that many developing countries already impose and thus reduces the incentive to overcharge for service fees. Late in 2019 the OECD published a consultation document on the "undertaxed payments" and "subject to tax" rules in the Pillar Two approach of its response to digitalization of the economy (OECD, 2019c). The consultation document notes that these rules may operate by way of imposition of source-based taxation (including withholding tax) for a payment to a related party if that payment was not subject to tax at or above a minimum rate. Further work will develop the parameters of these rules, but an important feature is that the right will be to tax the "payment" and so apply to the gross amount. However, the country of the payer would have to investigate the tax treatment in other countries (to determine if the minimum tax is reached) before it can impose the tax. This is not the case with regular withholding taxes and may add substantial complexity to the administration of the rules.

Anti-avoidance Measures Targeting Other Forms of Tax Avoidance

While related-party payments reduce the domestic corporate income tax base, some of these income flows are still taxed domestically: withholding taxes apply

---

[27] The introduction of these restrictions was triggered by the spread of intellectual property boxes throughout Europe, where royalty income was taxed at low rates.

[28] The applicable rate was 5 percent in 2018 and 10 percent in 2019; it will rise to 12.5 percent in 2026.

in most countries on cross-border interest-, royalty-, and service-fee payments. For multinational enterprises, these taxes increase the effective costs of intragroup transactions with low-tax affiliates and limit incentives to engage in tax arbitrage.[29] They can thus act as a second line of defense in safeguarding the domestic tax base, especially when administrative capacity is limited, the scope of antiabuse provisions is narrowly defined (see Balabushko and others 2017), or tax incentives have eroded the corporate tax base. For instance, Brazil levies withholding taxes at a rate of 15 percent on royalty and interest payments. However, this rate is increased to 25 percent if the recipient is domiciled in a low-tax jurisdiction.

Yet many countries have concluded double tax treaties that limit their right to tax passive income payments. Reduced withholding taxes vis-à-vis low-tax jurisdictions are especially problematic, eroding a country's tax base both directly and indirectly: the direct effect is a reduction in withholding tax revenue collected on existing income flows, because these flows are now taxed at lower rates. In addition, behavioral responses imply that the bilateral volume of flows with both the treaty partner country and all other countries will change, with potentially more important revenue implications. Specifically, reduced withholding tax rates increase the tax differential between the source country and the low-tax jurisdiction the treaty was concluded with. Multinational enterprises will respond with the following actions:

- *Restructuring operations:* By setting up intermediate holding companies in the treaty partner country, multinational enterprises can benefit from lower bilateral taxation. Intermediate holding companies are especially effective in reducing the group's tax bill if the treaty-partner country (1) taxes business income minimally, (2) does not apply withholding taxes on outgoing income flows, and (3) has weak substance requirements associated with its treaty benefits. These conditions provide for an easy flow of money to the ultimate parent's location.[30] The restructuring will lead to increased flows through the low-tax jurisdiction and reduced flows through all other jurisdictions that apply higher effective taxes on income payments.

- *More aggressively pricing related-party transactions:* With a larger tax differential, the return to transfer mispricing increases, which is what multinational enterprises can exploit by charging higher royalty and service-fee payments than they otherwise would. As a consequence, not only the quantity but also the price of related-party payments going to the low-tax jurisdiction will likely increase.

---

[29] Withholding taxes increase the effective tax cost of transactions with affiliates in low-tax jurisdictions only because high-tax countries typically provide some form of tax relief—a credit or a deduction—for the foreign taxation of passive income. Consequently, withholding taxes allocate the tax base between high-tax countries, with limited effects for multinational enterprises. However, they increase the tax burden for entities in low-tax jurisdictions.

[30] Empirical evidence suggests that the misuse of countries' double taxation treaties with investment hubs has historically reduced corporate income tax revenue in Sub-Saharan Africa by an average of between 15 and 20 percent. At the same time, these treaties did not attract additional investments (Beer and Loeprick 2018).

A structured approach to concluding double taxation treaties is one of the most effective anti-avoidance measures against treaty abuse (see also Chapter 8). Ministries of finance should scrutinize the cost and benefits of treaty conclusion on a case-by-case basis and abstain from concluding double taxation treaties with countries that do not tax or minimally tax the income of their residents. To minimize variation in the tax treatment of bilateral income flows, countries should rely on a model treaty that provides the same terms to all countries with which this treaty is concluded. The model should limit source countries' taxing rights as little as possible. For instance, the treaty should allow source countries to withhold substantive amounts on passive income payments and fully tax the capital gains derived from a sale of location-specific assets, such as mining rights or telecommunication licenses, even if the ownership of these assets has been transferred and sold abroad (see Platform for Collaboration on Tax 2018). Finally, the treaty should include robust antiabuse measures that effectively limit treaty benefits to residents of the treaty partner country.

Under current rules, multinational enterprises can avoid being subject to tax altogether by avoiding physical presence (although, as discussed above, there are also discussions and in some countries recent actions about changing definitions of permanent establishments). For instance, selling goods usually requires local marketing and sales functions. Foreign multinational enterprises can either establish a subsidiary that performs these functions, or they can commission another entity, possibly part of the same group, to perform these functions on its behalf. While the profit from selling goods would be taxed at the branch or subsidiary level in the former case, it is not taxed in the latter. The United Kingdom and Australia have introduced diverted profits taxes to target, among other things, the avoidance of permanent establishments. While these taxes differ in some respects, there are important commonalities: both taxes target (primarily) the international tax avoidance of large multinational enterprises, apply punitive rates on profits that businesses are considering diverting, and are sufficiently broad in scope to act as an effective deterrent device for a range of abusive structures. For instance, the UK Diverted Profits Tax applies at a rate of 25 percent, which is higher than the standard corporate income tax rate of 19 percent.[31] While the tax primarily targets the avoidance of corporate taxes by large multinational enterprises with turnover exceeding €50 million, it may also apply to purely domestic firms. Moreover, the diverted profits taxes target the avoidance of both nonresidents (that avoid a permanent establishment) and residents that abuse tax deductibility of related-party payments. For instance, if tax deductible payments in the United Kingdom are not subject to an effective tax rate of at least 80 percent of the UK tax rate abroad, these payments are also considered as diverted profits.

Alternatives to Arm's Length Allocation Mechanisms

Instead of attempting to estimate arm's length prices, profits can also be allocated by simple formulae to different locations. Chapter 14 discusses how such formula apportionment could be used to allocate consolidated profits across jurisdictions, as well as the pros and cons of such an approach.

---

[31] For firms in the oil and gas sector, it is levied at 55 percent.

The formulae used in such approaches can include different apportionment factors, such as capital, labor, or sales. It is possible to allocate aggregate profits using a unique formula, or to distinguish between routine and residual profits (residual profit allocation), with different allocation mechanisms for both. Specifically, under residual profit allocation, the ordinary profit is typically allocated only to capital, while residual profit may include more factors, including sales.

The choice of factors used in the formula is crucial for determining whether the approach aims at maintaining source-based taxation—at least as an approximation—or includes a move to destination-based taxation. Specifically, factors such as capital and labor still imply source-based taxation, because they suggest that profits are allocated to where production takes place. The use of sales, however, especially if defined by the destination rather than their origin, would imply a move away from source- to destination-based taxation. That is certainly a reform option—and as discussed in detail in Chapter 13, a very powerful one— but it would not be a way to strengthen source-based taxation.

A full move to formulary methods is not the only option. Already now, for certain transactions, transfer pricing methods allow a transaction-level profit split, which could include remuneration of routine functions with some split of residual profits.

ADDRESSING TAX COMPETITION

With the increasing implementation of antiabuse measures, multinational enterprises' tax avoidance opportunities are likely to decrease in the future. However, even if all loopholes to artificially move tax bases to low-tax jurisdictions were effectively eliminated—which will be hard to achieve—multinational enterprises could still minimize their global tax burden by relocating actual production to these places. Empirical research provides ample evidence for the sensitivity of real investments to tax. For instance, in a metastudy, De Mooij and Ederveen (2008) show that foreign direct investment increases by an average of 2.4 percent in response to a 1 percentage point reduction in the domestic corporate income tax rate. When profit shifting opportunities as a tax minimization device cease to exist, the sensitivity of real investments to tax will likely increase.

Governments are keenly aware of the risk that neighboring countries could offer more attractive tax terms to invite investments that might otherwise be made domestically. And since foreign direct investment is a vital source of growth for many developing countries, generating employment, technology, and skill transfers and increasing demand for local production through backward linkages, the willingness of many governments to trade tax revenue against an increased likelihood of attracting investments is not surprising. Indeed, in a static environment, providing tax incentives can be rational or even revenue maximizing. But in a dynamic context where other countries react to a given country's policy changes, tax competition leads to suboptimal outcomes globally. Take the corporate income tax rate competition as an example. By lowering the cost of capital, a reduction in a country's corporate income tax rate should attract real investments, with positive effects on a country's growth and tax revenue in the short run. However, historically, other countries have responded to foreign tax rate reductions by reducing their rates too (Leibrecht and Hochgatterer 2012). While the average corporate income tax rate was at around 40 percent in 1990, it was around 23 percent in 2019. If the decline in rates were to continue at the same pace, the average rate will have declined to below 20 percent well before 2030. Gains from tax competition thus tend to be short lived, with all countries collecting less revenue than before.

Tax competition is inherently tied to source-based taxation. Alleviating the mutually adverse effects from competing over an internationally mobile tax base requires strong commitment devices or tax instruments that will reduce the strategic interdependency between domestic tax rules. For instance, more reliance on residence-based taxation—where countries tax the income of their residents from both domestic and foreign sources (see Chapter 12)—that is, a return to more residence-based taxation—would reduce the dependency of overall tax burdens on the tax treatment in source countries.

While complete residence-based taxation is unlikely to return any time soon, minimum taxes on outbound investment are one important example of a residence-based tax instrument. Minimum taxes are already in use. For instance, the United States introduced the Global Intangible Low Taxed Income (GILTI) provision in its latest tax reform. The tax targets intangible returns accruing abroad by specifying as the tax base all active business income exceeding 10 percent of the group's tangible assets. It is levied at 10.5 percent and provides a nonrefundable tax credit for 80 percent of foreign taxes paid, implying that usually no tax is due if the group's intangible returns are taxed at a rate of 13.125 percent or above (see Beer, Klemm, and Matheson 2018). One aspect that weakens the implications of these provisions is that the tax is assessed globally, rather than on a country-by-country basis. This means that it is often not binding for multinational enterprises that also have operations in high-tax countries. As long as their average tax rate is sufficiently high, they still gain by shifting profits into low-tax countries.

Recent developments in the Inclusive Framework show that outbound taxes may spread quickly. Specifically, the income inclusion proposal tabled in the OECD's Inclusive Framework suggests taxing the income of foreign subsidiaries and permanent establishments if this income is subject to a low effective tax rate abroad. The proposal has much in common with existing controlled foreign company rules that are primarily used by capital-exporting countries. However, while controlled foreign company rules are typically targeted at passive income payments, the income inclusion rule is broader and would also include active income. Clavey and others (2019) propose translating the OECD's income inclusion proposal into a rule designed to better meet developing economy interests (see Box 11.2). As more capital-exporting countries apply taxes on lightly taxed income abroad, source countries will see less need to reduce their own tax rates. Minimum taxes can thus provide a floor in the race to the bottom. While minimum taxes can be implemented unilaterally, multilateral adoption by all important capital exporters would be particularly powerful, as it would immediately provide such a floor, below which it would not be worth cutting taxes.

Box 11.2. An Income-Inclusion Rule for Developing Economies

Based on the concept of diverted profits, the approach of Clavey and others (2019) would target profit shifted to low-taxed and low-substance entities and use a simple redistributive formula to reallocate any excess of these profits above what is justified by the observable indicators in these locations.

Specifically, the rule would be implemented as follows:

- The rule would apply to taxpayers with related parties, possibly with a de minimis rule to exclude small and medium sized enterprises. It would target cases of tax mismatches.
- Identification would be relatively mechanical, targeting low-taxed entities in a group with "super profits" (either absolute or relative to the multinational enterprise group). An amount of profit representative of the earning capacity would be determined for these low-taxed entities based on a mechanical approach using observable indicators of substance, such as the direct cost of labor.
- Profit in excess of the representative earning capacity would be reallocated to all countries involved in the relevant multinational enterprise supply chain. A formulaic approach (potentially based on sales) could be used to determine a country's share of the diverted profits.

Moreover, several multilateral initiatives aim at improving international cooperation to overcome the mutually damaging outcomes of uncoordinated tax policies. For instance, in 1997 the European Union adopted a non-binding legal instrument, the Code of Conduct on Business Taxation, to curb harmful tax competition within the European Union. While the Code of Conduct was initially designed as a commitment device so that member states would reexamine, amend, or abolish any tax measures that constitute harmful tax competition (and refrain from introducing new ones), it has since morphed into a standard the European Union uses to evaluate the national systems of third countries.

In 2017 the EU Commission published its first blacklist of jurisdictions that are subject to punitive measures because their national tax systems do not conform with the Code of Conduct. Similarly, the OECD's Forum on Harmful Tax Practices has been conducting reviews of national tax systems since 1998. In 2000 the OECD published its first blacklist, which included the names of 35 countries where elements of the national tax systems were considered harmful. The specific inclusion criteria differ across lists, but a common feature is that a ring-fenced preferential treatment of nonresidents, or of activities that do not impinge on the domestic market, is considered especially problematic by both the OECD and European Union. Keen (2001) shows, however, that these regimes may, in fact, reduce negative spillovers by confining tax competition to the most mobile parts of the international tax base. In contrast, undifferentiated tax incentives might attract investment at higher government cost. Care thus needs to be taken in coordinating national policies, as discussed in detail in Chapter 6.

Another simple and effective—though politically hard to agree upon—measure targeting tax competition might be self-imposed constraints on applicable tax rates. For instance, the European Union allows all member states to levy VAT at a standard rate, which cannot be below 15 percent, and a maximum of two reduced rates, which normally cannot be less than 5 percent. The Western and Central African Economic and Monetary regions prescribe minimum excise tax rates as well as bands for the VAT and corporate income tax rates that countries can apply. While excise and VATs are levied on goods and services, leaving little ambiguity on the base, the situation is different for the corporate income tax, where definitions of the tax base are more complex and standardized tax bases across countries are less prevalent. Source-based taxes, like corporate income taxes, however, are precisely those under competitive pressure and will potentially benefit from coordination, while such pressure on destination-based taxes, like VATs, is much more limited.

CONCLUSION

Digitalization and, more broadly, the globalization of the economy are disrupting traditional business models and challenging definitions of value creation. The fundamentals of the international tax framework, in contrast, still reflect the logic of a brick-and-mortar economy. This dislocation has provided multinational enterprises with vast opportunities to avoid source-based taxation. In the aftermath of the global financial crisis, when public coffers were depleted, international taxation became a priority area for public policy coordination. The OECD/G20 BEPS Project has been one of the most ambitious efforts in this respect, raising awareness about international tax avoidance risks and guiding a multilateral dialogue. However, national business models differ, as do perceptions of what is an appropriate tax burden. These differences complicate a multilateral solution process, and larger countries have moved unilaterally, increasing the pressure on the international community.

However, the international tax system is tightly interlinked, and policy reactions of one country can have ramifications on public revenues globally. Source-based taxation induces tax competition. This means that even if legal definitions of source were aligned with today's business realities and the allocation of profits properly strengthened with anti-avoidance rules, multinational enterprises might nevertheless end up paying minimal taxes due to a race to the bottom.

This chapter has described both incremental and more radical deviations from the current system that would allow maintaining source-based taxes in the future. The chapter proposed three main approaches:

- *Defining source:* The concept of permanent establishment allows for a qualitative threshold, self-imposed by the source country, that limits its taxing possibility. A broader permanent establishment concept could strengthen source-based taxation. In addition, source countries should refrain from giving up withholding rights on investment income and ensure—both domestically and under their treaty policy—that capital gains on business assets, securities, and real property are taxable.

- *Strengthening the allocation of profits:* Documentation requirements can support an effective implementation of the arm's length principle.

However, deviations from pure arm's length pricing, such as mechanical or formulaic approaches, including safe harbors or residual profit allocation mechanisms, might be better suited to fit the needs of developing countries. Restrictions on the deductibility of expenses can strengthen the allocation of profits.

- *Addressing tax competition:* Minimum taxes on outbound investments—especially if coordinated multilaterally—are potentially the most effective measure in strengthening residence-based taxation components in the international tax system and thus relaxing source countries' need to reduce their tax rate to attract investment. But regional cooperation is another potential tool for reducing pressure on corporate tax rates.

REFERENCES

Balabushko, Oleksii, Sebastian Beer, Jan Loeprick, and Felipe Vallada. 2017. "The Direct and Indirect Costs of Tax Treaty Policy: Evidence from Ukraine." Policy Research Working Paper Series 7982, World Bank, Washington, DC.

Beer, Sebastian, Ruud de Mooij, and Li Liu. 2020. "International Corporate Tax Avoidance: A Review of the Channels, Magnitudes, and Blind Spots." *Journal of Economic Surveys* 34(3): 660–88.

Beer, Sebastian, Alexander Klemm, and Thornton Matheson. 2018. "Tax Spillovers from US Corporate Tax Reform." IMF Working Paper 18/166, International Monetary Fund, Washington, DC.

Beer, Sebastian, and Jan Loeprick. 2015. "Profit Shifting: The Drivers of Transfer (Mis)pricing and the Potential for Countermeasures." *International Tax and Public Finance* 22(3): 426–51.

Beer, Sebastian, and Jan Loeprick. 2018. "The Cost and Benefits of Tax Treaties with Investment Hubs: Findings from Sub-Saharan Africa." IMF Working Paper 18/227, International Monetary Fund, Washington, DC.

Best, Carlos, Anne Brockemeyer, Henrik Kleven, Johannes Spinnewijn, Mazar Waseem. 2015. Production vs. Revenue Efficiency with Limited Tax Capacity: Theory and Evidence from Pakistan.

Buettner, Thiess, and Georg Wamser. 2013. "Internal Debt and Multinational Profit Shifting: Empirical Evidence from Firm-Level Panel Data." *National Tax Journal* 66(1): 63–95.

Clavey, Colin, Jonathan Pemberton, Jan Loeprick, and Marijn Verhoeven. 2019. "International Tax Reform, Digitalization, and Developing Countries". MTI Global Practice Discussion Paper No. 16. World Bank Group.

Cooper, Joel, Randall Fox, Jan Loeprick, and Komal Mohindra. 2016. *Transfer Pricing and Developing Economies: A Handbook for Policy Makers and Practitioners.* Directions in Development. Washington, DC: World Bank.

De Mooij, Ruud. 2011. "The Tax Elasticity of Debt: A Synthesis of Size and Variation." IMF Working Paper 11/95, International Monetary Fund, Washington, DC.

De Mooij, Ruud, and Sjef Ederveen. 2008. "Corporate Tax Elasticities: A Reader's Guide to Empirical Findings." *Oxford Review of Economic Policy* 24(4): 680–97.

Desai, Mihir A., C. Fritz Foley, and James R. Hines. 2004. "A Multinational Perspective on Capital Structure Choice and Internal Capital Markets." *Journal of Finance* 59(6): 2451–87.

Desai, Mihir A., C. Fritz Foley, and James R. Hines. 2006. "The Demand for Tax Haven Operations." *Journal of Public Economics* 90(3): 513–31.

Dischinger, Matthias, and Nadine Riedel. 2011. "Corporate Taxes and the Location of Intangible Assets within Multinational Firms." *Journal of Public Economics* 95(7–8): 691–707.

Griffith, Rachel, Helen Miller, and Martin O'Connell. 2014. "Ownership of Intellectual Property and Corporate Taxation." *Journal of Public Economics* 112: 12–23.

Grubert, Harry. 2003. "Intangible Income, Intercompany Transactions, Income Shifting, and the Choice of Location." *National Tax Journal* 56(1): 221–42.

Hebous, Shafik, and Niels Johannesen. 2015. "At Your Service! The Role of Tax Havens in International Trade with Services." CESifo Working Paper 5414, Center for Economic Studies, Munich.

Heckemeyer, Jost H., and Michael Overesch. 2017. "Multinationals' Profit Response to Tax Differentials: Effect Size and Shifting Channels." *Canadian Journal of Economics* 50(4): 965–94.

Huizinga, Harry, Luc Laeven, and Gaëtan Nicodème. 2008. "Capital Structure and International Debt Shifting." *Journal of Financial Economics* 88(1): 80–118.

International Monetary Fund. 2019. World Economic Outlook, August 2019. Chapter 2: The Rise of Corporate Market Power and its Economic Effects.

Keen, Michael. 2001. "Preferential Regimes Can Make Tax Competition Less Harmful." *National Tax Journal* 54(4): 757–62.

Leibrecht, Markus, and Claudia Hochgatterer. 2012. "Tax Competition as a Cause of Falling Corporate Income Tax Rates: A Survey of Empirical Literature." *Journal of Economic Surveys* 26(4): 616–48.

Organisation for Economic Co-operation and Development (OECD). 2015. "Transfer Pricing Documentation and Country-by-Country Reporting, Action 13 - 2015 Final Report", OECD/G20 Base Erosion and Profit Shifting Project, OECD Publishing, Paris. http://dx .doi.org/10.1787/9789264241480-en

Organisation for Economic Co-operation and Development (OECD). 2017. *Transfer Pricing Guidelines for Multinational Enterprises and Tax Administrations 2017.* Paris: OECD Publishing. http://dx.doi.org/10.1787/tpg-2017-en.

Organisation for Economic Co-operation and Development (OECD). 2019a. "Addressing the Tax Challenges of the Digital Economy." Public Consultation Document, OECD/G20 Base Erosion and Profit Shifting Project, OECD, Paris.

Organisation for Economic Co-operation and Development (OECD). 2019b. "Secretariat Proposal for a 'Unified Approach' under Pillar One." Public Consultation Document, OECD/G20 Base Erosion and Profit Shifting Project, OECD, Paris.

Organisation for Economic Co-operation and Development (OECD). 2019c. "Global Anti-Base Erosion Proposal – Tax Challenges Arising from the Digitalization of the Economy." Public Consultation Document, OECD/G20 Base Erosion and Profit Shifting Project, OECD, Paris.

Platform for Collaboration on Tax. 2018. *The Taxation of Offshore Indirect Transfers—A Toolkit.* Washington, DC: International Monetary Fund, Paris: Organisation for Economic Co-operation and Development, New York: United Nations, and Washington, DC: World Bank Group.

Platform for Collaboration on Tax. 2017. A Toolkit for Addressing Difficulties in Accessing Comparables Data for Transfer Pricing Analyses, https://www.oecd.org/tax/toolkit-on -comparability-and-mineral-pricing.pdf

Platform for Collaboration on Tax. 2019. "Practical toolkit to support the successful implementation by developing countries of effective transfer pricing documentation requirements (Draft version)". https://www.oecd.org/tax/beps/draft-toolkit-transfer-pricing -documentation-platform-for-collaboration-on-tax.pdf

Schindler, Dirk, Jarle Møen, Guttorm Schjelderup, and Julia Tropina. 2013. "International Debt Shifting: Do Multinationals Shift Internal or External Debt?" Annual Conference 2013 (Duesseldorf): Competition Policy and Regulation in a Global Economic Order 79749, Verein für Socialpolitik / German Economic Association.

Tørsløv, T., L. Wier, and Gabriel Zucman. 2018. "The Missing Profits of Nations." NBER Working Paper 24701, National Bureau of Economic Research, Cambridge, MA.

CHAPTER 12

Residence-Based Taxation: Is There a Way Forward?

Kiyoshi Nakayama, Victoria Perry, and Alexander Klemm

INTRODUCTION

The world is in a state of fairly deep confusion regarding whether the international tax system is to be moved toward or away from residence-based corporate taxation. Chapter 7 outlined the parameters of that confusion and described the historical and recent steps that have been taken to strengthen the application of the residence basis; these steps have included combatting both the erosion of the tax base and the practice of shifting taxable profits. This chapter explores ways in which those efforts could be, and are being, strengthened still further. Yet, at the same time, as also described in Chapter 7, most advanced economies—the primary capital exporters—have now moved away from worldwide taxation toward territorial systems that in theory tax active business income at the source only, by one mechanism or another, largely for reasons of tax competition.

It may be that this confused state is inevitable in a world in which no profound principles underlie the international allocation of the tax base constituted by the economic return to business capital.[1] In that case, we must ask of the potential reforms affecting residence-based taxation—from minimal fixes to more fundamental changes—what their impact will be on efficiency (economic and administrative), overall tax revenue generation, and perceptions of inter-nation fairness. While the first two of these at least permit of objective, if complex, answers, the last—fairness—is viewed very differently by various observers.

This chapter discusses options for the way forward for residence-based taxation, beginning where Chapter 7 left off—with what might be termed loophole closers—and proceeding through more fundamental changes that could be (and in some cases are being) considered. It should be emphasized that in many of these areas, effectiveness will depend upon multilateral agreement to proceed, though this is more true of some cases than others. And, as will be mentioned below, it must also be noted that the lines between some of these possibilities are themselves not bright. Where do territorial—source-based—taxes leave off and

---

[1] See, for example, Mirrlees and others (2011, 430).

controlled foreign corporation (CFC) rules begin, for example, or minimum taxes end and worldwide taxation begin?

CONTINUED STRENGTHENING OF ANTI-AVOIDANCE PROVISIONS

Controlled Foreign Corporation Rules

As discussed in Chapter 7, CFC rules have been implemented widely in advanced economies as a means to counter tax deferral under worldwide tax systems or to bring some types of income earned abroad into the residence country tax net under otherwise territorial systems. In other words, such provisions represent partial movements toward contemporaneous worldwide taxation. Although varying in details across jurisdictions, these provisions are intended to tax immediately the undistributed income of overseas subsidiaries of a resident company as income of the resident company, thus combatting the planning device of shifting taxable income from the source country into an intermediate (generally low-taxed) jurisdiction where it can remain untaxed by the residence country because of deferral. However, as also discussed, tensions between the desire to enforce residence taxation, and to permit deferral or avoidance of tax for competitive (or other) reasons, have led to increasingly complex, and avoidable, CFC rules. The OECD/G20 Base Erosion and Profit Shifting Project, launched in 2013 (or BEPS 1.0), attempted to give guidance on implementing more stringent criteria for these rules—but was unable, for those reasons, to get OECD/G20 countries to agree to adopting these more stringent rules as BEPS minimum standards.

While the European Union Anti-Tax Avoidance Directive (ATAD) that followed BEPS was more forceful in its mandatory CFC provisions, those, too, are not unavoidable, at least with regard to transfers among EU countries. Restricting the application of CFC rules to artificial arrangements or to the nondistributed income of CFCs arising from "non-genuine arrangements which have been put in place for the essential purpose of obtaining a tax advantage"[2] not only increases administrative costs and difficulties of application, but allows countries concerned about tax competitiveness to interpret artificial or essential purposes in an overly restrictive manner, thus undermining the purpose of the rules.

To avoid discretionary application and uncertainty for taxpayers, CFC rules should rather be based on objective criteria. For example, there should at a minimum be a clear distinction between active business income and passive income (the payment of interest, dividends, or royalties from foreign subsidiary companies), and the rules should apply to prescribed passive income regardless of the existence or nature of business activities that may have given rise to that income. If CFC rules allow any exceptions with regard to passive income, such exceptions should also be subject to very restrictive and objective criteria. Policymakers could

---

[2] Council Directive (EU) 2016/1164 of 12 July 2016, Article 7, 2(b).

usefully reflect in developing these criteria, for example, upon how the "active financing exception" has undermined the effectiveness of the US CFC rules, as described in Chapter 7.

CFC rules may not be an urgent issue for economies from which outbound investment by their resident companies is still limited and for those that do not host headquarters of multinational enterprises. However, it is important for these economies to introduce good CFC rules early on and to keep track of outbound investment by their resident companies, as it will become more difficult to start this monitoring after any substantial amount of outbound investment has begun. Such expanding companies in these economies may not be required at early stages to comply with international accounting standards, unless and until they plan to list their shares in stock exchanges in advanced countries. Their residence country governments, therefore, should legally require taxpayers to provide data on their outbound investment. Data on controlled foreign subsidiaries can also be useful in detecting risks of transfer price manipulation and other base erosion problems. It should also be noted that residents of emerging and developing countries may make round trip investments into the resident country through a nonresident company that the resident owns, as disguised foreign investment (Vann 1996). If the country provides tax incentives for foreign investors, the incentives for this circular investment will only increase. While the actual application of CFC rules to such circular investment can only be accomplished by penetrating such a disguised structure, nonetheless CFC rules and accompanying disclosure requirements could have deterrent effects.

Effective enforcement of CFC rules is premised on the accurate reporting of the existence of all CFCs to the residence country tax authorities. While this can be to some extent verified through financial statements of multinational enterprises under international accounting standards, as noted, this is unfortunately no guarantee. Accounting standards define a subsidiary as a company with stock that is more than 50 percent controlled by another company—similar to the commonly used definition of CFCs. But the standards do allow a company to exclude certain categories of subsidiaries from consolidated financial statements, though these unconsolidated subsidiaries should be listed in consolidated balance sheets as investments and their information (such as name, place of business, and ownership interests held) should be disclosed.[3] However, as witnessed in the Enron case, in which Enron notoriously did not disclose its 3,500 special purpose vehicles in low-tax jurisdictions, tax authorities need measures other than financial statements to verify the accuracy of CFC reporting by taxpayers.

To this end, a corporate register with extensive beneficial ownership information would help tax authorities to detect noncompliance with CFC reporting requirements. At the G8 summit meeting in 2013, members agreed on the need to make available to tax collection and law enforcement agencies information on who really owns and profits from companies and trusts, for example through

---

[3] International Financial Reporting Standard (IFRS) 12: 19B.

central registers of company beneficial ownership (Group of Eight 2013). Three countries, the United Kingdom, Denmark, and Ukraine, implemented public beneficial ownership registers for companies by October 2017 (Global Witness 2017). In addition, the European Union agreed to establish a centralized and public register of companies and their ultimate beneficial owners by January 10, 2020.[4] According to a report by Global Witness, only five EU members, Bulgaria, Denmark, Latvia, Luxembourg, and Slovenia, met the directive's deadline (Global Witness 2020).[5] If a multilateral agreement could be reached on establishing a universal public corporate register of beneficial ownership information, it could greatly strengthen the implementation of residence-based taxation.

Residence Definitions

While most advanced countries use the place of effective management,[6] sometimes along with the place of incorporation, as the criterion for defining the residence of a company,[7] the United States uses the place of incorporation as the sole criterion.[8] This formalistic and objective criterion provides taxpayers with predictability. However, as described in Chapter 7, in interacting with different criteria in other countries this criterion also permits manipulation, including the creation of companies that technically are not resident anywhere. It has also allowed US companies to be inverted into existing or new subsidiaries, thus becoming nonresident for US purposes without changing anything of substance— a technique that has given rise to various rounds of anti-avoidance rules and increased complexity.

Using the place of effective management criterion can also lead to dual residence—as opposed to no residence—which was the only problem that was considered when these rules were originally created. This was then to be dealt with under bilateral treaties and tie-breaking rules, with the OECD Model Treaty,

---

[4] Fifth Anti-Money Laundering Directive (Directive 2018/843 of the European Parliament and of the Council), entered into force on July 9, 2018. https://eur-lex.europa.eu/legal-content/EN/TXT/PDF/?uri=CELEX:32018L0843&from=EN.

[5] According to the Global Witness (2020) report, in addition to the five members that are compliant with the directive, five other members have a centralized register of the beneficial owners of companies that is available to the public, but it contains significant restrictions that hinder its effective use. Harari and others (2020, 31–32) examined 133 jurisdictions through the Financial Secrecy Index and found that, as of April 2020, 44 jurisdictions have effective beneficial ownership registration; out of these 44 jurisdictions, Denmark and the United Kingdom have updated beneficial ownership information available online for free in open data format, and Ecuador and Slovenia have updated beneficial ownership information available online for free.

[6] Some common law countries such as the United Kingdom and Canada use central management and control as a test to determine the residency of a company. For a fuller description, see Vann (1996).

[7] The OECD Model Tax Convention provides place of management as a criterion (Article 4(1)). The UN Model Tax Convention provides both place of incorporation and place of management (Article 4(1)).

[8] Japan and Korea use head or main office to determine the residency of a corporation, though given applicable law, this results in place of incorporation also counting.

for example, expecting that dual residence issues would be solved by means of mutual agreement procedures on a case-by-case basis.[9] It can be helpful, if not dispositive, for tax authorities to provide guidance on how the place of effective management criterion will apply. For example, India, which introduced the place of effective management criterion in its Income Tax Act in 2016,[10] issued detailed guiding principles in 2017.[11]

How can these problems be solved? This is an area in which multilateral agreements and standards are crucial. As is evident, and increasingly so over the past 25 years of globalization of the economy, any differences in the definitions of residence of corporations across jurisdictions virtually beg for aggressive tax planning to take advantage of the interstices thereby created.[12]

Yet the greater the enhancement of effective enforcement of worldwide taxation, the greater the incentives for competition to host the headquarters of multinational enterprises, effected by reducing the local tax rate on the income of such resident companies—and the greater the incentives for the owners of such companies to move, or form, their headquarters in lower-taxed jurisdictions.

How can that problem be addressed?

MINIMUM TAXATION

> *"In international tax policy debate, global minimum taxes are currently having their moment."*
>
> (Shaviro 2020)

Tax competition can be mitigated—and the corporate income tax thus safeguarded—by ensuring that "all internationally operating businesses pay a minimum level of tax" (OECD 2020, 13). This is a phrase easily said, but less easily achieved. International minimum taxes[13] can be used to protect either (or both) the source base or the residence base. This section addresses the latter—minimum taxation of the return to outbound capital investment by the residence country.

The astute reader may ask how this approach differs from CFC rules, on the one hand, and from immediate (without deferral) worldwide taxation, on the other. The technical answer to these questions is, on the one hand, that CFC rules

---

[9] The OECD's Committee on Fiscal Affairs recognized that although situations of double residence of entities other than individuals were relatively rare, there had been a number of tax-avoidance cases involving dual-resident companies (commentary on Article 4(3)).

[10] Section 6 (3)(ii) of the Income Tax Act. Previously, the Income Tax Act had used a place of incorporation criterion.

[11] Central Board of Direct Taxation (CBDT) Circular 06/2017, January 24, 2017.

[12] Some examples are given in Chapter 7.

[13] Corporate minimum taxes have also been used extensively in the domestic context, generally to guard against the complete erosion of the tax base through preferences arising in the tax country's tax code. This chapter, though, focuses on their use in the international context.

as typically implemented and in their usual meaning apply only to passive sources of income generated abroad—interest and royalties in particular—and, for example in the case of US rules, explicitly not to the return on active business income even if channeled through an intermediate CFC. If CFC rules applied to any and all income derived by an overseas subsidiary, regardless of business activities, where the actual tax burden of the subsidiary is zero or extremely low, this would be such a minimum tax. And minimum taxes differ from pure worldwide taxation by virtue of not being applied at the full rate applicable in the residence (capital-exporting) country. Thus, such an outbound minimum tax constitutes not only a floor under the total tax paid by a multinational enterprise, but a step back from the implementation of territorial taxation on active business income—with the tax competition that such a source-based system entails. In a system that is not based on an underlying allocation principle, minimum taxes represent a messy, but perhaps advisable, compromise.

While such outbound minimum taxes apply directly in the residence country, if adopted widely among capital exporters, they can nonetheless help to protect the tax base of source-only, capital-importing, countries by setting a floor beneath which it will not benefit the source country to reduce its tax burden. Any further reduction would, in a pure minimum tax system, simply result in the balance of tax up to the minimum applicable rate being paid to the residence country—just as in the case of the former worldwide systems, at least in theory, before the addition of the element of deferral and the manipulation of the location of the residence tax bases.

These taxes are, indeed, having their moment—but they are by no means easy to design. The United States has led in the area, by enacting as part of the 2017 Tax Cuts and Jobs Act the global intangible low-taxed income (GILTI) provision. GILTI is calculated as the total active business income earned by a US resident firm's foreign affiliates that exceeds an amount equal to 10 percent of the foreign affiliates' tangible assets. Thus, the idea is that an excessive return (over 10 percent)—theoretically attributed to *intangible* assets, including, it is to be supposed, excess returns attributable to market dominance—will be brought into the US residence tax net on a current basis, but at a rate equal to only half of the US domestic corporate tax rate. Additional complexities—of effective rate and otherwise—arise as a result of the partial crediting of the GILTI tax for foreign tax credit purposes, as well as from the fact that the calculation of the tax base, relative to the foreign tangible assets, is done on an aggregate basis, rather than by looking at each foreign country and the assets and income therein. This opens the way to—again—extensive tax planning by US-resident multinational enterprises. Somewhat counterintuitively, for example, an incentive arises to invest more tangible assets abroad in order to minimize the GILTI base.

More recently, a coordinated effort on minimum taxes has also been underway. Under the Inclusive Framework, a two-pillar approach to reforming international taxation is under preparation. For the purposes of this chapter, the relevant component is the outbound minimum tax, which is part of Pillar Two (along with an inbound minimum tax). The details of the proposal are still subject to change (a blueprint was published in October [OECD 2020]), but the basic idea is to have a globally coordinated minimum outbound tax. Unlike GILTI, this would likely be on a country-by-country basis, and foreign tax credits would be granted fully (rather than at only 80 percent). One complication is the need to determine the order of taxing rights, when both inbound and outbound minimum taxes may apply. If ultimately consensus is reached and such a tax adopted, it could have a powerful impact on tax competition: unlike a unilateral minimum tax, this would not leave source countries competing for investment from other capital exporters. And a country-by-country approach reduces the scope for avoidance found in GILTI from the mixing of income from high- and low-tax jurisdictions.

MORE RADICAL REFORMS

This chapter, and Chapter 7, have made clear that the national residence of a legal entity is, at least in today's world, essentially an arbitrary concept—one that now facilitates tax avoidance and does not eliminate tax competition. How, then, to proceed? The foregoing sections have discussed ways in which steps can be taken to make more effective the use of residence as a concept for base allocation— essentially retaining the current system with some improvements. This section looks at more radical reforms, which would completely change the way profits are allocated. The first radical option considered is to do away with source and residence definitions, as well as separate accounting, and allocate profits by formula. The second option is to maintain a definition of residence but to base it on the ultimate human owners of firms rather than the entities themselves.

Allocation by Formula

A fundamental reform—discussed in more detail in Chapter 14—would be to give up on the separate entity or arm's length method of allocating the corporate tax base altogether, and instead to adopt a unitary approach to calculation of the tax base, with allocation by means of a formula. In most countries that use such formula apportionment in the subnational context, and in most proposals for adopting this approach in the supranational context (including under the proposed EU consolidated corporate tax idea), allocation of the unified tax base of a multinational enterprise depends upon the locations of physical capital, labor, and consumption. In this case, the place of ownership of capital—as well as the so-called residence of the unified multinational enterprise—becomes irrelevant to the allocation of the tax base. Beyond transition problems, a problem with this approach lies in the use of physical capital location as part of the allocation formula. Again, this approach was developed in a world largely addressing physical goods rather than services. Where more and more of the capital inputs to world production are intangibles—intellectual property, in essence—some might argue that a formula that leaves such intangibles out of the allocation process is missing the point. Arguably, though, on the other hand, this could be seen as exactly the point. A formula that explicitly includes the location of such easily "moveable" intangibles bring back all the difficulties of valuation and arbitrary location. And indeed, as discussed in Chapter 14, the value of intangibles is implicitly allocated to the locations at which the labor and physical capital used in their creation is located.

Moreover, such a formulary approach would essentially allocate profits based on a mix of the source (capital, employment) and destination (sales) principle. So far, it is very rare to include proxies for a residence base.[14] Hence, while addressing the difficulty of defining residence, typically formulary apportionment effectively also does away with residence-based taxes and hence with their mitigating impact on competition over source-based taxes.

Taxing Owners of Corporations

While the concept of residence of a company—which is, after all, just a legal fiction—is inherently artificial, for the great majority of human beings, residence is a very natural concept. Moreover, while the country of residence of a human is not fixed, it is much harder to change than it is for a company, given that there are financial and emotional costs as well as restrictions on migration. It therefore makes sense to explore reforms that use the residence of owners in allocating taxing rights.

One approach would be to assign the residence of an entity to the ultimate beneficial (human) owners of all of its capital. The great majority of multinational enterprises are, however, owned by stockholders resident in many different countries, and for many firms the investor base is likely to be so diverse that no country of residence represents an absolute majority among all stocks owned.

Hence, instead of assigning the entire tax base of the entity to one country, a solution more directly tied to ownership would allocate the tax base to the ultimate owners and tax it in their country of residence, with no need for defining a corporate residence.

Would this be possible? Or, put another way, can transparency and technology save the residence basis? Until recently, the answer would certainly have been negative without a shadow of doubt and, as discussed in Chapter 2, the impossibility of collecting and enforcing a personal income tax on business profits was one of the motivations for having a corporate income tax in the first place. It is still likely not possible at this moment, but technological advances coupled with multilateral approaches to information exchange and crackdowns on tax evasion by individuals are coming together to make this possible in the foreseeable future.

As noted in Chapter 10, digitalization provides many challenges to corporate tax systems and intensifies existing problems. Another aspect of digitalization is that it may—at least at some point in the future—also strengthen global data tracking to the extent that tax authorities in one country could monitor information on profits of their residents in corporations worldwide. Devereux and Vella (2017, 99–103) discuss the issues that would arise if profits were taxed in such a manner. They note

---

[14] This could be done through an additional allocation factor for the country of residence, one that would take into account typical definitions of residence, such as location of headquarters, incorporation, and effective management. Another approach would be to allocate based on the residence of a firm's owners, an approach similar to the one that will be discussed in the following section. (At the subnational level, China allocates 50 percent of profit to the location of the corporation's headquarters, as mentioned in Chapter 14.)

that there are two ways of taxing profits at the level of the owner: either by treating firms as pass-throughs, allocating a share of their calculated profits to each owner, or simply by taxing dividends and capital gains. The second option is only relevant for listed shares, where capital gains can be determined.

Data requirements would be high, especially in the case of pass-through treatment of firms, where it is not sufficient to know share prices and dividends, and one country's tax authority would need access to information on profits elsewhere.[15] Auditing such information in another jurisdiction would also prove challenging, and the country where a firm is located might not have a strong incentive to be vigilant, in case the share of foreign owners (and hence related taxing rights) is high. Another difficulty relates to ownership changes during the course of the year, which would require some allocation rules among owners at different points in time.

Even if restricted to listed firms only (possibly combined with a mandate that multinational enterprises above some size be listed), the data and information requirements are extensive. First, a universal system of corporate ownership registration would be required. To be effective, this would have to reveal beneficial ownership so that avoidance through indirect holdings (located in low-tax jurisdictions) would not be an option. Obtaining information is not just a technological issue but also requires transparency and willingness to share data, that is, a robust exchange of information across all jurisdictions for individuals. And while the world has made enormous strides in the latter regard over the past decade, through the mechanism of the Global Forum on Transparency and Exchange of Information, this process is nowhere advanced enough to support such a radical reform, although it helps in enforcing the current personal income tax (Box 12.1).

In addition to technological and data transparency issues, a system based on the residence of owners would need to tighten definitions of residence and deal with people resident in more than location.[16] As noted, residence is both clearer and harder to change for individuals than it is for firms, but for some individuals determining a residence can still be complicated because it involves various countries. Moreover, a system of international business taxation based on owner residency would present greater incentives to move such residency than does the current framework. Even more problematic than actual international relocation would be cases where the country of residence is changed on paper only, which would then raise a similar issue to the one currently encountered with corporate residence.

Even now, where the issue is just personal income tax, there is some competition over high-income or high-net-worth individuals. Countries with no or low personal income taxes, or a personal income tax that does not tax foreign source income of a resident, whether or not remitted (what might be called preferential

---

[15] Indeed, as the calculation of taxable profits differs across jurisdictions, there might be a need for detailed access to accounting items—some of which might not be collected if not relevant in the location of the firm.

[16] The tax base for such people could be either allocated to the country of principal residence (however defined) or among all residence countries, for example, based on time spent in each one.

Box 12.1. Global Forum on Transparency and Exchange of Information

The Global Forum is a body with 161 members that monitors global standards on transparency and exchange of information, both on request and automatically (the newer and more demanding standard). Compliance is assessed through a system of peer reviews.

The OECD/G20 publishes a list of jurisdictions deemed noncooperative with the Global Forum, and the G20 has at least raised the possibility of countries adopting "defensive measures" on this basis. This will not be enough to ensure success, though. The terms of reference for peer reviews of implementation of automatic exchange of information include assessment of beneficial ownership information. However, a country that is not compliant with the beneficial ownership requirement will not be rated as noncompliant with the standards for exchange of information, automatic or not, if the country or jurisdiction complies with other elements of the review standards. This lack undermines the purpose of the G20's decision to include beneficial ownership information in tax transparency standards. Beneficial ownership information should be included as one of the criteria identifying noncooperative jurisdictions to be reported to the G20 and subjected to defensive measures.

The present mechanism for exchange of information works as follows. Under the rules for automatic exchange of information—the present standard—when an individual resident of Country X opens a bank account in Country Y, he or she must self-certify that he or she is a resident of country X, providing certain required documents. The Country Y bank will report financial information of the nonresident's account to the tax authority of Country X through its own tax authority in Country Y, annually. Thus, the tax authority of Country X can in theory obtain data on its residents' foreign earned income or foreign assets and cross-match this information against its residents' tax returns. If the tax authority needs further information regarding taxpayers' bank accounts in Country Y or their transactions with residents of Country Y, it may make a request for information to its counterpart in Country Y.

personal income tax systems) can serve to undermine the taxation by other countries of residence by allowing individuals to assert and declare their residency in the preferred jurisdiction, without requiring actual long-term physical presence. The United States taxes its citizens irrespective of their place of residence, but even that can be—practically though not legally—circumvented by jurisdictions that offer "citizenship by investment."[17] Although safeguards are intended to prevent dual citizens in such jurisdictions from evading tax in their other location(s) of residence or citizenship, this is not always effective, as financial institutions have no way of knowing about additional citizenships of customers presenting local identification papers only and hiding their other nationalities. Moreover, people with citizenships and (claimed) residence of countries in nonreciprocal jurisdictions (that is, countries providing *automatic exchange of information* to other countries but not requesting it for their own residents) may manage to escape taxation irrespective of where their funds are held, because financial

---

[17] There are more than 30 countries that have both preferential personal income tax systems and a program of citizenship or residency by investment (Knobel and Heitmüller 2018).

institutions are not required to collect and report to local authorities information on their nonresident clients who are residents of such jurisdictions.[18]

And while financial institutions can be put under strict due diligence requirements to ascertain the citizenships and residence countries of their customers, it is hard to imagine corporations doing this for each of their stockholders. If one is willing to assume away all technological and transparency constraints, though, none of the issues are insurmountable: with a global taxpayer register, giving each human being a unique taxpayer identification number and determining residency based on a single agreed set of criteria, combined with extensive data sharing for detection of fraud, it would become workable.

Another issue with taxing corporations on a purely pass-through basis would be that a significant proportion of the ultimate shareholders of major multinational enterprises are tax-free entities—particularly pension funds as well as major universities and the like. In the United States, for example, this represents at least 25 percent of shareholdings. Thus—if the ultimate tax burden were not to be changed—it would be necessary to impose a compensating tax on those tax-exempt shareholders.

CONCLUSION

Residence-based taxation, though at first sight on the way out with countries moving to territoriality, is making a comeback, notably through minimum taxes on outbound investment. Avoidance is harder than in the past, both because the new minimum taxes avoid the deferral that typically featured in previous residence-based taxes and because of tightening anti-avoidance legislation, covering stricter definitions of the place of residence and advanced CFC rules.

More fundamental reforms, notably tying taxation to the residence of owners rather than entities, address more directly the problems of the current system: given that human beings are less mobile than investment or corporations, this would significantly reduce pressures for tax competition, even for the location of corporate headquarters. For now, the technological and data requirements appear insurmountable, but this is an area with rapid, and often unpredictable, changes. It is worth remembering that one of the motivations for taxing corporations is the enforcement of the personal income tax. If that can be done through other means, then taxing owners rather than corporations would be a more efficient approach to taxation. It would, however, imply major redistribution away from source countries with little ownership in multinational enterprises, that is, from developing countries, which would be a strong counterargument even if all technological obstacles could be overcome.

---

[18] The Tax Justice Network calls them "voluntary secrecy" countries. Knobel and Heitmüller (2018) listed Barbados, Belize, Cayman Islands, Costa Rica, Cyprus, Montserrat, Samoa, St. Lucia, and Turks and Caicos Islands as voluntary secrecy countries. Residence of a country that does not participate in the automatic exchange of information could achieve the same.

REFERENCES

Devereux, Michael P., and John Vella. 2017. "Implication of Digitalization for International Corporate Tax Reform." In *Digital Revolutions in Public Finance*, edited by Sanjeev Gupta, Michael Keen, Alpa Shah, and Genevieve Verdier, 91–112. Washington, DC: International Monetary Fund.

Global Witness. 2017. "Learning the Lessons from the UK's Public Beneficial Ownership Register." https://www.openownership.org/uploads/learning-the-lessons.pdf.

Global Witness. 2020. "Patchy Progress in Setting Up Beneficial Ownership Registers in the EU." https://www.globalwitness.org/en/campaigns/corruption-and-money-laundering /anonymous-company-owners/5amld-patchy-progress.

Group of Eight. 2103. *2013 Lough Erne G8 Leaders' Communique.* https://assets.publishing .service.gov.uk/government/uploads/system/uploads/attachment_data/file/207771/Lough _Erne_2013_G8_Leaders_Communique.pdf

Harari, Moran, Andres Knobel, Markus Meinzer, and Miroslav Palanský. 2020. "Ownership Registration of Different Types of Legal Structures from an International Comparative Perspective: State of play of Beneficial Ownership—Update 2020." Tax Justice Network. https://www.taxjustice.net/wp-content/uploads/2020/06/State-of-play-of-beneficial -ownership-Update-2020-Tax-Justice-Network.pdf.

Knobel, Andres, and Frederik Heitmüller. 2018. "Citizenship and Residency by Investment Scheme: Potential to Avoid the Common Reporting Standard for Automatic Exchange of Information." Tax Justice Network. http://taxjustice.wpengine.com/wp-content /uploads/2018/03/20180305_Citizenship-and-Residency-by-Investment-FINAL.pdf.

Mirrlees, James, Stuart Adam, Tim Besley, Richard Blundell, Stephen Bond, Robert Chote, Malcolm Gammie, Paul Johnson, Gareth Myles, and James M. Poterba. 2011. *Tax by Design.* Institute for Fiscal Studies. Oxford: Oxford University Press.

Organisation for Economic Co-operation and Development (OECD). 2020. *Tax Challenges Arising from Digitalisation—Report on Pillar Two Blueprint: Inclusive Framework on BEPS.* OECD/G20 Base Erosion and Profit Shifting Project. Paris: OECD Publishing.

Shaviro, Daniel. 2020. "What Are Minimum Taxes, and Why Might One Favor or Disfavor Them?" Law and Economics Paper Series Working Paper 20-38, New York University School of Law, New York.

Vann, Richard. 1996. "International Aspects of Income Tax." In *Tax Law Design and Drafting,*" edited by Victor Thuronyi, 718–810. Washington, DC: International Monetary Fund.

CHAPTER 13

Destination-Based Taxation: A Promising but Risky Destination

Shafik Hebous and Alexander Klemm

INTRODUCTION

Country-specific origin-based profit taxes are marked by profit shifting and tax competition (see Chapter 6). Incentives for profit shifting can be mitigated, but not eliminated, by stricter rules and strengthening tax administration, while coordination can reduce the scope of tax competition but is hard to agree on (Chapter 11). Moreover, tighter anti-tax-avoidance rules often raise compliance and administrative costs and may intensify tax competition (Chapter 9).

The origin of a profit or "where value is created" is not only in practice but also conceptually a vague notion (Chapter 5). Even in the absence of tax-motivated profit shifting, "assigning" profit to a location is an imprecise science, especially in the case of complicated cross-border supply chains. If a profitable product is produced using many intermediate goods and services, it is not clear which ones give rise to routine profits and which ones allow earning supernormal profits.

Given these difficulties with origin-based taxation, a range of fundamental reform proposals contain a move away from this approach and toward destination-based taxation, with the aim to reduce or eliminate profit shifting and tax competition. This shift can be full, for example through a border adjustment, or it can be partial, for example if profits are allocated across countries through an agreed formula that contains destination elements, such as the destination of sales (see Chapter 14).

Under a border adjustment, a country taxes all domestic sales—with no requirement of a permanent establishment—allowing deduction of all local costs, such as labor and domestically purchased intermediates. A pure exporter would therefore obtain a tax refund, as only costs occur (tax would be paid in the country of sales). A pure importer would pay tax on all sales, with no deductions in the country of sale (but deductions and tax refunds in the producing country if that country also employs a destination-based tax). Any cross-border transactions become irrelevant for tax, which is a function only of sales and domestic costs. Conceptually, moreover, the location of sales is in most cases clear cut. An exception is the case of cross-border shopping, especially of small high-value consumer durables.

Destination-based consumption taxation is already common in the form of value-added and sales taxes. However, no country thus far applies the destination-based

TABLE 13.1.

Location of Taxation for Major Taxes on Bases That Include Profits			
Taxation of Sales at ⟍ *Labor Cost Deduction at*	*Source*	*Destination*	*Nowhere*
Source	Standard corporate income tax		
Destination	DBCFT (and other border-adjusted taxes)	Formulary apportionment with sales factor	VAT, sales tax

principle to taxes of corporate profits or rents, with the key difference being the deductibility of labor costs. Various proposals for destination-based business taxes have been made, with the destination-based cash-flow tax (DBCFT) being the best-known example. Apart from being in the academic debate, a variant of it has also been proposed recently in the United States by Senators Brady and Ryan, although it was ultimately not implemented.

Table 13.1 classifies the main taxes paid by businesses by where sales are taxed and where labor costs are deductible.[1] For the existing corporate income tax, both take place at source.[2] For the VAT and sales taxes, there is no labor deduction. The DBCFT, or other border-adjusted taxes, would tax sales at the destination, but labor (and other cost) deductibility would remain in the country of origin—a point that has implications for revenues and trade effects, as will be discussed. The table also shows an example of a tax where all would take place at the destination country. This would be a corporate income tax with formulary apportionment, with sales as the only apportionment factor. If sales were one of various factors, the result would be partial apportionment of both costs and sales to the origin and destination countries.

To the extent that moving to a destination basis successfully reduces profit shifting and tax competition, this opens up new possibilities for tax reform. In particular, while tax competition pushes countries toward broad bases and low rates, in its absence a narrower base could be chosen, with revenue shortfall made up by a higher rate. This is why the destination base is often combined with taxation of economic rents, that is, on profits that exceed the normal rate of return (see Chapter 2).

This chapter is structured as follows: The next section discusses the DBCFT as the best-known example of a destination-based rent tax. The third section,

---

[1] Costs other than labor are also deductible; labor is shown in the table to allow a distinction between profit taxes (where it is deductible) and consumption taxes, such as VAT and sales taxes, where it is not.

[2] There may be additional taxation in the country of residence, but even if that occurs, it would typically allow the deduction of costs incurred at the source and it would credit the source tax. Moreover, it is typically restricted to repatriated profits.

"Destination-Based Allowances for Corporate Equity or Capital," discusses other possible implementations of destination-based rent taxes. The fourth section, "Destination-Based Corporate Income Taxes," analyzes options for implementing a more standard corporate income tax system on a destination basis and the likely problems to which this would lead, as well as the extent to which formulary apportionment could achieve a destination base. The fifth section, "Equivalent Reforms," discusses equivalencies between different tax reform options and how they may facilitate reforms. The final section offers concluding remarks.

THE DESTINATION-BASED CASH-FLOW TAX

Design

The DBCFT is a simple implementation of a destination-based tax on rents. This tax, developed by Bond and Devereux (2002), combines a cash-flow tax with a destination base.

The DBCFT typically starts from an R-base cash-flow tax, which allows immediate deduction of all investment and taxing all proceeds from selling investment goods, while disregarding any financial flows, such as interest (see Chapter 2). To turn this tax into a DBCFT, the cash-flow component is combined with a border adjustment. This is illustrated in Figure 13.1: domestic sales are included in the tax base, while export sales are exempt. Domestic costs are deductible. Imported items can be handled in two equivalent ways: they can be taxed at the border and be deductible, or they can simply be treated as nondeductible.[3] The implementation is administratively simple but implies that some firms, such as those whose sales are predominantly exports, will systematically run tax losses. These firms will require tax refunds, as they would not benefit from loss carryforward.

Figure 13.1. Destination-Based Taxation

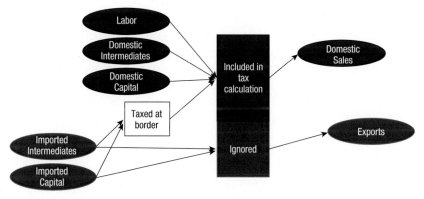

Source: IMF staff illustration.

---

[3] Goods imported by final consumers would have to be taxable at the border in any case.

Economic Implications of a DBCFT

Despite the border adjustment, the DBCFT is not about trade or competitiveness. Unlike a tariff, a DBCFT does not create a difference between traded and non-traded goods: all sales to final consumers, whether imported or domestically produced, are taxed, while all domestic costs are deductible whether used to produce for exports or the domestic market. Hence, theoretically, a DBCFT does not affect competitiveness, because changes in the real exchange rate undo the border adjustment (for example, Auerbach and others, 2017a). In practice, sticky prices or pricing in the currency of a DBCFT-adopting country could cause temporary effects (Barbiero and others 2018; Buiter 2017), but these would be small and not last long: Barbiero and others (2018) show in a dynamic stochastic general equilibrium model that, while there is no impact under local currency pricing, under US dollar pricing, DBCFT adoption in the United States would depress exports and imports by up to 0.3 percent, though the impact would largely run out after 10 quarters. Notwithstanding the economic analysis, there is legal uncertainty about the border adjustment under DBCFT in relation to tax treaties and WTO rules.

A global move to a DBCFT would remove all known profit-shifting channels. Auerbach and others (2017b) show that under universal adoption profit shifting through transfer pricing, the use of debt and the location of intangible assets becomes impossible. Under a DBCFT, exports are untaxed, so their price becomes irrelevant. Similarly, as imports are not deductible (or taxed and deductible, which washes out), their price is equally of no relevance to determining the tax base. Without interest deductibility, the amount of debt and the interest rate equally play no role.

Tax competition would also be addressed by a DBCFT. When choosing where to locate a factory, a firm will not care about the tax rate, because exports are tax free and local sales are taxed irrespective of whether they are produced in or outside a given country. As shown in Table 13.1, costs would remain deductible in the source country. This could be feared to encourage production in high-tax countries, allowing enterprises to obtain large tax refunds while exporting tax free. This incentive would, however, be completely undone by the exchange rate adjustment: as noted, the exchange rate should adjust by the tax rate (or the tax differential between two countries) to undo any effect on trade. This would simultaneously address such an incentive: the higher tax refund in a high-tax country would be exactly equal to the higher production cost resulting from appreciation.

If, however, adoption is not global but by one or a subset of countries, profit shifting and tax competition would not disappear. Instead pressures for the remaining countries would intensify. Shifting profits from an origin-based corporate income tax to a DBCFT system would be extremely lucrative, as such profits would face a tax rate of zero: if done through transfer pricing, they would appear as higher exports by the DBCFT country, which are exempt; if done through debt, they would show up as untaxed interest income. The same is true of tax competition: if an activity that exports produces an economic rent, it is attractive to locate it in a DBCFT country, because this rent will go untaxed.

The incidence of the DBCFT is on consumption financed out of non-labor income (Auerbach and others 2017a). Hence, for countries that have both a VAT and a DBCFT, the implication is that consumption financed out of labor income is taxed at a lower rate than consumption financed out of nonlabor income. Unlike a VAT, there is no concern about the tax being regressive, as low-income people, whose income source is typically labor, would not be affected.[4] In case of nonlabor income received from abroad or paid to capital owners in other countries, the effect is more complicated: resident capital owners bear the burden, irrespective of where in the world they hold assets, but foreign owners will not bear it (see the annex for details). This implies for natural resources that despite the destination base, revenues will be collected, provided they are owned by domestic residents. Otherwise, a special regime for the resource sector is needed to capture its location-specific rents. And in any case, another regime may be needed to ensure higher rates of tax in the resource sector.

Impact on Revenue

Global DBCFT adoption would not change average tax revenues much but would lead to a major reallocation across countries. Hebous, Klemm, and Stausholm (2020) show that, at unchanged tax rates, on a global average calculated over 80 countries, DBCFT revenues would remain similar to the existing corporate income tax revenue. For any individual countries, revenues could be very different, though (Figure 13.2), with the move to a border adjustment having greater impact than the introduction of a cash-flow base.

The following features increase the likelihood of gaining revenues from adopting a DBCFT:

- *Trade deficits:* As imports are taxed and exports exempt, trade deficits increase revenues (Figure 13.3). Intertemporally, these effects may be smaller as trade balances adjust. Countries with large positive initial international investment positions, who can finance future trade deficits, could gain even in the long term (Auerbach 2017).

- *Limited resource revenues:* Resources entail location-specific rents, so replacing an origin-based corporate income tax with a DBCFT can be expected to reduce revenues (Figure 13.4). For this calculation, any taxes beyond corporate income tax were held constant. In practice they could be increased to maintain the same level of origin-based taxation of resource rents.

- *Low income:* Countries with low incomes are more vulnerable to tax avoidance and evasion by companies and stand to gain more from a more robust system (Figure 13.5). One might also have expected such countries to lose, given their role as locations of production, but empirically the allocated rents to such production under the current system do not appear to outweigh the potential gains from a more robust system. Some countries can be expected to lose, though: those where foreigners own most of the capital, and trade surpluses finance income payments to nonresidents.

---

[4] An exception would be the case of benefit or pension recipients, if the real appreciation occurs through the price level rather than the exchange rate and benefits or pensions are not indexed.

Figure 13.2. DBCFT and Corporate Income Tax Revenues
(Averages over 2002–2011)

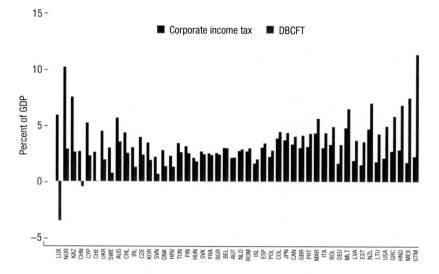

Source: Hebous, Klemm, and Stausholm (2020).
Data labels use International Organization for Standardization (ISO) country codes.

Figure 13.3. Trade Balance and Revenue Change, Excluding Resource-Rich Economies
(percent of GDP)

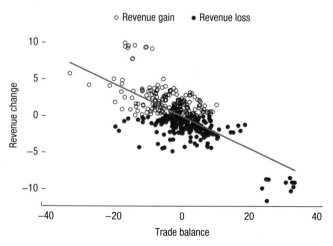

Source: Hebous, Klemm, and Stausholm (2020).

Figure 13.4. Revenue by Resource Dependence

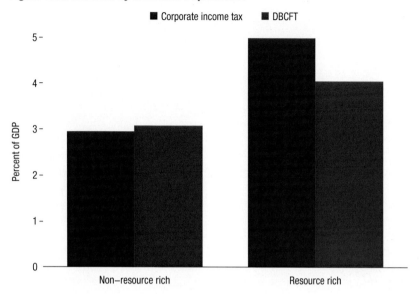

Source: Hebous, Klemm, and Stausholm (2020).

Figure 13.5. Revenue by Income Group

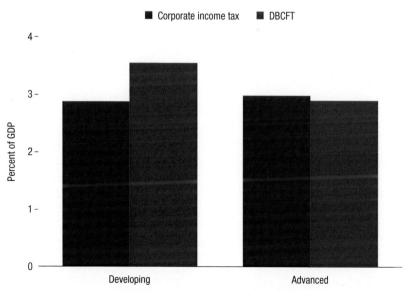

Source: Hebous, Klemm, and Stausholm (2020).

In many cases, revenue losses can be made up by changing the rate, given the absence of pressures from profit shifting and tax competition under a DBCFT. Countries with very high net exports, however, can even have a negative tax base—and there are two such cases in these estimates. If this holds up to more refined estimates using data available to tax authorities only, such countries are unlikely to support adoption of such a tax. As noted, intertemporally, some revenue losses and gains will be made up as trade rebalances.

DBCFT revenues would be more volatile than those of the current corporate income tax, which is already among the more volatile taxes. The DBCFT allows expensing of investment. Investment, which is a flow variable, will vary more over the cycle than depreciation, which is linked to a stock and averages out the flows of various past years. Another reason for greater volatility is the immediate refund of tax on losses, while most current corporate income tax systems merely allow carryforward (or very limited carryback) of losses, smoothing revenues over time. Empirically, Hebous, Klemm, and Stausholm (2020) confirm that the standard deviation of hypothetical DBCFT revenues is higher than the one for the current corporate income tax for most countries.

Revenue implications are very different if the DBCFT is adopted unilaterally rather than globally. As mentioned, there would then be strong incentives to shift profits and the production of rent-earning exporting activities into the DBCFT country. While this would not have direct revenue consequences for that particular country,[5] the outflow would reduce revenues elsewhere. Estimates by Hebous, Klemm, and Stausholm (2020) suggest that DBCFT adoption by a large integrated economy, such as the United States, could cause neighboring countries to lose about 40 percent of tax revenue from multinationals.

The Natural Resources Sector

A separate solution will need to be found for the taxation of location-specific rents, such as natural resources (see also Chapter 15). For this type of rent, taxation at the origin is efficient. Moreover, it is likely politically important, as natural resources belong to the nations where they are located. This does not amount to an obstacle for introducing a DBCFT, though. Already currently, in most countries the resource sector faces a different tax and regulatory regime from the general economy. License fees, royalties, and any special resource revenue taxes could continue under a DBCFT and could even be raised to compensate from any shortfall that arises from shifting from a corporate income tax to a DBCFT (in countries where the resource sector pays corporate income tax in addition to other fees and taxes). This sector would then continue to face pressures from profit shifting and require maintaining relevant anti-avoidance rules.

---

[5] There could be positive indirect effects if the increased capital stock raises employment or wages, thus boosting personal income tax revenue.

R+F and S-Base Cash-Flow Taxes with a Destination Base

One issue that arises in cash-flow taxation (even in a closed economy) is how to ensure that the financial sector is covered. The financial sector can be directly included by implementing a real and financial ("R+F") base (Chapter 2). Even under an R-base, which disregards financial flows, any economic rents earned by financial institutions in dealing with corporations are effectively taxed, but this occurs effectively in the hands of the borrower and is reflected in the interest rate (Auerbach and others 2017a). Only in the case of lending to households (or other DBCFT-exempt entities), any rents would indeed go untaxed, and hence Auerbach and others (2017a) discuss the option of using an R+F base for dealings with DBCFT-exempt entities, even if an R-base is used otherwise.

Another form of a cash-flow rent tax is the so-called S-base implementation (Chapter 2), meaning that only share transactions, which are defined as net distributions (roughly dividends less capital increases), are taxed. In an international context, this means that for a company to be liable for tax in a jurisdiction, it would not only need to have some permanent establishment, but it would have to be incorporated. An S-base cash-flow tax is therefore neither an origin nor a destination, but rather a country-of-incorporation-based system. It appears impossible to the authors to combine this with a destination base.

DESTINATION-BASED ALLOWANCES FOR CORPORATE EQUITY OR CAPITAL

Cash-flow taxes are not the only possible rent taxes (see Chapter 2). Other rent taxes include the allowance for corporate equity, which is implemented by exempting a notional return on equity from tax. Previous analysis (IMF 2009; 2016) has stressed its neutrality and the reduction of debt bias. This can also be border adjusted, turning it into a destination-based allowance for corporate equity (DBACE). Hebous and Klemm (2020) analyze the DBACE finding that transition to a DBACE rather than DBCFT might be easier, because a DBACE would (1) initially raise higher revenues (as it can be implemented with an incremental base, counting only postreform equity); (2) generally entail less volatile revenues; and (3) avoid the need for transitional arrangements on the initial capital stock (as depreciation is maintained) and debt stock (as interest deductibility is maintained).

On the other hand, a DBACE reduces profit-shifting incentives and tax competition, but unlike the DBCFT does not eliminate them. Notably, intercompany loans at inflated interest rates remain possible. More subtly, if the notional interest rate is not set at the correct level, there would still be incentives to change the global distribution of debt. There may even remain an incentive to manipulate transfer prices in certain situations. Assume that the destination base is implemented by taxing goods at the border and then allowing deductions—which is generally the safer implementation, as it reduces risks of goods being imported without paying tax and then diverted for final consumption. In that case, the tax collected at the border will depend on the reported import price. For intermediate goods, this does not matter much: any mispricing will wash out immediately. For capital goods, however, this is not necessarily the case (see bottom left of Figure 13.1): if the import price of a capital good is understated, it yields an instantaneous saving at the border. This also reduces the equity of the firm, so intertemporally there is theoretically no impact on tax payments. If, however, the notional interest rate is lower than the firm's discount rate, then there is an incentive for such underpricing of imported capital goods. This problem does not exist under the DBCFT, where capital goods are expensed, and any such effect washes out immediately. Overall, such a tax would be more complicated and less effective than a DBCFT, but still much more robust than the current system.

Closely related to the allowance for corporate equity, the allowance for corporate capital applies a notional return on all capital, including debt, but disallows deductibility of the actual interest cost (Kleinbard 2005). This means that debt neutrality is achieved, irrespective of the notional interest rate chosen, reducing the risks stemming from setting it at the wrong level. Hebous and Klemm (2020) also analyzed the destination-based version allowance for corporate capital (DBACC) and found that it eliminates all profit shifting related to changes in debt ratios. Like the DBACE it only eliminates transfer pricing manipulation and tax competition provided the notional interest rate is set at the correct level.

Both the DBACE and the DBACC have the advantage that no transitional arrangements are needed for the capital stock, as depreciation is maintained rather than replaced by expensing, as under the DBCFT. Regarding the debt stock, which was issued by firms assuming full deductibility of interest, transitional difficulties are: none with a DBACE, which maintains interest deductibility for debt, relatively small for the DBACC, where interest deductibility is reduced from the full to the notional return, and greatest for the DBCFT, where deductibility is abolished.

DESTINATION-BASED CORPORATE INCOME TAXES

Destination Base for Current Corporate Income Tax

In principle, the switch from an origin- to a destination-based approach to taxation could also be implemented without a change to a rent tax, but it would have disadvantages. Not only would it be a lost opportunity for moving to a more efficient tax, it would also fail to eliminate profit shifting. First, because interest would remain deductible, tax planning through international debt shifting would remain attractive. Second, there would be some incentives for transfer price manipulation, because underreporting the cost of capital goods would lower import taxes. While it would also lower future depreciation, there would be a net present value gain (which would be stronger than under the DBACE, where such gain only occurs to the extent that there is a difference between the notional rate and the firm's discount rate).

Formulary Methods

Another, related, reform would be the move to a consolidated unitary base for multinationals, which would be allocated to countries by formula (see Chapter 14). Typically, formulary apportionment proposals suggest allocation based on factors including the capital stock, employment, and sales. With sales as an apportionment factor, there is thus a destination-based element.[6] The greater the weight on sales, the stronger the link to the destination. In the United States, where formulary apportionment is used for subfederal taxes, the development over the last few decades has been toward increasingly high weights on sales.

However, even with sales as the only factor of apportionment, formulary apportionment would not be fully equivalent to a border adjustment. This is because costs would be deducted at the consolidated level (and hence also apportioned), rather than where they are incurred (see Table 13.1). As discussed in Bond and Devereux (2002),[7] this means that such a tax cannot be fully neutral to trade and investment choices, because the exchange rate cannot simply adjust to undo the effect of the tax. Nevertheless, this implementation has the advantage of allowing a gradual movement toward more destination-based taxation over time, with the weight on sales rising. This would possibly allow a later move to a full DBCFT or other such tax.

Moreover, formulary apportionment could be combined quite flexibly either with a tax base resembling the current one, or with a more efficient rent tax. As there is still tax competition under formulary apportionment (Chapter 14), the tax base could be kept broad while origin-based factors are important, and it could be narrowed toward a rent tax as the weight on sales rises.

Another partial implementation of the destination base would be through residual profit allocation. Under this proposal, a normal return is taxed in the country of origin using standard separate accounting, but residual profit is allocated by sales.[8]

EQUIVALENT REFORMS

The DBCFT strongly resembles a VAT, except that it allows deduction of domestic labor costs. A DBCFT is a tax on consumption financed out of nonlabor income. Hence, an increase in the VAT combined with a reduction in labor

---

[6] Strictly speaking, sales could be defined on an origin or destination base, with the latter harder to observe, but more useful (and used in subnational applications, such as for US state taxes).

[7] In their terminology, the DBCFT is labeled "VAT-type DBCFT," while formulary apportionment based on sales is called "full DBCFT."

[8] If the tax rate on both types of profits is different, additional options arise. For example, if countries choose a tax rate of zero on the normal rate of return, then the system is close to a DBACC.

Figure 13.6. Average Income Tax and VAT Rates, 1999–2019
(Percent)

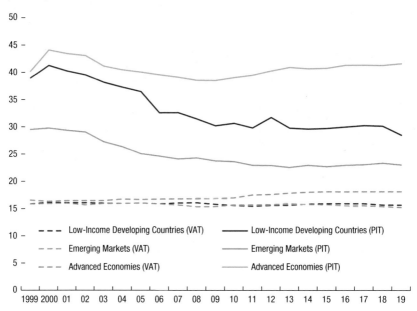

Source: IMF FAD TP Rates database.
Note: PIT = personal income tax.

taxes (including social security contributions) can achieve an economically similar outcome. As neither the VAT nor reductions of labor taxes are internationally controversial, these reforms allow countries to have similar outcomes. Indeed, over the last few decades, there has been a relative rise in consumption and a decline in income tax rates (Figure 13.6), suggesting that such a move is already underway.

There are, however, reasons why in practice such a combination of reforms would not precisely match the introduction of a DBCFT. First, VATs tend to have exemptions and differentiated rate structures; similarly, labor taxes differ by labor income types and levels, with social security contributions often charged only up to an upper limit. Second, despite the economic equivalency, there could be differences in short-run effects depending on the legal incidence and how contracts are fixed. For example, a VAT increase would typically boost the price level, combined with a labor tax cut that would increase net earnings. This would represent a real appreciation. A DBCFT, however, collected from firms, would likely not affect the price level: firms would pay tax on sales less labor and capital costs. If they make a normal profit, there is no tax and no reason to raise prices. If they earn rent, they do pay tax, but only on the rent part. To prevent a relative increase in the price of imported goods, it is likely that in this case the real appreciation would be achieved by nominal appreciation.

CONCLUSION

Destination-based taxation has many attractive features. Most importantly, it reduces profit-shifting opportunities and softens tax competition. When combined with a rent tax, it is, moreover, neutral to investment, improving efficiency. The DBCFT, as the most well-known and studied version, has the advantage of fully removing all known profit-shifting and tax-competition channels, with cross-border shopping remaining as one of few avoidance risks.

Despite these advantages, the DBCFT and other destination-based profit taxes remain controversial. To some extent, this is likely due to suspicions that such a tax would distort trade, for example, because skeptics may not believe that the theoretical claims of full exchange rate adjustment hold in practice. This is hard to prove wrong, because no empirical observations are available as no country has yet undertaken such reform.

Even in the absence of an effect on trade, the diverging revenue impact of such a tax on countries would make it difficult to agree on a global adoption, as the revenue losers would be unlikely to support it. Countries with significant foreign-owned or licensed resources would stand to lose the most revenues, although this point should not cause undue concern, as they would be able to maintain an alternative taxation system for the resource sector. Moreover, countries with only small revenue losses could address them by simply raising rates, which would not drive away investment or reported profits.

Global adoption would be crucial to reap the full benefits. Unilateral adoption would entail major negative spillovers on countries maintaining origin-based taxation, whose tax bases would be strongly attracted by the DBCFT country so that tax competition and profit shifting for remaining countries would intensify. This would risk triggering political reactions, such as legal challenges and even trade wars. From a purely economic point of view, however, introducing a DBCFT is a stable choice for a country, because even if no other country follows, the benefits can be reaped, and a DBCFT adopter would not face incentives to revert to origin-based taxes.

Apart from the DBCFT, other implementations are feasible and may have transitional advantages. The DBACE would initially raise more, and generally less volatile, revenue, but it would remain susceptible to various profit-shifting schemes. The DBACC would be almost as robust as the DBCFT but would also require a more fundamental change than the DBACE. Finally, moving to formulary apportionment with a sales factor would allow transitioning toward destination-based taxation by raising the weight on the sales factor over time. To reap the full efficiency impact and avoid distortions to trade, a shift to a DBCFT is, however, ultimately required.

Given that the options discussed in this chapter are unlikely to be considered, the question arises of why they are worth studying. One reason is that their simplicity, combined with robustness with respect to a major issue in the current architecture, makes them very appealing. Understanding them sheds light on other reform proposals, that contain elements of these pure ones. Another reason is that they may occur through the back door, by countries raising VAT while reducing taxes on labor income.

ANNEX 13.1: INTERNATIONAL REVENUE AND INCIDENCE IMPLICATIONS OF A DBCFT

This appendix provides a theoretical comparison of the incidence and revenue implications of DBCFT considering different company profiles. The results on incidence have been previously described (for example, Auerbach and others 2017a).

The following assumptions are made throughout: A country, labeled DB, introduces a DBCFT at rate t. There is one other country, labeled ROW, that does not change its tax system. The currency of country DB appreciates in textbook fashion by exactly $\frac{t}{1-t}$. Hence, there is no adjustment in prices.[9] Wages are unchanged: as prices are the same, labor supply is unaffected. As wages remain untaxed, labor demand is unaffected. As normal profits are untaxed, investors will not need to shift the DBCFT burden onto labor.

First Experiment: Impact of Location of Sales and Production

As shown in Annex Table 13.1.1, the tax collection depends on whether firms are purely domestic operations, exporters, or importers. For now, all firms are assumed to be owned by residents. Domestic firms pay tax on sales less cost. Exporters pay no tax and get a refund on their costs. Importers pay tax on sales but are not allowed a deduction. As long as exports and imports balance, revenue from the external sector will mirror those from domestic operations.

The incidence aligns with the tax payment only in case of a purely domestic operation. For exporters, the appreciation means that their revenues from foreign sales decline. Because they get a tax refund on their costs, their normal profits remain tax free and the rent is reduced by the same amount as if they had sold domestically. Exporters therefore bear the same tax burden, even though they are net recipients of tax refunds. The mirror image applies to importers: while their sales are fully taxable, their costs decline thanks to the appreciation. Despite remitting very high taxes, they bear the same tax on rents as firms producing domestically.

To sum up: the tax is equally borne by all types of firms located in DB, irrespective of where they produce and sell their goods. No revenues are collected

---

[9] If the exchange rate were fixed and adjustment occurred through the price level, the same results would be obtained, but given the likely slow adjustment, there may be some time periods of disequilibrium. Going beyond the examples discussed here, which are all about firms, there would be further real differences, because of the impact on other nominal assets.

ANNEX TABLE 13.1.1.

Tax Payments and Incidence for Firms Located in DB			
	Domestic Operation	**Exporter**	**Importer**
Production	DB	DB	ROW
Sales	DB	ROW	DB
Sales	p^{DB}	$p^{ROW} = p^{DB}(1-t)$	p^{DB}
Costs	c^{DB}	c^{DB}	$c^{ROW} = c^{DB}(1-t)$
Tax Payment	$(p^{DB} - c^{DB})t$	$-c^{DB}t$	$p^{DB}t$
Net Profit[1]	$(p^{DB} - c^{DB})(1-t)$	$(p^{DB} - c^{DB})(1-t)$	$(p^{DB} - c^{DB})(1-t)$
Tax Borne	$(p^{DB} - c^{DB})t$	$(p^{DB} - c^{DB})t$	$(p^{DB} - c^{DB})t$

Source: Authors' calculations.

_____

[1] Calculated as sales less costs less tax payment.

from exporters, but very high revenues from importers, evening out tax revenues, provided trade is balanced.

Second Experiment: Impact of Ownership

Firms located in DB could be owned by resident or foreign investors. Moreover, residents of DB could own domestic and foreign firms.

The tax implications are shown in Annex Table 13.1.2. The first column shows a domestically owned firm in DB, that is, it condenses the information of Annex Table 13.1.11 into one column. The second column shows the tax consequences for DB residents of owning firms in ROW. Even though no DBCFT is payable when owning a firm abroad (as this analysis abstracts from any foreign tax), the owners still bear the incidence of the DBCFT, because the profits earned in foreign currency are worth less. The third column shows foreign investors owning firms in DB. The investors remit DBCFT just as domestically owned firms do (that is, depending on where sales take place). However, the foreign investors do not bear any tax burden, because the appreciation compensates them for the tax. Finally, for completeness, firms in ROW owned by ROW investors are not affected by the DBCFT.

To sum up: tax payments and refunds are only due to firms located in DB, with the tax payment/refund depending on the location of sales, and ownership not having a bearing. The tax incidence, however, depends only on the residence of the firms' owners, and is borne by DB residents.

Untaxed Assets

DB residents owning assets denominated in ROW currency, such as bonds or land, also bear the burden of the DBCFT, because of appreciation of DB's

ANNEX TABLE 13.1.2.

Tax Payments and Incidence Depending on Ownership			
Residence of Owner	DB	DB	ROW	ROW
Location of Firm	DB	ROW	DB	ROW
Net Profit	$(p^{DB}-c^{DB})(1-t)$	$\begin{aligned}&p^{ROW}-c^{ROW}\\&=(p^{DB}-c^{DB})(1-t)\end{aligned}$	$\begin{aligned}&(p^{DB}-c^{DB})(1-t)\\&=p^{ROW}-c^{ROW}\end{aligned}$	$p^{ROW}-c^{ROW}$
Tax Borne	$(p^{DB}-c^{DB})t$	$(p^{DB}-c^{DB})t$	0	0
Tax Payment				
Domestic Operation	$(p^{DB}-c^{DB})t$	0	$(p^{DB}-c^{DB})t$	0
Exporter	$-c^{DB}t$	0	$-c^{DB}t$	0
Importer	$p^{DB}t$	0	$p^{DB}t$	0

Source: Authors' calculations.

currency. No tax is remitted, though. There is no difference between owning a foreign firm or a fixed asset.

DB residents owning assets denominated in DB currency (including pensions or benefit rights) do not bear any tax burden.

ROW residents do not bear any burden on assets denominated in ROW currency and enjoy a gain if they own assets denominated in DB currency, but are not subject to DBCFT.

Putting It All Together

From a government perspective, taxes are collected from all firms located in DB, with tax losses by exporters compensated by revenue on importers, provided they are in equilibrium.

From a taxpayer perspective, however, the burden is borne by rent-earning investors resident in DB, with foreign residents unaffected.

This has the following implication: suppose DB's residents own relatively much foreign capital. At the time of DBCFT introduction they then bear a high burden. In the long term, this translates into high revenues: owning foreign capital entitles them to income streams from abroad, which can finance a trade deficit, which boosts revenues. Hence, countries with a strong international investment position will ultimately benefit in revenue terms from a DBCFT.[10] Even though this is collected on imports, the burden is still on residents.

Suppose there is a large location-specific rent earned by exporters in DB (for example, a natural resource, or a network benefit from Silicon Valley). If the asset is domestically owned, the burden of the DBCFT will be borne by owners

---

[10] Auerbach (2017) also points out that it will depend on the rates of return on assets. For example, a negative IIP need not require future trade surpluses, if income earned on the smaller foreign assets is higher than the financing cost of the larger foreign liabilities.

even though no tax is collected from the exporting firm. The owners will (ultimately) use their income from exports to finance imports, which are taxed. If the asset is foreign owned, however, there is no tax burden. There are revenue losses: the profits of nonresidents weaken the income balance, requiring trade surpluses.

REFERENCES

Auerbach, Alan. 2017. "Demystifying the Destination-Based Cash-Flow Tax." *Brookings Papers on Economic Activity* 48(2): 409–32.

Auerbach, Alan, Michael P. Devereux, Michael Keen, and John Vella. 2017a. "Destination-Based Cash Flow Taxation." Oxford University Centre for Business Taxation Working Papers 17/01, Oxford University Centre for Business Taxation, Oxford, UK.

Auerbach, Alan, Michael P. Devereux, Michael Keen, and John Vella. 2017b. "International Tax Planning under the Destination-Based Cash Flow Tax." *National Tax Journal* 70(4); 783–802.

Barbiero, Omar, Emmanuel Farhi, Gita Gopinath, and Oleg Itskhoki. 2018. "The Macroeconomics of Border Taxes." NBER Working Paper 24702, National Bureau of Economic Research, Cambridge, MA.

Bond, Stephen, and Michael P. Devereux. 2002. "Cash Flow Taxes in an Open Economy." CEPR Discussion Paper 3401, Centre for Economic Policy Research, London.

Buiter, Willem H. 2017. "Exchange Rate Implications of Border Tax Adjustment Neutrality." *Economics: The Open-Access, Open-Assessment E-Journal* 11: 1–41.

Hebous, Shafik, and Alexander Klemm. 2020. "A Destination-Based Allowance for Corporate Equity." *International Tax and Public Finance* 27(3): 753–77.

Hebous, Shafik, Alexander Klemm, and Saila Stausholm. 2020. "Revenue-Implications of Destination-Based Cash-Flow Taxation." *IMF Economic Review* 68(4): 848–74.

International Monetary Fund (IMF). 2009. "Debt Bias and Other Distortions: Crisis-Related Issues in Tax Policy." IMF Policy Paper, Washington, DC.

International Monetary Fund (IMF). 2016. "Tax Policy, Leverage, and Macroeconomic Stability." IMF Policy Paper, Washington, DC.

Kleinbard, Edward. 2005. "The Business Enterprise Income Tax: A Prospectus." *Tax Notes*, January 3.

CHAPTER 14

Formulary Apportionment in Theory and Practice

Thornton Matheson, Sebastian Beer, Maria Coelho, Li Liu, and Oana Luca

INTRODUCTION

The current international tax system, which is based on separate accounting for corporate affiliates trading at arm's length prices, is increasingly viewed as prone to abuse, as noted in Chapters 5 and 6. Multinational enterprises have become adept at manipulating the rules of the current system to shift profits from high-tax to low-tax (or no-tax) jurisdictions. Several recent studies of worldwide revenue losses due to profit shifting suggest that short-term losses range from 5 to 10 percent of total corporate income tax revenues (Cobham and Janský 2018; Crivelli, De Mooij, and Keen 2016; OECD 2015; Tørsløv, Wier, and Zucman 2018; UNCTAD 2015).[1] On average, revenue losses in OECD countries are found to be about twice as high as those in developing countries; however, revenue losses as a share of GDP are about one-third higher for developing countries (Crivelli, De Mooij, and Keen 2016).

In addition to being porous, the prevailing corporate tax system is also extremely complex. Each country's law sets corporate income tax rates as well as bases, which may be eroded by tax incentives provided via legislation or ministerial discretion. These laws are further overlaid by a network of bilateral tax treaties, which alter the tax treatment of investment depending on the particular source and residence countries involved. This makes administration and enforcement of the corporate income tax costly, especially for developing country governments. Corporate compliance costs also increase with complexity, although sophisticated multinationals are often able to turn complexity to their advantage by practices such as treaty shopping and the use of hybrid entities.

One fundamental reform proposal is to replace the current system of separate accounting by formulary apportionment.[2] In contrast to separate accounting,

---

[1] Crivelli, De Mooij, and Keen (2016) further estimate long-term losses from profit shifting to be as much as 25 percent of corporate income tax revenues.

[2] This has been proposed by some experts and civil society organizations. See, for example, Avi-Yonah and Clausing (2007); ICRICT (2018); OECD (2019b); and Picciotto (2016).

formulary apportionment would consolidate corporate profits at the regional or global level and then allocate them among jurisdictions according to a formula, leaving the decision on the tax rate to individual jurisdictions. Typically, the allocation formula is some combination of real resources used (employment, payroll, or fixed assets) and sales (usually destination-based sales). This method has been used successfully by federal states including Canada, Germany, Japan, and the United States to allocate corporate income tax revenues among subnational governments. The current EU initiative for adoption of the Common Consolidated Corporate Tax Base (CCCTB) would constitute the first application of formulary apportionment at a supranational level.

This chapter considers a range of questions, including the following:

- Would formulary apportionment in fact be simpler than the current system? This depends on the trade-off between eliminating the complexity inherent in the current international tax system, notably in the need to determine transfer prices, and new complexities that may be created (regarding, for example, decisions as to what entities or activities are to be consolidated; separation of activities subject to different sectoral regimes, such as finance or extractive industries; and, in a regional system, determination of income within the so-called water's edge).

- How would formulary apportionment affect the distribution of tax revenues? This depends on the system's design and notably the factors of apportionment: Some countries are more likely to gain from factors mimicking source, such as capital and employment, while others would benefit from destination-based factors, notably destination-based sales.

- How would formulary apportionment affect economic efficiency? This again depends on the factors of apportionment. If productive factors such as assets and employment are used, formulary apportionment would retain the incentive to locate such factors in low-tax jurisdictions, perpetuating tax competition. Apportionment on the basis of destination-based sales would avoid these distortive pressures (see Chapter 13).

- Is formulary apportionment politically feasible? This depends not only on who loses and gains from such a reform, but also on international trust and the willingness to cooperate, including among low-income and high-income economies in the case of global adoption.

The remainder of this chapter explores these questions in greater depth, drawing inferences from recent studies as well as historical experience. The next section considers the various design options for a formulary apportionment system and how they affect corporate and government incentives. The chapter then looks at how formulary apportionment has performed in practice at the subnational level (in the United States, Canada, and China), and its prospects for implementation in the European Union. The following section discusses economic sectors, in particular finance and the extractive industry, that require special treatment under formulary apportionment due to their specific features. Finally, the chapter discusses residual profit allocation and then concludes.

THEORETICAL AND PRACTICAL DESIGN ISSUES

Design Considerations

Implementation of formulary apportionment requires several important design considerations that affect potential efficiency and equity gains relative to separate accounting. In particular, the definition of the consolidated tax base and the allocation formula used to apportion consolidated profits are key features determining the impact of any formulary apportionment system.

Defining the Consolidated Tax Base

The first step in the design of formulary apportionment is determination of the tax base (that is, taxable profits), which should be commonly defined across participating jurisdictions. This includes determining depreciation allowances, deductible expenses, and deductibility limits implemented as anti-avoidance measures. More substantially, participating jurisdictions need to decide whether to consolidate taxable income at the corporate group level or on a business activity basis.

One option consists of a corporate group's total earnings, where the group is defined according to some choice of ownership threshold. Consolidating a group's total earnings likely implies a reduction in administrative and compliance costs relative to a more granular approach: most jurisdictions already have a working definition of an affiliated group that relates multiple corporations through some threshold of common ownership, such as share of equity ownership or voting rights. Moreover, publicly listed firms are already required to prepare consolidated financial accounts for majority-owned affiliates. Therefore, a consolidated tax base at the corporate group level would be relatively straightforward to define and implement in domestic law, given the current legal and regulatory background. However, consolidation based on ownership structure can introduce incentives for increased vertical integration for tax purposes (for example, if the combined structure offsets intragroup losses, as described in the next section). Furthermore, differences in production functions, business models, and risk exposure across industries imply that consolidation of income for tax purposes could distort the allocation of resources and impair tax burden neutrality across sectors, as the same regulation could favor one sector over another.

Another option is consolidation on an activity-by-activity, business, or product-line basis. This may be easier to align with the current international tax architecture. Double tax treaties allow countries to tax nonresidents, on either a gross or net basis, if they are sufficiently economically connected with the country or if there is taxable income whose source is in the taxing country. Under the current system of bilateral tax treaties, taxation on a gross basis is usually imposed by withholding taxation on payments that are considered to have a domestic source, such as interest or service payments. Taxation on a net basis, on the other hand, requires the identification of a permanent establishment. The digitalization of the economy has raised significant challenges with respect to both approaches, and new proxies for what constitutes sufficient economic presence are actively being discussed (see Chapter 10). Significant ties of a nonresident to a country are easier to establish for a nonresident establishment providing intermediate inputs to the production of a good or service that is sold domestically than for another nonresident arm of the same corporate group that is not directly involved in the production of the domestically sold good. Consolidation of a group's income along business lines is thus likely simpler to align with the current international tax framework, as it would align tax bases more closely with the activities performed within a given jurisdiction. However, many functions within multinational enterprises, such as support and service activities, serve multiple business lines, complicating the delineation of a unitary business (see Picciotto 2017).

Finally, consolidation of a group's income can either be restricted to the participating jurisdictions (often referred to as "water's edge") or done on a worldwide basis. For instance, the EU Common Consolidated Corporate Tax Base proposal foresees a formulary apportionment system that applies only to income generated within the European Union, while traditional transfer pricing methods and the network of double tax treaties would continue to determine the allocation of profits between the European Union and third countries. Conversely, by eliminating the ambiguity over geographical reach, global income consolidation should be less affected by profit shifting. However, if not all countries participate or apply the same apportionment formula, global consolidation could easily lead to double taxation (or nontaxation), in which case multiple uncoordinated formulary apportionment and separate accounting systems might be applied to the same base by different countries.

Distribution Mechanism

Formulary apportionment allocates the consolidated tax base of a multinational using proxy weights for economic activity. Historically, countries with subnational formulary apportionment systems have relied on a combination of (proxies for) production factors—such as payroll, headcount employment, or tangible assets—and on third-party sales. Similarly, the European Union's Common Consolidated Corporate Tax Base proposal suggests using three equally weighted factors: fixed assets, sales by destination, and labor (comprising an equal weighting of payroll and employees).

The use of production factors as an allocation base reflects the idea of taxing the underlying factors that generate profits. The market value of a firm's tangible assets is sometimes not readily available, but corporate accounting generally tracks acquisition costs, depreciation expenses, and depreciated book valuations for both financial and income tax purposes. As a consequence, the value of tangible assets is straightforward to compute. It is, however, subject to some manipulation, particularly in accounting systems that give some leeway on depreciation amounts. Payroll usually involves third-party transactions, increasing this factor's robustness to manipulation. In contrast, headcount employment is independent of wage levels but may be easier to manipulate for tax reporting purposes, since nominal positions can be created without significant associated labor costs.

Third-party sales, an increasingly prevalent factor in policy choice, can be measured either on an origin basis (where the seller resides) or on a destination basis (where the purchaser resides). Using sales by destination as an apportionment factor has the advantage that consumers are relatively immobile, so the tax base should be fairly inelastic with respect to such a factor. However, profit taxation based on the destination of the final consumers requires adjustments to the nexus definition in existing tax treaties.

For certain lines of business, the inclusion of industry-specific factors in the allocation formula may be justified. For example, as elaborated later in the chapter, natural resource assets could be used as a key allocation factor for the extractives sector. This would likely benefit commodity-exporting developing countries in particular. Although intangible assets are an important production input for several industries, such as pharmaceuticals and information technology, their manipulability (due to ease of "relocation" and current lack of accounting measurability in the case of self-developed intellectual property) has thus far excluded intangible assets from consideration as an apportionment factor. Nonetheless, to the extent that the value of intangible assets is derived from employment (research and development workers) or tangible investments (such as laboratories), they are arguably at least partially captured by those other factors.

Efficiency Implications

Moving from separate accounting to formulary apportionment would change the nature of tax avoidance and the potential for real factor distortions and thus impact the efficiency of the global tax system. Moreover, by eliminating the need to document and verify group-internal price setting, formulary apportionment would reduce administrative and compliance costs substantially. However, other administrative and compliance costs under formulary apportionment would depend on the specifics of the system and are hard to quantify.

Factor Distortions

Production efficiency requires that the marginal pretax return of production factors be equalized across sectors and jurisdictions. Taxes generally drive a wedge between pre- and posttax returns, thus distorting this optimal allocation and leading to production inefficiencies. Under formulary apportionment, the corporate income tax effectively becomes a tax levied on the factors of the formula (McLure 1981). Hence, tax rate differences between countries may distort the allocation of mobile factors as multinationals relocate workers and physical assets to low-tax jurisdictions that are otherwise not the most productive. In addition, definition of the tax base on a consolidated corporate group basis may compromise tax neutrality across sectors of economic activity, where the group's activities span structurally different industries that are asymmetrically affected by the unitary tax formula.

Several studies try to quantify the distortive impact on real factors of production, with most, but not all, showing nontrivial misallocation. For instance, some studies using US state data from the 1980s and 1990s find that employment and investment are sensitive to the use of payroll and asset weights, respectively, in the state-level allocation formula (Goolsbee and Maydew 2000; Gupta and Hofmann 2003). Riedel (2010) likewise finds a very elastic response of the payroll-to-capital ratio of German affiliates in response to tax rate differentials under Germany's local business tax, which uses payroll as a single apportionment factor. In contrast, Clausing (2016b) examines the effects of US tax rates on employment, investment, and sales, depending on state-level formula weights, and finds that these variables have not been particularly sensitive to tax rates, suggesting that distortions might in fact be modest.

Tax Avoidance

Tax avoidance can reduce the distortive effects of tax systems on the allocation of real productive factors, for example under the current system. However, spending time and resources unproductively to avoid taxes increases the deadweight loss of the tax system, in addition to direct tax revenue erosion. Under separate accounting, multinationals use tax planning techniques to shift reported taxable income between entities in the group in order to minimize their overall corporate income tax liability. By contrast, when taxing multinationals on a consolidated basis for formulary apportionment, the arm's length principle and the availability—or absence—of comparable prices are immaterial to the determination of taxable profits. Formulary apportionment thus eliminates tax avoidance through the manipulation of intragroup payments or through the abuse of a country's double tax treaty network (at least if income is consolidated globally). However, this does not mean that profit shifting will disappear altogether.

Under formulary apportionment, related and unrelated companies are treated differently for tax purposes, engendering arbitrage or avoidance in organizational form and ownership. Combining two independent firms would generally change their combined tax liability under formulary apportionment, while such a group would be treated the same under separate accounting if transfer prices were set at arm's length. Gordon and Wilson (1986) show that companies have an incentive to spread excess returns to low-tax jurisdictions under formulary apportionment by merging with companies in low-tax states. Hines (2010) also finds that even a distortion-minimizing formula can create large incentives for inefficient ownership reallocation due to the variation in profitability that is unexplained by formulary factors. Nielsen, Raimondos, and Schjelderup (2003) posit that such incentives might be especially large under conditions of imperfect competition.

Tax avoidance opportunities also depend on the apportionment formula and the simplicity of manipulating apportionment factors. For example, Eichfelder, Hechtner, and Hundsdoerfer (2017) study the German context of local business taxes that use payroll as a single apportionment factor. The authors conclude that payroll expenses are driven by both reallocation of real labor and tax-planning strategies that affect the payroll expense at the establishment level without implying changes in the production process or the allocation of input factors. In addition, while the location of final consumers is inelastic and hence a theoretically appealing factor for apportioning profits, the recorded location of third-party sales is open to abuse. If, for example, origin-based sales are used as a factor, corporate groups may have an incentive to establish sales subsidiaries in low-tax jurisdictions and serve the markets in high-tax countries through independent distributors. Thus, if destination-based sales were used, multinationals would have an incentive to sell to independent distributors located in low-tax jurisdictions.

Moreover, if formulary apportionment were restricted to the water's edge of participating jurisdictions, all currently available profit-shifting strategies would remain for transactions with affiliates outside the water's edge.

Despite these potential distortions, formulary apportionment is generally thought to be less vulnerable to manipulation than separate accounting. This was stressed, for example, by Musgrave (1973) and is confirmed by Mintz and Smart (2004), where firms are taxed either by formulary apportionment or separate accounting, depending on their ownership structure across provinces. The latter find that the elasticity of taxable income for firms subject to separate accounting is more than double that for firms under formulary apportionment.

Revenue Implications

Formulary apportionment would impact both the aggregate level of global corporate income tax revenues and their distribution, with modest but mostly positive effects for emerging market economies. Directly, global revenues would decrease due to intragroup loss consolidation and increase due to a redistribution of the tax base from low-tax to high-tax countries. In the long run, revenues would also change indirectly due to evolving tax competition incentives among governments.

In addition, IMF (2019) indicates that the global distribution of taxable income is highly sensitive to apportionment factors. For example, a heavy weight on headcount employment would tilt the taxable income base in favor of developing countries, which have a relatively large concentration of workers; but these countries would lose from a system based on payroll, due to their relatively lower wages. In turn, advanced economies are more likely to gain revenue if apportionment is by value added, payroll, or sales.

Direct Revenue Implications

Corporate income tax systems typically allow companies the opportunity to carry forward losses, offsetting future profits with current losses incurred. Under separate accounting, this opportunity to offset losses applies separately to each subsidiary or, if there is domestic group taxation, to the group of subsidiaries within the borders of a country. Under formulary apportionment, however, the global consolidation of entity-level earnings would imply an immediate loss offset for all globally profitable multinationals, leading to a reduction in their overall tax base. Fuest, Hemmelgarn, and Ramb (2007) assess the base effect of loss consolidation in the European Union using data for German multinationals and find a reduction in the EU-wide corporate income tax base of more than 20 percent. Using a larger set of unconsolidated firm-level data from ORBIS, Cobham and Loretz (2014) report a potential revenue loss of about 10 percent under global formulary apportionment due to similar drivers. Computable general equilibrium simulations for Europe by Bettendorf and others (2010), however, find a smaller reduction in the tax base from loss consolidation of close to 7.5 percent in the long term, that is, once the stock of losses carried forward from past years has stabilized.

The second effect on corporate income tax revenue is due to the reallocation of the tax base among countries. In particular, as the base is shifted from low-tax to high-tax countries, the previously described narrowing of the tax base is largely offset, boosting aggregate tax revenue. For the European Union, Devereux and Loretz (2008) find that this reallocation effect would more than offset the effect of loss consolidation and that EU-wide tax revenues would therefore rise by 2 percent under regional water's edge formulary apportionment. For global formulary apportionment, Cobham and Loretz (2014) also report a net increase in total potential tax revenue in the order of between 2 and 4 percent.

Inter-nation equity goals concerning the allocation of taxable income across jurisdictions (Musgrave and Musgrave 1972) are also affected by apportionment factors, but by and large formulary apportionment is estimated to distribute potential tax revenues more uniformly across jurisdictions than the existing system does. Using various data sets and allocation factors, De Mooij, Liu, and Prihardini (2019) confirm that the distributional consequences of global formulary apportionment on potential revenue are highly sensitive to the system design choices and data used. Notwithstanding, investment hubs are consistently estimated to experience large revenue losses of up to 80 percent of multinational enterprise tax payments. In contrast, many large economies are estimated to benefit from higher revenues. Developing countries gain mostly if employment receives a large weight in the formula, yet also tend to benefit on average from formulae based on sales by destination, as shown in Figure 14.1.[3]

Indirect Revenue Implications

Under the current separate accounting framework, governments have an incentive to attract investment by reducing corporate taxation. Tax competition is seen as the major driver behind the decline in corporate tax rates worldwide over the past decades. Under formulary apportionment, tax competition does not disappear, as countries can continue to compete with their tax rates to attract whatever factors are given high weight in the formula. The incentive may be even stronger

---

[3] Figure 14.1 shows the median impact per region. Due to the large aggregate impact of the United States, the median impact for other countries is highly dependent on what happens in the United States, which is markedly different between the asset and employment share. For another analysis, see also Cobham, Faccio, and Fitzgerald (2019).

Figure 14.1. Revenue Effect from Implementing Formulary Apportionment for Different Allocation Factors
(Percent of corporate income tax revenue)

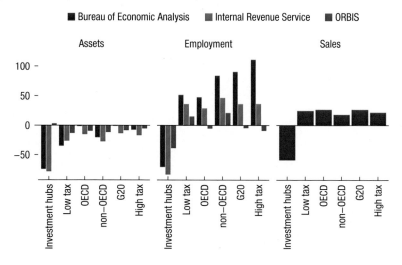

Source: De Mooij, Liu, and Prihardini (2019).

than under separate accounting, since the revenue gain from attracting such factors is not merely from a marginal increase in some local tax base, but from the greater share of the group's overall profit that is brought into tax (Nielsen and others 2010). This effect on tax competition, however, will depend on the choice of apportionment factors and their weights.

Namely, under a formulary system built on relatively immobile factors, such as destination-based sales, the pressure for a race to the bottom on rates might soften, and the trend could even reverse. Empirically, Pethig and Wagener (2007) find that tax competition under formulary apportionment results in lower equilibrium tax rates if the formulary share of a particular factor is more elastic. Thus, tax competition is most intense when apportionment is based on assets, followed by payroll and then sales, which are the least elastic. More promisingly, Eichner and Runkel (2008) show that formulary apportionment with a sales factor may mitigate or even eliminate fiscal externalities associated with tax competition. Calibrating the model for the European Union, they show that formulary apportionment with a sales-only formula raises average steady-state corporate income tax rates by 2 percentage points and generates positive welfare effects. Some studies have also explored tax competition through the choice of formula factors, which applies only if jurisdictions are granted full fiscal autonomy with respect to formula design—as is the case in the United States. US states have increasingly converged toward a greater weight of the sales factor. Anand and Sansing (2000) find that states with a current account deficit generally have incentives to increase the sales factor, whereas states with a current account surplus tend to increase input factors. (This aligns well with the discussion about the revenue implication of destination-based corporate income taxes in Chapter 13).

Lastly, sharing a common tax base across countries could produce novel fiscal externalities. Deductible expenses, such as social security contributions or non–corporate income tax state-specific taxes, could translate into *de facto* cross-subsidization if they continued to be deductible from a cross-country consolidated income base before apportionment (Schreiber 2008). Under international formulary apportionment, concerns have surfaced over the moral hazard associated with governments increasing taxes on relatively immobile domestic bases (such as payroll), provided those taxes are deductible from the consolidated international corporate tax base. In doing so, they would capture the full marginal increase in state-specific taxes, while sharing the reduction of corporate income tax revenue with other countries in the consolidated tax base. In general equilibrium, however, this would be constrained by the fact that as firms will not keep investing in countries where profitability is lower due to higher payroll costs.

SUBNATIONAL AND SUPRANATIONAL EXPERIENCES

A number of countries, including the United States, Canada, and China, use formulary apportionment to tax the income of multijurisdictional enterprises at the subnational level. This section summarizes the experiences in these countries, focusing on the prospective benefits and costs of introducing formulary apportionment at a supranational level. It then discusses the main features of the European Commission's Common Consolidated Corporate Tax Base, which introduces an apportionment formula for distributing the consolidated corporate tax base among EU member states.

The United States

The United States has used formulary apportionment to distribute multistate companies' taxable income among its states since the early twentieth century. In determining state-level tax liabilities, states first need to determine whether they have the authority to tax a business, that is, whether a company has economic nexus in a state. Loosely speaking, if a firm has physical presence in the state—specifically, property or employees—then the state has the power to tax it.[4] If a firm does not have physical presence in the state, and its activities are limited to "mere solicitation of orders," then it does not have nexus in the state. Many states use "throwback" rules that attribute taxable income back to the source state if a company has no nexus in the state where its goods are sold.

However, the nexus rule has also been evolving, in particularly with regard to the sales tax. On June 21, 2018, the US Supreme Court ruled granted South

---

[4] The term "nexus" is thus closely linked to the concept of a permanent establishment.

Dakota authority to impose sales tax on sales into South Dakota of companies with no physical presence in the state (*South Dakota v. Wayfair*). Since the ruling, several states have responded by implementing legislation to adopt economic nexus provisions requiring remote sellers to collect and remit sales tax without having a physical presence in the state.[5] Expanding the nexus rules to cover international transactions by remote sellers without a permanent establishment could be the next step. For new international formulary apportionment proposals, some of which consider taxing residual profits in "market countries"—that is, countries where final sales are located--nexus can be defined more broadly from the start to include the presence of (nontrivial) sales.

In the early days of formulary apportionment, virtually all US states apportioned taxable income on the basis of the Massachusetts three-factor formula, which gives equal weight to property, payroll, and destination-based sales within a state. Over the past twenty years, however, many states have reduced the weights of property and payroll factors. As of 2017, only six of the 47 states that tax corporate income[6] use the traditional evenly weighted three-factor formula. Fifteen states use double- or triple-weighted sales formulae, in which a company's in-state sales are at least twice as important as each of the other factors. Some 23 states and the District of Columbia use a single sales factor formula (that is, a 100 percent weight on destination-based sales).

Evidence from empirical research suggests that local investment and employment tend to increase following reduction in the weight on the property and payroll factors (Goolsbee and Maydew 2000; Gupta and Mills 2002; Weiner 1994). Under a pure single-sales factor, the only variable that matters in apportioning income to the state (assuming that the firm has nexus) is the share of within-state sales. The effective tax rate on property and payroll is thus zero, regardless of the level of the statutory corporate income tax rate.

Other aspects of state policies also vary substantially. Most states use federal taxable income as the baseline, making subsequent adjustments to determine the state tax base. Some 26 states require combined reporting by multistate firms, including profits of all US subsidiaries regardless of their location. Some states offer options among formula types or reporting requirements, and as noted, many states also have throwback rules. Further, states have frequently changed tax rates, although on average these rates have been fairly stable over time, declining from 7.2 percent in 1986 to 6 percent in 2017 (Clausing 2016a).

---

[5] Hawaii, Kentucky, and Vermont, for example, have adopted South Dakota style economic nexus laws that went into effect on July 1, 2018. Each state's threshold is $100,000 or 200 individual sales in any preceding 12-month period (Vermont) or in current or previous calendar year (Kentucky and Hawaii). Several other 18 states already have economic nexus rules similar to South Dakota, each with different statutory start dates and sales/transactions requirement that trigger nexus.

[6] Nevada, South Dakota, and Wyoming do not tax corporate income. Ohio and Texas use a gross receipts tax instead of corporate income tax.

Canada

As in the United States, Canadian provinces typically use the federal tax base, while each province imposes its own tax rate. The federal government, by entering tax collection agreements with 8 of 10 provinces, plays a strong role in the legislation and administration of the common tax base. The two non-acceding provinces (Quebec and Alberta) have independent corporate income taxes, but they coordinate closely with the federal government and rely largely on federal audit and enforcement. Tax rates range from 7 percent in Quebec to 16 percent in New Brunswick, Newfoundland, Manitoba, and Saskatchewan.

Canadian formulary apportionment applies to corporations that have permanent establishments in more than one province on the basis of a formula that equally weights payroll and destination-based sales.[7] However, as Canada does not allow group consolidation, formulary apportionment is in effect elective for taxpayers, as it only applies to those operating by permanent establishment (branches or other unincorporated entities) in different provinces. Companies operating through separate affiliates can shift tax losses and profits across provinces, often through leasing, financing, and transfer pricing. These tax avoidance behaviors increase the elasticity of taxable income and reduce the sensitivity of investment decisions based on differences in tax rates. Indeed, Mintz and Smart (2004) show that the reported taxable income of single-province subsidiaries is twice as responsive to provincial tax rates (with an estimated elasticity of 4.6) as that of large firms that are subject to formulary apportionment (with an estimated elasticity of 2.3). The findings thus suggest that tax avoidance is likely to be larger under separate accounting than formulary apportionment in Canada.

The federal equalization program, a system of transfers designed to reduce fiscal disparities across provinces, plays a key role in limiting provincial tax competition. The equalization formula is based on each province's revenue-raising capacity (using commonly defined tax bases at national average tax rates) compared to a representative standard. Increases in own-source tax revenue reduce equalization grants almost dollar for dollar (Smart and Vaillancourt 2019). Currently, seven provinces receive equalization payments.[8]

Canada's equalization system essentially removes incentives for provinces to engage in horizontal and vertical tax competition (since revenues are shared with the federal government). While federal corporate income tax rates in Canada have significantly declined, provincial rates have been relatively stable. As shown in Smart (2007), tax rates are typically higher in grant-receiving provinces, where they would be 38 percent lower if grants were abolished. Provinces respond to expansions of equalization transfers by increasing their own corporate tax rates.

---

[7] Special types of formulary apportionment are used for insurance companies, banks, lending companies, railways, crop companies, freight transportation, shipping, and pipelines (Weiner 2005).

[8] These include Manitoba, New Brunswick, Newfoundland, Nova Scotia, Prince Edward Island, Quebec, and Saskatchewan. These seven provinces have a combined population of approximately 12 million, or 39 percent of the national population.

China

Though its use of formulary apportionment is less well known, China also applies it to companies that have permanent establishments, including branches or other unincorporated entities, in more than one region.[9] Similar to the system in Canada, formulary apportionment only applies to those operating by permanent establishment but not by separately incorporated entities in different regions.

The apportionment formula has two tiers. First, the headquarters is responsible for 50 percent of total corporate income tax. Second, all other unincorporated businesses are liable for the remaining 50 percent. The liability for each establishment is determined by a three-factor formula that includes origin-based sales, payroll, and total assets, with respective weights of 35, 35, and 30 percent. Effectively, the formulary apportionment in China uses a mix of source and residence principles, with equal weights for the residence and source locations.

European Union

The European Commission introduced its supranational formulary apportionment proposal, the Common Consolidated Corporate Tax Base, in 2011 and relaunched it in 2016. The Common Consolidated Corporate Tax Base is a water's edge system that applies only to the EU-source income of multinationals operating in more than one EU state. It is mandatory for multinationals with global sales of at least EUR 750 million and optional below this threshold. Where optional, the Common Consolidated Corporate Tax Base system applies on an all-in-or-all-out basis: in other words, a company belonging to a covered group cannot individually opt for the Common Consolidated Corporate Tax Base, but only jointly with all other members of the corporate group. Further, intergroup shareholding must exceed 50 percent, and more than 75 percent of the capital must be owned by the parent.

Under the current proposal, each multinational enterprise calculates its consolidated taxable profits under the rules for a common tax base, with losses of one affiliate automatically offsetting profits of others in the same group. The principal taxpayer of the group—generally the regional headquarters—consolidates all individual tax bases in a single return to the tax authority of the regional headquarters' country. A formulary apportionment system is then used to distribute the tax base among the member states in which the group is active. The Common Consolidated Corporate Tax Base formula consists of three equally weighted factors of assets, labor, and destination-based sales. The labor factor is a 50-50 weighting of payroll and employees to compensate for labor productivity and wage differentials across the European Union. Member states are free to set their own tax rates. There are sector-specific formulae for several industries: For financial institutions and insurance companies, financial assets and sales are included

---

[9] With exceptions for 15 large state-owned enterprises, whose revenue goes entirely to the central government. Formulary apportionment is also not applicable for the transportation sector in China.

in the common tax base. For the oil and gas industry, sales are attributed to the jurisdiction of extraction or production. There are also specific provisions for shipping, inland waterways transport, and air transport.

The consideration of adopting the Common Consolidated Corporate Tax Base has been progressing very slowly since its relaunch, highlighting the political challenges in reforming the corporate tax regime in the European Union, which requires unanimity among members. An EU-wide Common Consolidated Corporate Tax Base also implies that corporate groups in Europe would have to deal with different income tax systems within and outside the EU single market. Nevertheless, the recent OECD (2019a) report on the digital economy could accelerate work on the Common Consolidated Corporate Tax Base and formulary apportionment in general. The OECD's Inclusive Framework has launched a new initiative to explore changes to the international tax system, with the aim of reaching consensus by mid-2021. One of the pillars under consideration would allocate at least some part of the residual profits of multinationals by means of a formula, that includes a sales factor (see Chapter 10).

SECTOR-SPECIFIC FORMULAE

For both technical and political reasons, any introduction of formulary apportionment on a global or regional basis would likely require special provisions to reflect the inherent characteristics of certain industries. This section examines some of the specific characteristics in the financial sector and extractive industry that highlight the design issues in allocation factors warranting special consideration.[10]

Financial Sector

Two distinct features of the financial sector call for special consideration in the choice of apportionment factors. First, compared to other capital-intensive sectors, fixed assets comprise only a small fraction of the total assets of financial companies, as most of their assets consist of loans, deposits and other financial obligations. For example, fixed assets typically account for one-third of total assets among the world's largest 10,000 nonfinancial, nonutility multinationals, but less than 5 percent of total assets among the top 500 financial companies. Thus, fixed assets are likely to be a weak indicator of the overall economic activities of financial companies.

Moreover, sales conducted by financial companies are of a different nature than those of other companies, whose activities typically involve exchange of goods and services for money. For financial companies, only some receipts come in the form of explicit fees for service, which is a straightforward sale. Instead,

---

[10] Special apportionment formulae also apply to other sectors, including construction contractors, transportation, television and radio broadcasting, and publishing.

much financial intermediation is compensated by a financial margin such as an interest markup or bid-ask spread.

Given these considerations, the formula applied to the financial sector is generally different. Canada uses an allocation formula based on both payroll (one-third) and loans and deposits (two-thirds, as a proxy for sales). In the United States, the sales factor for financial companies is replaced by a gross receipts factor. In the European Common Consolidated Corporate Tax Base proposal, 10 percent of the value of financial assets is added to the asset factor.

Extractive Industries

Extractive industries, such as mining and petroleum, have distinct features that set them apart from other sectors of the economy—most saliently, immobile and exhaustible natural resource assets that can generate substantial rents (Daniel, Keen, and McPherson 2010). Applying the standard allocation formulae with (an often heavy) destination-based sales weighting would thus omit the principal factor involved in their value generation. It would also fail to address international equity concerns, whereby low-income source countries would receive little of the extractive industry revenue, since projects typically generate scant local employment and the bulk of production is sold abroad. Moreover, extractive industry projects tend to inflict considerable environmental damage while depleting a nonrenewable local resource. All these concerns suggest that a destination-based sales factor would not be appropriate for the extractive industries (see also Chapter 13).

The experience of formulary apportionment applied to extractive industries at the subnational level illustrates various design options:

- In the United States, several states have special formulary apportionment provisions for the sector, but only Alaska explicitly includes natural resources in the allocation formula. Alaska allocates income for petroleum and pipeline companies on the basis of sales and tariffs, property, and an extraction factor consisting of total production of barrels of oil plus one sixth of thousand cubic feet of natural gas.

- In Canada, although some sectors benefit from special formula rules, extractive industries are subject to the general formula based on payroll and destination-based sales. This reduces revenue for resource-rich provinces, where the capital-intensive extractive industry sector generates comparatively few jobs (Siu and others 2017). Nevertheless, some of the distortions are leveled off through the federal capacity equalization grants system.

- Under the Common Consolidated Corporate Tax Base, the petroleum sector (but not the mining sector) has a sector-specific formula, according to which sales are attributed to the jurisdiction of extraction and production and not to the jurisdiction of consumption.

For a broader regional implementation, many complexities need to be addressed, including clarification of the definition of extractive industry activities subject to the tax, composition of extractive industry income, interaction with other domestic taxes and levies, and the formula for apportionment.

- *Definition of extractive industry activities:* International accounting and disclosure requirements for the sector—such as those laid out in the US Dodd–Frank Act,[11] in the EU Accounting and Transparency Directive,[12] and in the Extractive Industries Transparency Initiative—point to a broad definition in which extractive industries include all upstream activities within the mining or petroleum value chain (that is, exploration and extraction activities), but generally exclude downstream activities (such as processing). If formulary apportionment were to reflect the inherent characteristics of the industry and its underlying economic activities, the industry definition should arguably include entities from both upstream and downstream activities (Phionesgo 2015). Such consolidation has the additional advantage of removing incentives for transfer pricing between upstream and downstream operations; however, it is likely distortionary as upstream activities have very different risk profiles compared to the downstream.

- *Extractive industry income subject to taxation:* In defining the base at an international level, a critical element will be the treatment of other domestic extractive industry taxes, which in many countries yield more revenue than the corporate income tax in this sector. These include bonuses (upfront payments on the acquisition of mineral exploitation rights), royalties (production-based taxes), additional profit taxes, resource rent taxes, and "profit oil or gas" in production-sharing contracts. The host government may also have an equity stake in resource projects, either paid or unpaid. The consolidation approach would have to account for the interaction between such payments and corporate income taxation (IMF 2012). In particular, it will be important to specify whether royalties and rent taxes are deductible from the unitary tax base, and whether project-specific economic rents are determined before or after netting out corporate income tax liabilities. The existing literature does not discuss such interactions but acknowledges that formulary apportionment could considerably improve project-level tax accounting through improved top-down reporting (Siu and others 2017).

- *Apportionment formula:* The literature is split on the design of the apportionment formula, and the US and Canadian experiences indicate that it is

---

[11] The Dodd–Frank Act, Section 1504, Rule 13(q), mandated that the Securities and Exchange Commission issue a rule requiring issuers engaged in the "commercial development of oil, gas, or minerals, or the license for any such activity" disclose annually the amount of expenses by type, project, and government. The scope of the Dodd–Frank Act excludes marketing, transportation, refining or smelting activities, and logging activities (US Securities and Exchange Commission 2012).

[12] The EU Accounting and Transparency Directive, Article 41, defines extractive industry activities as undertakings involving "exploration, prospection, discovery, development, and extraction of minerals, oil, natural gas deposits or other materials within the economic activities."

possible to operate both with and without incorporating a sector-specific weight. Phionesgo (2015) argues that the traditional formula of equally weighted sales, assets, and labor factors provides a reasonable apportionment that removes the need for a sector-specific formula (except perhaps for an adjustment in the labor factor to strike a balance between remuneration and headcount employment, as under the Common Consolidated Corporate Tax Base). However, for developing countries to strengthen their source taxation, the asset factor could be replaced or supplemented by an extraction factor tied to the production level. Siu and others (2017) argue in favor of using source-based factors for extractive industries to satisfy source entitlement concerns, such as special extraction factors (following the Alaskan formula) or origin-based sales factors (following the Common Consolidated Corporate Tax Base proposal).

RESIDUAL PROFIT ALLOCATION[13]

What Is Residual Profit Allocation?

Residual profit allocation has been widely discussed in recent proposals as a potential solution to the tax challenges arising from the digitalization of the economy, and more fundamentally as a future alternative to the current international tax regime (IMF 2019). As a hybrid system that combines elements of formulary apportionment and separate accounting under the arm's length principle, residual profit allocation takes the entire profit of a multinational corporate group and divides it into routine and residual components on a unitary basis.

- Routine profit refers to an acceptable return to some activity or function—broadly equivalent to a normal return (that is, the minimum after-tax return required by shareholders). As the name suggests, in transfer pricing analysis routine profit is usually assumed to be the return on routine activities, such as assembling a product's subcomponents or providing warehousing services.[14] Calculation of routine profit is in practice context specific, the general aim being to identify the return earned by an entity undertaking that activity on an outsourced basis.

- Residual profit refers to the difference between aggregate profit and routine profit, which may be negative. If routine profit can be identified with a normal return on investment, residual profit can be identified with economic rent. It will include that part of profit that—due to intangibles or risk bearing, for instance—is hardest to allocate across jurisdictions by standard transfer pricing methods.

---

[13] This section draws heavily on IMF (2019) and Beer and others (2020).

[14] Auerbach, Devereux, Keen, Oosterhuis, Schön and Vella (2019) argue that the two coincide when, as in the simplest capital asset pricing models without taxation, the required return on an investment is the same for all firms undertaking it.

In most proposals under discussion, routine profits are typically allocated where the associated costs (purchases from third parties) are incurred, while residual profits are generally allocated on a formulaic basis. Countries may then choose to tax these two types of income allocated to their jurisdictions at different rates. The OECD's Inclusive Framework proposes using variants of residual profit allocation to tax digital consumer-facing companies, or more generally, the return to selected intangibles. A common feature of these schemes is that they envisage taxing rights being established in the destination country, even in the absence of a traditional permanent establishment. Examples of such proposals include the following:

- Avi-Yonah, Clausing, and Durst (2009) propose calculating routine profit by applying an agreed markup on third-party costs and apportioning residual profit on the basis of destination-based sales.

- Auerbach, Devereux, Keen, Oosterhuis, Schön and Vella (2019) propose allocating residual profit in proportion to destination-based sales less third-party costs that can be attributed to sales in particular markets.[15]

Other proposals seek to distinguish among different types of residual profit or to address the income tax challenges introduced by the digital economy:

- The United States has proposed allocating part of residual profit attributable to "marketing intangibles"[16]—trademarks, brand recognition, and the like—to the market country with which they are associated.[17]

- A proposal put forth in the United Kingdom envisages allocating residual profit in part by some indicator of the value created by user participation, such as revenue or the number of active users (HM Treasury 2018).

The implementation issues raised by these proposals differ, but they share the fundamental principle of extending taxing rights to destination or 'user' countries. The UK proposal, for instance, raises the practical issue of how to quantify user value and leaves open the allocation of other sources of residual profit. Schemes that allocate in part by destination face the possibility, as under standard formulary apportionment, of avoidance by multinationals selling final products to third-party distributors in low-tax jurisdictions. Schemes that operate on a product or product line basis can add their own complexities and opportunities for manipulation by strategic choice of product groupings.

A common feature of destination-based apportionment schemes is that they envisage taxing rights being established even in the absence of a traditional permanent establishment. This is a fundamental shift of principle that is likely to

---

[15] The merit of this approach, relative to fully sales-based allocation, is that it allocates less residual profit to jurisdictions that are demonstrably costlier to serve. This scheme also has the feature—which may make it more familiar to practitioners—that the final allocation can be reached not only by apportionment but by intuitive hypothetical transfer pricing adjustments.

[16] As opposed in particular to product or trade intangibles reflecting, for example, research and development and product design.

[17] See, for example, reported comments made by US Treasury officials at the 31st Annual Institute on Current Issues in International Taxation, held December 13–14, 2018, in Washington, DC.

require amendment of existing tax treaties—either to create a "virtual permanent establishment" as discussed earlier, or to establish a generalized right to tax in the destination country. Essentially the same issues as for formulary apportionment arise in the sharing of residual profit.

The interest in residual profit allocation signals a recognition that although the arm's length principle has proved capable of dealing with relatively straightforward operations, it is not capable of addressing the full complexities of transactions within modern multinational enterprises. While preserving a significant element of source taxation, the residual profit allocation approach thus provides a framework within which progress might be made while retaining familiar elements of current arrangements. The taxation of normal returns retains a distortion inherent in most current corporate income taxes and creates an incentive for countries to attract mobile routine activities. Incentives to compete for residual profit depend on an apportionment formula: using formulary apportionment to allocate residual profits means that the same forces potentially encouraging tax competition between governments (and game playing by firms) identified earlier remain. They are lessened, however, if apportionment is by destination-based sales.

What Is the Potential Revenue Impact of Residual Profit Allocation?

There is little analysis of the revenue implications of residual profit allocation. Avi-Yonah and others (2009) and Auerbach and others (2019) describe how their proposals would work, how they can be implemented, and what the benefits are of such reforms, but not their revenue implications. Conjecturally, the revenue impact of residual profit allocation would be proportional to the size of the residual profit, as only the allocation of that share of income would be modified—the routine return would continue to be taxed according to the current system. If so, then the economic implications (for example, on investment, profit shifting, and tax competition) would also be proportionally adjusted. However, there can be profound nonlinearities in the system that can create disproportional effects. For example, profit shifting might currently be disproportionally associated with residual profit allocation, rather than with routine profits. Residual profit allocation would then, like formulary apportionment, virtually eliminate profit shifting.

The impact of residual profit allocation will depend critically on two aspects: (1) how routine profit is determined, and (2) how residual profit is subsequently apportioned across countries. On the first, some initial empirical analysis is reported in Beer, de Mooij, Hebous, Keen, and Liu (2020), based on consolidated income statements of the 10,000 largest global companies. The analysis shows, for instance, that for a routine return on tangible assets of 7.5 percent, the average residual profit of a multinational enterprise would be about 60 percent of total income. Assuming this routine rate of return, between 20 and 30 percent of the multinationals would report a negative residual. This may be an artifact of assumptions underlying the calculations, but it highlights the practical issue of how to apportion residual losses. There would also be significant variation across sectors and countries. Most global residual profits are earned by US-based

Figure 14.2. Excess of Current Corporate Income Tax Bases over Routine Return

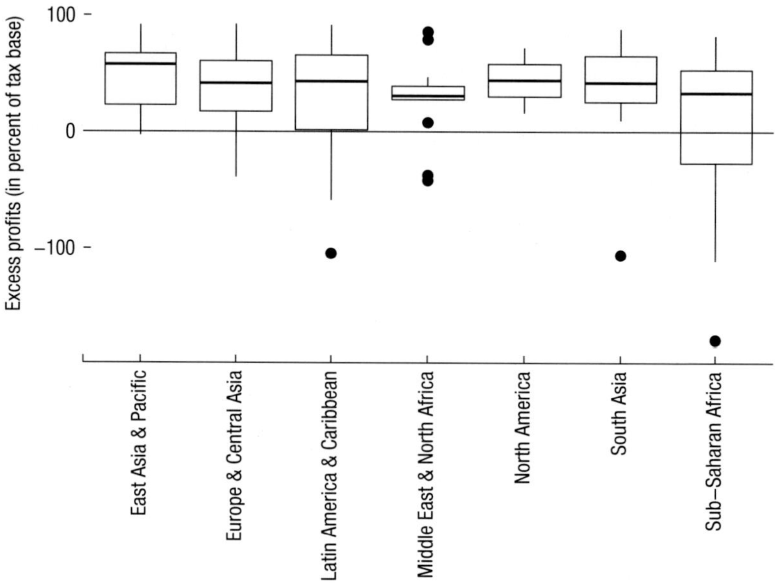

Source: IMF staff calculations.
Note: Figure shows boxplots by country groups. The lower and upper hinges correspond to the first and third quartile of the region-specific distributions. The middle line depicts the median of the distribution, and points represent outliers.

multinational enterprises, and one third of global residual profits are earned by the largest 1 percent of multinationals in terms of revenue.

On the second issue, the focus in Beer, de Mooij, Hebous, Keen, and Liu (2020) is on apportionment to the destination country using a sales factor and, alternatively, a fixed assets factor. Two complementary assessments shed light on the potential revenue implications of residual profit allocation proposals, including (1) the scale of revenue from taxing only the routine return component, and how the revenue under this approach compares to current tax revenue; and (2) the full revenue effect from taxing both the routine return and the residual profit. The main data set used for these assessments is a sample of 114 countries and their corporate income tax rates, revenue, capital stock, and a proxy for sales by destination.[18] One insight from this assessment is that many countries, particularly in sub-Saharan Africa, may currently collect less revenue than they would by fully taxing routine returns (computed as 7.5 percent of tangible assets) (Figure 14.2).

---

[18] Data set developed from the IMF's WEO and WoRLD databases, available at: https://data.imf .org/?sk=77413F1D-1525-450A-A23A-47AEED40FE78.

Figure 14.3. Effect of Sales-Based Residual Profit Allocation on Corporate Income Tax Revenue

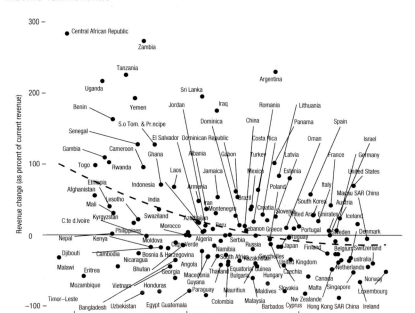

Source: Beer, de Mooij, Hebous, Keen, and Liu (2020).

Reducing profit shifting under residual profit allocation could benefit many countries, but its impact on the distribution of tax revenues depends on how residual profit is allocated. Analysis of wholly sales-based residual profit allocation suggests that the effects of reduced profit shifting may be modest relative to those from reallocation of residual profits. Figure 14.3 summarizes the results from this simulation, showing the revenue change from sales-based residual profit allocation as a percentage of current corporate income tax revenue. Interestingly, lower-income countries stand to gain more from sales-based residual profit allocation, as illustrated by the downward slope of the regression line. Reallocation of residual profits also implies that high-tax countries gain at the expense of low-tax countries, so that global revenue is likely to increase as a result of the reallocation.

One important qualification of the assessment is that it does not capture the reduction in taxable profits inherent in moving to the taxation of enterprises on a consolidated basis (through the cross-border jurisdiction offsetting of losses). Previous work suggests that this effect can be substantial, perhaps in the order of 10 percent of aggregate corporate tax revenues.[19] Indeed, far more research is

---

[19] See, in particular, Cobham and Loretz (2014); and De Mooij, Liu, and Prihardini (2019).

needed on routine and residual profit patterns and the potential impact of alternative residual profit allocation schemes.

Efficiency Aspects of Residual Profit Allocation

A primary concern with the adoption of a residual profit allocation scheme, as with any major reform of the corporate tax system, is its impact on investment. This matters for revenue as well as for the efficiency of the tax system. Again, the specific impact would depend on the rates at which the routine and residual profits were taxed. Analysis in Beer, de Mooij, Hebous, Keen, and Liu (2020) shows that if the tax rate on routine profits was equal to current statutory tax rate, the marginal effective tax rate—defined as the amount by which the marginal value product of capital in a country exceeds the required pretax return, as a proportion of the latter—would rise significantly (from an average of 0.13 under the current system to 0.28 under residual profit allocation) and efficiency would decline. However, if the tax on routine profits is set in a way as to leave the effective tax on capital unchanged, the marginal effective tax rate will hardly change; that is, the weighted average will increase by 0.01—reflecting the elimination of profit shifting.

CONCLUSION

The weaknesses of the global corporate tax system—particularly its complexity and manipulability, which along with tax competition have contributed to revenue erosion—have spurred debate on how to amend or replace it. Apportioning multinational enterprise revenues among their countries of operation according to a formula, rather than the separate accounts of their affiliates, may offer greater simplicity and fewer opportunities for manipulation. Both of these aspects are particularly important for developing countries.

In terms of revenue implications, the effect of formulary apportionment on the international allocation of corporate income tax revenues depends on the system's design. Developing countries gain mostly when headcount employment receives a large weight in the formula, yet also tend to benefit on average from a formula based on sales by destination. While *low-income* jurisdictions may gain or lose, depending on the formula, *low-tax* jurisdictions would lose tax base under all formulae under consideration.

In terms of efficiency, to the extent that the formula contains production factors, such as assets and employment, the corporate income tax effectively turns into a tax on those factors and distorts productive efficiency. Moreover, the incentive to locate such factors in low-tax jurisdiction remains, also perpetuating tax competition. Experience from federal states confirms that such distortions arise in the allocation of formula factors. Apportionment on the basis of destination-based sales would reduce these distortive pressures (see Chapter 13), although it could encourage turning low-tax investment hub jurisdictions into marketing hubs. While classic profit shifting would become impossible, new opportunities for tax planning will arise, related to manipulation of factors.

In terms of simplicity, the elimination of the need for transfer price estimation and enforcement would be a major advantage. Clearly this is maximized in the case of global adoption, while regional adoption would still require transfer pricing at the water's edge. In any case, while possibly simpler, the system would still feature some new complexities, such as which entities and activities are to be consolidated and how to distinguish between different sectoral regimes (such as the finance or extractive industries). In the case of residual profit allocation, the additional difficulties of distinguishing between types of profits and using two allocation mechanisms arise.

Given that formulary apportionment represents a significant departure from the current system, its adoption faces substantial political obstacles. These would likely stem less from opposition by corporations than from national governments. Global loss offsetting would be an attractive feature for many multinational enterprises, while national governments may not find a smaller tax base appealing, nor would they wish to cede control over that base, which is a valuable fiscal tool. Developing countries might be especially reluctant to join a formulary apportionment union with developed countries for fear that they would have relatively little bargaining power in central decision-making. Formulary apportionment adoption may therefore be more feasible—at least in the medium term—regionally among countries with similar income levels.

Nonetheless, continued integration of global markets and rapid growth of the digital economy create increasing pressure to reform the current system, and the dialogue among the more than 130 member countries of the Inclusive Framework on Base Erosion and Profit Shifting (BEPS) continues to deepen: the OECD's (2019b) *Programme of Work* discusses several formulary options, one of which ("fractional apportionment") is supported by the G24 group of developing economies. Overall, the policy relevance of the discussions goes beyond formulary apportionment. For instance, the analysis makes transparent how profit would be allocated if it were to closely resemble the allocation of production factors or sales (either by origin or destination). This informs debates on the desirable allocation of taxing rights and profit attribution. Moreover, the analysis sheds light on the revenue implications of more incremental reforms that would only partly use formulary elements. For example, proposals for so-called residual profit allocation use formulary apportionment for a fraction of the total profit.

REFERENCES

Anand, Bharat N., and Richard Sansing. 2000. "The Weighting Game: Formula Apportionment as an Instrument of Public Policy." *National Tax Journal* 53: 183–99.

Auerbach, Alan Jeffrey, Michael P. Devereux, Michael Keen, Paul Oosterhuis, Wolfgang Schön, and John Vella. 2019. "Residual Profit Allocation by Income." Oxford University Centre for Business Taxation Working Paper WP19/01.

Avi-Yonah, Reuven, and Kimberly Clausing. 2007. "Reforming Corporate Taxation in a Global Economy: A Proposal to Adopt Formulary Apportionment." Discussion Paper, Hamilton Project, Brookings Institution, Washington, DC.

Avi-Yonah, Reuven, Kimberly Clausing, and Michael Durst. 2009. "Allocating Business Profits for Tax Purposes: A Proposal to Adopt a Formulary Profit Split." *Florida Tax Review* 9(5): 498–525.

Beer, Sebastian, Ruud de Mooij, Shafik Hebous, Michael Keen, and Li Liu. 2020. "Exploring Residual Profit Allocation." IMF Working Paper 20/49, International Monetary Fund, Washington, DC.

Bettendorf, Leon, Michael Devereux, Albert van der Horst, Simon Loretz, and Ruud de Mooij. 2010. "Corporate Tax Harmonization in the EU." *Economic Policy* 25:3 537–90.

Clausing, Kimberly. 2016a. "The Effect of Profit Shifting on the Corporate Tax Base in the United States and Beyond." *National Tax Journal* 69(4): 905–34.

Clausing, Kimberly. 2016b. "The U.S. State Experience under Formulary Apportionment: Are There Lessons for International Reform?" *National Tax Journal* 69 (2): 353–86.

Cobham, Alex, Tommaso Faccio, and Valpy Fitzgerald. 2019. "Global Inequalities in Taxing Rights: An Early Evaluation of the OECD Tax Reform Proposals." SocArXiv. https://doi:10.31235/osf.io/j3p48.

Cobham, Alex, and Petr Janský. 2018. "Global Distribution of Revenue Loss from Corporate Tax Avoidance: Re-estimation and Country Results." *Journal of International Development* 30: 206–32.

Cobham, Alex, and Simon Loretz. 2014. "International Distribution of the Corporate Tax Base: Implications of Different Apportionment Factors under Unitary Taxation." Working Paper 11176, Institute of Development Studies, International Centre for Tax and Development, London.

Crivelli, Ernesto, Ruud de Mooij, and Michael Keen. 2016. "Base Erosion, Profit Shifting, and Developing Countries." *FinanzArchiv* 72: 268–301.

Daniel, Phillip, Michael Keen, and Charles McPherson. 2010. *The Taxation of Petroleum and Minerals: Principles, Problems and Practice.* Washington, DC. Routledge.

De Mooij, Ruud, Li Liu, and Dinar Prihardini. 2019. "An Assessment of Global Formula Apportionment." IMF Working Paper 19/213, International Monetary Fund, Washington, DC.

Devereux, Michael, and Simon Loretz. 2008. "The Effects of EU Formula Apportionment on Corporate Tax Revenues." *Fiscal Studies* 29: 1–33.

Eichfelder, Sebastian, Felix Hechtner, and Jochen Hundsdoerfer. 2017. "Formula Apportionment: Factor Allocation and Tax Avoidance." ARQUS Discussion Paper No. 220, ARQUS Consulting, Berlin. http://www.arqus.info/mobile/paper/arqus_220.pdf.

Eichner, Thomas, and Marco Runkel. 2008. "Why the European Union Should Adopt Formula Apportionment with a Sales Factor." *Scandinavian Journal of Economics* 110(3): 567–89.

Fuest, Clemens, Thomas Hemmelgarn, and Fred Ramb. 2007. "How Would the Introduction of an EU-Wide Formula Apportionment Affect the Distribution and Size of the Corporate Tax Base? An Analysis Based on German Multinationals." *International Tax and Public Finance* 14(5): 627–29.

Goolsbee, Austan, and Edward L. Maydew. 2000. "Coveting Thy Neighbor's Manufacturing: The Dilemma of State Income Apportionment." *Journal of Public Economics* 75(1): 125–43.

Gordon, Roger, and John Wilson. 1986. "An Examination of Multijurisdictional Corporate Income Taxation under Formula Apportionment." *Econometrica* 54(6): 1357–73.

Gupta, Sanjay, and Mary Ann Hofmann. 2003. "The Effect of State Income Tax Apportionment and Tax Incentives on New Capital Expenditures." *Journal of American Taxation Association* 25 (1): 1–25.

Gupta, Sanjay, and Lillian Mills. 2002. "Corporate Multistate Tax Planning: Benefits of Multiple Jurisdictions." *Journal of Accounting and Economics* 33(1): 117–39.

Hines, James R., Jr. 2010. "Income Misattribution under Formula Apportionment." *European Economic Review* 54: 108–20.

HM Treasury. 2018a. Corporate Tax and the Digital Economy: Position Paper Update, https://assets.publishing.service.gov.uk/government/uploads/system/uploads/attachment_data/file/689240/corporate_tax_and_the_digital_economy_update_web.pdf.

Independent Commission for the Reform of International Corporate Taxation (ICRICT). 2018. "A Roadmap to Improve Rules for Taxing Multinationals." Buckinghamshire, UK, https://www.icrict.com/icrict-documents-a-fairer-future-for-global-taxation.

International Monetary Fund (IMF). 2012. "Fiscal Regimes for Extractive Industries—Design and Implementation." IMF Policy Paper, Washington, DC.

International Monetary Fund (IMF). 2019. "Corporate Taxation in the Global Economy." IMF Policy Paper, Washington, DC.

McLure, Charles E., Jr. 1981. "The Elusive Incidence of the Corporate Income Tax: The State Case." *Public Finance Review* 9(4): 395–413.

Mintz, Jack, and Michael Smart. 2004. "Income Shifting, Investment, and Tax Competition: Theory and Evidence from Provincial Taxation in Canada." *Journal of Public Economics* 88: 1149–68.

Musgrave, Peggy. 1973. "International Tax Base Division and the Multinational Corporation." *Public Finance* 27: 394–411.

Musgrave, Peggy B., and Richard A. Musgrave. 1972. "Inter-Nation Equity." In *Modern Fiscal Issues*, edited by Richard M. Bird and John G. Head, 63–85. Toronto: University of Toronto Press.

Nielsen, Søren Bo, Pascalis Raimondos, and Guttorm Schjelderup. 2003. "Formula Apportionment and Transfer Pricing under Oligopolistic Competition." *Journal of Public Economic Theory* 5(2): 419–37.

Nielsen, Søren Bo, Pascalis Raimondos-Møller, and Guttorm Schjederup. 2010. "Company Taxation and Tax Spillovers: Separate Accounting versus Formula Apportionment." *European Economic Review* 54: 121–32.

Organisation for Economic Co-operation and Development (OECD). 2015. *Measuring and Monitoring BEPS, Action 11—2015 Final Report.* OECD/G20 Base Erosion and Profit Shifting Project. Paris: OECD Publishing.

Organisation for Economic Co-operation and Development (OECD). 2019a. "Addressing the Tax Challenges of the Digitalisation of the Economy." Public Consultation Document, OECD/G20 Base Erosion and Profit Shifting Project, OECD, Paris.

Organisation for Economic Co-operation and Development (OECD). 2019b. *Programme of Work to Develop a Consensus Solution to the Tax Challenges Arising from the Digitalisation of the Economy.* Paris: OECD. https://www.oecd.org/tax/beps/programme-of-work-to-develop-a-consensus -solution-to-the-tax-challenges-arising-from-the-digitalisation-of-the-economy.pdf.

Pethig, Rudiger, and Andreas Wagener. 2007. "Profit Tax Competition and Formula Apportionment." *International Tax and Public Finance* 14(6): 631–55.

Phionesgo, Einsny. 2015. "Using Global Formulary Apportionment for International Profit Allocation: The Case of Indonesia's Mining Industry." Master's thesis, Queensland University of Technology.

Picciotto, Sol. 2017. "Unitary Alternatives and Formulary Apportionment." In *Taxing Multinational Enterprises as Unitary Firms*, edited by Sol Picciotto, 27–34. Brighton, UK: International Centre for Tax and Development, Institute of Development Studies.

Riedel, Nadine. 2010. "The Downside of Formula Apportionment: Evidence on Factor Demand Distortions." *International Tax and Public Finance* 17: 236–58.

Schreiber, Ulrich. 2008. "Evaluating the Common Consolidated Corporate Tax Base." In *A Common Consolidated Corporate Tax Base for Europe—Eine einheitliche Körperschaftsteuerbe messungsgrundlage für Europa*, edited by Wolfgang Schön, Ulrich Schreiber, and Christoph Spengel. 113–127. Berlin, Heidelberg: Springer.

Siu, Erika, Sol Picciotto, Jack Mintz, and Akilagpa Sawyerr. 2017. "Unitary Taxation in the Extractive Industry Sector." In *Taxing Multinational Enterprises as Unitary Firms*, edited by Sol Picciotto, 48–58. Brighton, UK: International Centre for Tax and Development, Institute of Development Studies.

Smart, M., and F. Vaillancourt. 2019. "Formula Apportionment in Canada and Taxation of Corporate Income: Current Practice, Origins and Evaluation." Unpublished, University of Toronto.

Tørsløv, Thomas, Ludvig Wier, and Gabriel Zucman. 2018. "The Missing Profits of Nations." NBER Working Paper 24701, National Bureau of Economic Research, Cambridge, MA.

United Nations Conference on Trade and Development (UNCTAD). 2015. *World Investment Report 2015: Reforming International Investment Governance.* Geneva, Switzerland: United Nations.

US Securities and Exchange Commission. 2012. Disclosure of Payments by Resource Extraction Issuers. https://www.sec.gov/info/smallbus/secg/resource-extraction-small-entity-compliance -guide.htm

Weiner, Joann. 1994. "Company Taxation for the European Community: How Substantial Tax Variation Affects Business Investment in the United States and Canada." PhD diss., Harvard University.

Weiner, Joann. 2005. "Formulary Apportionment and Group Taxation in the European Union: Insights from the United States and Canada." Taxation Papers 8, Directorate General Taxation and Customs Union, European Union.

CHAPTER 15

Resource-Rich Developing Countries and International Tax Reforms

Thomas Baunsgaard and Dan Devlin

INTRODUCTION

Resource-rich countries can collect revenues from natural resources to support economic development and structural transformation, although often the revenue potential is not fully realized. Profit shifting often poses a challenge undermining the ability to effectively apply the fiscal regime.[1] Multinational enterprises through tax planning and transfer pricing may shift profits away from the source country, conflicting with the government's objective of collecting a fair share of economic rents realized from the resource extraction. Further complicating this, the concept of where value is added as natural resources are extracted is not always straightforward to establish.

This chapter examines the international tax debate focusing on the extractive industries in resource-rich developing countries.[2] Often developing countries are finding it challenging to effectively collect revenue from multinational enterprises, including in the mining and petroleum sectors.[3] This has led to consideration of a more fundamental overhaul of the global corporate tax regime (IMF 2019). There are particular characteristics of the extractives sector, not least the globally integrated supply chains and the prevalence of multinational enterprises as well as the commonly higher tax rates, that increase vulnerabilities to profit shifting. While the physical nature of commodities reduce some monitoring challenges, commonly encountered profit-shifting risks relate to the valuation of commodities, transfer pricing affecting services and goods used during the development and production phases, and intracompany financing arrangements.

---

[1] The fiscal regime includes tax and nontax instruments to collect the government share of the cash flow generated by a mining or petroleum project. See, for example, the discussion in IMF (2012).

[2] The IMF has contributed to the international debate (for example, *International Taxation and The Extractive Industries*, IMF 2017) in addition to its country level work providing technical assistance to developing countries on fiscal issues relating to extractive industries.

[3] See, for example, United Nations (2013).

This chapter contributes to the tax debate by proposing reforms to extractive industries fiscal regimes that could complement a more fundamental overhaul of the international tax architecture.[4] Current proposals for reforms of the international corporate tax architecture recognize that the potential location-specific economic rents from nonrenewable resources provide a justification for having a special fiscal regime for the extractives. However, it is generally left unstated whether this implies maintaining the current status quo or rather if this provides a springboard for sector-specific reforms.

This chapter considers what such a reformed extractives fiscal regime might look like for developing countries, taking into account international profit shifting channels, local capacity constraints, and the importance of balancing investment attractiveness with revenue mobilization. It is premised on the sector being "carved out" of wider international tax reform.

The reform proposal preserves the primary taxing rights for mining and petroleum upstream activities at the level of the source country by replacing the corporate income tax on extractive industries with a cash flow tax targeted at resource rents, combined with a royalty to ensure a reasonable minimum tax payment. Disallowing interest deductions would close one profit-shifting channel, while other safeguards—including benchmark commodity pricing, safe harbor rules, and non-resident withholding taxes—would reduce, albeit not eliminate, the risk of profit shifting. A less fundamental reform variant would retain the corporate income tax but more carefully sequence the interaction with the cash flow-based resource rent tax using the latter as a backstop against corporate income tax profit shifting.

CHARACTERISTICS OF EXTRACTIVE INDUSTRIES AND TAX IMPLICATIONS

Structural Characteristics

Natural resource extraction provides a desirable tax base from both an efficiency and equity perspective. Notable features of natural resources relevant for tax policy formulation include the following:

- *Location-specific rents that reflect the fixed supply of nonrenewable resources:* When producers are awarded the exclusive right to extract resources, they are often able to sell those resources above their cost of extraction (including a normal return on the investment). The associated economic rents can be taxed, in principle, without distorting investment decisions.

- *High-risk/reward:* Exploration is highly uncertain and may not necessarily lead to commercially viable discoveries. In return for carrying this risk, the investor would expect a higher return. Fiscal regimes that provide for fiscal certainty and a relatively faster investment recovery reduce investor risk.

---

[4] The latter was the topic of a 2019 IMF Policy Paper and is also covered in Chapters 11–14.

- *Substantial capital outlays:* The costs of developing a resource and bringing it to production are large, and the investment recovery period can be long. This implies that revenue from profit-based taxes tend to be more back loaded.

- *Cyclicality and the sensitivity of project profits to prices:* The economic rents can vary considerably over the life of a project as commodity prices and other parameters change. This means government revenues can also fluctuate significantly over time.

To realize the potential benefits from extracting mineral and hydrocarbon assets, developing countries frequently seek the technical expertise and financial investment capital of multinational enterprises. This generally allows for the most efficient development of the natural resources. These companies allocate business functions to achieve the most efficient and financially advantageous corporate structures (for example, marketing functions can be located closer to customers and borrowing sourced where there are more efficient capital markets), but these structures can also facilitate profit shifting.

Fiscal Regimes for Extractive Industries

The main economic motivation for having a special fiscal regime for extractive industries is to tax potential economic rents. The fiscal regime, therefore, is the main tool for sharing risk and reward between government and investors. Host governments must consider three aspects when designing these regimes:

- *Type of fiscal regime:* For mining, usually countries use a combination of tax and royalty. For petroleum, some countries use a tax–royalty combination, whereas others have a contractual production-sharing regime. Hybrid fiscal regimes that combine production sharing with tax and royalty are also common, while many countries also include direct state participation in projects.

- *Legislative and contractual arrangements:* Some countries include fiscal terms as part of project-specific contracts with resource companies, others in generally applicable legislation. To reduce the risk associated with their large upfront investments, many investors seek protections against future tax changes.[5] Policymakers need to avoid unduly limiting the room for subsequent policy adjustments. A more flexible fiscal regime that ensures the government take adapts automatically to different profitability outturns will provide more predictability and hence reduce the need for explicit stability provisions.

- *Fiscal instruments:* These range from royalties imposed on the value of production, specialized resource rent taxes that are usually assessed on a cash-

---

[5] Stabilized fiscal terms may serve to prevent future changes in law from applying to the investor or to restore the investor to approximately the same economic position if a change adversely affects the profitability of the project (Daniel and Sunley 2010).

flow basis for each project, and corporate income tax that is often (but not always) levied on consolidated corporate income rather than ring-fenced within a project or license area. In production-sharing contracts, the profit oil is also calculated on a cash-flow basis. It is common to have withholding taxes on outbound payments (for example, interest, dividends, and subcontractor service payments).

The current international tax architecture gives producing countries a mandate to tax resource extraction. Producing countries (that is, the source countries) effectively have the right to tax resource extraction, with the mine or well constituting a fixed place of business. This is recognized in UN and OECD model tax treaties by including mines and wells in the definition of permanent establishment.[6] But residence-country tax arrangements are also important: this is because they impact the final tax burden imposed on a project. As more countries move their corporate income tax toward a territorial basis, this is diminishing as an issue, but may strengthen the pressures for tax competition.

Revenue from Extractive Industries in Developing Countries

Resource revenues collections vary across developing countries. Countries with petroleum have generally higher revenue collections than those with mining, and middle-income countries, which tend to have higher capacity in policy and administration, are faring better than low-income countries (see Figure 15.1):

- *Low-income economies:* Countries with mining receive relatively little resource revenue; most are below 3 percent of GDP. Countries with petroleum production are generally collecting more resource revenue (around 9 percent of GDP or higher). This pattern is reflected in a lower resource revenue share in total revenue in mining (most countries at 13 percent or lower) relative to petroleum (most above 50 percent of total revenue).

- *Middle-income economies:* With one exception (Botswana), countries with mining receive no more than approximately 3 percent of GDP in resource revenues. Again, those countries with petroleum generally fare better—some have very low revenue (9 of 20 countries at less than 5 percent of GDP), but others are higher (4 countries at 20 percent or more). As a percentage of total revenue, countries with mining are receiving at most 11 percent of total revenue (Botswana again is the exception), while for petroleum producers, revenues make a larger contribution to the budget with 13 countries at 20 percent of total revenue or higher.

The different revenue patterns of countries with mining and petroleum sectors may be explained by several factors. Effective tax rates for petroleum are generally

---

[6] Article 5.2 of the UN Model Double Tax Treaty defines a permanent establishment to include "a mine, an oil or gas well, a quarry or any other place of extraction of natural resources." This would typically be interpreted also to include an offshore installation used to extract and process oil and gas.

Figure 15.1. Number of Countries Sorted by Resource Revenue Collections in Percent of GDP and of Total Revenue
(Percent of GDP and of total revenue)

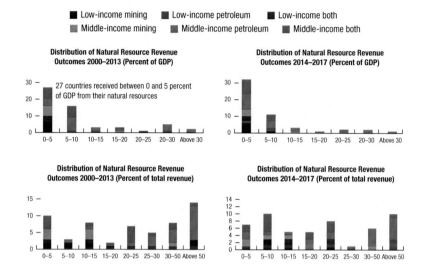

Source: IMF based on forthcoming dataset.

higher than for mining,[7] perhaps reflecting an expectation of lower economic rents and more employment and other non-fiscal benefits from the latter.[8] Mispricing of oil products may be harder than for many mineral products, given their transparent international markets; the use of norm pricing to determine the value for tax purposes; and, because upon exiting the upstream, petroleum products often do not require much additional spending on transformation (for example, refining) as a proportion of their final price.[9] Some also argue that the greater prevalence of joint-venture arrangements in petroleum, whereby joint-venture partners monitor each other closely, indirectly assists revenue authorities.[10]

---

[7] An IMF (2012) policy paper, entitled "Fiscal Regimes for Extractive Industries—Design and Implementation," found that effective tax rates are commonly higher in petroleum (approximately 65–85 percent) than in mining (45–65 percent).

[8] As noted by Cameron and Stanley (2017) p.41: "[at the time of writing, t]here is nothing in mining that equates to . . . US$8 per barrel production costs of Saudi Arabia and the Islamic Republic of Iran." Indeed, Saudi Aramco's 2019 Initial Public Offering prospectus estimated the company's lifting costs at $2.80 per barrel.

[9] An exception may be long-term contractual pricing for gas deliveries (in particular, liquefied natural gas).

[10] See Delahay and Schmalz (2019). "No profit" rules prevent any partner from charging a markup above the cost of providing a good or service to the group, limiting scope for inflated costs (Calder 2014).

INTERNATIONAL TAX CHALLENGES FACING RESOURCE-RICH DEVELOPING COUNTRIES

In many developing countries, there is a perception that revenue collected from mining and petroleum does not provide a "fair" compensation for the extraction of their natural resources. Often this is directly related to revenue risks from transfer pricing and international tax challenges. It is common to encounter pessimism by fiscal authorities regarding the capacity to effectively counter profit shifting or hear concern that the tax base has been eroded either in legislation or in contracts.[11] In response, some countries are reconsidering the balance between profit-based and production-based fiscal instruments, as the latter provide more certain revenue from the start of production.[12] However, unless handled in a measured fashion, this may increase distortions that will discourage investment or limit the scope of government sharing fully in the upside of more profitable projects. This section discusses common challenges in resource-rich developing countries, while the following section, "A Tax Reform Proposal for the Extractive Industries Sector," presents a novel approach on how to address these concerns.

Profit Shifting

Profit shifting can occur through the mis-pricing of transactions between related parties (that is, vertically integrated entities within the same corporate structure or with shared ownership). Companies can transfer profits to low-tax jurisdictions in order to avoid the typically higher tax burden imposed by the source country in the upstream (where the extraction of the commodity takes place). The three common channels for transfer pricing are to lower the valuation of commodities extracted, inflate costs incurred, or charge excessive financing costs.

Challenges

The value of the extracted commodity can be underpriced when sold to related parties. Through associated sales to a nonresident affiliate, a multinational enterprise can undervalue the minerals or oil and gas production by applying discounts or charging marketing fees above the cost of services provided.[13] The challenge for

---

[11] "Base erosion" refers to policies that narrow the tax base (for example, tax incentives), while "profit shifting" refers to strategies to shift profits abroad to lower-tax jurisdictions (for example, through transfer pricing).

[12] For example, dissatisfaction with the capacity to control costs in Indonesia led to a switch in the model production-sharing contract from a profit oil calculation to a gross production split in 2018 (effectively turning the production sharing into a royalty arrangement). Nigeria has been considering fiscal regime changes that would introduce additional price-based royalties for example, as evidenced in amendments to the Deep Offshore Act in 2019).

[13] For some commodities such as oil and gold, norm pricing—either determined in legislation or contracts—can limit these opportunities, but these come with their own risks if poorly designed or implemented.

developing countries of verifying the pricing arrangements becomes more difficult where products are not openly traded or there is substantial vertical integration of the supply chain. This makes it more difficult to find comparable sales prices between unrelated parties on terms that match the characteristics and economic context of the transactions under review.[14] Identifying an appropriate benchmark price poses specific challenges for sales of natural gas, which are often based on long-term contracts, and for unrefined minerals, where downstream smelting and refining costs may be large.

Multinational enterprise entities can also inflate payments for goods, services, and assets provided within the firm or procured from associated parties. It is common practice for extractive industries to make extensive use of nonresident subcontractors to provide services and equipment for developing and operating mining and petroleum projects. A transfer pricing risk arises whenever the subcontractor is an associated party to the multinational enterprise, and it can be nontrivial for the tax authorities to establish this if the corporate structures are complex. A parent company may also charge a subsidiary in the source country a royalty for the use of intellectual property or specialized knowledge, or payments for support services, including an allocation of overhead costs or a management fee. Alternatively, offshore entities may sell assets to the local entity at inflated prices or with financing embedded, reducing taxable income and circumventing interest withholding tax.

A perennial challenge arises from the use of related-party debt financing.[15] Given the high risk, exploration activities are usually financed by equity-funded capital injections, but it is common for a multinational enterprise to use debt financing for the substantially higher investment costs during the development phase of an extractives project. Large multinational enterprises can raise corporate finance on global capital markets, which in turn can be on-lent to subsidiaries to finance individual project development. In principle, this reduces the cost by having the most efficient project-level financing. But the benefits of lower financing costs may not necessarily flow through to the source country. In practice, by charging an interest premium above their corporate level cost of financing in the subsidiary, the multinational enterprise may shift profits by inflating interest deductions at the project level in the source country. This can be achieved by increasing the interest rate, the amount of debt, or both. It can be challenging for many tax authorities to analyze these financing transactions and establish whether they are in line with usual industry practice. The origin of financing can also be hidden through "back-to-back" financing arrangements, where a third party is inserted into a transaction between the affiliates to disguise the underlying related party dealing.

---

[14] See Calder (2017) and Platform for Collaboration on Tax (2018) for discussion.

[15] See a general discussion in de Mooij and Hebous (2017).

Possible Safeguards

Countries, however, can implement safeguards to reduce the risk of commodities being undervalued. To maximize fiscal benefits, it is generally preferable to value production for fiscal purposes as close as possible to the actual point of sale or delivery. For exports of oil and minerals, this would usually be based on the free-on-board value (excluding freight and insurance costs only); for commodities with domestic processing, it may be based on the inlet point to an oil refinery or liquefied natural gas plant or the net smelter return for minerals.[16] To provide more certainty, the legislation or project agreement can specify a benchmark price or formula to use for the valuation when assessing royalty, income tax or profit oil payments. This can either take the form of a general valuation rule for all sales of a particular commodity or only apply to associated party sales (Calder 2017).[17] A benchmark approach is more feasible for commodities with international price indices (for example, quoted prices on the London Metal Exchange for gold or for different types and qualities of oil by Platts or other price-reporting services). For commodities without a relevant price index or with subsequent smelting costs incurred after the fiscal valuation point, an alternative is to articulate a valuation formula to be applied through an advance pricing agreement.

For the use of subcontractor services, the mining or petroleum subsidiary in the source country should report related party transactions. Tax legislation or contracts should specify that transactions be valued at market prices (guided by transfer pricing rules). This, however, can be challenging to effectively enforce as the specialized nature of goods and services used for extractive industries projects makes it difficult to identify comparators.[18] Withholding taxes on payments for services provided by nonresidents can provide a blunt safeguard mechanism (albeit the lower withholding tax rates still provide a tax saving compared to the higher taxes in the extractive industries fiscal regime). A particular challenge arises when services are rendered outside of the source country even if they relate directly to the extractive industries project in the source country. Some countries have sought to overcome this through a source rule deeming that a service even if provided abroad falls within the scope of the withholding tax if payments for the service originate from the entity in the source country.[19] Withholding taxes can also be applied on payments to the parent company for management fees, royalties, and other technical service fees. Contracts or even legislation can also provide

---

[16] In cases involving associated sales there is a need for rules to clarify allowable treatment and refining cost to calculate permissible netback costs for unrefined commodities, or a mechanism to value gas as an input into a liquefaction plant (Calder 2017).

[17] There may be a need to detail transparent adjustments for differences in quality and grade differences.

[18] In response, tax authorities are often interested in establishing cost benchmarks, but this is also challenging, as they may have incomplete information (Calder 2017).

[19] But, in turn, this can give rise to disputes with tax authorities where the service provider is resident.

a safe harbor by capping certain parent-related payments to a percentage of total costs or revenue.[20]

Clear tax rules establishing when a subcontractor has a permanent establishment also provide certainty. Usually this is based on whether the subcontractor is incorporated in the source country or has a fixed place of business; there may be rule-of-thumb guidance on the minimum period of time required to be present in a country to trigger a permanent establishment (and an antifragmentation rule to prevent a splitting of contracts between related parties). This is important for delineating the scope of the nonresident-withholding taxes versus taxing economic activity by subcontractors under the corporate income tax. Without these legislative provisions—which are reinforced in tax treaties—substantial economic activity may go untaxed. Although if withholding taxes on gross payments exceed the corresponding corporate tax on net income, there may, of course, be an incentive for subcontractors to set up a permanent establishment in the source country. This is particularly an issue during the exploration and development phases of a project.

For financing, tax legislation can limit allowable deductions for interest and other financing costs. The traditional approach has been to have a debt leverage limit capping the allowable project debt to equity at a certain ratio (say, 2:1 or 3:1). While the cap limits the volume of debt, it does not provide protection against excessively high interest rates but can be combined with a requirement that the interest rate shall reflect comparable arms-length market rates. In some cases, the contract or legislation may even specify a numerical interest rate cap, usually linked to a specific cap above a market rate (for example, LIBOR). Challenges with the debt leverage limit relate to the definition and measurement of debt and equity (best practice is to follow international financial reporting standards).

A more recent variant is an interest limitation rule based on company-earnings. This effectively caps deductible net interest payments as a share of earnings before interest, tax, depreciation and amortization allowances (EBITDA) (see OECD 2014a). It is a broader measure reducing the risk of both high volume of debt and high interest rates. The downside is that the limit can become procyclical, potentially denying interest deductions during price downturns when earnings are lower, while permitting excessive deductions when prices are high.[21] This is a particularly relevant issue in the extractives sector, where commodity price boom and bust cycles are prevalent. In both variants, it is common to apply withholding taxes on nonresident interest payments as an additional safeguard.[22]

---

[20] With the inherent risk that the "ceiling quickly becomes the floor" (Calder 2017, p. 100).

[21] The procyclical effect can be mitigated by allowing denied interest deductions to be carried forward for future years. However, this, in turn, implies the cap has more of an impact on the timing of revenue rather than protecting total revenue over the life of the project.

[22] Although project-specific exemptions may limit effectiveness.

Protecting Source Country Taxing Rights

Source countries often do not effectively protect taxing rights in double tax treaties. Countries primarily negotiate tax treaties to promote crossborder investment, but sometimes also for political or diplomatic reasons (see also Chapter 8). Treaties that reduce withholding taxes (sometimes set to zero), remove an important backstop to the corporate income tax, an outcome hard to rationalize for mainly capital-importing countries. Developing countries may not effectively analyze the relative strengths of different treaty models, inadvertently leading to a greater allocation of taxing rights to residence countries, or omit safeguards such as on treaty shopping.[23] There may also be unanticipated interactions with contractual stability obligations, as Mongolia experienced (see Box 15.1).

Transfers of interests in mining and petroleum agreements have international tax implications. Following a significant natural resource discovery, there may be subsequent changes in ownership of the right to exploit those resources. Exploration companies may sell their interests, or smaller companies may bring in other partners with capital and technical expertise to develop the resources. The original owners of the resource rights may realize significant capital gains which, if the transaction occurs offshore or if it involves changes higher up in the ownership structure, can be hard for the source country to detect and to tax.[24] Model tax treaties recognize that source countries have taxing rights over gains from direct and indirect transfers of immovable property, including interests in mining or petroleum rights (in Article 13(1) and 13(4)). The key to effectively exercise this taxing right is to ensure these clauses are included in treaties, and that domestic tax legislation is carefully designed by determining the scope of taxation of the associated capital gains.[25]

Base Erosion and Tax Competition

Adding to these potential profit-shifting revenue losses are policy decisions related to tax competition. Many developing countries continue to offer tax incentives and tax holidays, perhaps responding to pressure from investors and with an eye on regional developments. These incentives can come at a direct cost to revenue, but they can also inadvertently weaken the domestic tax system. The incentives can extend to reduce or completely remove withholding taxes either in extractive industries contracts or in treaty negotiations.

Responding to these (self-inflicted) revenue losses, some countries attempt to claw back revenue in ways that may harm the overall fiscal regime. This may be through imposing other levies on the project or by delays in processing VAT

---

[23] Older tax treaties may also reflect outdated treaty models unless subsequently updated and renegotiated.

[24] An example of an indirect transfer is if ownership of a mine changes through the sale of shares in a company that owns the mining operation rather than the direct sale of the mine asset.

[25] *The Taxation of Offshore Indirect Transfers: A Toolkit* explores both the policy and legislative aspects in more detail (Platform for Collaboration on Tax 2020).

Box 15.1. Mongolia's Canceled Double Tax Treaties

Tax treaties are an important element in encouraging inbound investment. But these investment benefits need to be evaluated against any tax revenue losses from withholding tax reductions and any associated risk of increased international profit shifting.

In the case of Mongolia, the government became concerned with the treaty shopping by investors via several treaties, including the treaty with the Netherlands, which had been used by some mining investors to structure their inbound investments. There was a perception that this may have been motivated by the desire to benefit from reduced withholding tax rates (in particular on dividends at a zero tax rate).[1] Following a review and some attempt at renegotiations, Mongolia took the extraordinary step of canceling its existing tax treaties with the Netherlands, Luxembourg, Kuwait, and the UAE from the beginning of 2013 (PWC 2012), arguing they were susceptible to treaty shopping.

However, in the case of the inbound mining investor agreements, authorities had afforded the stabilization of fiscal terms extending to tax treaty provisions. This meant the change to the treaty (effectively increasing withholding taxes on the investor) was not actually applied to the mining project that had primarily triggered the authorities' concerns.

---

[1] Hubert (2017) refers to estimates that 70 percent of foreign direct investment into Mongolia at the time was via the Netherlands.

---

refunds to exporters. These measures, however, can have unintended effects, adding to project costs and worsening the investment climate.

Stabilization provisions benefiting investments can also unintentionally hinder tax system improvements. Given the substantial investments required, long repayment period, and risk involved, it is understandable why investors might seek assurances against unforeseen changes to the tax system. But these stabilization provisions, if written broadly, can limit the ability of countries to update their legislation in benign ways (for example, in line with international peers such as under the BEPS process, or to correct legislative errors) (Readhead 2018). They can also complicate a tax system transition, since typically, the country must either attempt a renegotiation or wait for the clause to expire.

Gaps in Local Capacity

Lower than expected revenue collections can be attributed to several causes, but a lack of capacity is common. Many developing countries struggle to implement and administer fiscal regimes that could limit both base erosion and profit shifting.

Countries may have deficiencies in the fiscal regime that applies to resource extraction. A legislative framework that is piecemeal or poorly drafted opens opportunities for multinational enterprises to find legal loopholes to exploit. This risk may be further exacerbated in countries with contractually agreed, project-specific fiscal terms that can introduce additional loopholes (while recognizing that these agreements, if well designed, can also close them and provide certainty for both taxpayers and tax authorities). Legislative gaps can also extend to measures such as those that help ensure taxpayer compliance (for example, to encourage information provision).[26]

Countries also often lack capacity in revenue administration to gauge and prioritize revenue risks, detect profit shifting, and audit multinational enterprises. Tax authorities often have highly constrained budgets, leading to a shortfall of officers allocated to audit roles,[27] and often those auditors lack the skills and time needed to review the complex structures and contracts that multinational enterprises may adopt. In addition, lengthy court cases to challenge profit shifting may constrain available resources of many authorities, even where there is a reasonable prospect of success. There are also cases where contracts limit audit rights more than is permitted under the general tax legislation. Underlying this is a difficult trade-off: ensuring tax compliance of an extractive industries project requires auditing expenditures from the start of the development phase before a project is profitable for tax purposes; while the overall revenue implications may be large in the longer run, for a cash-constrained government it may be more appealing to focus audit resources on activities with more immediate revenue benefits.

Another difficulty is keeping track of subcontractors for income tax purposes. Companies may bring in expertise employed by another arm of the business abroad. Depending on the length of stay, it may be legally possible to connect the income of these subcontractors to the source country, but it can be difficult to keep track of these employees and time intensive for tax authorities to review their activities and apply domestic income tax law.[28]

A TAX REFORM PROPOSAL FOR THE EXTRACTIVE INDUSTRIES SECTOR

Reinforcing the concerns regarding the revenue contribution of the mining and petroleum sectors, the international architecture for corporate taxation is under increased scrutiny. The push for international tax reform reflects challenges in applying the arm's length principle and limitations in using the physical presence concept in establishing the basis for taxation. For mining and petroleum, the former is arguably more of a challenge than the latter. There are three broad reform directions: ensuring minimum taxes on inbound (Chapter 11) and outbound investment (Chapter 12); allocation based on formulae, including through taxing the normal return in the source country and allocating residual profit using a

---

[26] According to an Ernst and Young survey, only 21 percent of multinational enterprise survey respondents said they were fully compliant with transfer pricing laws in every country they operate in. See Ernst and Young (2016).

[27] For example, tax authorities in Democratic Republic of the Congo, The Gambia, Guinea, Liberia, Mozambique, Sierra Leone, Uganda, and Zambia each have less than 10 auditors for the extractives sector.

[28] Since their legal employer is abroad, many subcontractors may not register under the local tax system.

formulaic basis (Chapter 14); or allocating taxing rights to destination countries (Chapter 13).

Notably, these fundamental reform options carve out natural resource activities for special treatment. This recognizes the principle that the location-specific economic rents provide a basis for the primary taxing rights remaining with the source country. This is best realized by having a special fiscal regime for extractive industries predominantly geared toward taxing rents, recognizing that rents may be project specific and vary over time (Annex 15.1 provides comments on the implications of these options if no carveout was made). Sufficient safeguards against profit shifting are also necessary to ensure that there is a reasonable minimum tax payable from the start to the end of production.

This section presents a conceptual proposal for extractive industries fiscal regime reform that could accompany reforms to the international tax architecture (although it could also be implemented in the absence of wider international reform). The proposal envisages the replacement of the corporate income tax for upstream resource projects with a simplified cash-flow tax and royalty system. The proposed fiscal regime would meet policymakers' dual objectives of (1) capturing a share of the location-specific economic rents via a cash-flow-based fiscal mechanism; and (2) ensuring a reasonable minimum revenue stream from the start of production. Depending on country preference, this could either be designed as a tax-royalty or a production-sharing fiscal regime.

An alternative proposal retaining the corporate income tax is also examined. The sequencing of the cash flow tax relative to the corporate income tax then becomes critical: if the resource rent tax applies to the cash flow after corporate income tax payments, profit shifting through the corporate income tax will be partly offset by higher payments of the cash-flow tax, providing a backstop against revenue leakage in the corporate income tax.

A New Fiscal Regime for Resource-Rich Countries

For the taxation of upstream production (i.e., the extraction of commodities at source), a fiscal regime package could combine several elements:

- Royalty on the value of mining and petroleum production, providing a minimum revenue share from the start of production, or, under a petroleum production sharing fiscal regime, a cost recovery limit having a similar effect.

- Resource rent tax targeted at project cash flows with appropriate ring fencing arrangements; importantly, with the cash flow base providing for immediate expensing of capital expenditure, there would be no basis for allowing interest deductions. The cash flow tax could also be implemented through an equivalent production sharing arrangement.

- Either replacing the corporate income tax entirely from mining and petroleum activities in the source country by the resource rent tax or applying the resource rent tax to the cash flow after the corporate income tax payment.

- Norm pricing for valuing production for royalty and tax calculations based on international price indices or independent analysis for product sales to related and unrelated parties.
- Withholding taxes on dividends, interest, and service payments to nonresidents, and management fees and other intracompany payments.

Benefits from this proposal are as follows:

- The fiscal regime can be designed to ensure that the resource rent tax provides a higher share of rents from more profitable projects, offsetting the regressive impact of the royalty, and vice versa for less profitable ones; as a rule of thumb, the higher the royalty rate, the more progressive the resource rent tax structure needs to be to ensure that the government take of rents is broadly the same across a range of pre-tax project profitability levels.[29]
- The fiscal regime would ensure a reasonable minimum tax payment, from the start of production, providing a bulwark against tax avoidance and evasion. This would be by either a royalty or, in a production sharing arrangement, a ceiling on cost recovery in each period with any excess costs carried forward.[30] The minimum tax payment reduces the political economy risk a government may face if extraction takes place from a low profitability project with no revenue payable and serves as a minimum "reserve price" on the option of keeping the resources in the ground.[31] On the other hand, if the royalty rate is set too high, this would lead to earlier shutdown of extraction.
- The regime would be attractive to investors by providing immediate expensing of capital expenditure, facilitating a faster investment recovery and less distortive impact of the tax regime.
- An important vulnerability to profit shifting would be eliminated by removing the interest deductibility or cost recoverability, although the risk of financing costs being embedded in financing leases would remain (Annex 15.2 examines impact of debt on different regimes).[32]
- The regime would be simpler to administer by having fewer tax instruments, which could all be managed by the revenue authority (collaborating as needed with the sector regulator). Moreover, increased use of benchmark pricing and safe harbor limits on certain deductions should also lessen the compliance burden on authorities by reducing the number of related-party transactions.

---

[29] An IMF working paper revisited conceptual issues related to the progressive taxation of extractive resources (Wen 2018).

[30] It is common in a production-sharing contract to have a ceiling on the amount of petroleum produced in each monthly or quarterly "tax" period that can be applied by the contractor to recover incurred cost. Any unrecovered costs will be carried forward to the next period. When combined with a minimum government share of profit oil, the impact is equivalent to a royalty—see IMF (2016).

[31] For fossil fuels, the reserve price could be higher, reflecting the carbon price, if this were to be imposed at the point of production rather than consumption.

[32] See Devlin (2018), Case Study 5, where interest charges are embedded into mine asset purchases.

Design and Implementation Issues

Compared to current fiscal regimes for extractives, the proposed reform package could be made broadly revenue neutral in terms of the overall government take. That said, the time profile of profit-based revenue could change; in particular, the resource rent tax may be more "back loaded" relative to corporate income tax because the latter limits the deduction of investment expenses (that is, capital equipment is depreciated). In countries with accelerated depreciation, this timing difference would be less significant. The removal of interest deductions would broaden the base for the resource rent tax. The overall timing effect on revenue could be counterbalanced by adjusting the royalty rate.

The royalty will play an important role by ensuring that there is a minimum tax payment due from the start of production. In addition to the usual interpretation of the royalty as a compensatory payment to the resource owner for the right to extract the resource (usually the government), it provides a minimum tax on inbound investment. To provide such a safeguard, the tax base for the royalty should be as broad as possible, minimizing any deductions of expenses. If combined with price benchmarking, this may be best achieved by assessing the royalty on the gross value of production at the point when the commodity changes ownership (usually the free-on-board value of exports excluding freight and insurance costs). If the royalty is instead imposed on a net basis (for example, on the mine-head or well-head value), it is important that the netback calculation is aligned with the fiscal valuation point and the ring fence. If the price used for the royalty calculation is determined by an international price index, a comparable netback mechanism would allow deductions for transportation and other operating expenses incurred beyond the fiscal ring fence. However, this runs the risk that the benefits from using benchmark pricing be undone by inflated costs claimed through the netback mechanism.[33]

The design of the resource rent tax is crucial, and it must be robust to international profit-shifting strategies. The cash-flow base simplifies the tax calculation by allowing immediate expensing of capital expenditure rather than applying depreciation allowances. Correspondingly, this removes the justification for providing deductions for interest expenses, directly removing incentives for profit shifting by intracompany financing.

An essential policy design matter is whether to apply an uplift on the negative cash flow, and, if so, at what rate. The theoretically first best option is to apply an uplift on negative cumulative cash flow at the rate of the investor "normal investment return," ensuring that the tax will only apply on economic rents.[34] The challenge is, however, that the normal return is not observable. If the uplift is set

---

[33] n addition, the same valuation practices should be used as much as possible for both royalty and rent tax (or corporate income tax) purposes, so that analysis to ascertain these pricing methods are only done once.

[34] A "pure" cash-flow tax would require refunding tax losses (an example is the Brown Tax), which can be approximated by alternatively providing an uplift on losses carried forward at a rate reflecting the investor's targeted minimum return.

too high, the tax will rarely, if at all, apply. In practice, countries that have introduced rate-of-return-based rent taxes often set the uplift quite high, which, in turn, may explain the disappointing experience with rate-of-return-based rent taxes from a revenue perspective.[35] This experience contrasts with profit oil calculations under production sharing contracts, which typically are cash flow based and in most cases without an uplift, without adverse implications on investments. A practical solution would be either not to provide an uplift on the balance of negative cash flows carried forward or to apply this at a suitably low rate (for example, a risk-free international interest rate with a reasonable country risk premium).

The cash flow tax would be underpinned by ring fencing at the project or license area, rather than allowing consolidation of activities at the corporate entity level. Ring fencing prevents a taxpayer from reducing tax paid on a producing mine or petroleum field by offsetting losses from other activities by the corporate entity (including other projects under development). While partly a timing issue, ring fencing plays a key role in preserving the economic rents at the upstream project level and ensuring the fiscal regime captures a fair share of that rent.[36] A well-designed ring fence is especially important if the tax rate is higher for upstream activities than for midstream or downstream activities. If the resource rent tax or profit oil sharing rates are progressive, consolidation across multiple projects may lower the overall revenue; if the rates are proportional (fixed), the impact of consolidation may be a deferral of revenue (reducing the value of revenue in discounted terms).

With a resource rent cash flow tax in place, it is not immediately obvious why a corporate income tax should also apply to upstream activities. The rent tax would target the location-specific rents more directly than a corporate income tax. One argument favoring retaining the corporate income tax is to tax the normal return on an investment in addition to the excess return. But especially with some rebalancing in the fiscal regime toward a higher contribution from royalty, the benefits from having two profit-based taxes are likely to be outweighed by the additional complexity and economic distortions.[37]

Still, if policymakers are uncomfortable removing the corporate income tax on extractive industries, an alternative would be to rethink the interaction with the resource rent tax. To preserve the tax base for the source country, the resource rent tax should be applied on cash flows *after* deducting payments of the corporate income tax. This will help shield the taxation of rents against profit shifting through

---

[35] Typically affording an uplift exceeding what the company likely would have required to undertake the investment, eroding the tax base. See, for example, discussion in Land (2010). In practice, countries apply uplift rates at 15 percent or even higher.

[36] Separating what is "upstream" from the later value chain can also be a thorny issue, with some natural resources—for example, natural gas—raising design questions of how to include midstream activities when there is no market-based transaction at an earlier point. This would need to be worked through for each commodity that would be subject to the new regime.

[37] Some aspects of the corporate income tax may need to be retained or replicated under the new rent tax, such as legislative definitions of key concepts for example, interest, income).

the corporate income tax: by applying the resource rent tax as a backstop on the cash flow after corporate income tax payments, any profit shifting that reduces corporate income tax liabilities will result in a larger tax base for the resource rent tax.

Some investors may have concerns that replacing the corporate income tax with a resource rent tax means they may not be able to receive tax credits in their residence country for the rent tax payments. Tax creditability may partly depend on whether the tax is comparable to the income tax in the residence country; uncertainty would be clarified by making it clear in tax treaties that such specialized resource rent taxes are covered.[38] Admittedly, with the general move globally toward territorial taxation, at least for active business income, this may become a lesser concern. But to the extent this remains an issue, this is another argument for sequencing the resource rent tax to be assessed on the post–corporate income tax cash flow. This would allow tax credits for corporate income tax payments while protecting the source-based taxation of rents on a post–corporate income tax basis. For production-sharing contracts, a pay-on-behalf scheme with a notional accounting of income tax paid out of the government's share of profit oil would provide the basis for tax credits.

Withholding taxes would be needed on payments to nonresidents on dividends, interest, and subcontractor services. This may at first seem odd since the corporate income tax would not apply to the extraction activities. However, the withholding taxes are targeted at income that originates from the natural resource asset but is otherwise not taxed by the source country; moreover, withholding taxes also provide a crude safeguard against profit shifting. In setting the rate, it is important to take into account that the withholding taxes may be passed on to the project cost if contracts allow for grossing up of withholding taxes (as is very common in extractives projects).[39]

Norm pricing would reduce the scope for profit shifting via price adjustments for associated party sales. This could be implemented through pricing formulas set by the authorities either through legislation or negotiation including by advance pricing agreements. For commodities with readily available benchmark price indices or limited downstream transformation of the commodity, this would be relatively simple to implement. For others, the design of an appropriate pricing formula would require expert advice. The norm pricing could be applied to all transactions or as a minimum price that authorities would accept for royalty and tax purposes.[40] It would need to be complemented by safeguards on associated party payments,

---

[38] In the United States, this requires that the tax is imposed on net income by reducing gross receipts by attributable costs and expenses (see Box 13.1 in Mullins 2010). Model tax treaties generally apply to taxes on income and capital, but specific taxes covered under the treaty can be listed (usually under Article 2).

[39] This may reduce the resource rent tax payment but would still lead to more front-loaded tax payments. The impact in net present value terms depends on the tax rate differential and the discount rate applied for the analysis.

[40] To minimize disputes under double tax treaties, the actual price attained by the seller could be used for arm's-length sales, with the norm price applied to associated party sales (as a "sixth method"). Source countries must also ensure the pricing method used reasonably approximates an arm's-length price, so that treaty partners accept its approach (and make corresponding adjustments where needed).

such as fees or commissions to related parties. Norm pricing is not without its own complexities, however, and requires specialist expertise and transparency in both design and implementation to retain the confidence of taxpayers.

Despite the potential advantages of the proposed fiscal regime, some challenges would remain. Profit shifting could still take place, particularly via inflated costs through related-party provision of goods and services for the project. This is of particular concern if the cash-flow nature of the resource rent tax (with an uplift) incentivizes excessive investment. Interest charges could also pose a risk if embedded into purchases or financing lease arrangements for equipment. This is a reminder that there is no shortcut escaping the need to build capacity to effectively identify revenue leakage risks and to challenge these through regulatory oversight and risk-based audits.

There may be a need for additional ad hoc safeguards against profit shifting. An example is safe harbor limits on expenditure deductions (for example, on overhead payments to parent companies) with a general starting point that the onus is on companies to demonstrate their compliance with the safe harbor. Another necessary protection would be that the legal entity concerned could not earn income from other activities that would typically be subject to corporate income taxes.

Country Practice

The reform proposal entails changes compared to the fiscal regime for extractive industries currently in place in many countries. The most noticeable difference would be the replacement of the corporate income tax by a combination of royalty and cash-flow-based resource rent tax; countries that already have these two fiscal instruments could simply adjust the rates and base to offset the repeal of the corporate income tax. Generally speaking, to yield similar revenue the resource rent tax rate would be higher if the corporate income tax were replaced than in an alternative regime where both the corporate income tax and the resource rent tax were to apply.

Even in countries that may not be ready to pursue more ambitious reforms, there is scope to reduce vulnerabilities moving in the direction of the fiscal regime reforms advocated. This would include removing interest deductibility from existing cash flow-based taxes and applying these on the cash flows after deducting corporate income tax payments. In practice, of course, contractual stability clauses may reduce the room for maneuver, especially regarding the application of reform changes to existing extractive projects.

A closer look at structural features of the fiscal regime for main petroleum producers provides the following insights (see Table 15.1):

- For countries with a production sharing fiscal regime, it is common that profit oil is calculated before the corporate income tax (so called, pre-tax production sharing); this forgoes the potential safeguard from the profit oil share acting as a backstop against profit shifting in the corporate income tax by applying production sharing on a post-tax basis.

TABLE 15.1.

Selected Petroleum Fiscal Regimes, Key Structural Features

	Royalty	Profit oil sharing						Resource rent tax					Corporate income tax		
	Rate (percent)	Profit oil sharing	Rate (percent)	Cost recovery limit	Capex	Interest cost recoverable	Interaction with CIT	RRT type	Tax rate (percent)	Capex	Interest cost recoverable	Interaction with CIT	Tax rate (percent)	Capex	Interest cost deductible
Angola	n/a	ROR	30–90	50	Expensing	No	Post-tax	n/a					50	SL, 4-yr	Yes
Australia	n/a	n/a						ROR	40	Expensing	No	Pre-tax	30	SL, 15-yr	Yes
Azerbaijan	n/a	R-factor	40–90	100	Expensing	No	POB	n/a						DB	Yes
Bolivia															
Brazil	10	n/a						DROP	10–40	SL, 10-yr	No	Pre-tax	34	SL, 10-yr	Yes
Canada (Alberta)	10–40	n/a						Price-based royalty					27	DB	
Congo, Rep. of	15	DROP	40–60	60	Expensing	No	POB	n/a							
Egypt	n/a	DROP, Price	75–90	40	SL, 5-yr	Yes	POB	n/a							
Equatorial Guinea	13	DROP	10–70	70	Expensing	No	Pre-tax	n/a					35	SL, 5-yr	Yes
Gabon	Variable	DROP	50–63	65–80	Expensing	No	Pre-tax	n/a					0	SL, 5-yr	Yes
Ghana	5–12.5	n/a						ROR	15–25	Expensing	No	Post-tax	35	SL, 5-yr	Yes
Guyana	2	Fixed	50	75	Expensing	Yes	POB	n/a							
Kazakhstan	5–18	n/a						Excess profi	10–60	SL, 5-yr	Yes	Post-tax	32	SL, 5-year	Yes
Kenya	10	R-factor	50–75	60	SL, 5-yr	No	POB	n/a					25	SL, 4-yr	Yes
Indonesia (pre-2017)	20	Fixed		100	DB	No	Pre-tax	n/a							
Iraq	10	R-factor	65–84	45	Expensing	No	Pre-tax	n/a					35	SL, 5-yr	Yes
Israel	12.5	n/a						R-factor	20–50	Expensing	No	Pre-tax	26.5	SL, 7-yr	Yes
Lebanon	5–12	R-factor	30–55	60–65	Expensing	No	Pre-tax	n/a					15	SL, 5-yr	Yes
Liberia	5	DROP	40–60	70	Expensing	Yes	Pre-tax	n/a					30	SL, 5-yr	Yes
Malaysia	10	DROP	30–60	70–75	Expensing	No	Pre-tax	n/a					38	SL, 5-yr	Yes
Mauritania	n/a	R-factor	31–42	55	Expensing	Yes	Pre-tax	n/a						SL, 5-yr	Yes

(continued)

TABLE 15.1. *(continued)*

Selected Petroleum Fiscal Regimes, Key Structural Features

	Royalty	Profit oil sharing						Resource rent tax					Corporate income tax		
	Rate (percent)	Profit oil sharing	Rate (percent)	Cost recovery limit	Capex	Interest cost recoverable	Interaction with CIT	RRT type	Tax rate (percent)	Capex	Interest cost recoverable	Interaction with CIT	Tax rate (percent)	Capex	Interest cost deductible
Mexico (Entitlement)	Variable	Fixed	65	60	SL, 4-yr			n/a		n/a	n/a	Pre-tax	30	SL, 4-yr	Yes
Mexico (PSC)	Variable	ROR	Biddable	60	Expensing	No	POB	n/a					30	SL, 4-yr	Yes
Mongolia	12.5	DROP	44–64	40	Expensing	No	POB	n/a							Yes
Mozambique (EPCC Area 1)	3	R-factor	10–60	65	SL, 4-yr	Yes	Pre-tax	n/a					32	SL, 4-yr	Yes
Mozambique	10	R-factor	15–60	60	SL, 4-yr	No	Pre-tax	n/a					32	SL, 4-yr	Yes
Myanmar	12.5	DROP	60–85	60	SL, 4-yr	Yes	Pre-tax	n/a					25	SL, 4-yr	Yes
Nigeria JV	20	n/a						n/a					85	SL, 5-yr	Yes
Nigeria PSC (1993)	Variable	Cumulative	20–60	100	SL, 5-yr	Yes	POB	n/a					50	SL, 5-yr	Yes
Norway	n/a		n/a					SPT	55	Uplift	Yes	Post-tax	23	SL, 6-yr	Yes
Papua New Guinea	2	n/a						ROR	30	Expensing	No	Post-tax	30	SL, 10-yr	Yes
Russia	20–50							Export duty	0–45				20	SL, 5-yr	Yes
Saudi Arabia (2018 regime)													50–85	SL (b), 20 years	Yes
Senegal		DROP	15–40	75	SL, 5-yr	No	Pre-tax	n/a					25	SL, 5-yr	Yes
Timor Leste	5	DROP	50–70	100	Expensing	No	Pre-tax	ROR	32.1	Expensing	No	Pre-tax	30	SL, 5-yr	Yes
Trinidad & Tobago	12.5	n/a						Price-based	0–55	n/a	n/a	Pre-tax	50	DB	Yes
Trinidad & Tobago PSC	0	DROP	45–68	60	Expensing	Yes	POB	n/a							
Uganda	5–12.5	DROP			Expensing	Yes	Pre-tax	n/a				Post-tax	30	SL, 6-yr	Yes
United Kingdom	n/a	n/a						Cashflow w	32	Expensing + No			30	Expensed	Yes

Source: FARI Fiscal Regime Library and Sub-Models

Notes: DROP (daily rate of production), ROR (rate of return), POB (pay on behalf), SL (straight line depreciation), DB (declining balance depreciation), SPT (Special Petroleum Tax)

- Most petroleum fiscal regimes ensure early revenue through a royalty. In some countries without an explicit royalty, the similar impact is achieved by a cost recovery limit providing minimum government share of production (when the limit on cost recovery is binding).

- In a small number of countries, profit oil is calculated on a post-tax basis by having the corporate income tax paid out of the government share of profit oil under a "paid-on-behalf" production sharing (profit shifting through the corporate income tax therefore has no material impact on government revenue).

- Most production-sharing fiscal regimes calculate profit oil on a cash flow basis with immediate expensing of capital expenditure and no interest deduction. However, a few fiscal regimes in addition also redundantly allow cost recovery of interest expenses, providing a debt bias.

- For tax-royalty countries with a resource rent tax, it is common to have this apply to pre-corporate income tax cash flow, again not benefiting from the safeguard against corporate income tax profit shifting that the resource rent tax can provide. This risk is further accentuated by providing for reduced interest withholding rates.

Table 15.2 summarizes structural features of the fiscal regime in major mining countries. Countries with a resource rent tax are about evenly split between having this applied to the pre- and post-corporate income tax cash flows. Some countries also allow interest deductibility under the resource rent tax despite providing for expensing of capital expenditure. Moreover, a number of countries only apply the corporate income tax which allows for interest deductions, without a tax targeted at resource rents.

Countries with extractive industries are also vulnerable to profit shifting through reduced withholding tax rates. For the majority of countries, the tax treaty network provides withholding tax rates significantly below the generally applicable ones, in many cases with the rates at least in some treaties reduced to zero (see Annex 15.3).

TABLE 15.2.

Selected Mining Fiscal Regimes, Key Structural Features

	Royalty		Resource rent tax					Corporate income tax		
	Rate (percent)	Base	RRT type	Tax rate (percent)	Capex	Interest cost recoverable	Interaction with CIT	Tax rate (percent)	Capex	Interest cost deductible
Argentina	3	Net	n/a					35	SL, 5-yr	Yes
Australia	Variable	Net						30	SL, 10-15-yr	Yes
Bolivia	Sliding scale	Gross	Mining surtax	25	SL, 8-yr	Yes	Post-tax	25	SL, 8-yr	Yes
Botswana	3–10	Net	Variable income tax	22–70	Expensing	Yes	n/a	n/a	n/a	n/a
Brazil	1–3.5	Gross	n/a					34	SL, 5-10-yr	Yes
Burkina Faso	Price-based	Gross	n/a					17.5	SL, 10-yr	Yes
Canada	n/a		Provincial mining tax	Varies	Expensing	No	Pre-tax	15 + 12	DB, 25%	Yes
Chile	n/a		Specific mining tax	5–34.5	SL, 9-yr	No	Pre-tax	27	SL, 9-yr	Yes
China	2.5–10	Net	n/a					25	SL, 10-yr	Yes
Colombia	4–10	Net	Rate of return	25	Expensing	No	Post-tax	27	SL, 5-yr	Yes
Congo, DR	1–3.5	Net	n/a					30	DB, 25%	Yes
Cote d'Ivoire	3.5	Gross	n/a					25	SL, 5-yr	Yes
Ghana	5	Net	Rate of return	10	Expensed	No	Pre-tax	25	SL, 5-yr	Yes
Guinea	3–5	Gross	n/a					30	SL, 3-yr	Yes
India	2–15	Gross	CIT surcharge	5–10				30	SL, 5-yr	Yes
Indonesia	3–10	Net	n/a					25	SL, 5-16-yr	Yes
Lesotho	7–10	Net	n/a					25	DB	Yes
Liberia	4.5	Gross	Rate of return	20	Expensed	No	Pre-tax	30	Expensed	Yes
Mali	3	Gross	n/a					25	SL, 3-yr	Yes
Mauritania	Price-based	Gross	n/a					25	SL, 3-yr	Yes
Mexico	n/a		Special mining right	7.5	SL, 10-yr	No	Post-tax	30	SL, 10-yr	Yes
Mongolia	5	Gross	Price-based royalty	Variable	n/a	n/a	Deductible	25	SL, 10-yr	Yes
Mozambique	3–6	Gross	n/a					32	SL, 7-yr	Yes
Namibia	3–10	Gross	n/a					37.5	Expensed	Yes
Niger	Variable	Gross	n/a					30	SL, 5-yr	Yes
Papua New Guinea	2.25	Gross	Rate of return	30	Expensed	No	Post-tax	30	SL, 10-yr, DB	Yes

(continued)

TABLE 15.2. *(continued)*

Selected Mining Fiscal Regimes, Key Structural Features

	Royalty			Resource rent tax				Corporate income tax		
	Rate (percent)	Base	RRT type	Tax rate (percent)	Capex	Interest cost recoverable	Interaction with CIT	Tax rate (percent)	Capex	Interest cost deductible
Peru	1–12	Oper. income	Special mining tax	2–8.4	Expensed	No	Pre-tax	29.5	Expensed	Yes
Philippines	5	Net	Additional govt share			Yes		30	SL, 5-yr	Yes
Sierra Leone	4–7.5	Gross						30	DB	Yes
Solomon Islands	3	Gross	Rate of return	20	Expensed	No	Post-tax	35	Expensed, DB	Yes
South Africa	5–7	Gross	Variable income tax	0–32	Expensed	Yes	Post-tax	n/a	n/a	n/a
Tanzania	3–5	Gross	n/a					30	SL, 5-yr	Yes
Zambia	5–6	Gross	Export duty					30	SL, 4-yr	Yes
Zimbabwe	1–15	Net	Rate of return	28–31	Expensed	No	Post-tax	15	Expensed	Yes

Source: FARI Fiscal Regime Library and Sub-Models

Notes: SL (straight line depreciation), DB (declining balance depreciation). Net (gross value exlcuding transportation, refining and processing cost).

CONCLUSION

The international tax architecture is under new scrutiny, with an apparent willingness to explore more fundamental reform changes. Some reform options under consideration may leave natural resource-exporting developing countries vulnerable to a revenue loss. The tax reform options under consideration recognize this and emphasize the need for a special fiscal treatment or "carve-out" for extractive industries. This follows the principle that the location-specific rents should be taxed primarily at source by producing countries through a fiscal regime reform that provide a fair share to government of economic rents, while ensuring a reasonable minimum share of revenue from the start of production.

This chapter has presented a conceptual proposal for what such an extractive industries fiscal regime could look like. Based on international experience with fiscal regimes and the pressures facing the international tax system, this proposal emphasizes three elements to ease pressure on source countries: i) greater simplification wherever possible; ii) narrowing the instances where full transfer pricing analysis is required; and iii) narrowing the tax planning opportunities from related-party lending. It ensures a minimum government share of revenue from the start of production through a royalty (or in production-sharing regimes, by a cost recovery limit having the same effect), possibly with some rebalancing toward production-based taxes relative to current practice. To better target rents, the corporate income tax could be replaced by a cash-flow tax applied to each project allowing for immediate expensing of capital expenditure with no interest deduction, removing a perennial profit-shifting risk. The tax neutrality advantages from applying an uplift on losses should be weighed against how this may encourage tax avoidance if the uplift is set too high. The corporate income tax could be retained for extractives, either to tax the "normal" return or to facilitate tax credits, with the cash flow tax applied on cash flows after the payment of corporate income tax to provide a backstop against profit shifting through the corporate income tax. Additional safeguards would be provided through commodity price benchmarking for tax and royalty valuation, safe harbor rules on expenditure deductions, and withholding taxes on nonresident payments (for dividends, interest, sub-contractor services, and intracompany payments).

Some challenges would remain. A fiscal regime preserving taxing rights for the source country would be vulnerable to continued pressure for tax competition. While the natural resources are naturally not mobile, there is competition for technical know-how and investment capital. This may warrant some international coordination between producing countries including on minimum tax payments. The proposal also does not close all loopholes for revenue leakage (although it reduces the more problematic ones). There is no panacea that circumvents the need for strengthening capacity to effectively enforce tax rules, including by improving tax auditing of extractive industries. Care is also needed to ensure that a country's tax treaty network preserves the domestic taxing rights, including for withholding taxes on nonresident payments and the taxation of gains on transfers of interest.

Fiscal regime reform should be carefully designed at the country level to provide a fair sharing of risk and reward between the investor and government without discouraging investment. Tax policies that are simple to administer and comply with would be desirable for both investors and government. Wider changes to current fiscal regimes for extractive industries should involve consultation between governments and investors in current resource projects. This recognizes the prevalence of fiscal stability provisions in legislation and contracts that limit the flexibility to introduce reforms. International coordination may be necessary, as will finding the right forum in which to discuss the issues, given the intricacy and interconnected nature of the issues involved.

ANNEX 15.1. INTERNATIONAL TAX REFORMS AND IMPLICATIONS FOR RESOURCE-RICH DEVELOPING COUNTRIES

This annex briefly looks at alternative corporate tax regimes discussed in Chapters 11–14 of this book and the implications for resource-rich developing countries if considered for implementation.

Minimum Tax

For developing countries that are net recipients of investment into natural resources, the "inbound" version of a minimum tax is the most relevant variant to examine. A minimum tax may require companies to pay the greater of either their corporate income tax liability or an alternative tax calculation that, for example, has a lower rate but that disallows certain deductions on payments commonly associated with profit shifting. It can also simply be a minimum tax on turnover.

Royalties effectively serve as a minimum turnover tax, in that payments are received from the start of production, even if there is no taxable profit. In principle, royalties could be made to work more like a minimum tax by making them creditable against income tax,[41] effectively smoothing corporate income tax collections. Alternatively, maintaining the tax deductibility of the royalty makes the tax marginally more distorting than the crediting option, but entails more revenue.

In a more ad hoc fashion, there may be scope to have some (arguably arbitrary) limits on expenditure deductions for payments to related parties abroad. Safe harbors could also apply to overhead or management charges paid by a subsidiary to the parent company.

A Destination-Based Cash-Flow Tax

A destination-based cash-flow tax (DBCFT) combines a destination base with cash-flow treatment. The country where the purchaser is located is allocated some taxing right, while there is immediate expensing of investment. Based on cash flows, these taxes target economic rents, much as resource rent taxes do. But a key difference is that there are "border adjustments," whereby the tax is adjusted to

---

[41] As was the case for example in Papua New Guinea until 2017, and which Australia contemplated in tax reform in 2012. For the latter, see Australian Government (2012).

ANNEX TABLE 15.1.1.

Comparison of Corporate Income Tax, DBCFT, and Resource Rent Tax			
	Corporate Income Tax	**DBCFT**	**Resource Rent Tax**
Tax Concept	Income	Cash flow	Cash flow
Tax base	Total income less allowable deductions	Company receipts less expenses with border adjustments	Sales of mine or well production minus all costs of production
Capital Spending	Depreciated over time	Immediate expensing	Immediate expensing
Interest expenses	Deductible (but can be limited)	Excluded	Excluded
Losses	Carried forward to offset profits in future years	May be refunded or carried forward (with or without an uplift)	Usually carried forward (often with an uplift)

apply where products are sold, on the basis that the buyer is contributing to profitability via their purchase (see comparison of taxes in Annex Table 15.1.1.).

A DBCFT presents some compatibility difficulties for the taxation of extractive industry projects, especially predominantly export-oriented ones. The border adjustments under a DBCFT typically entail the exclusion of exports from the tax calculation and, likewise, either the exclusion of imports from deductions or the taxation of imports, with a deduction for imports used in the production process. A country with a foreign-owned export-oriented natural resource sector would find itself with little left to tax under the DBCFT. Indeed, this is the primary reason the 2019 IMF Board Paper recognized the need for a separate tax treatment of extractives (IMF 2019).

The design of the extractives fiscal regime would be crucial, in particular the interaction with the DBCFT. Applying a cash-flow-based profit oil sharing or resource rent tax on a post-DBCFT basis would provide some protection against revenue loss in the producing country if the corporate income tax is replaced by a DBCFT—the resource rent tax would then tax any rents not captured by the DBCFT. An even simpler solution would be simply to apply the cash-flow tax on an origin basis for extractives (as is proposed in the preceding section).

Formulary Apportionment

An alternative is formulary apportionment, consolidating the accounts of all affiliates of a multinational enterprise, with the tax base then apportioned across jurisdictions according to a formula. This apportionment could be based on, for example, the shares of assets, payroll, employees, or sales located in each jurisdiction. Each country would then apply its own tax rate to the apportioned base.

For developing countries, this approach appears to have some simplicity advantages and reduces the need for defenses against international profit shifting. Whether this is advantageous from a revenue perspective depends on the design of the formula. Profits that have been moved artificially to intermediary low-tax countries as part of sales could be potentially reallocated based on the allocation metrics but depending on the metrics used (the "allocation key"), it would not necessarily all be afforded to the resource producing country. Moreover, as IMF (2019) notes, specific metrics used could stoke international competition to attract those factors. Alternatively, profit allocation connected to employee numbers may unintentionally strengthen the lure of mine automation and reduce local mine employment levels.

Special apportionment rules would be required to preserve the taxing rights of the location-specific rents in resource projects. As an example, the EU 2016 proposal for a common consolidated corporate tax base proposed that the sales of production from resource projects should be allocated based on source rather than destination.[42] This would (from the perspective of producing countries) be preferred relative to an allocation based on payroll or number of employees, given the capital-intensive nature of the industry, and would also capture the cyclical impact of price fluctuations.

But a sales basis would raise questions of how to value those sales, requiring careful design across several dimensions. Issues related to natural resource production would include determining how to allocate the profits of diversified resource companies. If based on total sales from each resource project, this could benefit countries with projects that have recently commenced production. Since it is common to have a long investment recovery production after production commences, this implies that formulary apportionment based on sales may lead to more front-loaded revenue relative to current arrangements.[43] But this could result in some thorny situations (for example, if a multinational enterprise made a loss in one country, how would remaining profits be shared?).[44]

Another question relates to mining or petroleum intangible assets (specifically the value associated with the license to extract natural resources within a certain area and time period). The EU proposal only includes tangible assets; if all intangible assets instead were to be included, this would open another avenue for tax planning, given how easy it is to move these intangible assets.

Residual Profit Allocation

Residual profit shifting splits the actual profit of a multinational enterprise between a notional routine return and a residual profit. The tax would make a distinction between allocating a rate of return to each function of the multinational enterprise (which would be, broadly speaking, the minimum return required for companies to undertake that activity), with any additional profits allocated across jurisdictions by some mechanism. This has conceptual parallels to a resource rent tax that only applies to resource rents after the investor has realized a minimum return on the investment.

The IMF (2019) acknowledges that for natural resources, associated residual income should largely be allocated where the natural resources are located. One question is how this would be most easily done, with similarities to the discussion of formulary apportionment.

---

[42] Proposal for a Council Directive on a Common Consolidated Corporate Tax Base, European Commission, October 2016.

[43] A formulary apportionment based primarily on sales would also be expected to have a similar economic impact on royalties since taxes are based on sales, not project economics.

[44] There may be also profit-shifting risks based around the boundary of the consolidated group that would need to be watched for (for example, by creating entities that just fall outside the control test).

Moreover, setting the normal return to functions may keep developing countries beholden to transfer pricing analysis.[45] Depending on implementation, affected countries might need to undertake this analysis themselves. Alternatively, it might be possible for a third party to do the analysis for all. The latter approach would lessen the administrative burden but would raise questions concerning how the analysis would be coordinated as well as who that third party would be.

ANNEX 15.2. ANALYSIS OF VULNERABILITY OF DIFFERENT OPTIONS TO DEBT LEVERAGE

Fiscal modeling is useful to illustrate the benefits from the reform proposal presented in this chapter and, in particular, how the reform proposal reduces the risk of profit shifting through related-party debt financing.[46]

With a representative offshore petroleum project, the IMF's Fiscal Analysis of Resource Industries (FARI) model is used to evaluate the impact of the government take and investor return of increasing debt financing. Starting from a base case of 50 percent of development cost at a market interest rate (LIBOR plus 3.5 percent), debt is then increased to 100 percent of development costs, financed through intracompany loans at an above-market interest rate (LIBOR plus 8 percent).

The following four fiscal regime types are modeled. These are stylized but still representative of fiscal regimes that countries can apply to mining and petroleum.

- *Corporate income tax regime:* The base case fiscal regime is a tax–royalty regime combining a 10 percent royalty with a 44 percent corporate income tax rate (it is assumed that a higher tax rate applies to extractives to capture resource rents). There is no interest withholding tax applied, and no limitations on interest deductibility. The generally applicable dividend withholding tax applies.

- *Corporate income tax/resource rent tax regime:* This regime combines the 10 percent royalty with corporate income tax at the ordinary rate of 26 percent and a resource rent tax of 30 percent that applies after the investor has realized a return on the investment of 15 percent. The resource rent tax is applied on the cash flow on a post-tax basis (that is, the tax base is the cash flow after corporate income tax payments).[47] Importantly, there is no deduction of inter-

---

[45] In practice, it might be necessary to analyze what the normal return would be for each and every business function in the corporation, unless a general rate is adopted.

[46] Multinational mining and petroleum companies often finance projects through intracompany loans. In fiscal regimes with few safeguards against excessive debt leverage or interest rates charged, this can, from the company perspective, be a tax-optimizing strategy that effectively shift profits out of the source country. Common safeguards in the income tax include applying interest withholding tax on payments to nonresidents, or other limitations on interest deduction either from a ceiling on net interest deductions relative to income, a cap on the debt-to-equity ratio, or a requirement that the interest rate will be commensurate with market costs.

[47] The resource rent tax could also be applied on a pretax basis, but this will reduce the safeguard benefits if there is concern about profit shifting reducing the base for the corporate income tax.

est costs under the resource rent tax. This regime also preserves the generally applicable withholding tax of 10 percent on dividend payments.

- *Resource rent tax regime:* This regime departs from common practice by replacing the corporate income tax with a 10 percent royalty and a 50 percent resource rent tax on positive cash flows after the investor has realized a 15 percent return on the initial investment. There is no deduction of interest expenses under the resource rent tax as this provides for immediate expensing of capital expenditure. The regime also applies a 10 percent withholding tax on interest and dividend payments.

- *Production sharing contract regime:* This models a production sharing agreement (common for petroleum) with a progressive sharing of profit oil with rates rising from 36 to 50 percent linked to the R-factor (an indicator of investment recovery). There is no corporate income tax or alternatively only a notional allocation of the corporate income tax amount paid out of the government's share of profit oil. The base for the profit oil calculation is effectively the cash flow with no interest expense being recoverable to the contractor, and with the additional limitation that recovered cost can only reach 60 percent of petroleum production in any period (any unrecovered costs are carried forward to the next period). The generally applicable 10 percent withholding tax applies to interest and dividend payments.

In the base-case scenario with moderate debt financing at market cost, the simple tax–royalty regime performs adequately, and in line with alternative cash-flow based regimes. The government take as measured by the average effective tax rate amounts to about 56 percent of cumulative cash flow from the project (in undiscounted terms) (Annex Figure 15.2.1). The alternative fiscal regimes have been parameterized to result in similar average effective tax rates.

When taking account of the risk of profit shifting from excessive debt leverage however, the assessment of the fiscal regime alternatives changes.

- In the debt leverage scenario, the government take falls to 47 percent of cumulative cash flow (undiscounted) as the investors take advantage of the tax planning opportunities by the unrestricted deductibility of interest costs.

- The fiscal regime having a resource rent tax applied on a post-tax basis without deductibility of interest (corporate income tax/resource rent tax) provides some limited safeguards, and the average effective tax rate only drops to 51 percent of cumulative cash flow (undiscounted).

- However, the government would be better off by replacing the corporate income tax entirely with either a royalty–resource rent tax combination or a production-sharing arrangement. In those alternative regimes, the government take is almost unchanged despite the excessive debt leverage (see Annex Table 15.1.1).[48]

---

[48] Despite interest payments not being deductible for tax purposes, the higher related-party debt financing reduces the dividends payments, which, in turn, reduces withholding tax on those payments that is only partially offset by higher interest withholding tax.

Annex Figure 15.2.1. Government Take under Different Fiscal Regime and Debt Assumptions

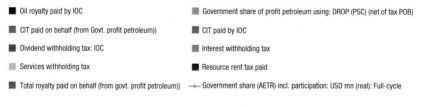

- ■ Oil royalty paid by IOC
- ■ CIT paid on behalf (from Govt. profit petroleum))
- ■ Dividend withholding tax: IOC
- ▨ Services withholding tax
- ■ Total royalty paid on behalf (from govt. profit petroleum))
- ▨ Government share of profit petroleum using: DROP (PSC) (net of tax POB)
- ■ CIT paid by IOC
- ▨ Interest withholding tax
- ■ Resource rent tax paid
- ━●━ Government share (AETR) incl. participation: USD mn (real): Full-cycle

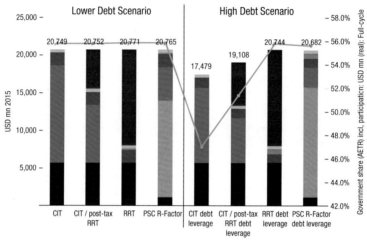

Source: Author's calculations.

ANNEX TABLE 15.1.1.

Comparison of Fiscal Regimes Using a Stylized Offshore Petroleum Project			
(Change in parentheses are under a high debt scenario)			
	AETR	**Total Revenue**	**Breakeven Price**
CIT	47.0% (−9.0%)	17.5 bn (−3.3 bn)	28.7 US$/bbl (−3.6 US$)
CIT/Post-tax RRT	51.5% (−4.5%)	19.1 bn (−1.6 bn)	28.7 US$/bbl (−2.0 US$)
RRT	56.0% (..)	20.7 bn (−0.03 bn)	29.6 US$/bbl (..)
PSC R-Factor	56.0% (..)	20.7 bn (−0.08 bn)	33.5 US$/bbl (..)

Source: Author's calculations.
Note: .. denotes not zero but rounded to zero. Calculations of AETR/total revenue based on undiscounted cash flows.

ANNEX 15.3. WITHHOLDING TAX RATES IN EMERGING ECONOMY TAX TREATIES

ANNEX TABLE 15.3.1.

Withholding Tax Rates

	Dividends		Interest		Royalties		
	Generally applicable	Lowest Treaty rate	Generally applicable	Lowest Treaty rate	Generally applicable	Lowest Treaty rate	Number of treaties
Algeria	15	0	10/40	0	4.8/24	5	32
Australia	0/30	5	10	10	30	5	45
Brazil	0	12.5	0/15/25	10	15/25	10	33
Canada	25	5	0/25	10	25	10	92
P.R. China	10	3	0/10	3	10	3	101
Colombia	7.5	0	0/5/15/20/33	10	20/33	10	12
R. Congo	15	0	20	0	20	0	8 (a)
Cote d'Ivoire	10/15	10	1–18	10	20	5	18 (d)
Egypt	10	0	0/20/32	5	20	0	58
Equatorial Guinea	25	n/a	10	n/a	10	n/a	1
Gabon	20	15	0/15/10/20	10 (e)	0/20	0	6 (b)
Ghana	8	10	8	0	15	8	9
Guinea	10	0	10	0	15	0	3
Guyana	20	0	20	15	20	10	3 (f)
Indonesia	20	7	20	5	20	5	66
I.R. Iran	0	0	0/3	5	2.5–10 (g)	5	47
Israel	25/30	0	0/24	0	24	0	54
Kazakhstan	15	5	15	10	15	10	52
Kenya	10	5	10	10	15/25	10	13
Kuwait	0/15	0	n.a.	n.a.	n.a.	n.a.	65
Lebanon	0/5/10	0	5/10	0	7.5	0	28
Liberia	5/15	15	0/5/15	20	15	20	1
Malaysia	0	0	15	5	10	0 (h)	79
Mali	7/10	5	0–18	5	30	0	12 (d)
Mauritania	10	10	10	10	0	0	4 (i)
Mexico	10	0	4.9–40	0	5/25/35/40	0	59
Mozambique	20	0	20	0	20	5	9
Myanmar	0	5	15	10	15	10	8
Namibia	20	10	10	10	10	0	10
Niger	7	10	0–20	15	16	0	2 (d)
Nigeria	10	7.5	10	7.5	10	7.5	13
Norway	25	0	0	0	0	0	87
Russian Federation	15	5	9/15/20	0	20	0	84
Senegal	10	0	8/13/16/20	0	0/20	0	15
Sierra Leone	10	0	15	0	25	0	3
Tanzania	10	0	0/10	0	15	0	9
Thailand	10	10	15	10	15	5	62
Timor-Leste	10	10	10	10	10	10	1
Trinidad and Tobago	5	0	15	10	15	5	6 (f)
Uganda	15	0	15/20	10	15	10	9

Source: IBFD database. Dividend rates are for direct investments with >10% ownership Interest WHT rates do not include lower rates for payments from public bodies or banking in several treaties.

a) excludes OCAM Treaty 1971 countries, as treaty was terminated
b) CEMAC Treaty includes 4 partner countries
c) so long as taxable in state of recipient
d) treaty with WAEMU has 7 partner countries
e) also zero rates, but unclear what qualifies
f) CARICOM treaty includes 9 partner countries
g) rate is 25%. applicable to 10% to 40% of total annual receipts, resulting in effective tax rates of 2.5%–10%.
h) royalty rate not applied to petroleum sector payments
i) excludes Arab Maghreb Union treaty, which has no withholding tax limitations

REFERENCES

Australian Government. 2012. *Australia's Future Tax System Review*. Canberra.

Calder, Jack. 2014. *Administering Fiscal Regimes for Extractive Industries: A Handbook*. Washington, DC: International Monetary Fund.

Calder, Jack. 2017. "Transfer pricing—Special extractive industries Issues." In *International Taxation and the Extractive Industries*, edited by Philip Daniel, Michael Keen, Artur Świstak, and Victor Thuronyi, 79–110. New York: Routledge.

Cameron, Peter, and Michael Stanley. 2017. *Oil, Gas and Mining: A Sourcebook for Understanding the Extractive Industries*. Washington, DC: World Bank.

Daniel, Philip, and Emil Sunley. 2010. "Contractual Assurances of Fiscal Stability." In *Taxation of Petroleum and Minerals: Principles, Problems and Practice*, edited by Philip Daniel, Michael Keen, and Charles McPherson, 405–24. New York: Routledge.

de Mooij, Ruud, and Shafik Hebous. 2018. "Curbing Corporate Debt Bias: Do Limitations to Interest Deductibility Work?" Journal of Banking and Finance 96(C): 368–78.

Delahay, David, and Karl Schmalz. 2019. "Why Upstream Oil and Gas Poses Lower Transfer Pricing Risks Than Other Industries." *Tax Notes International*, January 11.

Devlin, Dan. 2018. *Limiting the Impact of Excessive Interest Deductions on Mining Revenue*. IGF-OECD Series on BEPS in Mining. Paris: OECD.

Ernst and Young. 2016. *Operationalizing Global Transfer Pricing*. 2016–17 Transfer Pricing Survey Series. London: Ernst and Young.

Hubert, Don. 2017. *Many Ways to Lose a Billion*. Ottawa: Publish What You Pay Canada.

International Monetary Fund (IMF). 2012. "Fiscal Regimes for Extractive Industries—Design and Implementation." IMF Policy Paper, International Monetary Fund, Washington, DC.

International Monetary Fund (IMF). 2016. "Fiscal Analysis of Resource Industries (FARI) Methodology" Technical Note, Washington DC.

International Monetary Fund (IMF). 2017. "International Taxation and The Extractive Industries", International Monetary Fund, edited by Philip Daniel, Michael Keen, Artur Swistak and Victor Thuronyi, New York, Routledge.

International Monetary Fund (IMF). 2019. "Corporate Taxation in the Global Economy." IMF Policy Paper, Washington DC.

Land, Bryan. 2010. "Resource Rent Taxes: A Re-appraisal." In *The Taxation of Petroleum and Minerals: Principles, Problems and Practice*, edited by Philip Daniel, Michael Keen, and Charles McPherson, 241–62. New York: Routledge.

Mullins, Peter. 2010. "International Tax Issues for the Resources Sector." In *The Taxation of Petroleum and Minerals: Principles, Problems and Practice*, edited by Philip Daniel, Michael Keen, and Charles McPherson, 378–402. New York: Routledge.

Organisation for Economic Co-operation and Development (OECD). 2014a. *BEPS Action 4: Final Report*. Paris. OECD.

Organisation for Economic Co-operation and Development (OECD). 2014b. *Impact of BEPS in Low Income Countries*. Report to G-20. Paris: OECD.

Platform for Collaboration on Tax. 2018. *A Toolkit for Addressing Difficulties in Accessing Comparables Data for Transfer Pricing Analyses*. Paris.

Platform for Collaboration on Tax. 2020. *The Taxation of Offshore Indirect Transfers: A Toolkit*. Washington DC.

PriceWaterhouse Coopers (PWC). 2012. *Tax Alert Issue 11*.

Readhead, Alexandra. 2018. *Tax Incentives in Mining: Minimising Risks to Revenue*. IGF-OECD Program to Address BEPS in Mining. Ottawa: International Institute for Sustainable Development.

Saudi Aramco. 2019. *International Offering Circular (Prospectus)*. Riyadh: Kingdom of Saudi Arabia.

United Nations. 2013. *Secretariat Report on the Expert Group Meeting on Extractive Industries Taxation*. New York: United Nations.

Wen, Jean-Francois. 2018. "Progressive Taxation of Extractive Resources as Second-Best Optimal Policy." Working Paper 18/130, International Monetary Fund, Washington, DC.

CHAPTER 16

The Evolution of Tax Law Design within an Increasingly Destabilized International Tax Law Framework

Christophe Waerzeggers, Cory Hillier, and Irving Aw

INTRODUCTION

This chapter brings a legal perspective to the pressures in the international corporate tax system that have been discussed in other chapters largely from an economic point of view. In addition to the economic drawbacks of the current architecture, the current system is also marked by major legal weaknesses leading to continued uncertainty and providing opportunities for ongoing tax arbitrage and aggressive tax planning. The proliferation of anti-avoidance rules to combat these opportunities has made the international corporate tax system more complex. Failure to address the core structural weaknesses in the system has intensified the debate surrounding the fair allocation of taxing rights, particularly over lightly taxed residual profits—amplifying the need for fundamental reform.

This chapter is structured as follows: The following section summarizes the current state of the international tax law framework, and the gaps and mismatches in that framework that have been exploited. The third section identifies the weaknesses and deficiencies in the current international tax system that remain in the aftermath of the G20/OECD Base Erosion and Profit Shifting (BEPS) Project. The fourth section provides a legal assessment of future reform options and directions that the international tax system may take. It takes a broad perspective, drawing on fundamental proposals,[1] but is also of relevance to the assessment of the recent, more concrete, and narrower proposals under the two-pillar approach outlined in the program of work being carried out by the G-20/OECD Inclusive Framework on BEPS (hereafter referred to as "Inclusive Framework"). The fifth section emphasizes the need for greater tax cooperation in order to implement any agreed reforms. The sixth section specifically discusses the distinct problems faced by, and capacity limitations of, low-income countries, which require tailored responses. The final section offers concluding remarks.

---

[1] Especially those laid out in the IMF Board Paper "Corporate Taxation in the Global Economy" (2019).

CURRENT STATE OF THE INTERNATIONAL TAX LAW FRAMEWORK

Historically, international tax cooperation has focused primarily on the conclusion of double tax agreements with the principal aim of reducing double taxation. This cooperation has established a series of international concepts and norms underlying a current network of over 3,000 bilateral double tax agreements with which domestic tax systems have historically sought to comply in order to minimize inappropriate interaction issues that could lead to adverse consequences and distortions, particularly double taxation of cross border trade and investment (column 1 of Table 16.1).

More recently, international tax cooperation has focused on limiting the ability of multinational enterprises to exploit loopholes from existing gaps and mismatches between domestic tax systems and double tax agreements (column 2 of Table 16.1). This includes the 2015 BEPS package, which was intended to provide a comprehensive, coherent, and coordinated reform of the international tax rules. The BEPS package—which was subsequently endorsed by the G20 leaders—consists of 15 actions that produced a consensus on four minimum standards. The BEPS package was intended to provide governments with coordinated solutions for closing the gaps in existing international tax rules that allowed corporate tax bases to be eroded or artificially shifted to low- or no-tax jurisdictions, where typically little or no economic activity (substance) takes place. While the BEPS package represents the most comprehensive and internationally coordinated effort to date to strengthen the existing international concepts and norms, those underlying concepts and norms—being bolstered by a series of tax integrity and anti-avoidance rules (column 3 of Table 16.1)—have remained fundamentally unchanged.

The immediate aftermath of the BEPS Project saw a strong trend toward countries adopting anti-avoidance rules to address remaining weaknesses and deficiencies in the current international tax system (column 4 of Table 16.1). In response to the BEPS package, the European Union, for instance, adopted its own measures in the form of the Anti-Tax Avoidance Directive (ATAD) in July 2016 (Table 16.2). A number of the mandatory ATAD measures go further than the four minimum standards under BEPS. The ATAD measures were required to be transposed into law by EU member states by January 1, 2019, with the exception of the interest limitation rule (January 1, 2024, if existing rules are equally effective) and exit taxation (January 1, 2020).

SHORTCOMINGS IN THE CURRENT INTERNATIONAL TAX SYSTEM

While various tax integrity or anti-avoidance rules are important to effectively counter tax avoidance practices and protect the integrity of the tax system, the current trend to strengthen existing rules and develop more novel rules—as discussed hereafter—has also made the current international tax system relatively

TABLE 16.1.

BEPS Impact on International Concepts and Norms for International Tax Law Design			
International Concept and Norm	**Gap or Mismatch Being Exploited**	**BEPS Focus**	**Remaining Deficiencies and Weaknesses after BEPS**
Residents are taxed on worldwide income (residence principle) and nonresidents are taxed on domestic source income (source principle).[11]	Ability to strip and shift profits out of high-tax (residence or source) countries (for example, through base-eroding payments such as interest deductions or profit shifting by minimizing assets or risks in those high-tax countries)	For example Actions 2, 4, 8–10, directed at limiting base erosion through interest and other deductions; neutralizing the (deduction) effects of hybrid mismatch arrangements; and seeking to align transfer pricing outcomes with value creation	Other base eroding payments (for example, cross-border service or management fees) are unaddressed, and intangible and risk-related returns are still capable of being shifting to low-tax jurisdictions using the arm's length principle (see below in this table)
The source country has the primary right to tax active income, subject to finding a sufficient economic presence (nexus), defined by reference to a permanent establishment in its jurisdiction.	Weakness of existing nexus requirement exacerbated by digitalization because a permanent establishment does not arise when businesses sell remotely from abroad, even though there is a significant internet and economic presence in a local market	For example, Action 7, directed only at preventing the artificial avoidance of a (physical) permanent establishment	No fundamental change to nexus test, which has focused attention on the fairness of existing allocation of taxing rights, particularly in the context of the digital economy
The residence country has the primary right to tax passive income (other than from immovable property in the source country), with the source country typically accepting rate limits on locally sourced passive income (for example, by entering into double tax agreements).	Engaging in treaty shopping or arbitrage of domestic tax rules to achieve low or no withholding tax on payments made from the source country	For example, Action 6, directed at preventing the granting of treaty benefits in inappropriate circumstances.	Reduced source country taxation under double tax agreement not otherwise dependent on passive income being subject to a minimum level of taxation in residence country
Residence country taxation of foreign income is deferred until repatriation, unless controlled foreign corporation rules apply to combat inappropriate deferral.	Ability to achieve inappropriate tax deferral by exploiting the absence of (effective) controlled foreign corporation rules	For example, Action 3, directed at designing effective controlled foreign corporation rules	Residual profit still capable of being shifted to low tax jurisdictions using arm's length principle, and often left untaxed by controlled foreign corporation rules

(continued)

[1] Some countries have pure territorial systems, that is, they impose tax only on a source basis.

TABLE 16.1. *(continued)*

BEPS Impact on International Concepts and Norms for International Tax Law Design			
The residence country provides relief from international double taxation, either through domestic law or double tax agreements, typically by way of a credit or exemption method.	Trend toward territorial system of taxation in residence countries enables residual profit shifted to low-tax jurisdictions to remain untaxed	Not specifically dealt with by BEPS, and often left untaxed by controlled foreign corporation rules.	Tax competition not fundamentally addressed (for example, no or nominal tax jurisdictions), with arm's length principle still enabling substance (assets or risks) to be shifted to justify the location of large residual profits in low-tax jurisdictions.
Income is allocated between jurisdictions based on the arm's length principle.	Ability to produce transfer pricing outcomes that do not align with value creation	For example, Actions 8–10 seeking to align transfer pricing outcomes with value creation	Intangible and risk-related returns still capable of being shifted to low- or nominal-tax jurisdictions under arm's length principle, exacerbated by unconstrained tax competition.

Source: Authors' compilation.

TABLE 16.2.

The EU's Anti-Tax Avoidance Directive (ATAD)		
ATAD Measure	**BEPS Action/ Minimum Standard?**	**Description**
Interest limitation rule	Yes/No	ATAD prescribes an earning-stripping rule that denies interest deductions if the ratio of net interest payments to EBITDA exceeds 30 percent. Unused deductions can be carried forward.
Controlled foreign corporation rule	Yes/No	Under the ATAD, EU member states must implement legislation in their national laws incorporating certain legal design features.
Hybrid mismatches rule	Yes/No	This rule counters tax planning that exploits differences in countries' legal characterization of an entity or a financial instrument leading to double deductions or a deduction without an equivalent income inclusion. The rule was extended in March 2017 to also cover arrangements between EU and nonmember states (ATAD II).
GAAR	No/No	Under the GAAR (general anti-avoidance rule) in the ATAD, nongenuine arrangements that are put in place for the main purpose of obtaining a tax advantage that defeats the object or purpose of the applicable law should be ignored when determining a tax liability.
Exit taxation	No/No	EU member states must apply an exit tax to prevent companies from avoiding tax in the country of origin by moving their tax residence or closing a permanent establishment.

Source: Authors' compilation.

more complex and uncertain. Tax certainty is increasingly recognized as important for economic agents (see IMF and OECD 2017; 2018; and 2019), but countering tax avoidance (especially through general anti-avoidance rules) necessarily creates uncertainty for taxpayers, implying a trade-off.

At the same time, tax competition issues remain fundamentally unaddressed, in particular through the continued existence of no or nominal tax jurisdictions, which, in combination with the existing arm's length principle, effectively enable substance (assets or risks) to be shifted to low-tax jurisdictions, leaving large residual profits subject to no or low levels of taxation (see Table 16.1). The increasingly digitalized economy—exacerbating the limitations of the current nexus requirement of a permanent establishment—further intensifies the debate surrounding the fair allocation of taxing rights and the need for fundamental reform. These factors also continue to inform the design of more novel unilateral international tax law reform measures that countries are adopting in the absence of longer-term multilateral solutions.

Countries' newly designed or proposed unilateral tax law reform measures generally seek to effectively tax a greater portion of offshore residual profits that otherwise remain lightly taxed post BEPS. In this regard, many countries have already gone further than BEPS and have unilaterally implemented their own tax law measures under the ambit of anti-avoidance.

Examples of such unilateral and uncoordinated measures include the United Kingdom's diverted profits tax and Australia's Multinational Anti-Avoidance Law, which are designed to counter the erosion of the tax base by multinational enterprises using artificial or contrived arrangements to avoid establishing a permanent establishment in, and attributing related business profits to, those jurisdictions.

Furthermore, the 2017 US tax reform similarly includes measures that go beyond those set out in the BEPS package, such as the GILTI (global intangible low-taxed income, which is a residence-based minimum tax on outbound investment from the United States) and the BEAT (base erosion antiabuse tax, which is a residence-based minimum tax on inbound investment into the United States). While generally aimed at combatting broader BEPS issues that were otherwise left unaddressed (for instance, because of the application of the existing arm's length principle), those measures are also uncoordinated in their design and operation, thereby giving rise to double taxation concerns, particularly in relation to the BEAT (which does not take into account the effective rate of tax paid by the recipient of the base-eroding payments in regard to which the BEAT is seeking to reverse the benefit). The US tax reform also contains other novel features that lessen the tax motivation to adopt international base-eroding and profit-shifting structures, including a specific measure that seeks to regularize previously untaxed foreign earnings of US multinational enterprises through a deemed repatriation tax.[2] This measure was deliberately designed to address the historic

---

[2] At 15.5 percent for foreign earnings held in cash or cash equivalents (or 8 percent otherwise).

US tax deferral on foreign earnings of US multinational enterprises that gave some of the impetus to the BEPS Project in the first place.

In the meantime, others (for instance, the European Union, France, Spain, the United Kingdom, Mexico, India, Chile, and Kenya) are exploring or adopting short-term (interim) measures such as a digital services tax—also with a view to maintaining pressure toward reaching international consensus on a more modern allocation of taxing rights. Many of these short-term (interim) measures diverge with respect to underlying principles and tax law design (for example, the EU measure takes a volume-based approach, whereas the UK measure takes a value-based approach with respect to user participation in certain highly digitalized business models).

While generally legally designed to be compatible with existing domestic laws and double tax agreement obligations, these unilateral tax measures may still create distortions and spillovers because of their uncoordinated nature. Furthermore, anti-avoidance instruments—typically designed to counter tax avoidance practices—are not particularly well suited to operate as a backstop to address what are considered by those adopting countries to be structural deficiencies in the existing international tax law framework. Similarly, bespoke turnover taxes like a digital services tax generally impose a levy on gross income from specified transactions, which raise all the efficiency concerns generally associated with these types of taxes. While countries may feel pressure to take immediate action, uncoordinated interim measures may also create significant spillovers and distortions, including from retaliatory measures other countries might take in response to the real or perceived targeted nature of such measures.

LEGAL ASSESSMENT OF FUTURE REFORM OPTIONS AND DIRECTIONS

Previous chapters have explored a number of alternative directions that the international tax system could take. This chapter assesses their feasibility from a legal perspective, focusing on the following policy options: (1) a strengthened nexus requirement to include a significant economic presence without the need for a physical presence or permanent establishment (as currently defined); (2) a residence-based minimum tax on outbound investment (like the GILTI), combined with a residence-based minimum tax on inbound investment (modified BEAT); (3) unitary taxation with formulary apportionment (combined formula); (4) residual profit split, with sales factor; and (5) a destination-based cash-flow tax (DBCFT), with an exclusion for location-specific rents. The features of policy option (4) reflect those being explored under Pillar 1 of the Inclusive Framework, with the features of policy option (2) reflecting those being explored under Pillar 2 of that Framework.

The degree of implementation feasibility of each option or direction needs also to reflect the current legal and other constraints (Box 16.1), beyond those international concepts and norms embodied in double tax agreements as

Box 16.1. Existing International Institutions and Frameworks Imposing Tax Reform Constraints

World Trade Organization: The multilateral trading system is governed by World Trade Organization (WTO) agreements, which have been negotiated and signed by the bulk of the world's trading nations. These documents provide the legal rules for international commerce. They are essentially contracts, binding governments to keep their trade policies within agreed limits, complemented by a dedicated dispute settlement mechanism. The WTO agreements recognize that countries' tax laws can undermine the proper functioning of international trade rules in two main ways: First, taxes can serve as tariff barriers if they are imposed on imports but not on domestic sales of similar commodities. Second, remission of taxes on exports can amount to prohibited export subsidies.[1]

European Union: The European Union imposes constraints on member states' policies and protects certain freedoms to foster intra-EU trade. For example, the EU single market seeks to guarantee the freedom of movement of goods, capital, services, and labor—the "four freedoms"—within the European Union. The legal framework seeks to remove or reduce barriers to intra-EU trade and prevent the creation of new ones, so enterprises can trade freely in the EU and beyond—indeed, the free movement of capital also applies to capital movements between EU and non-EU countries. The functioning of the single market is monitored by a central authority—the European Commission—including through infringement proceedings brought against EU countries that do not comply with governing EU law and principles. Domestic tax policy is also constrained by other obligations and commitments in the European Union, notably the Code of Conduct for business taxation and the state aid rules. The Code of Conduct for business taxation is a political commitment by member states to refrain from engaging in "harmful tax competition," which covers many preferential tax regimes. EU Treaty–based state aid rules also prohibit member states from offering government support, including through the tax system, that gives a company an advantage over its competitors in the European Union. Cases can be simultaneously within the ambit of the Code of Conduct and state aid rules.

Other regional blocs/agreements: Many of these were inspired by the process of European integration and have adopted common and institutional legal frameworks to achieve economic integration, which also shapes and constrains national policy reform, although often with relatively weaker monitoring and enforcement mechanisms compared to the European Union. This includes the Andean Pact, now the Andean Community, which aims to liberalize intraregional integration between members (Bolivia, Colombia, Ecuador, Peru). Similarly, other regional economic communities have been established such as those throughout Africa including the West African Economic and Monetary Union, the Economic and Monetary Community of Central Africa, and the Southern African Development Community, all with various legal obligations binding on members. The use of soft law rules is also a feature of a number of these regional economic communities, which can still be highly persuasive and enjoy considerable political legitimacy, while preserving required flexibility.

Source: Authors' compilation.

---

[1] In particular with respect to the trade in goods there are also legally binding instruments imposed on members of the World Customs Organization that sign them that are not covered here.

strengthened by BEPS. However, double tax agreements are still expected over the short to medium term to remain a means for settling—on a coordinated basis—common problems that arise in international taxation, including with respect to settling disputes, with the present multilateral instrument or a similar new multilateral instrument providing an efficient implementation mechanism.

A residence-based minimum tax could be designed and implemented through unilateral domestic tax law measures, and in a manner that is consistent with existing norms and double tax agreements (for example, because of the savings clause in double tax agreements, which does not prevent a jurisdiction from adopting a residence-based measure to tax its own residents, provided the measure is nondiscriminatory).

Greater legal implementation complexities arise whenever there is a need to establish new norms, such as ones that need to be embodied in double tax agreements (for example, altered allocation of existing taxing rights under a new nexus concept, or the reallocation of taxing rights based on a new formula or factor, and so on). This would require the new norms to be adopted in all existing and new double tax agreements, which could be facilitated by a new multilateral instrument. Optionality with respect to core features relating to the reallocation and attribution would need to be minimized—underpinned by a robust dispute resolution mechanism—in order to avoid double taxation and reduce the risk of other adverse spillovers occurring, which could lead to increased cross-border tax disputes that would jeopardize the collection of any reallocated revenues.

Where the scheme retains significant aspects of current norms and practice (for example, the arm's length principle for routine returns), then the legal implementation will be relatively less difficult (for example, a residual profit split will be relatively easier to implement legally when compared to full unitary taxation with formulary apportionment). The key legal challenges will center around ensuring the consistent calculation of residual profits (total profits less routine returns) in order to, in turn, enable the determination of the reallocated residual profits based on a globally agreed formula or allocation factors—again, to be implemented through new double tax agreement norms. Greater implementation complexity will arise where residual profits are determined with regard to multilayered segmentation, such as by business lines, product lines, and geographic regions, and so on. In all cases where some global consolidation of profits is required—whether in respect of residual returns or of all profits under full unitary taxation—there would also be a need for significant harmonization of the calculation of the apportionable profits across jurisdictions, noting that harmonized tax base rules over residual profits will be more likely to be agreed to as compared to full unitary taxation at a global level. All deviations from current norms and practices (for example, taxing in the absence of a physical presence) would also need to be implemented through domestic law, with their reallocation supported by double tax agreements. The design, drafting, and implementation of these new rules and norms will again be critical to avoid double taxation and manage the risk of other adverse spillovers occurring across jurisdictions. The imperative to maximize the ease of legal implementation and administration—of particular relevance to low-income countries[3]—would tend toward the adoption of more formulaic approaches over apportionable (for example, residual) profits and losses, rather than seeking to replicate the complexity inherent in the current system which apportions profits and losses on an individual entity and transaction basis, commonly involving complex segmentation.

While implementation of the DBCFT can draw on experience with the VAT, it represents a more fundamental shift giving rise to significant legal questions relating to consistency with World Trade Organization (WTO) rules and double tax agreements (although these double tax agreement issues also arise under any alternative that departs from the current norm by seeking to create a taxing right in the absence of a physical presence). These questions warrant further discussion, but when combined with the WTO sensitivities make this option the most difficult legally to implement. A DBCFT that is designed in a way that (1) denies deductions for imports or imposes a withholding tax on imported goods or services to achieve the border adjustments; and (2) implements the wage subsidy via a deduction within the tax system itself (rather than by way of separate direct relief or credit), gives rise to significant WTO and tax treaty consistency issues.

The consistency issue arises under WTO rules because border adjustability resulting in imports and exports being taxed differentially is not currently permitted for direct taxes, including corporate income taxes. The DBCFT raises key national treatment concerns on the import side because the purchase cost of imports would not be deductible, whereas the purchase costs of domestic inputs would be deductible. Further, wage deductions would be available to domestic businesses, whereas the tax would likely be imposed on importers without a similar wage deduction. The wage deduction could also amount to a prohibited export subsidy. It is possible that a DBCFT could be designed in alternative ways to better defend against a WTO challenge (for example, by treating import and exports consistently or by reducing labor costs through mechanisms other than embedded tax deductions). A more direct way would be to change WTO rules, which would be possible in the (admittedly unlikely) case of an agreed global adoption of such tax.

Similarly, consistency issues arise in relation to the DBCFT with respect to double tax agreements. The threshold question with respect to the DBCFT and double tax agreements revolves around whether the DBCFT is an income tax or "substantially similar" tax and therefore within the scope of double tax agreements. This ultimately depends on how a country chooses to design and draft the implementing legislation. While consistency between characterization of the nature of the tax for WTO and double tax agreement purposes might be

---

[3] See the fourth section, "Legal Assessment of Future Reform Options."

desirable, this is not guaranteed. If characterized as a tax within the scope of double tax agreements (which would be considered the more favored characterization based on the design features outlined above), the key legal issue would seem to be that existing double tax agreements would need to be renegotiated or terminated because of the following reasons:

- Taxing importers (for example, remoter sellers) without a permanent establishment would violate existing double tax agreements.

- There would be a potential violation of the nondiscrimination provisions (for example, where providing benefits to local exporters as compared to others).

- The impact on existing withholding taxes would also be uncertain. In theory, withholding taxes should not be imposed by the DBCFT country in relation to imports by taxable entities, as tax is "collected" via disallowances of deductions, with payments for exports giving rise to exempt income. However, at the opposite end, there will be little incentive for non-DBCFT countries (or DBCFT treaty partners) to reduce their withholding taxes (given that export income is likely to be untaxed in the DBCFT country). This also highlights the foreign tax credit–related issue. As the DBCFT more closely reflects a territorial system, there may be little need for the DBCFT country to give foreign tax credits (see also the following discussion, from the perspective of the non–DBCFT country, which may still seek to deny a foreign tax credit for the DBCFT paid abroad). On the other hand, if the DBCFT country were to collect the DBCFT in relation to imports by nontaxable entities by way of withholding, that could be problematic in a double tax agreement context.

- A number of other tax treaty modifications would also be required to achieve full implementation of the DBCFT —for example, in order to subject cross-border royalties and derivative payments to import treatment (which seems essential to preserve the intention and proposed benefits of the tax, particularly compared with current profit shifting and transfer pricing practices).

However, if characterized as something other than an income tax, then the DBCFT would be outside the scope of existing double tax agreements (which would simplify the implementation somewhat), but this could mean that:

- Parties have no access to tax treaty based bilateral dispute mechanisms regarding the operation of the DBCFT.

- A non-DBCFT country would not be obliged to give any credit for tax levied by the DBCFT country under an existing double tax agreement (although double tax relief is now commonly conferred through domestic law rather than relying on double tax agreements). In any case, given the unique nature of the DBCFT, particularly the bespoke expensing mechanism on imports, treaty partners may argue that any DBCFT is not creditable (this is a common issue for withholding taxes levied on gross payments of services income, for instance).

TABLE 16.3.

Assessment of Legal Implementation Feasibility of Reform Options	
Global Reform	**Implementation Feasibility**
New nexus definition (expanded permanent establishment concept to capture digital permanent establishment/significant economic presence)	Medium
Residence-based minimum tax on outbound investment combined with a residence-based minimum tax on inbound investment	High-Medium
Unitary taxation with formulary apportionment (combined formula)	Medium-Low
Residual profit split, with sales factor	Medium
DBCFT, with exclusion for location-specific rents	Low

Source: Authors' compilation.

Table 16.3 summarizes the assessment of legal implementation feasibility in simple overall ratings ranging from low to medium-high in respect of the various reform options.

NEED FOR GREATER TAX COOPERATION TO IMPLEMENT GLOBAL REFORM

Irrespective of the chosen longer-term reform, greater tax cooperation is likely to be required. To avoid undesirable spillovers from double (non) taxation, tax competition, proliferation of unilateral measures and trade distortions, the international tax system should continue to be based on mutually accepted concepts and norms, but appropriately adapted to the modern economy. A multilateral approach to international tax reform producing consensus-based solutions should also be preferred because of its capacity to take into account the interests of all parties involved. For example, the recent EU listing of noncooperative tax jurisdictions exposed the shortcomings of not adopting a more inclusive multilateral approach. The EU listing process seeks to impose EU and OECD standards on non-EU and non-OECD countries (with the exception of also applying to OECD countries outside the European Union), which were not involved in setting those standards. For instance, the EU Code of Conduct, which was initially developed to apply to EU member states, does not translate easily to low-income countries, which often face capacity constraints. Low-income countries can—and many do—join the Inclusive Framework on BEPS, within which they are expected to adhere to BEPS standards that have already been set. While the BEPS (or EU Code of Conduct) principles should generally be supported, these are not necessarily reform priorities for low-income countries, which often require more structural and critical reforms to their domestic tax systems before turning to the implementation of those standards.

However, the Inclusive Framework on BEPS still serves as a practical and useful model for bringing about a consensus-based solution under a multilateral approach. This was reconfirmed at the virtual G20 meeting of finance ministers and central bank governors in October 2020, where further progress on addressing the tax challenges arising from digitalization was encouraged, and the blueprints for Pillars 1 and 2 were welcomed as a solid basis for negotiations and possible political consensus.[4] The Inclusive Framework generally embodies very efficient features enabling the production of soft law standards, supported by review and monitoring mechanisms to ensure more effective implementation outcomes. A framework of this kind also avoids the legal and institutional complexities associated with seeking to develop a forum or body based on "hard" law or legally binding obligations (for instance based on one-country-one-vote or quota-based systems). The "soft" law approach also more naturally lends itself to a consensus-based mechanism and arguably better reflects the current geopolitical reality, balancing the need for multilateral solutions with the desire to maintain tax sovereignty. Any consensus-based framework should also be underpinned by a functioning dispute settlement mechanism, with supporting mechanisms to put pressure on countries to abandon harmful tax policies that are inconsistent with the agreed soft law principles.

IMPACT FOR LOW-INCOME COUNTRIES

The distinct problems faced by, and capacity limitations of, low-income countries require tailored responses. The main forms of profit shifting affecting them are typically less sophisticated than those affecting more advanced economies, while tax incentives often give rise to an especially prevalent form of tax competition. While external support can help to develop capacity, attention is needed to the design of legal rules and norms themselves. Capacity limitations put a premium on the use of simpler methods to protect developing countries' tax bases. Not least, their interests—since they host no major multinational enterprises—can be quite different from those of advanced economies. For example, as capital importing countries, inbound measures are typically even more important for low-income countries.

Pending more fundamental reform of the international tax system, low-income countries' primary focus should be on further strengthening their domestic legal framework (beyond BEPS) to counter base erosion and increase domestic revenue mobilization. Any such additional measures should be rules based to achieve greater tax certainty and designed to mitigate against distortions and the risk of double taxation. In this regard, the current trend is toward domestic tax law measures (to complement existing traditional measures) in the form of minimum taxes, particularly in respect of inbound investment, to counter the continued erosion of the corporate income tax base, especially of low-income countries. As noted above, an inbound minimum tax measure is more relevant and crucial for low-income countries. In contrast, an outbound minimum tax measure will

---

[4] Communique, G20 Finance Ministers and Central Bank Governors Meeting, virtual, October 14, 2020, https://www.mof.go.jp/english/international_policy/convention/g20/g20_201014.pdf.

typically be of limited relevance since low-income countries typically host no major multinational enterprises. Low-income countries have a sovereign right to implement a well-designed inbound minimum tax measure and should be cautious about agreeing—whether bilaterally or multilaterally—to constrain their ability to enforce that right, including by agreeing to allow another country's outbound measure to apply in priority to their own inbound measure. Such inbound measures are also capable of being designed to ensure consistency with double tax agreements. Further, care needs to be taken when designing these minimum taxes so that they achieve their policy objective without jeopardizing trade and foreign investment. Therefore, the current trend toward minimum taxes on inbound investment into low-income countries should conform to the following general legal design principles:

1. They should be residence based so as to maintain consistency with existing double tax agreements, which do not typically affect a contracting state's right to tax their own residents, such that:

   a. the measure operates to tax a resident entity or local permanent establishment;

   b. by denying tax benefits (for instance, deductions or treaty benefits), and/or as a separate minimum tax assessment to essentially reverse those tax benefits,[5] and

   c. in each case, with the denial of tax benefits or separate minimum tax assessment being calculated with regard to base-eroding amounts/payments, including high risk profit shifting payments giving rise to deductions in the low-income country, which could cover payments for both goods[6] and services.[7]

---

[5] This leaves open the possibility of adopting an assessment mechanism of a similar kind to the BEAT. While much of the current debate revolves around the denial or scaling back of base-eroding deductions under the regular tax, a key difference with the BEAT mechanism is that it produces a minimum by applying a different rate (currently, 10 percent) to a narrowed base and imposing a separate minimum tax (BEAT) liability. It has been suggested by various commentators that this difference in the BEAT mechanism (while somewhat more complex) could be legally significant (for example, could arguably overcome the nondiscrimination article depending on terms of individual double tax agreements because the BEAT does not actually formally limit deductions, which still apply under the regular system at the corporate tax rate of 21 percent), but instead operates to impose a separate BEAT liability with the effect of eroding some of the tax benefit of the relevant deductions (at the different 10 percent BEAT rate) without ever formally denying them. This legal assessment is untested, but see, for example, the arguments advanced in Avi-Yonah and Wells (2018).

[6] Measures affecting trade in goods (such as those affecting the cost of goods sold) also need to be carefully designed with regard to applicable WTO rules.

[7] The rule should cover a broad range of payments (for example, any payment giving rise to a deduction or tax base reduction in the hands of the payer) to avoid planning around the rule by taxpayers and should also combat "conduit" or "imported" arrangements.

2. The denial of tax benefits or the assessment of a minimum tax relating to base-eroding amounts should depend on those amounts not being subject to minimum effective taxation in the hands of the recipient (not minimum level of substance in recipient jurisdiction),[8] with the onus to be placed on taxpayers claiming the tax benefit to prove that adequate tax has been paid. This design feature will better mitigate against the risk of double taxation and more specifically target asymmetric related-party arrangements (that is, deduction for payment in the low-income country, without corresponding taxation of the payment in the hands of the related recipient); and

3. They should be nondiscriminatory (meaning provisions should apply equally to like domestic transactions).

Further, low-income countries should consider domestic law measures that seek to specifically target the taxation of location-specific rents in their jurisdiction.[9] The BEPS objective of "taxing where value is created" has in part had the effect of embedding existing norms in the allocation of taxing rights. The case for allocating the right to tax income from location-specific rents to the location country appears widely accepted—though putting this economic concept into legal language is challenging. It should be formulated to include—for example—location-specific rents clearly linked to natural resources and rights (such as those embodied in licenses) to explore for, develop, and exploit those natural resources. It could possibly be extended further to also cover income from rents linked to other national assets, such as from licenses to exploit public goods (for instance, electricity, gas, or other utilities; telecommunications and broadcast spectrum and networks and so on). Irrespective of the direction taken in terms of future reform options (Table 16.3), source/location countries should retain substantial taxing rights in relation to natural resources. Beyond this, however, is a longstanding tussle for taxing rights between "source" and "residence" countries—an issue of particular importance for low-income countries, which, though not the only ones acting as a source of income, rarely host the parent of significant multinational enterprises. Location-specific rents are an attractive tax base because they can in principle be taxed without distorting investor behavior. Although more common in the extractive sector, low-income countries could think about designing tax rules that specifically target location-specific rents more broadly. If one were to design a very simplified tax on location-specific rents (without detailed calculation rules), the basic skeleton might resemble the simplified provisions set out in Box 16.2. These basic provisions are very general in nature and do not take into account the individual circumstances of any particular tax system but provide a

---

[8] Given substance is now required for the purposes of both the OECD's Forum on Harmful Tax Practices and the EU listing of noncooperative tax jurisdictions, a carve-out simply based on substance would significantly erode the policy intent, impact, and effectiveness of the rule for low-income countries.

[9] The issue of taxing location-specific rents is also explored in the draft toolkit on the Taxation of Offshore Indirect Transfers which was published under the framework of the Platform for Collaboration on Tax (IMF, OECD, UN, WBG 2020).

> **Box 16.2. Location-Specific Rent (LSR) Tax**
>
> (1) LSR Tax (LSRT) is charged and payable by an entity for any year of income in which the entity has a positive accumulated net cash position from the conduct of an enterprise under an LSR right.
> (2) The amount of LSRT payable under subsection (1) by an entity for a year of income is the aggregate of LSRT payable for the year with respect to each separate enterprise conducted by the entity under an LSR right.
> (3) LSRT payable by an entity with respect to an enterprise conducted by the entity under an LSR right is calculated as [25 percent] of the accumulated net cash position of the entity for the year.
> (4) LSRT is imposed in addition to any other tax or charge, including income tax.
> (5) Payments made and received in respect of an LSR right have a source in [Source Country].
> (6) In this section, "LSR right" means
>   (a) an exploration, prospecting, development, or similar right relating to land or buildings, including a right to explore for mineral, oil or gas deposits, or other natural resources, and a right to mine, develop, or exploit those deposits or resources, from land in, or from the territorial waters of, [Source Country];
>   (b) information relating to a right referred to in paragraph (b); or
>   (c) a right or other authorization granted by or on behalf of the government (whether or not embodied in a license) to be an exclusive or semiexclusive supplier or provider of:
>   (i) goods (such as radioactive material);
>   (ii) utilities (such as electricity or gas); or
>   (iii) other services (such as telecommunications and broadcast spectrum and networks).
>   Countrywide or within a geographic area of [Source Country].
>
> Source: Authors' formulation.

first insight into what sort of rights could give rise to income from location-specific rents when expressed in legal language. The ultimate form of any such provisions to be adopted by a given country would need to take into account the country's specific legal tradition and system—including any constitutional and international law limitations, including double tax agreements[10]—as well as its political and administrative structure and fiscal policies.

CONCLUSION

The proliferation of anti-avoidance rules following the BEPS Project has made domestic tax systems more complex and uncertain without addressing the fundamental shortcomings in the current international tax system. Tax competition issues remain fundamentally unaddressed, in particular through the continued

---

[10] To the extent that any existing double tax agreements constrain a country's policy intention of taxing location-specific rents in accordance with their domestic law, then that country should consider revising their tax treaty policy to address the misalignment, and existing tax treaties should also be reassessed and possibly renegotiated in line with that revised policy.

existence of no or nominal tax jurisdictions which, in combination with the existing arm's length principle, effectively enable substance (assets or risks) to be shifted to low-tax jurisdictions, leaving large residual profits subject to no or low levels of taxation. The increasingly digitalized economy—exacerbating the limitations of the current nexus requirement of a permanent establishment—further intensifies the debate surrounding the fair allocation of taxing rights and the need for fundamental reform.

These factors continue to inform the design of more novel unilateral international tax law reform measures that countries are adopting in the absence of longer-term multilateral solutions. Countries' newly designed or proposed unilateral tax law reform measures generally seek as a common objective to tax a greater portion of offshore residual profits that otherwise remain lightly taxed post BEPS, either on a destination basis (in the market jurisdiction) or as a residual minimum tax (in the country of residence of the parent company of multinational enterprises). However, few substantial multinational enterprises are headquartered in low-income countries, but many multinational enterprises operate in the relatively smaller markets that exist there—making inbound rules more critical for them.

Pending more fundamental reform of the international tax system (which gives rise to relatively more legal complexity and difficulty in reaching agreement with respect to adoption and implementation), low-income countries' primary focus should be on further strengthening their domestic legal framework (beyond BEPS) to counter base erosion and increase domestic revenue mobilization. Any such additional measures should be rules based to achieve greater tax certainty and designed to mitigate against distortions and the risk of double taxation. In this regard, the current trend is toward domestic tax law measures (to complement existing traditional measures) in the form of minimum taxes, particularly in respect of inbound investment, to counter the continued erosion of the corporate income tax base, especially of low-income countries. Care needs to be taken when designing these minimum taxes so that they achieve their policy objective without jeopardizing trade and foreign investment. Therefore, the current trend toward minimum taxes on inbound investment should conform to the general legal design principles outlined in the preceding section. Further, low-income countries should consider domestic law measures that seek to specifically and more comprehensively target the taxation of location-specific rents in their jurisdiction.

Greater legal implementation complexities arise whenever there is a need to establish new norms, such as ones that need to be embodied in double tax agreements (for example, altered allocation of existing taxing rights under a new nexus concept, or the reallocation of taxing rights based on a new formula or factor, and so on). This means that a more fundamental reform of the international tax system is likely to have a longer lead time, despite the recent extension of the goal of achieving a more comprehensive consensus-based solution within the Inclusive Framework on BEPS by mid-2021 (previously set for 2020). However, reform options that retain significant aspects of current norms and practice (for example, arm's length principle for routine returns) will be relatively less difficult to implement legally (for example, residual profit split will be relatively easier to implement legally when compared to full unitary taxation with formulary apportionment). While implementation of the DBCFT can draw on experience with the VAT, there are significant legal questions such as those relating to consistency with WTO rules and double tax agreements, which would need to be resolved before this solution can be implemented. It is possible that a DBCFT could be designed in alternative ways to make the case for WTO and double tax agreement consistency (for example, a new tax that treats imports and exports consistently, with separate measures to lower labor costs). However, an implementing country could expect to be challenged where material adverse spillovers arise. Alternatively, multilateral adoption of a DBCFT would imply some consensus on the need to overcome these legal obstacles and challenges.

REFERENCES

Avi-Yonah, S. Reuven, and Brett Wells. 2018. "The BEAT and Treaty Overrides: A Brief Response to Rosenbloom and Shaheen." Law & Economics Working Papers 157, University of Michigan Law School Repository, University of Michigan, Ann Arbor, MI.

International Monetary Fund (IMF) and Organisation for Economic Co-operation and Development (OECD). 2017. *Tax Certainty*. IMF/OECD Report for the G20 Finance Ministers and Central Bank Governors. Washington: IMF and OECD.

International Monetary Fund (IMF) and Organisation for Economic Co-operation and Development (OECD). 2018. *Update on Tax Certainty*. IMF/OECD Report for the G20 Finance Ministers and Central Bank Governors. Washington: IMF and OECD.

International Monetary Fund (IMF) and Organisation for Economic Co-operation and Development (OECD). 2019. *Progress Report on Tax Certainty*. IMF/OECD Report for the G20 Finance Ministers and Central Bank Governors. Washington: IMF and OECD.

International Monetary Fund (IMF). 2019. *Corporate Taxation in the Global Economy*. IMF Board Paper (Washington, IMF).

International Monetary Fund (IMF), Organization for Economic Co-operation and Development (OECD), United Nations (UN), and World Bank Group (WBG). 2020. *The Taxation of Offshore Indirect Transfers – A Toolkit*. Washington: The Platform for Collaboration on Tax (PCT).

Index